Interreligious Dialogue in the Catholic Church Since Vatican II

An Historical and Theological Study

Robert B. Sheard

Toronto Studies in Theology
Volume 31

The Edwin Mellen Press
Lewiston/Queenston

Library of Congress Cataloging-in-Publication Data:

Sheard, Robert B.
   Inter-religious dialogue in the Catholic Church since Vatican II : an
historical and theological study / by Robert B. Sheard.
      p.   cm. -- (Toronto studies in theology : vol. 31)
      Bibliography: p.
      Includes index.
      ISBN 0-88946-774-9
      1. Christianity and other religions--History--20th century.
2. Catholic Church--Relations. 3. Catholic Church Secretariatus
pro Non Credentibus. 4. World Council of Churches. Sub-unit for
Dialogue with People of Living Faiths and Ideologies. I. Title.
II. Series: Toronto series in theology : v. 31.
BR127.S44 1987   87-21181
261.2'09'04--dc19   CIP

This is volume 31 in the continuing series
Toronto Studies in Theology
Volume 31 ISBN 0-88946-774-9
TST Series ISBN 0-88946-975-X

All rights reserved. For more information contact:

The Edwin Mellen Press   The Edwin Mellen Press
P.O. Box 450   P.O. Box 67
Lewiston, New York   Queenston, Ontario
USA 14092   CANADA L0S 1L0

Printed in the United States of America

TABLE OF CONTENTS

PART TWO
THE SUB-UNIT FOR DIALOGUE WITH PEOPLE
OF LIVING FAITHS AND IDEOLOGIES

CHAPTER FOUR. TOWARDS THE ESTABLISHMENT
OF THE DFI

PART III
DIALOGUE AND THE DEVELOPMENT OF AN
ADEQUATE THEOLOGY OF RELIGIONS

CHAPTER SEVEN. DIALOGUE AND ITS
THEOLOGICAL IMPLICATIONS: A SUMMARY
AND CRITICAL REFLECTIONS............................273

     1. The Multivalent Nature of Dialogue.........273
        (a) Informational Dialaogue................274
        (b) Solving Common Problems................276
        (c) Seeking Truth.........................278
        (d) Indigenization........................279
     2. The Inevitable Tension in Dialogue.........281
     3. The Persistent Problem of Mission..........283
     4. Some Final Comments on Dialogue............285

II. Dialogue and a Theological Evaluation of
     Religions: Observations and Critique..........286

     1. Observations on the Theology of
        Religions in the Secretariat
        for Non-Christians........................286
     2. Some Critical Reflections on the
        Theology in the Secretariat
        for Non-Christians........................289
     3. Observations on the Theological Re-
        flections in the Work of the DFI..........292
     4. Some Critical Reflections on the
        Theological Problems in the
        Work of the DFI...........................298

III. Towards An Adequate Theology of Religions......299

     1. The Important Change in Context
        and Mood..................................299
     2. The Inherent Superiority
        of Christianity?..........................301
     3. The Exclusivist Statements in the Bible....305
     4. Towards An Adequate Theology
        of Religions..............................306

x

INTRODUCTION

One of the affirmations that has structured the consciousness of Christians from the New Testament times to the present has been that it is through Jesus Christ that knowledge of God and salvation are mediated to human beings. During the course of the twentieth century, however, the situation in which Christians have found themselves and thus the context for making this claim have changed dramatically. Because of communications technology and improved means of transportation, men and women are able to know more about peoples in cultures other than their own and are coming into real contact with them as never before. Christian claims about Jesus run up against the religious claims of others who are no longer distant and easily dismissed. Moreover, the Enlightenment ideals of tolerance and religious freedom, while often honoured more in the breach than in practice, have influenced the outlook of contemporary men and women, and so play a role in the way human beings interact with one another.

Coupled with the above aspects of the contemporary world situation, and probably because of them, are others which have notable effects on the Christian self-understanding. The increasing emergence of pluralistic societies is one of these. Peoples from different cultures and, most importantly for this book, peoples with different religious convictions, are living side by side in larger and larger numbers. Whether to pursue educational goals or because of economic factors, significant numbers of men and women of various religious traditions are meeting and working with one another. In certain areas of the world, India, for example, this living and working together of peoples of differing religious traditions has taken on the intensified focus of nation-building with the retreat of former colonial masters. In an effort to build up national unity and independence from colonial domination, citizens in these countries of different faiths have been forced to work together despite their religious differences to further the national welfare.

There are other important factors present in the contemporary world situation that bear mentioning. Men and women of all cultures and all religions and ideologies are experiencing a call to work for the welfare of all of humanity. Common problems are being recognized as people struggle for peace and justice and freedom. International organizations have been formed to address these problems. Indeed, it is fair to say that human beings are becoming increasingly aware that they live in a global village, that they are fashioning one common human history.

The increasingly real living together and contact between people of different faith affirmations has resulted in a new situation in which Christians must reflect upon their own faith and upon how to relate to other believers. In this new situation, a new form of activity has emerged--interreligious dialogue. Such dialogue, in fact, has become an institutional part of two of the world's major Christian organizations, the Roman Catholic Church and the World Council of Churches. Interreligious dialogue is an official activity which these two major bodies promote and upon which they comment.

In the case of the Roman Catholic Church, the dialogue agency concerned is the Secretariat for Non-Christians. In the case of the World Council of Churches, it is the Sub-Unit for Dialogue With People of Living Faiths and Ideologies, more commonly called simply the DFI. This book attempts to examine and analyze the work of these two agencies. The focus of attention will be twofold. Firstly, it will document what the two agencies are saying about the nature and purpose of interreligious dialogue. Secondly, it will analyze the underlying theology of religions that underpins their activity. By "theology of religions" I mean that evaluation of the nature and value of the world's various religious traditions and how they related to one another. Thus, Christians dialogue with representatives from other religious traditions and reflect upon this, they betray definite attitudes towards these other believers, their traditions, and how Christianity is related to them.

The period of time covered by this examination is as follows. In the case of the Secretariat for Non-Christians, this study looks at this agency's work from its beginnings in 1964 to the issuance of a major set of dialogue guidelines by the Vatican in 1984. In the case of the DFI, this study examines the beginnings of the movement towards interreligious dialogue among Protestant circles that led to the formation of the DFI, and that agency's workings up to 1979 with the emergence of a major WCC statement on dialogue.

The study of these two dialogue agencies will provide the basis for a series of reflections on interreligious dialogue and the Christian self-understanding, and so this book is more than simply an historical study as important as that may be. The problems that have surfaced during the course of the activity of these agencies are still problems facing Christians today. Interreligious dialogue is really a new form of

Christian activity and Christians have different attitudes towards it. There are insights evident in the work of these two bodies that are the focus of concern that are useful, indeed, essential for the development of what I consider to be a proper Christian attitude towards the men and women of other faiths. There are also attitudes and views that are of dubious fruitfulness. Moreover, there are questions that arise that necessitate a close look at some of the very basic affirmations Christians make about reality. Thus the examination of the work of the two dialogue agencies named above will provide, I believe, an excellent introduction into the problems Christians face as they reflect upon their faith in a new situation.

There are three major sections to this book. The first section outlines the activity of the Secretariat for Non-Christians and the reflections of some of its key personnel. The treatment of the Secretariat's work is not intended to be exhaustive. I have selected events and writings which provide an understanding of its thinking on dialogue and the world's religions. The second section deals with the activity of the DFI, primarily the various meetings that led to its establishment and the meetings it itself sponsored. The many statements that emerged from these meetings provide an overview of its attitudes and the problems it faced in this new form of Christian activity. The third section will be a summary and evaluation of the work carried on by the Secretariat and the DFI. It will also outline my own thoughts concerning the direction I think Christian activity and reflection should take as Christians encounter men and women of other religious traditions. The various Christian communities are entering a new phase in the history of Christianity, I think, one which must include serious reference to the other major religions of the world and which may mean a radical revision of Christianity's very identity. I hope that this book can contribute in some way to the advancement of Christian thinking in a time that is placing serious demands on basic Christian ideas.

PART ONE
The Secretariat for Non Christians

CHAPTER ONE
LAYING THE GROUNDWORK
FORMATION AND EARLY YEARS
(1964 - 1967)

I. Foundation, Purpose and Structure:
Some General Remarks

The establishment of a special Secretariat by Pope Paul VI in 1964 to promote friendship and collaboration between the Roman Catholic Church and the followers of non-Christian religious traditions occurred within the context of general interest by the Roman Catholic Church to open itself up in a serious way to the outside world. The Second Vatican Council (1961-1965) was the most visible manifestation and catalyst of this opening out. This interest was reflected institutionally within the Church's organizational structure by the formation of a number of Secretariats in the early 1960's, namely, the Secretariat for Promoting Christian Unity, the Secretariat for Non-Christians, and the Secretariat for Non-Believers. These focused on particular groups outside the boundaries of the Roman Catholic Church with which the Church's officials wished to enter into contact.

The idea of a special Secretariat to be concerned with the Church's relations with non-Christians appeared in a letter of Paul VI to the head of the College of Cardinals, Cardinal Tisserant, at the opening of the second session of Vatican II.[1] This was consistent with a desire by some of the Council Fathers, then engaged in a debate on the Church's relationships with the Jewish people, to include in their deliberations the followers of all religious traditions.[2] The fol-

lowing year, on Pentecost, May 17, 1964, the Pope con-
firmed his intention to set up a special Secretariat
dealing with non-Christians.[3] Two days later, he issued
the official proclamation which established it and
named a former Apostolic Delegate to Japan, Cardinal
Paolo Marella, as its first President.[4]

There were, it seems, two major factors which gave
impetus to the Pope's actions. The first was a general
spirit of openness present in the Church and exemplified by the Second Vatican Council. The Secretariat
emerged out of this spirit.[5] The second was the interest of Paul VI himself who seems to have been personally eager to establish friendly contacts with the followers of other religions. His concern was to show the
Church's care and love for all human beings and thereby better demonstrate its catholic nature.[6]

The general aim of the Secretariat, as the Pope
initially indicated, was to promote "dialogue" between
the Church and those who believed in God.[7] The Pope
seems to have had in mind a personal type of God and
this caused some confusion at first. The idea of a personal deity is absent from Buddhism and some forms of
Hinduism, while there are other forms of Hinduism and
many African religions that have a multiplicity of de-
ities. It seemed at first to many, then, that the
Pope's views would restrict the new Secretariat to encouraging friendly relations between the Church and
Muslims and Jews. The Pope, though, had no intention of
including either of these religious groups within the
scope of the Secretariat's concern because both were
considered to be special cases as a result of their
unique historical and theological ties with Christianity and because both were already being dealt with
by other Vatican agencies.[8] The matter was soon clar-

ified, however. The Secretariat's dialogue partners were to be all those who belonged to a religious tradition open to a "spiritual" dimension to reality.[9] Nonetheless, Jews and Muslims were still excluded, and in practice the Secretariat began its work intending to foster friendly relations with Hindus, Buddhists, and followers of what were called the "animist" religions of Africa. By 1965, however, Muslims had come to be included as prospective dialogue partners for the Secretariat and so the followers of the traditional major religions of the world except Judaism fell under its mandate.

During the year preceding its official foundation, Cardinal Marella in consultation with the Pope had worked out the structure and organization of the Secretariat. It was to have a small nucleus of full-time personnel stationed in Rome who would coordinate its activity. This nucleus consisted first of all of the President (Cardinal Marella), a Secretary (a Fr. Pierre Humbertclaude who had been a friend and associate of Cardinal Marella in Japan), an Under-Secretary (Fr. Pietro Rossano), office personnel, and later a special Under-Secretary for Islam (Fr. Joseph Cuoq). There were also to be two types of part-time personnel. The first of these, called Consultors, were to be appointed by the Pope on the advice of the President of the Secretariat. Their role was to advise the Secretariat on matters pertinent to its activity and to represent the Secretariat in meetings when the occasion arose. The second group was called Correspondents who were to be named by any interested episcopal Conference to act as liaisons between these groups of bishops and the Secretariat and to keep the Secretariat informed about the dialogue activities in their respective areas.[10] It is

important to note that the Secretariat saw itself as an
agency working through local bishops and developing dialogue through them. The local bishop was to be in
charge of any dialogue activity in his diocese and the
Secretariat had no intention of taking over this role.
Accordingly, the Secretariat considered all interested
bishops to be members of its organization and sent them
any information it had to offer.

Although the definite type of activity which the
Secretariat was to undertake had to be decided upon in
consultation with local bishops and its own Consultors,
there were some general tasks which the officials of
the Secretariat thought it necessary to undertake.
There was to be a two-fold focus in its activity.
Firstly, there was to be activity directed towards
those within the Church, informing them about the non-
Christian religions of the world and encouraging them
to make friendly contacts with the followers of these
religions. Secondly, there was to be activity directed
to those who were not Christian, informing them of the
beliefs of Christianity in order to break down prejudices and misunderstandings, in the hope that they
would join the Church in dialogue. The primary way by
which the Secretariat hoped to accomplish these goals
was by the publication of a number of informational
pamphlets and books directed to both of the groups noted above. Hence, very early it planned to publish a
regular "Bulletin" with information about other religions and about dialogue activity in the world.[11] It
also determined to publish guidelines for dialogue with
followers of specific religions and to publish a brief,
simple explanation of the Catholic faith for non-Christians. Other activities, notably participation in dialogue meetings, were to be undertaken as the opportu-

nity arose. The Secretariat did not, in its early
years, plan to organize any interreligious dialogue
meetings itself, leaving this in the hands of local
bishops and other organizations.

The preceding remarks have been intended to provide a general picture of the structure and plans of
the Secretariat for Non-Christians in its early years.
Later in this first chapter I will deal with its activities in some detail so as to bring to light the understanding the Secretariat's officials had of the nature and purpose of dialogue and its theological implications. Before proceeding with this, however, I want
to review certain theological currents that were "in
the air" in Roman Catholic circles during the initial
years of the Secretariat's work. This will show the
state of the question within Roman Catholic ranks concerning the relationship of the Church to other religious traditions and their followers and so will help
to shed light on some of the concerns the Secretariat's
officials had as they began their work of encouraging
dialogue.

II. Elaborating a Theology of Religions:
Roman Catholic Tendencies

Roman Catholic thinking on the religions of the
world has tried to balance a number of affirmations.
Perhaps one of the most important of these is that salvation, the fulfillment of the human person, is not
something attainable by human efforts alone but was
rather a supernatural gift from God. Human beings are
thus destined for an end beyond their natural abilities
to attain, often expressed in terms of a sharing in the
divine life itself. This supernatural salvation is made
possible by God's work through Jesus Christ and avail-

able if one has faith in Jesus Christ. One expresses
such faith by being baptized in the name of Jesus,
thereby becoming a member of the Church. The Church
itself was usually considered to have been instituted
by Christ to continue God's saving work on earth. It is
the Church that provides the means of salvation now,
then, chiefly through the sacraments and the preaching
of the gospel.

It is interesting and important to note, however,
that within the Roman Catholic tradition there has been
a tendency to allow for the possibility of salvation
for those who are not explicit members of the Church.
The concepts of what were called "implicit faith" and
"invincible ignorance" are part of a long tradition
that allowed for this possibility. No one was lost simply because of an accident of birth. God's saving help
was available in some mysterious way to everyone who
strove to do the best they could to live upright lives
and come to a knowledge of God.[12] During the 1960's,
when the Secretariat for Non-Christians was beginning
its work, such theological reflection by Roman Catholics on the world's religions was taking place probably
as never before. Two prominent Roman Catholic thinkers
engaged in such reflection were the French Cardinal,
Jean Daniélou and the German theologian, Karl Rahner.

1. Jean Daniélou's Theology of Religions

Jean Daniélou is one of the more prominent thinkers in Roman Catholic circles during the 1950's and
1960's to put forward a theology of religions, and, interestingly, he was among the first group of Consultors
named to the Secretariat for Non-Christians.[13] In his
writings on the relationship between Christianity and
the other religions of the world, Daniélou attempts to

come to what he calls a balanced position which avoids
the extremes of, on the one hand, a complete dismissal
of the non-Christian religions of the world as full of
error and corruption (what he calls a "sectarian" view)
and, on the other hand, an overly optimistic acceptance
of the non-Christian religions of the world as being on
a par with Christianity, all being equal paths to the
same God and equal paths to salvation (what he calls
"syncretism").[14]

A fundamental feature of Daniélou's position, as
he attempts to steer a course between the above-mentioned extremes, is the distinction he makes between
"religion" and "revelation." There is in humankind, he
holds, an essential religiosity, and this religiosity
manifests itself socially in the form of the great religions of the world. By an essential religiosity, Daniélou means that humankind implicitly has some appre-
hension of the divine and seeks communion with it. In
attempting to comprehend the divine, human beings are
not without help. God makes the divine Self manifest to
some extent in nature. The attempts by human beings to
understand and commune with the God whose presence is
evident in nature has resulted in the rituals, beliefs,
and traditions of the great non-Christian religions of
the world. Daniélou accordingly calls these religions
the "cosmic" religions.[15] Judaism, Islam, and Christianity do not, however, belong in this category because they are based upon what Daniélou refers to as
"revelation."

Revelation, for Daniélou, stands in contrast to
religion. He summarizes the fundamental difference between the two by calling religion the human search for
God while revelation is God's search for human beings.
In revelation, God breaks into human history. The Jew-

ish, Christian, and Muslim religious traditions are derived in various ways from this divine inbreaking, an inbreaking which has as its object the granting of salvation to human beings. These religions, then, are not simply the result of the human striving to know and associate with God. Revelation is a work of God, a series of interventions in which God works out the divine will for the welfare of humankind. These revelatory inbreakings are recorded in the Old and New Testaments which thus gives these writings the preeminent place in the religious writings of humankind.[16]

The importance of this distinction between religion and revelation emerges in Daniélou's discussion of how men and women attain salvation. Through the cosmic religions, men and women attempt to attain salvation, but this is an impossible task for them to do on their own. There are two main reasons for this, according to Daniélou. First of all, because of Original Sin, there is a profound alienation between God and humankind. The whole human person is the captive of evil which no human striving can overcome. Only God can liberate humankind from this situation and undo the alienation caused by Original Sin.[17] Secondly, the end that alone fulfills human existence, namely, participation in the life of God, is not attainable by human effort at all. God, through "grace," elevates human nature, introducing it into this new life. One receives this new life by accepting it in faith as a gift offered by God. It is in Christianity, based as it is on God's intervening activity, that the necessary means for overcoming the effects of Original Sin and receiving God's grace are made available. Christianity therefore transcends the other religions of the world.

Christianity also transcends the other religions

of the world, including Islam and Judaism, in another
way. Only it can provide a knowledge of God's inner
life, that is, what God is really like. Daniélou acknowledges that non-Christians can have some knowledge
of God, but their knowledge is very incomplete. In the
case of the followers of the "cosmic" religions, they
can know those things about God which can be discerned
in nature. This includes such things as the fact that
God exists and has certain perfections, for example,
immutability, omniscience, and infinitude. Judaism,
Islam, and Christianity, though, can say things about
God which are not accessible to observation or human
reason because God has revealed the divine inner life
and the divine will for humankind through the self-revelation captured in the Old and New Testaments. The definitive self-revelation of God occurs, however, in the
person and work of Jesus Christ, so that Christianity
is superior to both Islam and Judaism which do not
accept this final and definitive revelation.[18]

By insisting on the transcendence and uniqueness
of Christianity, Daniélou does not want to imply that
the non-Christian religions of the world have no value. They do, he insists, contain real spiritual and
moral values, and they do possess some real understanding of God. For example, they make use of prayers and
rituals which make their followers aware of a sacred
dimension to reality. They capture aspects of the truth
about God inasmuch as these can be known from nature,
and Judaism and Islam even know God, albeit incompletely, through revelation. Moreover, the religions
generally promote upright moral living. Christianity
ought not deny or depreciate these truths and values.
In fact, Christians must acknowledge them and praise
the religions for promoting them. However, while

acknowledging this goodness and value in the religions, Christians cannot simply accept them as they are. Rather, Christians must try to see that this good is assumed, purified, and transformed by the gospel. Indeed, assumption, purification, and transformation sum up Daniélou's position with respect to how Christianity is related to the values in the non-Christian religions.[19]

What does he mean by this? First of all, the revelation of God, on which Christianity is based, frees the values and truths in the non-Christian religions from their errors and corruption, or completes the partial revelation in them in the case of Judaism and Islam. The values in the religions, moreover, have been perverted and infected with error because of the effect of Original Sin. Daniélou points to the proliferation of idolatry which he sees all around as a manifestation of this. Instead of adoring the true God manifest in nature, the tendency of human beings to adore God has degenerated into the adoration of idols all too often. Thus rather than adore the God behind the visible realities of earth through which the invisible God is manifest, many adore the visible realities themselves. In addition, the world of the non-Christian religions is full of disquieting and harmful elements, Daniélou remarks, pointing to the presence in them of magic, superstition, sexual abuses, and pantheism. Christianity thus has to take up and purify the good that is evident in these religions, freeing it from the corruption of human error and perversion.[20] It can do so because it is based on the fullness of God's revealing activity which informs humankind what God was really like and how to respond properly to the divine presence.

There is also another element involved. Through
God's power, humankind is actually transformed and
enabled to share in the divine life. Even the signs of
nature which men and women use in their search for God
and which serve to reveal something about God are
transformed to become the signs of God's inner life and
saving activity. Daniélou explains this in the following remarks:

> If fire expressed God's purifying power, wa-
> ter his unifying power, wind his creative
> force, these images now designate the activ-
> ity of the divine persons. The Spirit is the
> fire which Christ came to light on the earth,
> the divine breath which animates the Apos-
> tles, the living water which flows from the
> throne of God and the Lamb.[21]

The relationship between Christianity and the non-
Christian religions of the world is a dialectical one
for Daniélou. On the one hand, because these religions
contain elements of goodness and true spiritual values,
they can be seen as "preparations" for the Gospel which
the Church preaches. They promote real values and turn
the attention of their followers to the spiritual.
These religions are preparations because the values and
truths they propose are assumed and completed by the
revelation in Christianity. This revelation does not
simply deny the good in these religions but perfects
it. The goodness and truth in the non-Christian religions, then, can be seen as "stepping-stones" to Christianity which fulfills them.

On the other hand, though, while the non-Christian
religions can be seen as preparatory to the Gospel,
these religions can also be stumbling blocks in the way

of the Gospel message. If the religions do not submit to the demands of the Gospel, if the goodness and truth they promote are not transformed and completed when the fullness of the revelation of Christ has entered into the consciousness of their followers, indeed, if these religions impede the spread of the Gospel message, then these religions, for Daniélou, are actually enemies of the Gospel. They have to die out when that which fulfills them comes onto the scene. Otherwise, they are not stepping-stones but hindrances.[22]

A final important thing to note about Daniélou's view of the non-Christian religions of the world is that he denies that they are "means of salvation." By "means of salvation," Daniélou has in mind those divinely ordained actions, ceremonies, and rituals through which one comes in contact with God's saving and elevating power. For Daniélou, these means of salvation are to be found in the preaching of the Gospel and in the sacraments, and these are to be found in the Christian Church alone.

The problem of how those are saved who do not explicitly belong to the Church, who do not acknowledge God through faith in Jesus Christ and who do not take part in the Church's sacramental system, remains. Here Daniélou's reply is simply that non-Christians can be saved, but through the mysterious workings of God's grace. Everyone can, in whatever situation he or she finds him or herself, respond to God's offer of salvation which is ubiquitous. How this occurs remains, though, ultimately a mystery. It does not necessarily occur by means of the rituals and beliefs of the non-Christians religions. Non-Christians may be saved in their religions, but not because of them. Their religions may make them open to God's presence and God's

grace, but these same religions may also make them
closed to God. The non-Christian religions are ambiguous at best.[23]

To sum up, Daniélou's theology of religions has
the following key ideas. Religion is a natural human
phenomenon. It is basically the human quest for God.
The religions in the world reflect this on the social
level. Revelation transcends religion; it is essentially God's movement to humankind. Christianity, inasmuch
as it is founded on God's definitive revelation, is
unique and transcendent. The other religions of the
world have values which can be considered stepping-
stones or preparations for God's revelation. Yet, they
can also be stumbling blocks if they do not disappear
and let their values be assumed, completed, and transformed by the Gospel. These religions are thus ambiguous. Finally, it is through faith in the Gospel message preached by the Church and through participating
in the Church's sacraments that one is saved, not by
means of participating in the rituals of non-Christian
religions or adhering to their beliefs. Any salvation
outside the Church (and this is possible) occurs because of the mysterious workings of God.

2. Karl Rahner's Theology of Religions

While Jean Daniélou advanced an influential view
concerning an understanding of the world's religions,
his view was not the only one being proposed by Roman
Catholic thinkers in the 1960's. Although he proposes
a view which esteems the values of non-Christian religions, in the final analysis he gives a negative evaluation of them. There were others, though, who were
somewhat more positive than Daniélou. The major difference concerned the salvific efficacy of non-Christian

religions. These other theologians argued that while
God has revealed the divine will and has effected it
primarily in and through Jesus Christ, this same divine
will has been and still is operative salvifically
everywhere, especially in and through humankind's religions. Thus the religions of the world could be
considered positive means by which men and women come
in contact with and respond to God's saving grace.

One of the more prominent theologians to argue for
this more positive evaluation of the non-Christian religions was Karl Rahner. Writing in the early 1960's,
Rahner argued that everyone must have the possibility
of entering into a real saving relationship with God,
for otherwise the idea of a universal saving will would
be meaningless. This relationship, though, could not be
simply an interior one, a mysterious inner colloquay
between God and individual human beings. Humankind is
social by nature, noted Rahner, and so the divine offer
of salvation has to have a social dimension to it.
Indeed, it must come through the social institutions in
which a person lives. Rahner thought that religion is
one of the prime social institutions through which this
occurs, and so he insisted that it is through the religion of a society that one comes in contact with the
divine offer of salvation. God is indeed present and
active in and through the non-Christian religions of
the world and reaches out to men and women everywhere
through them.[24]

Men and women are in touch with God to whom they
respond affirmatively or negatively, although often un-
consciously, through the attitudes and actions of their
daily lives, Rahner felt.[25] The non-Christian religions
provided one of the social contexts in which this is
done. There is, then, a history of salvation that takes

place in the more general history of the world and the non-Christian religions are part of this. Salvation history, that history in which God meets men and women and makes the divine saving grace available to them, is not restricted to the special history of salvation that is connected explicitly with the events of the life of Christ and which is now being continued in the life of the Church. The Church, though, is the visible, objective sign of this divine activity of salvation, an activity that is occurring everywhere throughout the world. The history of salvation in the world at large and the history of salvation made visible in the history of the Church are related as unthematic to thematic, unconscious to conscious, implicit to explicit.

For Rahner, however, the non-Christian religions of the world are illegitimate once their followers have come in contact in a meaningful existential way with the Gospel message preached by the Church. Until this happens, though, the religions are "lawful," that is, they are "loci" for the encounter with God's saving grace. As such, they are not purely "natural," the result simply of human strivings to know God. God is present and is active in them.[26]

3. A Brief Note on Other Roman Catholic Views

The view of Karl Rahner that men and women could receive salvation by means of the religious institutions provided to them by their culture was given a special twist by another Roman Catholic theologian, Heinz Robert Schlette, and repeated by Hans Kung in the mid-1960's. Both argued that most people in fact come in contact with God and respond to God through the religion of their culture. Since Christianity is not the major religion of the world but is in a minority situa-

tion in terms of the number of its followers compared
to all those who belong to other religions, other
religions must be considered **ordinary** means of salvation. The Church, or Christianity, is a special and extraordinary way since only a small portion of the men
and women in the world come into contact with God
through it. This idea reversed the more common Roman
Catholic view that the Church was the normal, ordinary
means of salvation instituted by Christ, all other
means being extraordinary.[27]

III. Papal and Conciliar Influences

Since it was an official body of the Roman Catholic Church, the Secretariat for Non-Christians had to
pay attention to and indeed promote the Church's official statements about the religions of the world and
about the attitude Christians should adopt towards
their followers. Significant statements emerged from
the Second Vatican Council and from the Pope himself
which were relevant to these questions. These statements provided theological principles and directions
which were to influence the Secretariat's work and reflection. They are thus important in the development of
the positions it took. The statements that are of most
importance were, from the Pope, an encyclical entitled
Ecclesiam suam, and, from the Second Vatican Council,
declarations on the relationship of the Church to non-
Christian religions, the nature of the Church, and the
nature of the Church's missionary activity.

1. The Encyclical "Ecclesiam suam"

One of the major early statements directly concerned with the work the Secretariat was to undertake
is the encyclical **Ecclesiam suam.**[28] Dialogue is one of

its major themes. One of the things to note in the encyclical is that the Pope's notion of dialogue includes
any type of non-hostile encounter between Christians
and men and women who are not members of the Church.

In the encyclical, the Pope divides humankind up
into a number of different groups, each being a group
with whom the Church wished to enter into friendly relations. He arranges these groups in a series of concentric circles. The outer circle comprises non-believers, those who do not believe in God. The second is
made up of worshippers of God, those who belong to the
great Afro-Asian religions on the periphery, then Muslims, and then Jews. Finally, the inner circle is
composed of Christians, Roman Catholics and those united with the Church of Rome forming the center.[29] In effect, the further one was away from the beliefs of the
Roman Catholic Church, the further one was from the
center.

The motivation for the Church's desire to enter
into dialogue with these groups is, insists the Pope,
the Church's love for all. Its origin lies in the divine loving activity which reaches out to all of humankind. The Pope describes this activity as that of a
continual dialogue, a dialogue of salvation, in which
God has been constantly throughout history calling men
and women to a share in the divine life. It was God who
initiated this dialogue, and the Church is called to
continue it.[30]

The dialogue as the Pope understood it, however,
has the definite character of a proclamation rather
than an exchange between equal partners. The Church has
a message for the world, the Pope says, a message it
feels compelled to communicate. Dialogue (friendly interaction) is an excellent way to do this, so that

while he insists that Catholics respect the freedom and
integrity of those outside the Church, the Pope sees
dialogue as a means of making them better disposed to
the message of the Church and the good things that God
has given it.[31]

The encyclical actually points to two types of dialogue, the first type concerned directly with the
preaching mission of the Church, and the second concerned with preliminary activities leading up to the
missionary proclamation. Thus the Pope recommends that
the missionary task of the Church should be carried out
in a dialogical way. Through dialogue, and not through
force or overt pressure, Christians ought to share with
others outside the Church its saving message. But in
addition to this missionary dialogue, the Pope urges
Christians to join with their non-Christian neighbours
in dialogue to face up to common human problems. This
type of dialogue, though, also has a missionary thrust,
for the Pope sees it as a means of predisposing non-
Christians to the Christian message by setting up
friendly contacts with them and thereby making them
more open to what their Christian partners are saying.[32]

Although the encyclical does not explicitly deal
with a theology of religions as such, there are a number of points that can be seen in it which do have implications relevant to such a theology and which indicate important directions for thought. Firstly, the
Pope affirms clearly the principle of the universal
salvific will of God. God desires the salvation of all,
without distinction. There is no people or group that
does not receive in some form the divine offer of salvation.[33] Significantly, moreover, the Pope recognizes
that this offer occurs only within a definite histor-

ical context and therefore has to take into account the cultural and historical situation of those receiving it. Since he presupposes that God's offer of salvation comes ultimately and in its most perfect form through the revelation and activity of Christ, the Pope remarks that there may be many obstacles because of these cultural and historical conditions to overcome in the completion of spreading the saving message of Christianity. The important point here is the recognition of the pervasive and deep-rooted influence of a person's historical connections which may make it difficult simply to accept the revelation of Christ when such revelation is preached. Any resistance need not necessarily be sinful and it could often be overcome only gradually.[34] The Pope sees dialogue, the establishing of friendly contacts, as a step in the process of advancing the Gospel. Finally, the Pope affirms that the various non-Christian religions do have certain real spiritual values. He urges Catholics to admire all that is good and true in the worship of God that these religions inspire.[35] They are not simply vain human strivings devoid of any goodness whatsoever.

In spite of this rather positive evaluation of non-Christian religions, however, the Pope at the same time insists that Catholics must affirm theirs to be the one and only true religion. Not all religions are equal, he says, and he warns against any diminution of the principles of the Christian faith by attempting to create harmony among men and women of various religions through sacrificing the integrity of the Christian faith.[36] There is, then, a "yes-no" stance towards non-Christian religious traditions in this encyclical, a stance that will appear in the remarks coming from the Secretariat for Non-Christians.

2. Statements of the Council

The document from Vatican II most directly concerned with the question of non-Christians and their religions is **The Declaration on the Relationship of the Church to Non-Christian Religions** promulgated on October 28, 1965.[37] This declaration is primarily a pastoral one rather than a doctrinal one, that is, it tries to elicit a positive attitude towards the major non-Christian religions and their followers from Catholics rather than provide a detailed theological evaluation of these religions. It does, however, point to certain themes for any such theological enterprise. The declaration first of all insists upon the essential unity of the human race, a unity based on the fact that all men and women have God as their creator and also as their ultimate goal.[38] In addition, the declaration notes that many cultures have developed a profound religious sense and have generated highly refined religions in an attempt to express what it calls an awareness of some "hidden power" that lies behind the course of events in the world.[39] Moreover, these religions also reflect the answers men and women in various cultures have given to fundamental questions about the meaning and purpose of existence. The declaration even attributes to these religions the possibility of reflecting elements of the divine Truth which it says enlightens all people.[40] The non-Christian religions of the world, then, inasmuch as they reflect the answers to basic human questions and reflect God's revealing presence in some way, share some common ground with Christianity. There is a basis on which Christians can begin a process of dialogue with their followers.[41]

One of the underlying images in the declaration is that of a pilgrimage in a history of salvation. Human

life is pictured as a pilgrimage towards final union
with God, a pilgrimage that God has initiated.[42] The
divine offer of salvation becomes visible in the history of the people of Israel and is fully and definitively manifest in the Christ-event. It is this definitive event which truly fulfills the human quest for
meaning and salvation, that quest which lies at the
root of the human religious drive and which is at the
base of humanity's religious history.[43]

The declaration, in a manner typical of the openness of the Council, pointed out that the Church was
related to other religious communities in different
ways. Judaism occupies a special place because of its
role in preparing the way for Christ and the Church.
Islam, too, has a special relationship to the Church
because it shares the same spiritual heritage and wor-
ships the same God as does the Church. The other religions, notably Hinduism and Buddhism, are of value to
the extent that they direct their followers towards the
true God and the divine offer of salvation, even though
they do this obliquely. There exists, then, an hierarchy among the religions of the world, an hierarchy with
the Church at the top and the other religions related
to it to the extent that they share in its revelatory
insights.[44]

Besides **Nostra aetate**, other conciliar declarations make important comments that bear directly on the
Church's attitude towards non-Christians and their religions, notably the **Dogmatic Constitution on the
Church (Lumen gentium)** and the **Decree on the Missionary
Activity of the Church (Ad gentes)**.[45] It is important
to keep in mind that there is no systematically developed theology of religions in the Council's decrees.
There are only scattered but important themes that

emerge. For example, in **Lumen gentium,** in a discussion
of the relationship of the Church to those outside its
boundaries, there is the insistence that God's saving
activity is mediated to humankind through Christ and
his Church, and so all men and women are ordained to
the Church for their salvation. However, the document
also affirms God's universal saving will, and so God
wills the salvation of all and provides them with the
means they need to receive it. God's saving grace,
then, is present everywhere. The particular means by
which God's offer of salvation reaches those outside
the Church, however, how they respond to it even though
they do not become explicit members of the Church, and
how they receive salvation through Christ even without
knowing him, are topics on which this decree does not
elaborate. The key thing to note is that the Council
does indeed affirm explicitly that salvation is possible to those who are not consciously members of the
Church. A key passage to this effect reads as follows:

> Those also can attain to everlasting
> salvation who through no fault of their own
> do not know the gospel of Christ or His
> Church, yet sincerely seek God and, moved by
> grace, strive by their deeds to do His will
> as it is known to them through the dictates
> of conscience. Nor does divine Providence de-
> ny the help necessary for salvation to those
> who, without blame on their part, have not
> yet arrived at an explicit knowledge of God,
> but strive to live a good life, thanks to His
> grace.[46]

Another important theme that recurs in these conciliar decrees is that the religions of the world do,

indeed, contain elements of truth and goodness and they do contain real moral and spiritual values.[47] Nevertheless, the decrees do not praise these religions unreservedly. Both **Lumen gentium** and **Ad gentes** see the good in them as being "preparations" for the Gospel message of Christ.[48] The religions are good and worthwhile to the extent that they point to God and direct people to their final goal, namely, a share in the divine life, but unless they are connected in some way with the fullness that comes through Christ, they cannot do so adequately. Moreover, **Ad gentes**, the missionary decree, notes that there is a tendency to pervert the truth and goodness that exist naturally in the world because of the effects of Original Sin.[49] The revelation of Christ must therefore purify and transform this truth and goodness if they are to be truly worthwhile and valuable. This affirmation, one should note, provides a motivation for the Church's missionary work.

A final noteworthy element in the Council's statements concerning non-Christians is the view that dialogue is a way for Christians to relate to them. This approach presupposes a genuine respect for the non-Christian and his or her beliefs. It involves a coming together of Christians and their non-Christian neighbours in mutual respect and a desire to get to know each other better. Moreover, it includes a recommendation that Christians collaborate with their non-Christian neighbours in facing common human problems.[50] This dialogical approach accords very well with the entire tone of the Council and marks a rather significant turning point in the history of the Church's relationships with those outside its boundaries.

In the missionary decree, as could be expected, this attitude of dialogue takes on a missionary dimension. Through a "patient and sincere" dialogue, the Christian is called to become more aware of the truths and values present in non-Christian religions so that he or she may show how Christ is the fulfillment of whatever is good and of value in these religions.[51] Dialogue is a first step in a gradual process of showing Christ as the "way, the truth, and the light."[52] Another interesting aspect of this missionary dimension is the use of dialogue as a means of making Christianity indigenous. Christians are urged to adapt their practices to the customs, outlooks, and culture of the various countries in which they live. They become familiar with these things through their dialogue with those living in the country concerned and through what the decree calls a "dialogue" with the culture concerned.[53]

Various documents from Vatican II, then, contain important themes related to the Christian attitude towards non-Christians and their religions. There are some important issues, however, which the Council did not address, and these became topics for discussion among Catholic theologians and hence among the members of the Secretariat for Non-Christians. Chief among these was the question of whether the non-Christian religions as such were positive means for the mediation of God's saving grace. The Council was clear in its assertion that anyone could receive salvation, but it did not explicitly deal with the matter of the role, if any, of the non-Christian religions in this simply beyond indicating that they can make their followers open to God. The relationship between dialogue and mission, moreover, seems problematic. The Council's missionary decree does lend some credence to the suspicion that dialogue is just another missionary tactic to be

employed by the Church, more overt and direct missionary activity having failed. These were to become important issues in the discussions by the Secretariat for
Non-Christians on its dialogue activity.

3. Comments by the Pope

During the years of his pontificate, Pope Paul VI
gave a number of addresses which touched upon the question of relations between the Church and non-Christians. Through his actions he also displayed a desire
to enter into contact with peoples of other religious
traditions. His trip to the Holy Land and then to India
in 1964 were occasions for displaying this, for on both
voyages he met with non-Christian groups. A number of
themes dominate the Pope's statements.[54] First of all,
the Pope consistently stressed that the Church wished
to work for the common good of all of humankind and
that it was an instrument of service, not of domination.[55] It desired to promote better mutual understanding and friendship through dialogue with the followers
of those religions outside its boundaries.[56] The Pope
also consistently praised the spiritual and moral values to be found in other religions and commended them
for promoting and preserving the sense of divine transcendence in the world.[57]

Yet there was also a continual insistence in the
Pope's remarks on the inherent superiority of Christianity which he saw as the only true faith.[58] Moreover, he repeated the idea that there were deficiencies
and imperfections in the values and truths proposed by
other religions, values and truths that could be fulfilled only by the message and grace that came from
Jesus Christ. Accordingly, the Pope compared the relationship between the Church and the world's non-Chris-

tian religions to the relationship between the first
glimmers of dawn and the fullness of light when dawn
completely shines forth. The religions contained the
glimmers of the truth that reached its splendor and
fullness in Christ. The image was expressed as follows:

> Every religion contains flashes of light
> which must not be depreciated or extin-
> guished, even if these are not sufficient to
> give to humankind the clearness which it
> needs and do not serve to duplicate the mir-
> acle of the Christian light which makes truth
> coincide with life. But every religion raises
> one to the transcendent Being, without whom
> there is no reason to exist, to discuss, to
> work responsibly, to hope without illusion.
> Every religion is a dawning of faith and we
> wait for the better daybreak, the most per-
> fect splendor of the Christian wisdom.[59]

Christianity as fulfillment, then, is one of the
dominant themes that is present in the Pope's remarks
on the relationship between the Church and the non-
Christian religions of the world.

With the preceding background in mind--Roman Catholic attempts to propose a theology of religions and
official statements coming from the Pope and the Second Vatican Council--it is now possible to examine in
some detail the work and thought in the activity of the
Secretariat for Non-Christians for the Secretariat's
activity and reflection evolved with this background in
mind.

IV. Early Problems and Clarifications

In the initial stages of the Secretariat's existence there was some discussion about the role the Secretariat was to play in terms of the Church's mission
and about the nature and goals of the dialogue activity in which it was supposed to be engaged. The dialogue activity recommended by both the Council and the
Pope was a relatively new form of activity for the
Church, at least on an organized, official level, and
there was no clear view of how it was to be carried
out. In the face of what they perceived to be some confusion concerning its activity, then, the officials of
the Secretariat issued a number of letters and statements in an effort to clear up misunderstandings. Two
of these, in particular, both directed towards bishops
interested in the Secretariat's work, indicate some of
the concerns the Secretariat's officials were facing as
well as some of the theological principles they saw as
motivating their work.

1. Explanatory Pamphlet to the Council Fathers

During the proceedings of the second session of
Vatican II, in late 1964, the Secretariat issued a
pamphlet to the Council Fathers explaining its nature
and its role.[60] In this pamphlet, the officials of the
Secretariat addressed two main questions. The first
concerned the definition of the dialogue partner. As
has already been mentioned, there had been some confusion in which it was thought that the Secretariat was
to be concerned only with those who believed in one,
personal God. This, the pamphlet points out, would have
limited the work of the Secretariat to Jews and Muslims
alone. Hence the pamphlet notes that the Secretariat's
activity was directed towards promoting dialogue with

everyone who, following some religious tradition, recognized a spiritual, transcendent realm beyond the material world. This expanded the dialogue partners to include the followers of all the major religions of the world, except, as already noted, Jews, who were dealt with by another agency.[61]

The second important issue, a recurrent one for the Secretariat as it turned out, concerned the relationship between the Secretariat and the Sacred Congregation for the Propagation of the Faith, that Vatican body in charge of the Church's missionary work. In short, the problem centered around the relationship between dialogue and mission. The pamphlet asserts that dialogue activity is distinct from missionary work. Each has its own proper objective and methods. Thus, the Secretariat's role was not to preach the Gospel directly in order to win converts, nor was it to engage in direct missionary activity. Rather, its role was simply to promote the establishment of friendly contacts between Christians and the men and women of other faiths on matters of mutual concern. The pamphlet states,

> It [viz., the Secretariat] proposes to create between Christians and followers of other religions a climate of great cordiality and understanding, with sincerity and charity. It is not its purpose to discuss doctrinal problems, much less to be charged with the mission of preaching and spiritual ministration, which is the duty of missionaries; rather, it will be bent on establishing contacts with non-Christians in regard to questions of common human interest.[62]

While claiming, however, that the dialogue with which it was concerned was distinct from missionary activity, the pamphlet points to some connection between the two. Dialogue, it says, is a means of "sowing the seeds" of the Gospel by setting up friendly contacts with non-Christians and thereby breaking down prejudices and hostility. Dialogue prepares the way for missionary work in areas where overt evangelization is impossible.[63]

It is necessary at this point to note an important element underlying the Secretariat's reflections on the nature and purpose of its activity, an element that emerges in this discussion of the relationship between dialogue and mission. The point of contact between Christians and non-Christians, that is, the common ground shared by Christians and non-Christians alike is, the Secretariat affirms, the common humanity that all share and the natural law that is present in all of creation. The latter is most important. The concept of natural law in Roman Catholic theology at this time involved the idea of the existence of a natural moral order, the following of which led one to a form of natural fulfillment.[64] It was the natural order and its natural fulfillment that was "transformed" and "elevated" to a "supernatural" state by God's grace since God ultimately directed humankind not to a natural end but to the supernatural end of divine life itself. This natural law, albeit obscured by the Fall, was nonetheless recognizeable in some way by all. It formed a moral base which all shared. It thus provided a basis for dialogue, since there were moral principles that all human beings could recognize and which they all shared. Dialogue on the purely "natural" level, then, could be grounded on this natural law present in creation.[65]

2. Explanatory Letter to the Bishops

Another explanatory note to the bishops, this time in the form of a letter sent to bishops who had attended informational meetings with officials of the Secretariat during the Council, appeared in February 1966.[66] As in the earlier 1965 informational pamphlet, this letter attempts to explain the activity of the Secretariat in the face of what its officials thought to be continuing misunderstandings. One of the main areas of confusion continued to be that of the relationship between dialogue and mission. The letter insists, as had the 1964 pamphlet, that there was no contradiction between the two, nor was there any overlapping in the work of the Secretariat and the work of the Sacred Congregation for the Propagation of the Faith. The letter states that the Secretariat's dialogue activities were directed towards those who had no interest at all in Christianity. The Secretariat simply hoped to encourage friendly contacts between the Church and these people. However, the letter also states that the eventual goal of this is to break down barriers and prejudices and to make those with whom the Church was dialoguing better disposed to the Church. Dialogue, then, was ultimately a means of preparing the way for more overt types of missionary work.[67]

The letter, though, expands on the reasons for the Church's involvement in dialogue with the followers of other religions. The Secretariat wanted to show that such dialogue was a proper form of Christian activity, wholly consistent with Christian ideals and traditions and not simply a new activity arising out of expediency. Thus the letter points to examples from the life of Jesus which would support the Secretariat's outreach to all. It notes that Jesus had died for all men and

women, implying thereby that the Church's concern
likewise extended to all since the Church was supposed
to continue Jesus' work after he left this world.
Moreover, there were times in the life of Jesus when he
found great faith among non-Jews, that is, among those
not belonging to the chosen people, and he had minis-
tered to them. Jesus, then, had exhibited a wide concern for others, a concern that went beyond the boundaries of his own nation and his own religious tradition.[68] Dialogue was, in this letter, a means of showing the universal concern which the life of Jesus had
exemplified.

V. Towards a Theology of Religions

One of the important tasks the officials of the
Secretariat undertook during this time of beginnings in
their work was that of trying to establish sound principles upon which to base a theology of religions. Mention has already been made of a number of tendencies in
Roman Catholic thinking on this topic during the 1950's
and 1960's.[69] The officials of the Secretariat were
very much concerned about the thinking taking place on
the topic of the world's religions. They had two major
concerns. First of all, they felt that there was too
much confusion in the Church because of divergent
views being advanced. Second, and perhaps most importantly, they felt that there was a tendency in many of
the views being put forward to be overly optimistic
about the chances for salvation for non-Christians.
They feared that there was a risk of casting into doubt
the need for missionary work.[70]

Members of the Secretariat discussed these issues
at a major Consultors' meeting in April, 1965. This
meeting is one of the key events in the Secretariat's

early years because during it the members of the Secretariat outlined a number of basic principles for the
elaboration of a theology of religions. The main theme
of the meeting was the salvation of non-Christians. In
discussing this question, the Secretariat wanted to
formulate a position that would first of all affirm
God's love for all of humankind, stressing the divine
universal saving will and the universal availability of
salvation, and, secondly, maintain the need for the
Church as the sole mediator of salvation. It hoped to
suggest a solid set of principles based on the Bible,
the Fathers and Doctors of the Church, and the pro-
nouncements of the magisterium. The Consultors discussed four traditional themes: 1) the knowledge non-
Christians have of God, 2) the manner in which non-
Christians receive God's saving grace, 3) the role of
non-Christian religions in furthering salvation, and 4)
the axiom "outside the Church, no salvation."

1. The Knowledge Non-Christians Can Have of God

Whether non-Christians can know God at all, and if
so, the type of knowledge they can have has been a
problem in Christian theology because Christians have
generally held that a real knowledge of God is possible
only through some form of divine revelation. This revelation, for Christians, has occurred in and through
the history of Israel and in the person and life of Jesus Christ. This knowledge of God is not simply knowledge for the sake of interest or to satisfy human cu-
riosity. There is a connection in Christianty between
knowledge of God and salvation. Salvation depends upon
one's acceptance of God's self-revelation which transforms one's consciousness and alters the way one understands the world and acts in it. Hence knowledge of God

is a crucial component of Christianity's understanding
of salvation.

The Roman Catholic tradition has generally been
open to the possibility that men and women can come to
some form of knowledge of God by their powers of reason
and by observing nature, but without the divine self-
revelation a deep and full knowledge of God is impossible. The Secretariat followed this general line of
thinking in its 1965 Consultors' meeting. The Consultors agreed that those outside the Church could know
something about God through the signs of the divine
presence in nature and in their conscience. By reflecting on creation, one could know of the existence, grandeur, and goodness of God. Through one's conscience,
one could be aware of natural moral principles implanted into creation by God. However, this "natural"
type of knowledge of God was at best ambiguous and, because of the vitiated human condition after the Fall,
often distorted.[71]

While following the traditional Roman Catholic position about the natural knowledge of God, the Consultors also affirmed the possibility of a type of "supernatural" or revealed knowledge of God even among those
outside the Church. They pointed to the Scriptures
which were full of examples of revelation being granted
to those outside the domain of the chosen elect. For
example, God revealed something of the divine nature
and will to Melchizedek, Job, and Noah, none of whom
were Jews. The Church's own theological tradition made
the same point: there is revelation outside the boundaries of the Church. Thus, although it was in the
Christian Church that one had access to the fullness of
God's revelation, the Secretariat's Consultors took the
view that revelation was not necessarily restricted to

Christianity. There were elements of supernatural revelation present among non-Christians, perhaps even in
their religions, although it was not complete and
although it was not possible to point to an actual
example in any particular religion.[72]

2. The Justification of Non-Christians

Just as the knowledge of God available to non-
Christians has been an issue in Christian theology, so
too has the question of the justification of those who
do not believe explicitly in Christ. Accordingly, this
topic received attention in the Consultors' meeting.
The point at issue was not really whether non-Christians could receive divine saving grace, but how they
did so. The position the Consultors' adopted followed
the lines of traditional Roman Catholic thinking on
this issue. The Consultors attempted to hold together
a number of different principles. First of all, then,
they insisted that God's salvation was mediated through
Jesus Christ alone, and, by extension, through the
Church he established. Second, they affirmed that God
desired the salvation of all men and women and provided
them with the necessary means of attaining it. Third,
they repeated the notion that men and women received
salvation not through their own merits but only through
God's freely given saving grace, a grace received by
responding to God's promptings, believing in Jesus
Christ and his saving work, and being baptized in his
name.

While faith in Jesus and baptism in his name were
the normal means by which one received God's saving
grace (normal because willed by God to be so), the Consultors followed the mainstream of Roman Catholic tradition by allowing for unusual means, notably baptism

of desire and implicit faith in Christ. Using these
categories, the Consultors likened the situation of
non-Christians living today to that of men and women
living before the coming of Christ. This distinction of
people living before and after the time of Christ
occurs in the Roman Catholic theological tradition to
excuse those living before the time of Christ from the
strict obligation of having explicit faith in Christ,
an obligation that is demanded in such biblical texts
as Acts 4:12: "For of all the names in the world given
to men, this [the name of Jesus] is the only one by
which we can be saved." Medieval theologians had placed
such an obligation on those living after the coming of
Christ because they assumed that the Gospel of Christ
had been preached to the ends of the earth and that all
people were thus in a position to accept or reject
it.[73] Such belief was impossible, of course, for those
who lived before Christ, yet so great was the conviction that faith in Christ was necessary for salvation
that some form of faith had to be attributed even to
them. Hence the notion of an implicit faith arose.[74]

    One of the examples of implicit faith in Christ to
which the summary article of the Consultors' meeting
points involves the medieval distinction between "majores" and "minores". The former were those who had received some form of special revelation about God and
God's will, the latter those who followed the former
thereby sharing implicitly in the faith these had in
the received revelation. These "majores" were not, one
should note, restricted to the ranks of those great
figures in the Jewish tradition, figures like Moses and
the prophets, who were thought to have received some
partial revelation about God's will. There were non-
Jews, too, who had received some form of revelation,

the great pagan philosophers being the most prominent.[75] All of these great figures had received some
type of revelation about God's plan for humankind, a
plan carried out finally by Christ. To the extent that
they believed this revelation and lived according to
the truth they saw in it, they had faith in God and implicit faith in Christ who finally effected God's saving plan for the world. Such implicit faith was even
possible, some theologians argued, for non-Christians
through their participation in the sacrificial rituals
of their respective religions. These sacrifices could
be considered proleptic "types" of Christ's perfect
sacrifice with those who took part in them exercising
an implicit faith in the perfect sacrifice of Christ of
which these sacrifices were but pale shadows.[76]

In applying the principles that Roman Catholic
theology had originally applied to those living before
the time of Christ to present day non-Christians, the
Consultors were recognizing that knowledge of God's
saving work in Christ and the realization of the necessity for explicit faith in Christ were not existential-
ly forceful or even possible even so long after the
time of Christ as the twentieth century. There were
many historical and cultural impediments to the acceptance of the Gospel message. Thus, the summary article
of the Consultors' meeting says,

> In short, one can still say today, as
> once before in the time of St. Prosper, that
> the **tempus gratiae revelatae** does not begin
> at a fixed and universal date, that of the
> birth or the Passion of the Saviour. It is an
> event that is realized gradually in the dif-
> ferent countries and the different communi-
> ties of humankind.[77]

Those who, through some form of implicit faith, had opened themselves up to God's justifying grace, were implicit Christians, the Consultors noted. They belonged to the Church in an extended sense. It was not necessary, then, to belong explicitly to the Church to be saved. The summary account of their conclusions says,

> It is necessary from the outset to note that all the justified will not necessarily end up belonging to the Catholic religion, either because it is impossible for them to know it, or because the knowledge they have is accompanied by prejudices and deformities that prevent them from receiving it. They will therefore remain to the end **implicit** Christians, while others, more fortunate, will become **explicit** Christians.[78]

This notion of implicit Christianity, though, referred only to those who were justified by God, not to anyone simply because he or she appeared to be leading a good life. These latter were "potential" Christians, not implicit ones.[79]

3. The Non-Christian Religions

While the Consultors discussed the justification of individual non-Christians, they also discussed the role of the non-Christian religions in the divine plan of salvation. The primary role of these religions was to act as preparations for God's saving grace. These religions reinforced belief in God and promoted high moral values. They could thus open their followers up to God's presence. Thus,

> [Any non-Christian religion], Hinduism for
> example, can constitute a serious obstacle to
> one's conversion to Christianity and yet its
> higher moral values and the stronger training
> it gives to the soul can prepare the soul to
> reply more easily and generously to the call
> of grace.[80]

Although the non-Christian religions might be
preparations for God's saving grace, in themselves they
were not the real divinely-willed means for the mediation of such grace. One could be saved in them, but
they were not the same as the Church. Their role could
be that of making their followers receptive to a spiritual realm and of encouraging an upright life thereby promoting the conditions which made an implicit
faith in Christ possible. Yet it was through the Church
that God wanted to mediate the divine saving grace. All
those saved were thus related to the Church in some
way, if only implicitly.[81] The summary of the position
advanced by the Consultors expresses this as follows:

> One cannot . . . say in the full and ab-
> solute sense of the word that the non-Chris-
> tian is saved by his or her religion, even
> though one can admit that it would have been
> more difficult to be saved without it unless
> there were some special grace from God. . .
> . [I]t does often happen that someone is
> saved in his or her religion and that God
> uses what is good or indifferent in that
> person's belief to attract the person in-
> volved. Yet one must not forget that the jus-
> tified Buddhist or Hindu has in fact become
> an **implicit** Christian, that he or she thus

belongs to the true Church and receives because of this the marks which are given to
it. One may be--and often is--more fervent in
one's former cult than one was before, but
one is nonetheless a member of the true
Church.[82]

The position that the Consultors advanced in their
April 1965 meeting concerning the non-Christian religions of the world recognized that there were, indeed,
real spiritual and moral values in these religions,
although they were only preparations for the values and
good in the Gospel revelation. But there was something
more in these religions that is of great significance.
These religions may actually contain elements of God's
revelation. The discussion above on the possibility of
revelation to the "majores" indicates the reason for
this. God does not restrict divine revelation to the
Judaeo-Christian tradition. Such revelation may be
contained in the various non-Christian religions of the
world whose founders could even be considered as "majores." Thus these religions may not simply be considered "natural," the result of human reasoning about
God.[83] Nonetheless, despite the value and good these
religions had and despite the elements of God's revelation they contained, this was deficient and could
even be perverted because it was not based on the fullness of divine revelation found in the Church. Christians should respect the non-Christian religions of the
world while at the same time work towards correcting
their errors.[84] It was through dialogue, interestingly
enough, that this might be done. The summary article
notes,

One cannot but speak well of **religion,** but
one must have reservations about any particular religion. On the whole, we must hope
along with the Holy Father, Paul VI, that
they preserve whatever good they have but we
must also hope to fill in their deficiencies
and redress their errors. This is one of the
goals of dialogue, a goal which should be
realized by speaking about it as little as
possible.[85]

In their reflections on the non-Christian religions of the world, then, the Consultors attempted to
tread a path between outright condemnation of these religions as totally false perversions, harmful to humankind's salvation, and an overly optimistic acceptance
of them which would put them on an equal footing with
Christianity. For the Consultors, Christianity was the
sole recipient of God's full saving revelation and it
alone contained the ordinary means set up by God to
mediate the divine saving grace. While there could be
elements of divine revelation in other religions, it
was only in Christianity, and to be more precise, only
in the Catholic Church, that such revelation was
complete. While the non-Christian religions contained
values and promoted proper moral action and a spiritual life, they were not the proper means willed by God
for the mediation of divine grace. Their goodness and
worth was of a preparatory nature insofar as they
directed their followers to God and to at least an implicit faith in Christ.

4. The Axiom "Outside the Church, No Salvation"

One of the problematic assertions arising in the Roman Catholic tradition on salvation was the assertion that there was no salvation for those outside the Church. This statement was part of the official magisterial teaching of the Roman Catholic Church, although the official interpretation of it did not mean that only those who were explicitly baptized into the Church could be saved. Implicit faith, noted above, was sufficient and made one a member of the Church in an extended sense.[86] However, at a time when the Church wanted to reach out in friendship to the people of other religious traditions, this axiom was particularly embarrassing because of the negative and uncompromising attitude it conveyed. What made the Consultors in this 1965 meeting even more sensitive to it was that during a meeting on world religions held in Bombay in 1964,[87] the Swiss theologian, Hans Kung, had been very critical of it.[88] In the face of this attack, the Consultors wanted to uphold the Church's tradition.

The summary article on the Consultors' meeting shows that they did not want to suggest that the Church simply repudiate the unfortunate axiom, mainly, as suggested above, because it was part of the Church's doctrinal teaching. Rather than suppress it entirely, then, the Consultors suggested that it be mentioned as little as possible when Christians dealt with people from other religions, and when it was mentioned, that its positive aspects be highlighted. By "positive" aspects, the Consultors apparently meant that Christians should talk about the doctrine as one which expresses the idea that all salvation was mediated through the Church, even that salvation attained through implicit faith. The summary of their discussion says,

We should employ [the saying] as little as
possible in our special task, and when we
have to use it, we must present it under its
positive aspect: the Church is the only ark
of salvation and offers it to all; it offers
it even to those who are outside of it
through no fault of their own by means of **implicit faith.**[89]

In not wanting to repudiate the doctrine completely, the Consultors were also being sensitive to questions being raised from missionary circles at this time
about the value of missionary activity.[90] The problem
raised by missionaries was quite simple, namely, that
if God's saving help was available to those outside the
Church just as it was for members of the Church, why
carry on missionary work at all? In reply, the Consultors argued that those within the Church were "more
fortunate" because of the tremendous help the Church
afforded in their journey towards salvation. Those outside the Church, for example, did not have the help of
the sacraments, the clear revealed doctrines about God
and God's relation to humankind, or the sound revealed
moral principles according to which one ought to
conduct one's life.[91] Missionary work was needed to
make them available to everyone.

VI. Summary Reflection on the Early Years

The 1965 Consultors' meeting brings to an end the
first part of this examination of the work and thought
of the Secretariat for Non-Christians. By way of summary, I would like to point out a number of important
points that surfaced about dialogue and about the
Christian understanding of the world's religions during

this time. The directions marked out by the Secretariat in these early years are directions that will recur, as will be seen in subsequent chapters.

The first thing to note about dialogue is that it
is seen very broadly by the Secretariat as a non-hostile encounter between Christians and the followers of
other religious traditions. It included, then, many
forms of such encounter. Secondly, a concern over the
identity of the dialogue partner was settled very early
in the Secretariat's work. The dialogue partner was any
follower of one of the major religious traditions of
the world except for Judaism, for reasons already noted
above. Thirdly, the relationship between dialogue and
mission was problematic. This emerges as a continual
question. For the Secretariat, dialogue and mission are
separate activities. Dialogue is not geared directly
towards conversion, yet it is seen as a form of pre-
missionary activity. Fourthly, there is a search for
"points of contact," the main ones being the common humanity Christians share with non-Christians, the natural law implanted in creation, and common human concerns. There is also present in the statements coming
from the Secretariat the grounds for affirming a shared
supernatural revelation as a point of contact, but this
receives no development during this time.

In carrying out its dialogue activity, the Secretariat reflected upon the religious traditions that influenced the lives of prospective dialogue partners. A
theological evaluation of humankind's religious traditions and how Christianity is related to other religions is apparent. There are some important aspects of
this evaluation to note. First of all, Christianity is
separate from all other religious traditions in that it
alone is based upon God's definitive revelation through

Jesus Christ. Christianity (or the Church, the two often being used synonymously) is divinely instituted, meant to continue and extend the saving work effected by Christ. Second, other religions may contain real moral and spiritual values, primarily "natural" ones. Third, the non-Christian religions may also contain traces of God's supernatural revelation that is present outside the Church. Fourth, because they may make their followers open to God's saving grace and arouse an implicit faith in them, non-Christian religions can be preparations for God's grace. Fifth, in themselves, these religions are ambiguous, that is, they contain not only spiritual and moral values but also perversions arising from their dependence on human reasoning, so vitiated by the Fall. Finally, the non-Christian religions are not as such means of salvation, equal to Christianity in mediating God's saving grace. Only the Church has the divinely-ordained means by which human beings receive God's grace. There is, though, salvation outside the visible Church, but such salvation is the result of implicitly holding the faith preached definitively by the Church and is mediated in a mysterious way.

CHAPTER TWO
PURSUING THE MANDATE
(1967 - 1973)

During the first three years of the Secretariat's existence, its officials were primarily engaged in laying the groundwork for their new organization and planning its activity. During the next few years under the presidency of Cardinal Marella, they began to carry through with their plans and projects. A glance at the Vatican's official record of the activities of its various Congregations and Secretariats, **Attività della Santa Sede,** during the years 1967-1973 shows the many activities in which the Secretariat became engaged. Among the most significant for this study was the publication of a series of books designed to provide guidance for those engaging in interreligious dialogue and to foster better understanding by Christians of the beliefs and practices of their non-Christian neighbours. These publications are important because they deal directly with the concerns the Secretariat had about dialogue and because they reveal the theological presuppositions concerning the religions of the world that undergirded the Secretariat's work. A large part of this present chapter, then, will be devoted to an examination of these publications. The officials of the Secretariat also continued to speak and write about the nature and role of the Secretariat in an effort to stimulate more dialogue activity on the part of Christians and to clarify misconceptions they perceived about this new activity. Moreover, while the Secretariat did not itself want to sponsor dialogue meetings, it sent representatives to selected meetings and, very importantly, became engaged in the dialogue activity then beginning in the World Council of Churches. Finally, through a series of general Consultors' meetings, the Secretariat continued a process of reflection and education in which its own members shared their knowledge and experience of other religious traditions and discussed strategies for the continuation of the Secretariat's work.

The general organizational structure of the Secretariat remained the same during this time, with two additions. To the existing special "Section" on Islam, the Secretariat added special Sections to deal with, firstly, the religions of Asia (Hinduism and Buddhism) and secondly, the so-called "traditional" religions, especially those in Africa. Each Section had its own head who could concentrate on the problems connected with dialogue in his own area of competence. The need for these additional Sections is an indication of the Secretariat's increasing activity and hence increasing work load.

I. The Secretariat's Publications

As noted above, the Secretariat began to follow through with a number of publications it had been planning during its initial years. It had already begun to publish a regular **Bulletin** in 1966 which came out three times a year. Officials of the Secretariat hoped that this **Bulletin** would provide the opportunity for its members to exchange information and express opinions on dialogue and on the religions of the world. It was a kind of link among the various people involved in the Secretariat's work. As well as this, however, the Secretariat also began to publish special works dealing with particular topics. These publications included various guides for dialogue, starting with a general guidebook which dealt with the principles of dialogue as such, followed by a series of special guidebooks concentrating on particular religious traditions. The first of these (**Towards the Meeting of Religions. Suggestions for Dialogue: General Section**) appeared as the third Supplement to the **Bulletin** in 1967. It was designed to deal with "concepts and guidelines which can be applied to a greater or lesser degree to all peoples and to all religions."[1] While a large portion of this guidebook concerns practical matters of information for those who take part in dialogue (such as pointing out occasions in one's daily life where opportunities for dialogue can occur), this general guide also indicates the Secretariat's view of the religions of the world and their followers and it provides theoretical reflections on the basis for and purpose of dialogue.

The special guidebooks that followed were designed to provide information to Christians in particular areas of the world about the religious tradition of the people with whom these Christians came in contact.[2] These guidebooks are largely concerned with describing the beliefs and practices of these particular religious traditions (insofar as the Secretariat understood them), but theoretical reflections do emerge concerning both dialogue activity and how Christians should evaluate the religious tradition in question. A final publication of note was a "manual" for religions (**Religions. Fundamental Themes for a Dialogistic Understanding**). This book was a collection of essays on various themes connected with the human search for God. Such themes included the general anthropological basis of

religion, the human quest for salvation, the understanding of the Absolute in the various major religions
of the world, and various views of good and evil. The
approach taken was phenomenological, that is, the book
describes the way various religions deal with these
themes. The section of the anthropological basis of religions, the introductory part of the work, does however discuss important principles for a theology of religions. All of these publications provide significant
indications of the Secretariat's view of the two general themes which are the focus of this book, dialogue
and the Christian approach to other religions, and so
are essential for a proper understanding of that organization's position.

1. Dialogue in the Secretariat's Publications

The general guide for dialogue and the various
special guidebooks set forth the Secretariat's understanding of the nature, basis, and purpose of dialogue
in a very consistent way. One of the first things to
note is that dialogue continues to be understood in the
Secretariat as almost any type of non-hostile encounter
between Christians and the followers of another religious tradition.[3] The Secretariat's publications,
though, make a distinction between "human" or "secular"
dialogue and "religious" dialogue. The former was any
type of coming together by the followers of different
religions to face some common human problem posed in
the society in which they lived. This was the most
usual type of dialogue that Christians could participate in and it occurred everywhere on many different
levels. The second type of dialogue involved the discussion of religious beliefs, practices, customs, and
the like. It was usually pursued by experts in a

formal, organized meeting. In both of these types of
dialogue, the guidelines noted, the emphasis should be
on the interpersonal encounter between the particpants.
Dialogue was primarily a meeting between persons, not
a meeting of systems of belief.[4]

If dialogue were a meeting of persons, it was also
a meeting of persons committed to their respective religious traditions. The persons involved in it did not
have to hide or minimize their beliefs. In fact, the
opposite was the case. The guidebooks insist that
Christians must bear witness to their faith in dialogue. This is done, they suggest, primarily through
leading a truly Christian life.[5]

The witness of Christians to their faith in dialogue did not mean that dialogue could be considered a
missionary activity. The guidebooks repeat the general
thrust of what has been pointed out in the preceding
chapter, namely, that dialogue and mission are separate
activities in the Church. Christians involved in dialogue were not engaging in a direct attempt to convert
others to Christianity.[6] Nevertheless, one repeatedly
finds the idea also seen in the earlier statements that
dialogue is a form of pre-evangelization, preparing the
way for missionary work in the proper sense.[7]

Since dialogue was a rather new form of Christian
engagement with peoples of other faiths, one of the
things the officials of the Secretariat continually
tried to do was to point out the common bond between
Christians and others, emphasizing that which they
shared and which therefore served as a basis for coming
together. One of these common bonds mentioned in the
guidebooks was the common humanity which all shared.
This notion actually includes a number of points. Most
prominent is that all of humankind is a pilgrim people

on a common journey towards God who is the source and
the goal of all. God was calling all people to a share
in the divine life and all were on the way towards this
divine fulfillment. The guidebook for dialogue with
Muslims expresses this idea as follows:

> It should be the source of very great joy for
> us to see them [viz., Muslims] engaging in a
> completely sincere and authentic search for
> God, for then we can share their journey and
> take part in their quest for the truth. Thus
> hand in hand we shall come under the influ-
> ence of that spiritual dynamism which will
> sweep us along through the vicissitudes of
> life towards union with God.[8]

As well as being pilgrims seeking after God, men
and women of differing religions were also co-workers
in the building up of the world, facing common tasks
and problems. The Secretariat's treatment of dialogue
on the "human" level brings out this aspect of the human condition. The guidebooks insist that Christians
must not remain aloof from joining with others in the
solution of problems in the societies in which they belong. Rather, they must cooperate with their fellow
citizens in overcoming these problems. Just as there is
an essential unity among all of humankind in its search
for God, so, too, is there an essential unity among all
men and women in facing up to the problems of their
particular society and of the world at large.[9]

The presence of "elements of truth and goodness"
in the religious traditions of the world provides another important basis for dialogue in the Secretariat's
guidebooks. These elements provide "points of contact"
upon which to base dialogue. Examples of this truth and

goodness remain rather unclear, however. What is clear is that the truth and goodness existing in the non-Christian religions of the world derive primarily from the natural truth and goodness that exist in creation itself which contains the divine imprint and which testifies to its divine source.[10] But is there also a "supernatural" truth and goodness somehow present in the world's non-Christian religions, elements of God's self-revelation captured in their beliefs and rituals? The guidebooks do not provide a very detailed discussion of this possibility, but they do say that God's "Word" is present to all men and women. There is at least an opening for the affirmation that God's supernatural revelatory presence may be found in these religions. The guidelines for dialogue with the African religions indicates this more clearly than the other guidebooks, saying,

> 'The Church does not reject anything that is true and holy in these religions. It has a serious respect for a way of living and acting, for rules and doctrines which, though they differ in many points from what it holds and teaches, nevertheless often bring **a ray of the Truth which gives light to all men'**.
>
> This essential passage, taken from the Gospel according to St. John, should direct our new attitude towards the African religions. It connects with the intuition of the Fathers of the Church of the first centuries: the Word of God was at work among the pagans, through the real values of their religions and apart from any preaching.[11]

The Secretariat's various guidebooks also discuss the goals of dialogue. One of the dominant goals that emerges has to do with the improving of relations between the members of various religious traditions. Dialogue is seen as a way of extending the Church's ministry of love for all. By getting to know the other better through dialogue, by establishing personal contacts between believers, hostilities and prejudices, the guidebooks hope, can be broken down.[12]

A second goal concerns the building up of the human community. Through a process of dialogue, the guidebooks note, the members of a particular community should be able to come together to face up to and overcome the problems their community faces. The emphasis is on a collective and cooperative approach to human problems. Christians are thus urged to work with others.[13]

Finally, dialogue is seen as a means of pre-evangelization, that is, it serves as a means of preparing the way for the spread of the Gospel message. It is important to keep in mind that throughout all of the guidebooks, and indeed, in all of the reflections emerging from the Secretariat on dialogue, there is the continued insistence that Christ alone is the "way, the truth, and the life," and that the revelation of God which comes through him is the fullness of revelation possible.[14] Thus, although dialogue is not aimed explicitly at overt preaching of the Gospel or at converting the non-Christian dialogue partner, there is always the hope that it will open the non-Christian up to the fullness that comes through Christ alone. The sharing of the spiritual resources and experiences of Christianity may have the result, then, of satisfying the aspirations and ideas left unsatisfied in other re-

ligious traditions.[15] The missionary aims of the Church
may thus be fulfilled.

The sharing of spiritual insights is not seen,
however, as a one-way affair. The Christian partner can
benefit from the dialogue with people of other religious traditions. This idea is most evident in the
guidebook for Hindu-Christian dialogue which states
more forcefully than do the other guidebooks that
Christians can, through dialogue, attain a deeper understanding of God by recognizing how God works through
the religious life of others. It says,

> [The dialogue partners] do not merely search
> for some "common denominator" between their
> religious convictions; they wish to enrich,
> deepen, broaden their own religious life by
> listening to God as He has spoken to men of
> other faiths, as He is speaking now to each
> dialogue partner, through the other's exper-
> ience and realization.[16]

More commonly, though, dialogue provides the Christian
partner with the opportunity of becoming more open to
certain dimensions of the truth which may have been ne-
glected in his or her own religious life or which may
not be stressed adequately. Thus Hinduism, for example,
with its sense of the sacred character of all material
reality, may help Christians influenced by Western em-
piricism and materialism to rediscover the sacred
depths to the created world.[17]

2. The Theology of Religions in the
Secretariat's Publications

In the course of their remarks on dialogue, the
various dialogue books provide an idea of the theolog-

ical evaluation of the religions of the world that the Secretariat favoured. One of the essential features of this evaluation is the anthropological basis upon which it rests.[18] Humankind, the Secretariat's dialogue books presuppose, is essentially "religious." Men and women have an innate self-transcending tendency and so reach out for the Absolute. This orientation to the Absolute is that which constitutes the specifically religious dimension of human existence.[19] In Christian terms, all men and women seek God.

It is this "religious disposition," this tendency to seek God or the Absolute, that is at the root of humankind's religious institutions. Human beings are social by nature, and express their inner dispositions in outer, visible, corporeal ways. Thus, the religious element in human nature has given rise to the religions of the world. These religions are the social expressions of humankind's religious nature.[20]

The notion that humankind is religious by nature fits in very well with the understanding of humankind as a pilgrim people on the march towards God, an understanding that is evident in the various dialogue guidebooks.[21] This march towards God, moreover, does not go without a response. If God has created human beings to seek their divine source, God has also responded to their quest. God has been engaged in a continual "dialogue of salvation," offering to men and women a share in the divine life which they so earnestly seek.

A question arises, at this point, as to whether the religions of the world, those institutional expressions of humanity's religious nature, are **loci** for the divine revelatory presence by which men and women are offered a share in the life of God. In my remarks on

dialogue in the Secretariat's publications, I showed
that there are indications in these publications which
point to a positive response. The religions of the
world need not necessarily be simply the expression of
humankind's search for God. They may also contain
aspects of the divine inbreaking. This idea is not common in the guidebooks, but it is expressed in the
guidebook for dialogue in Africa which says,

> If God is at work in the traditional African
> religions, and if man responds to this divine
> activity, the African religions contain an
> element of revelation and help of divine
> grace, because God, from the beginning of
> time, seeks to make himself known to men, and
> this response of man to God is religion. The
> man of dialogue should no longer use the
> terms "natural religion" or "human religion,"
> which reduce to the single dimension of a hu-
> man effort what is in reality an answer to a
> call.[22]

Nevertheless, although the non-Christians of the
world do contain worthwhile and praiseworthy truths,
spiritual and moral values, and even to some degree,
perhaps, God's revelation, in the Secretariat's guidebooks they remain predominantly the social expressions
of humankind's search for God. There is a profound difference between these religions and Christianity. The
latter is based upon God's definitive intervention in
history, God's saving work in the person of Jesus
Christ. It is in the Church that this saving work is
now continued. The Church (Christianity) is thus unique
and transcendent with respect to the other religions of
the world.[23] The general guide for dialogue points to

this fundamental difference very clearly, reflecting
the reason for the Secretariat's insistence on the superiority of Christianity, when it says,

> As an expression of man's seeking after
> God, they [the non-Christian religions] are
> on a different level to that of the Gospel
> which comes from above as Word and Spirit,
> gift of faith and charity, announcement and
> bestowal of salvation by God.[24]

As a result of the uniqueness and transcendence of
Christianity, based as it is on the Gospel message of
Christ and providing humankind with the means willed by
God for the mediation of salvation, the non-Christian
religions are seen as essentially "preparations" for
the Gospel. The notion of the non-Christian religions
as "preparations" for or "stepping-stones" to the
Christian proclamation is, in fact, one of the dominant
understandings of the non-Christian religions that is
present in the various dialogue guidebooks. They are
"stepping-stones" because the value and good they promote and the aspirations to which they give witness require the Christian message for their completion. This
message fulfills the longings for salvation and the
yearning after God which are present in the other religious traditions. Hence, the non-Christian religions,
inasmuch as they contain real value and truths, are
ordained to the Church, that institution established by
Christ which transmits the fullness of the Gospel message. As "preparations," the values promoted by the
non-Christian religions are not, then, complete in
themselves. They must be raised and purified by God.
One of the fundamental assertions of Christian theology is at work here. Humankind cannot attain salvation

by its own efforts. No matter what good human beings perform, salvation is always a free gift from God. And it is this free gift which is offered to all by the Church. The general guide for dialogue asserts, then,

> . . . the non-Christian religions in their primary and authentic elements, as expressions of man's aptitude for religion and of the moral law inscribed in his heart, can be considered as ways ordained by God beforehand in view of salvation and of the Church, to which the spiritual gifts of peoples lead, as was announced by the prophets.[25]

The theology of religions advanced by the Secretariat in its guidebooks, and indeed everywhere else, affirms that the revelation of God on which Christianity is based builds on and completes the human striving after the divine and on the natural good in creation. It does not deny this striving and this good or condemn it as totally corrupt. This understanding is important because of certain Protestant tendencies to insist on a contrary view.[26]

A final question to be considered in this discussion of the non-Christian religions of the world concerns their role in the mediation of God's saving grace. The question as posed by the Secretariat usually takes the following form: are they ways of salvation? In all of the guidebooks there is no question but that salvation is possible to those beyond the visible boundaries of the Church. But the normal method, ordained by God, is through the Church. It is ultimately the Church that mediates God's saving will to humankind. The general guide to dialogue sums up this position, a position that is also present in the other

guidebooks, and which highlights this key role of the
Church, as follows:

> A regime of personal graces . . . undoubtedly
> exists outside the Church and has existed
> prior to the Church. "God has other ways of
> saving souls outside the cone of light which
> is the revelation of salvation" (Paul VI,
> O.R., 15 May, 1965) despite the incertitude
> and the arguments carried on by theologians
> as to the channels by which this grace can
> reach individual souls, and on the nature of
> this grace. What is certain is the fact that
> God's action reaches men in the very experi-
> ence of life and of their conscience, that
> all divine grace is **grace of Christ through
> the Church** and that it "ordains these men" to
> take their place at the end of time among the
> People of God.[27]

The role of the non-Christian religions in the history
of God's saving activity on behalf of humankind is,
then, in general terms, to open their followers up to
the mysterious workings of God outside the visible
Church and arouse in them an implicit faith. These religions can be the occasions for this extraordinary way
of salvation.[28] They are useful, valuable, and even
providential to the extent that they do this.[29]

II. Articles and Addresses by Officials
of the Secretariat

The publications reviewed above were not the only
writings of importance during this time when the Secretariat began to pursue its mandate in earnest. The
major officials of the Secretariat, Cardinal Marella,

Fr. Pierre Humbertclaude, and Mgr. Rosanno, wrote a number of articles or gave addresses that were intended to explain the role of the Secretariat, their understanding of dialogue, or their view of how Christians should evaluate non-Christians and their religions. Many of these articles and addresses appear in the Secretariat's **Bulletin.** While it may repeat remarks already made, it is illuminating to review what these officials said.[30]

1. Dialogue in the Reflections of the Secretariat's Officials

One of the continuing topics of discussion about interreligious dialogue within the ranks of the Secretariat during this time was the relationship between dialogue and mission. In their articles and addresses, the three above-named officials of the Secretariat present a consistent view, the same view that has already been noted in the preceding section, namely, that dialogue and mission are separate activities in which the Church is legitimately engaged. Dialogue differs from missionary work in that it is not geared directly towards the conversion of non-Christians into the Church.[31] The Christian in dialogue, then, is not attempting to persuade his or her dialogue partner to become Christian, although this may happen as a result of the encounter. Nevertheless, there continues to be a certain underlying connection between these two forms of activity in the minds of the Secretariat's officials. Dialogue is a form of pre-evangelization, preparing the way for a future "harvest" as the non-Christian dialogue partner becomes more familiar with and more receptive to the Gospel message proclaimed in what the Christian partner says and does.[32]

Another repeated point about dialogue that emerges in the writings of the Secretariat's officials is that proper dialogue does not call for a weakening or a denial by Christians of their faith. Interreligious dialogue is a dialogue between believers firmly committed to what they believe. It does not lead to or require any form of syncretism, understood as the mixing up of elements of various elements of different religions. It does not lead to the watering-down of the Christian message. Whether it be a question of dialogue on the human level or dialogue at the religious level, the Christian can, and must, remain firmly committed in his or her faith.[33]

In discussing the basis for dialogue, the Secretariat's officials emphasize the points of contact that exist between Christians and their non-Christian neighbours. All share a common humanity. All share the same origin and all are called to the same end. Humankind is thus a pilgrim people on the road towards God. In the case of the dialogue concern of the Secretariat for Non-Christians, since it was interested in dialogue between followers of religious traditions, another common ground was an interest in the divine and in the spiritual dimension of reality. Moreover, all shared the natural law and could recognize and respect that which was naturally good.[34] Recognition of this natural law is a feature of the religions of the various cultures of the world, providing yet another basis of dialogue between believers, then. Finally, these religions may contain traces of God's self-revealing and saving presence and so Non-Christians may share with their Christian neighbours elements of divine revelation. Pierre Humbertclaude sums up some of these points of contact as follows:

All of us are men, sensitized as a result of human law which is the natural law.
We are, moreover, these others and ourselves,
religious men for whom the **spiritual** has a
meaning. We have a **moral** sense, a conscience,
and a respect for the divine. These are so
many points which bring us close together and
enable us to unite our efforts to live in
peace and concord on this common ground.

There are, moreover, some points which
are shared by our religions and our beliefs,
those rays of truth of which the Holy Father
has spoken and which enabled him to say: "Every religion is a dawning of faith and we
look forward to meeting it in a higher
dawn."[35]

While there was a basis for dialogue in the many
points of contact that existed between peoples of differing religious traditions, there was also another
type of basis for dialogue. Christians should reach out
in love to all, in imitation of the divine "dialogue of
salvation" in which God has continually reached out to
all, offering them salvation. Christians are called to
love and to show their concern for all people, and dialogue was, the Secretariat's officials insisted, one
of the ways by which they could do this. The Church's
desire to enter into dialogue, then, was an expression
of the Church's universal concern and followed the example of the divine activity on behalf of all humankind.[36]

A final major topic concerning dialogue in the reflection of the major officials of the Secretariat centered on the purpose of dialogue. Mention has already
been made of the "pre-evangelistic" intent that dia-

logue had. Insofar as the more immediate goals of dialogue are concerned, one of the chief ones was simply
that of promoting mutual respect, admiration and love,
and the building up of friendship among the dialogue
partners. [37] It is for this reason that there is a lot
of emphasis on getting to know the other better through
dialogue in the views of the Secretariat's officials.
The hoped for result is a better human community.

On the "religious" plane, however, one of the
goals of dialogue in the articles and addresses under
consideration here is that of enabling mutual enlightenment to take place among the dialogue partners in
their common journey towards God. In his writings, Mgr.
Rossano introduces the term "maieutic" to describe this
aspect of dialogue. The goal of dialogue, he remarks,
is not simply to get the dialogue partners to live in
a state of peaceful co-existence. Rather, it is also,
at its highest level, useful in helping the dialogue
partners in their search for answers to their deepest
aspirations, aspirations satisfied only by God. In dialogue, then, new insights into and new understandings
of the journey to God are the ultimate goals.[38]

On the part of Christians, this mutual edification
involved the recognition that there were values and
goods in the non-Christian religious traditions, that
God may indeed be at work in these religions, and that
Christians could actually learn from the religious
practices of their followers who respond to God's presence. It was through dialogue that Christians could
find new insights into God's activity among all peoples. On the part of non-Christians, the Secretariat's
officials all express the hope that they will come to
a fuller understanding of the truth revealed in Christ
and that they will allow the spiritual and moral values

of their religions to be "raised, purified, and transformed" by this truth.[39] Growth for non-Christians,
then, involves the realization that truth is found in
the Gospel message of the Church. Mgr. Rossano sums up
the maieutic purpose of dialogue as follows:

> Dialogue is essentially maieutic, that is to
> say, directed progressively towards the gen-
> eration of a new reality . . . . [A] dialog-
> ical attitude considered as an end in itself
> would mean the drying up of the religious
> conscience of mankind . . . . For this rea-
> son the Church seriously regards dialogue as
> a search. The Christians do not intend to
> throw away anything they possess, let alone
> jettison the treasure of Revelation; but they
> feel they have a duty to look more closely at
> the non-Christian religions, to look beyond
> the usual horizons of past generations. Simi-
> larly, the non-Christian religions are in-
> vited to have a confrontation with the man of
> today, to inspect their foundations critical-
> ly and to raise their eyes to the Church of
> Christ.[40]

2. A Theological Evaluation of the
Religions of the World

In the course of their written reflections on dialogue, the officials of the Secretariat provide valuable insights into the theological principles that
grounded their work. Since Mgr. Rossano was the most
prolific writer of this group on questions involving a
theological evaluation of the world's religions, much
of this section will deal with his comments, although
other officials will be examined as well.

In their articles and addresses, the officials of
the Secretariat repeat the idea that human beings are
essentially "religious", an idea found in the Secretariat's official publications. They also have the same
notion of the general nature of the world's non-Christian religions. Humankind by nature seeks God. The non-
Christian religions of the world are the social, institutional expressions of this.[41] There is, however, a
real fundamental difference between Christianity and
the other religions of the world. Christianity alone is
based upon God's full, explicit revelation and God's
definitive saving action in Christ. Thus, Christianity
can be considered unique and transcendent.[42]

An extremely important feature of the Secretariat's thinking on the non-Christian religions of the
world found in the writings of its officials is that
these religions may not simply be the result of the human quest for God. They may also, in some unspecified
way, contain elements of the divine self-revelation to
humankind. The Secretariat's officials affirm that God
does indeed work outside the Judaeo-Christian tradition, revealing the divine Self in some manner everywhere. Referring to the remarks of the Second Vatican
Council on the world's religions, remarks found in **Nostra Aetate** which indicate clearly the idea of the universality of God's revealing presence, Mgr. Rossano
says,

> . . . it was the very Council Declaration on
> the relationship between the Church and the
> non-Christian religions which indicated the
> common ground for the meeting between the
> Christian and the non-Christian in the reli-
> gious dimension of mankind. . . ; and the
> Council has gone even further confirming . .

. the existence of "elements of truth and
grace," of "true and holy things," common to
the Church and to non-Christian religions.
Whoever breaks up the elements of natural and
supernatural religious solidarity that exists
between Christianity and the religions of the
earth can only with difficulty keep to the
line of the Council and of the great Christian tradition.[43]

To discuss God's saving presence in the world, the
schema "general history of salvation" and "special history of salvation" emerges in the writings here under
consideration. The "special" history of salvation is
that history of God's dealings with humankind that is
recognized and remembered in the Judaeo-Christian tradition. For the officials of the Secretariat, this is
the normative and explicit history of salvation. In
this history, culminating in Christ, humankind receives
the definitive offer by God of salvation and the means
for attaining it, means found in the Church. The "general" history of salvation comprises God's secret dealings with all men and women everywhere who have not and
still do not take part in the special history of salvation. God has been, and still is, engaged in a "dialogue of salvation" with all human beings, offering
them a share in the divine life which alone fulfills
them. How this occurs, however, remains a mystery, but
it does occur. The religions of the world may facili-
tate this divine saving activity, and so they may be
included as part of the general history of salvation.[44]

The relationship between God's revelation on the
one hand and humankind's religious nature and the natural goodness of creation on the other hand is another topic of discussion in the writings of the Secretar-

iat's officials. The view of these officials is important when one compares it to certain major Protestant
tendencies current at the time. Because of his association with the dialogue movement then taking place in
the World Council of Churches, Mgr. Rossano gives a lot
of emphasis to this question in his writings, but the
views of both Cardinal Marella and Fr. Humbertclaude
are exactly the same. The neo-orthodox theological
movement in Protestantism, associated with the name of
Karl Barth, saw the non-Christian religions as emerging from the effort to know God and attain salvation by
human effort alone. In direct contradiction to this
stands God's revealed Word, addressed to humankind ultimately in Jesus Christ. God's Word condemns the human striving after salvation as pride and folly; only
God can give men and women the knowledge and salvation
they seek. Inasmuch as they try to attain these on
their own, they are acting in pride against God. Salvation and knowledge of God are free gifts, given by
God to those who accept them in faith, believing that
God has acted in the person of Jesus Christ. In short,
there is a sharp distinction between religion (the human striving after God and salvation) and revelation
(God's address to humankind and the divine offer of
salvation). The latter condemns the former.[45]

Against this view of the relationship between religion and revelation, the Secretariat's officials asserted that revelation does not condemn religion or humankind's natural ability to know God and do good.
Rather, it builds upon these, elevating, purifying, and
transforming them. God's grace, then, the divine self-
revelation, completes that which is natural; it does
not destroy it. Mgr. Rossano remarks,

The alternative Bible or religion, faith
or religion, revelation or religion, intro-
duced in a polemical way by Barth and supported with diverse nuances by his succes-
sors, is seen particularly to be antihistor-
ical and antiscientific in view of the facts.
Throughout the Bible, the history of salvation and revelation are intertwined with
religion and its forms. They meet humankind
and react in it through the forms and categories natural to the religious.

To limit oneself to the New Testament,
it seems evident that the divine gift of
faith (**pistis**) is grafted onto the preliminary dispositions of "the fear of God" and
submission to God, that fraternity and Christian communion (**philadelphia, koinonia**) perfect the aspirations for solidarity and association common in the religions. Even the
sacramentality of sacred actions (baptism,
Eucharist) answers the universal search for
effective ways of contact with the divine.[46]

One must remember in this that the Secretariat's officials were not denying that salvation was a free gift
from God or that the revelation of God added a new dimension to humankind's religious disposition. Their
point was that God builds up on what is already present, transforming it and making it able to serve as a
means of mediating divine saving grace. The natural
good of humankind and its natural aspiration to seek
God are completed, then, by God's revelation.[47]

A consequence of the above understanding of the
relationship between revelation, religion, and the human striving to do the good is that there is a conti-

nuity among them. Revelation does not condemn the human striving or the human religious disposition, but
rather fulfills them. Yet there is also a real discontinuity present. Revelation adds a qualitatively new
dimension to human existence. It is because of God's
revealing presence and activity that men and women can
truly know God, that they can direct their energies towards the real God, and that they are provided with the
means of being raised to the new life to which they are
called. None of this is possible through human effort
alone.

The relationship of continuity/discontinuity between revelation and religion and human striving
emerges in the comments of the Secretariat's officials
on the relationship between Christianity and the other religions of the world. Christianity is seen as that
religion based upon God's full revelation in Christ,
and furthermore it is in Christianity that God's saving, revealing work continues after the time of Christ.
Thus there is a continuity and a discontinuity between
Christianity and the other religions.

In pointing to the continuity between Christianity and humankind's non-Christian religions, the position of the Secretariat is directly opposed to that
neo-orthodox Protestant tendency mentioned above. In
stressing the discontinuity, the Secretariat's officials are in effect denying that Christianity is but
one religion among others. There is a real continuity
(Christianity, based as it is upon God's revelation,
builds upon the values and religious dispositions already present among men and women) yet there is a real
discontinuity (Christianity adds the new dimension of
the fullness of God's revelation, something unattain-
able by human striving). Mgr. Rossano, referring to St.

Paul's attitude to the religion of the Greeks, sums up
the attitude of the Secretariat as follows:

> . . . it seems to be going against the Apos-
> tle's method to raise the axe against the
> knowledge of God acquired on the basis of
> reason and of the universe, to apply to **the-**
> **ologia** and to **religio naturalis** (Greek or
> Asian) the verdict of impiety and of incon-
> sistency; but it is setting oneself also
> quite definitely against the Pauline course
> to claim the substantial identity of Chris-
> tianity with the religions, so that the bhag-
> avan Isvara of Hinduism, and the Tathagata of
> Buddhism are nothing but different denomina-
> tions, determined by culture, of Jesus of Na-
> zareth.[48]

The continuity--discontinuity type of relationship
existing between Christianity and the other religions
of the world also grounds the notion that appears in
the writings of the Secretariat's officials that the
non-Christian religions can be "preparations" for
Christianity. The elements of goodness and truth in
these religions, based upon the natural law, human reason, and even traces of divine revelation, are all oriented to a completion and fulfillment in Christianity.
It is the orientation of this goodness and truth to
Christianity that can make these religions the preparations or the "stepping-stones" to Christianity.[49]

The above aspects of the reflections of the Secretariat's officials all play a part in their remarks
on the role of the non-Christian religions in helping
their followers to attain salvation. One of the underlying assumptions always present in the remarks of

these officials on this topic is that it is in Christianity that humankind is provided with the ordinary
means of receiving God's offer of salvation. Christianity, based on the fullness of God's revelation in
Christ, has the means willed by God to mediate the divine saving grace.[50] But what about the non-Christian
religions? Do they mediate God's grace? Can they be
considered "ways of salvation?" In answer to these
questions, the response of Fr. Humbertclaude is negative. The non-Christian religions are not, in themselves, mediators of divine saving grace in the sense
that Christianity is. Their followers do not attain
salvation by devoutly participating in the rites and
ceremonies of these religions or by believing what they
teach. Rather, their followers attain salvation in what
Humbertclaude calls a "secret dialogue" between God and
each individual in that religion. The religion can at
best open its members up to God's secret action by reinforcing the idea of the divine, promoting spiritual
values, and encouraging an upright life. Humbertclaude
writes,

> . . . it is claimed . . . [that] since men
> and women have been created as social beings,
> the means of salvation must also be social
> and so they must therefore be found within
> the religions themselves. These thus become
> sacraments and transform without their know-
> ing it Buddhists or animists into "anonymous
> Christians." One must recognize however that
> neither the Scriptures, nor the Fathers, nor
> the texts of the [Second Vatican] Council al-
> low such a role to be accorded to the reli-
> gions. The salvation of non-Christians is of-
> fered only in a secret dialogue between God

who calls and the conscience of the individual who accepts or rejects it.[51]

He further insists that the non-Christian, because he
or she does not have the special aids granted to Chris-
tians--the sacraments through which grace is mediated,
and a full knowledge of God--is in a more precarious
position than the Christian with respect to his or her
chances of salvation. Missionary work, then, is still
an urgent task.[52]

A similar understanding of the salvific role of
non-Christian religions appears in the writings of Mgr.
Rossano. He insists that the non-Christian religions
are not what he calls "positive" means of salvation
which parallel the function of the Church. He notes,

> . . . the hypothesis which considers the non-
> Christian religions as positive and parallel
> ways of salvation, instituted by God, even if
> of an inferior quality to the Church, seems
> . . . to be irreconcilable with the biblical
> perspective.[53]

This view, however, receives some further comment by
Mgr. Rossano in other writings which will be noted in
the next chapter, where he explains that there is a
sense in which the non-Christian religions can be considered ways of salvation in that God's saving grace
can be encountered in them.

The evaluation of the non-Christian religions that
one sees in the writings of the above officials of the
Secretariat, then, is one that is both negative and
positive. These religions share with Christianity certain values and truths and even, possibly, traces of
God's supernatural revelation, and they can orient
their followers to God. Yet they do not contain the

fullness of God's revelation nor are they positive ways
of salvation willed by God. The goodness and truth they
contain is only a glimmer of the fullness to be found
in Christianity. They are therefore preparations for
that fullness which alone can complete them.[54]

III. Important Consultors' Meetings

During the period 1967-1973, the Secretariat convened a number of general meetings of its Consultors in
order to evaluate its activities and to allow the Consultors to exchange information and points of view.
These general meetings do not deal in any systematic
way with the theological issues involved in interreligious dialogue, but they do provide useful glimpses
into some of the theological and practical concerns
that these Consultors thought to be important in dialogue. By way of illustration of what these meetings
discussed and what they accomplished, this section will
examine briefly three of the most important ones.

1. The September 1968 Consultors' Meeting

The first general Consultors' meeting upon which I
want to comment took place September 25-26, 1968. The
main topic of concern was the publication of the various guidebooks for dialogue then in the process of being written. The Consultors were concerned primarily
with the factual details connected with the particular
religions discussed in the dialogue book under consideration.[55] They also discussed, however, the question
of a proper theological evaluation of non-Christian religions. The diversity of views among Catholic theologians, summarized by the Consultors, was a matter of
concern, and they wanted the Secretariat to contribute
to the establishment of a "sound" doctrine in this

area.[56] Although the Secretariat was not intended to be
a research institute dealing with theoretical issues,
the question of a sound theological evaluation of non-
Christian religions was important, they thought, because such an evaluation grounded the actual practice
of dialogue.[57] The Consultors do not, though, give a
detailed position of their own, but they do indicate
the general directions that a sound theological evaluation should take when they note approvingly those
who,

> . . . remaining in the direction of the
> teachings of the [Second Vatican] Council,
> recognize the presence of true and sound el-
> ements and authentic values in the various
> religions which nonetheless remain ambiguous
> complex realities.[58]

The non-Christian religions contain real goodness and
values, then, but they do not capture the fullness of
divine revelation and so are "ambiguous."

2. The September 1971 Consultors' Meeting

A second general Consultors' meeting of interest
took place at Paris, September 27-29, 1971. Its purpose
was to examine the problems of interreligious dialogue
and to suggest possibilities for the more effective
pursuance of the Church's dialogue activity. The Consultors were broken up into four groups, representing
the four major religious traditions or groups of religions with which the Secretariat in fact dealt: Hinduism, Buddhism, Islam, and the African religions. There
were major presentations given by Consultors special-
izing in aspects of each of these religious traditions
which gave those listening an opportunity for becoming

more familiar with the particular tradition in question
and which promoted reflection on the implications of
dialogue with their followers.[59]

An example of one of the recurring topics of discussion in the Consultors' deliberations was the search
for "points of contact" between a particular non-Christian religion and Christianity. These points of contact
were important because they provided a basis upon which
Christians could ground a dialogue with non-Christians
and because they were considered as examples of "preparations" for the Gospel message scattered throughout
the world by divine providence. In their presentations
before the Consultors, two of those giving talks, Henri Dumoulin and Victor Mulago, dealt with this issue.
Dumoulin, an expert on Buddhism, felt that Christians
should examine the religious experience of their Buddhist dialogue partners to find points of contact, and
when they did, he thought that one of these would be
the Buddhist desire for salvation from the painful human situation. This desire, he noted, could be an important basis upon which to build dialogue between
Christians and Buddhists.[60] Similarily, Victor Mulago
referred to points of contact between Christians and
the followers of traditional African religions by discussing the similarity between the symbolism of Bantu
ritual ceremonies and the Church's sacramental system.
The similarity resided in the fact that through their
rituals, occurring at key stages in the life of each
Bantu (initiation into the tribe, marriage, and death),
the Bantu people were attempting to become united with
the ultimate source of all things. They functioned in
a very similar way to the sacraments of the Church.
They therefore provided a common ground upon which both
Christians and the Bantu could meet.[61]

With respect to Mulago's discussion of the Bantu
rituals and the points of contact between them and the
Christian sacraments, it is important to keep in mind
that Mulago insists on the transcendence of the Christian sacraments and their superiority. Despite the similarities, there is a qualitative difference. In this,
Mulago echoes a point that occurs throughout the remarks of the Secretariat's officials, namely, that
Christianity transcends and fulfills the aspirations
found in other religions. The Christian message builds
upon the good that is already there, purifying it from
its defects, orienting it truly towards God, transforming it, making it capable of mediating the divine presence. Mulago said, then,

> Now we, in the Church, have realized
> these aspirations of the **muntu** soul in a re-
> markable and transcendent way. Symbolism
> reaches its highest point there in the sac-
> raments, ". . . that is to say, the union of
> the supernatural with the natural, corporal
> element."62

A final point of importance to be seen in this
conference is a corollary to what has just been mentioned. It concerns remarks Mulago made about indigenization, the expression of the Christian message in
terms appropriate to the particular culture in which it
finds itself. This concern emerges as a particularly
dominant one in Africa. It has to do with the use of
that which is good and valuable in the African religious mentality and giving this a Christian face,
transforming it in light of the Gospel.63 Thus, the
special character of the African spirituality and the
valuable religious intuitions of the African peoples,

can and should, insisted Mulago, become part of the
Christian proclamation and practice in Africa when they
do not contradict the Gospel.[64]

3. The October 1972 Consultors' Meeting

A third Consultors' meeting was held at Rome,
October 3-6, 1972. One of its main purposes, like that
of the Paris meeting the previous year, was to allow
the Consultors to exchange information about the religions in various parts of the world and to discuss ways
the Secretariat could further the dialogue activity in
these areas. There were two major themes in the presentations given at this meeting: (1) the self-understanding of the followers of the major religious traditions
of the world, and (2) how these major religious traditions were facing up to the problems of modernity which
the Secretariat felt involved technological change, the
quest for liberation from oppressive structures, increasing secularization, and the threat of Marxism with
its atheistic, materialistic philosophy.[65]

Perhaps the most significant aspect of this Consultors' meeting was that for the first time representatives from other religions were invited to take
part.[66] The Secretariat itself was beginning to actualize in a practical way the dialogue it was mandated
to promote in the Church. The meeting also points to a
rather important aspect of the Secretariat's dialogue
efforts, an aspect that is evident in the other general Consultors' meetings discussed above, namely, that
the Secretariat was concerned with dialogue on the "religious" level. It preferred to stay away from dialogue
on the level of discusing solutions to common human
problems. While it did encourage Christians to participate in such dialogue, the Secretariat saw its specif-

ic concern as that of engaging in dialogue that involved religious and spiritual topics.[67]

4. The Beginnings of Collaboration With
the World Council of Churches

It was during the period of time discussed in this
chapter that the World Council of Churches began to develop an interreligious dialogue program of its own.[68]
Those responsible for this program actively sought the
cooperation of members of the Secretariat, inviting
them to take part in the interreligious dialogue meetings the WCC was beginning to sponsor and the subsequent intra-Christian reflection on them. Thus various
Consultors from the Secretariat began to attend WCC
sponsored dialogue conferences. Mgr. Rossano, in particular, played a major role in the ecumenical collaboration in this area and became a regular observer-mem-
ber of the WCC's "sub-unit" for dialogue when it was
set up in 1971. It is useful at this point to make note
of Mgr. Rossano's views of the way he saw Protestants
evaluating the religions of the world. This will serve
to highlight his own position.

One of the places where Mgr. Rossano outlined what
he considered to be the Roman Catholic position with
respect to the world's religions was at a meeting of
the Joint Working Group in Gwatt, 1969. This Working
Group was a WCC-Roman Catholic body set up to examine
ways these two organizations could cooperate. In his
talk at the Gwatt meeting, Mgr. Rossano outlined the
questions dealt with by Roman Catholic theology in
dealing with the religious traditions of the world and
he identified what he thought were the major differences between the theological perspectives of his Secretariat and the WCC. The differences as he saw them

centered around the relationship between revelation and
the human religious spirit. The Secretariat's position
on this was quite clear. God's revelatory inbreaking
into human history builds upon human nature. It elevates, purifies, and transforms the natural good and
the natural religiosity present in the world.[69] In contrast to this, Mgr. Rossano noted, was the Protestant
view that revelation condemns nature. In point of fact,
one must note, this was but one view that was present
in Protestant thinking, albeit a very dominant one. As
will become evident later, the dialogue sub-unit of the
WCC itself spent much time discussing this very point.
Nonetheless, for Mgr. Rossano, it was characteristic of
the Protestant position. In the other major questions
about interreligious dialogue and its objectives and
bases, Mgr. Rossano thought that the Secretariat and
the WCC were in basic agreement. There could thus be
serious cooperation between them. He remarked, then,

> Catholic teaching is less absolute with re-
> spect to the corruption of nature and as a
> result its judgment on the non-Christian re-
> ligions is less negative. Catholic teaching
> distrusts any overly radical antitheses be-
> tween religion and faith . . . but on the ma-
> jor issues here in question the thought [of
> the Secretariat and that of the WCC] con-
> verge.[70]

A final point of interest in this ecumenical collaboration is that such collaboration was mainly the
result of the initiatives taken by the WCC. While officials of the Secretariat were beginning to take an
active role in the planning and execution of the WCC's
dialogue efforts, the reverse was not yet the case. Yet

the cooperation was there in incipient form and the opportunity was present for a certain cross-fertilization of reflection on this type of Christian activity, so new for many.

IV. Summary Reflections on the Years 1967-1973

During the years 1967-1973, the Secretariat for Non-Christians pursued the mandate to promote dialogue with men and women of other religious traditions. Its primary activity was the publication of various dialogue guidebooks in which the its views on dialogue and on a theology of religions became a little more clear.

The type of dialogue which the officials of the Secretariat were most interested in pursuing was "religious" dialogue, that encounter between men and women of different religions in which there was a sharing of their respective beliefs and practices. In focussing on this type of dialogue, a number of questions and emphases emerged.

First of all, the problem of the relationship between dialogue and mission remained ever present. The Secretariat's position on this remained the same as it had been in its early years. Dialogue is not mission, being directed to those who are not ready for missionary activity, although it may be seen as a form of pre-missionary work.

Secondly, a significant feature of the Secretariat's understanding of the goal of dialogue centers on the idea of dialogue as a "maieutic" activity, that is, one which leads to a mutual growth in the understanding of truth on the part of the dialogue partners.

Third, there is a continuing reflection on the grounds for dialogue. The most important of these is that Christians have much in common with their non-

Christian neighbours. For example, all people have the same origin and goal, all share a knowledge of the natural law, all have a religious disposition, and, importantly, all share traces of God's revealing presence.

In its reflections on the religions of the world, there continues in the Secretariat an affirmation of the five points that could be seen in its early years. One can see, though, the following major emphases during these latter years. First, the goods and values of non-Christian religions are taken up by God's revelatory activity, not denied. There exists, then, a continuity between the non-Christian religions and revelation. Yet there is at the same time a discontinuity. The goods and values in these religions must be completed and perfected by revelation.

The second emphasis is that God's revelation may be present in the non-Christian religions of the world, although not in a complete or satisfactory form. These religions, then, need not be merely reflections of the highest religious aspirations of human beings. Nonetheless, the Church remains the place where God's revelation fully abides.

A final emphasis is that the non-Christian religions of the world are not "ways of salvation." Only the Church is the real way of salvation willed by God for all human beings. The non-Christian religions, though, can be useful in opening their followers up to God's saving presence which is not restricted to those who are in the Church.

CHAPTER THREE
RENEWED EMPHASIS AND GUIDELINES

The period from 1973 to the promulgation of a new set of dialogue guidelines by Pope John Paul II in 1984 was a period marked by considerable changes among the personnel of the Secretariat for Non-Christians, to say nothing of the changes in the papacy itself. Early in 1973, Cardinal Sergio Pignedoli, former head of the Sacred Congregation for the Evangelization of Peoples, became President. Mgr. Rossano took over as Secretary, the most important office, in fact, in the Secretariat. Cardinal Pignedoli's unexpected death in 1980 necessitated a change in leadership, and so Mgr. Jean Jadot became President. During his tenure, Mgr. Rossano left the Secretariat to become rector of the Lateran University in Rome and was succeeded by Fr. Marcello Zago, a man with considerable experience in interreligious dialogue in Laos and Thailand.

This period of rather considerable change in the personnel was accompanied by a number of important activities and statements. There was, first, a period in which the Secretariat was engaged in the actual sponsorship of dialogue meetings. Previous to this, the Secretariat itself had not been eager to sponsor such meetings. Secondly, cooperation with the World Council of Churches also began. After some initial hesitancy, the Secretariat became more eager to make interreligious dialogue as much as possible an ecumenical effort. There were therefore visits by officials from both the Secretariat and the dialogue sub-unit of the

WCC to one another's headquarters in an effort to become better acquainted. The Secretariat took part in
the WCC's dialogue activity through its Consultors and
especially through Mgr. Rossano, and officials of the
WCC began to take part in some of the Secretariat's dialogue meetings. Finally, the Secretariat worked out a
draft statement on dialogue which was eventually promulgated by the Pope in 1984, a statement which reflects the current official position of the Catholic
Church on interreligious dialogue.

The emphasis during this period was clearly on the
sponsorship of meetings geared towards the discussion
of interreligious dialogue. There was a decided decrease in the Secretariat's publication efforts. During
the course of this chapter, then, I will be looking at
what took place in the dialogue meetings the Secretariat sponsored. I will also examine remarks that the
Secretariat's officials made during the meetings they
attended, other articles and letters of these officials, and the deliberations of the continuing Consultors' meetings. Out of these latter emerged a major
statement on dialogue which was promulgated by Pope
John Paul II. This statement will serve to bring my examination of the Secretariat's work to a close.

I. Important Presentations, Articles and Letters
of the Secretariat's Officials

It is in the presentations, articles, and letters
of the officials of the Secretariat that key considerations about dialogue and the world's religions are evident.[1] Mgr. Rossano, especially, and Cardinal Pignedoli make important statements on these topics, statements which continue to stress themes already present
in the Secretariat's work.

1. Dialogue in the Remarks of the
Secretariat's Officials

In their attempts to define the nature and role of the Secretariat and the sort of activity in which it was engaged, the officials of the Secretariat addressed the issue of the dialogue partner with whom the Secretariat itself wished to dialogue. They tried to define the dialogue partner as any "religious" person. In this context the Secretariat's officials were not using the term "religious" to mean religious in the sense simply of being open to the divine. All men and women were religious in that sense. Rather, what they meant was that their dialogue concern was with those whose lives were shaped by their participation in one of the world's religious traditions. In practice, this meant Islam, Hinduism, Buddhism, or one of the traditional African religions. In making this clarification, the officials of the Secretariat were trying to distinguish their activity from that of another dialogue Secretariat set up within the organizational structure of the Church, the Secretariat for Non-Believers. This latter Secretariat was concerned with dialogue with people espousing atheistic humanistic views.[2]

As well as insisting that their dialogue was with religious men and women, the Secretariat's officials tried to insist, as well, that the subject matter of the dialogue they desired to promote was religious. In their desire to emphasize the religious nature of their dialogue, these officials pointed to the existence of other bodies within the organizational structure of the Church which had responsibilities in the areas of social justice, economic development, world peace, and the like. In restricting their work to "religious" dialogue, the Secretariat's officials were defining the

specific work of their organization within the framework of a large body in which each part had its own
special sphere of activity.

What did they mean by "religious" dialogue? In
practice, the term was hard to define. On the obvious
level, it included dialogue which centered around a
discussion of what the dialogue partners believed,
their perceptions of God or the Absolute, humankind's
relationship to this divine Ground, and the religious
experience that was foundational for their particular
religion. Dialogue could not be restricted to these
topics alone, however, as the Secretariat's officials
soon came to realize. The understanding one had of God
and the God-humankind relationship had ethical and
therefore social implications. Moreover, the idea of a
"religious" place separated from a "temporal" plane met
objections from Muslims who did not make this distinction. Christians, they said, could not impose prior re-
strictions on interreligious dialogue by allowing only
the Christian agenda. Mgr. Rossano, aware of these difficulties, raised the problem at a general meeting of
Consultors in Rome in 1974 when he asked,

> How can we understand and assess the
> limitation of our program to the **homo reli-**
> **giosus**? The question here is the delicate
> connection existing between religion and the
> temporal order . . . . Our Secretariat holds
> to the classical position of the "religious
> order," the sphere of ultimate concerns com-
> mon to all which transcends the day to day
> empirical level and from which is derived new
> ethical-social behaviour which Christianity
> calls **fides quae per caritatem operatur.** But
> we remain reticent about discussing the prag-

matic concretization of this new conduct, for
there are other agencies to handle this domain. Other religions, though, for example,
Islam, have a different view and we are
called upon by dialogue groups and by the demands of the world today to confront non-religious problems, for example, the energy
crisis, the food crisis, world community,
etc. How then can we envisage our action? How
can we define it?[3]

Five years after these remarks, most likely as a result
of actual experiences of dialogues with peoples of other faiths, the Secretariat expanded its notion of religious dialogue to include all areas of common concern
shared by religiously committed people discussing the
contribution of their respective faiths to a particular question, even a "secular" one.[4]

The relationship between dialogue and mission continued to be a topic of discussion in the remarks of
the Secretariat's officials. The answer they gave remained essentially the same as previous answers. While
insisting that the two were separate forms of activity within the Church, the Secretariat's officials regarded them as interconnected. Dialogue was part of the
Church's mission to spread the good news it had received. It was an activity carried on from within the
context of a Church which by its nature was a missionary and evangelizing community.[5] Given the hostility or
indifference of many in the world today with respect to
the Church, and given the Church's desire to respect
the freedom of others, dialogue was an appropriate form
of making contact with non-Christians, thereby implant-
ing the "leaven" of the Gospel in the minds of those
who otherwise would not be touched by it.[6] Dialogue

during this period continued to be thought of, then, as
a form of pre-evangelization.

While dialogue was aimed at breaking down hostility or misunderstanding between believers from differing religions, promoting mutual collaboration, and ultimately introducing the Christian message into areas
where this would otherwise be impossible, dialogue was
also aimed at the indigenization of the Gospel message
throughout the world. Nowhere does this aim of dialogue
receive greater attention than in the Secretariat's dialogue activity in Africa. At this time, the Secretariat was becoming more involved in the sponsorship of
its own dialogue meetings as well as participating in
those sponsored by the WCC. Dialogues in Africa formed
a major part of this activity.[7] One of the dominant
features of dialogue in Africa was that dialogue primarily took the form of what came to be called "inner"
dialogue. Inner dialogue was dialogue, not between
Christians and representatives of traditional African
religions, but between African Christians and their own
traditional religious heritage. In a radio interview
following a dialogue meeting at Yaoundé in 1976, Mgr.
Rossano described this particular type of dialogue as
follows:

> Here [in Africa] dialogue takes on, I would
> say, a peculiar aspect which in English
> circles today has come to be called "inner
> dialogue." It is an interior dialogue in
> which a Christian alone or from within a com-
> munity confronts his or her cultural environ-
> ment, his or her cultural, religious, spiri-
> tual, and ancestral heritage.[8]

This form of dialogue emerged as a characteristic feature of dialogue in Africa as a result of the impossibility of engaging those who still practised the traditional African rites in dialogue. Qualified representatives from such religions were not inclined to enter
into dialogue.[9] Thus those engaged in dialogue in Africa were themselves Christians, but Christians who
shared the religious spirit of Africa and who were thus
influenced by the general outlooks and symbols African
spirituality promoted.

The purpose of such dialogue was to form a truly
African Christianity. This purpose is based upon a presupposition which is a consistent feature of the Secretariat's outlook, namely, the message of Christ assumes the values of a particular culture and transforms
them. God's redeeming activity, in other words, builds
upon the already existing moral and religious substratum and brings it to fulfillment.[10]

The ideas of spreading the Gospel message through
dialogue, collaboration with men and women of other religious traditions, and the assumption of the values in
their religious heritage are based upon a sincere respect for what non-Christians believe. Nowhere in the
remarks of the Secretariat's officials is this denied.
In fact, the opposite is the case.[11] Yet this attitude
gives rise to a certain degree of tension in the dialogue process because it is always coupled with the
insistence that the Christian must not minimize the
claims of Christianity to be transcendent and unique.
The fact that in dialogue the dialogue partner must
also have the right to claim superiority for his or her
religion gives rise to the tension. Mgr. Rossano noted
the fact of this necessary tension at a plenary meeting of Consultors in Rome, 1979, when he said,

Each of the parties in dialogue has the right
of adhering to his absolute, of feeling basically sure of his own position. He has the
right (and the duty, if he is a Christian) to
think that the other is not achieving human
and religious fulfillment as willed by God. A
Christian cannot place his own faith and other religions on the same level. He cannot
hold that the Holy Spirit dwells equally in
the Church, in Hinduism and in the dar-es-Is-
lam. There cannot be agreement that each
partner in the dialogue is equally in the
truth, or that different religions are only
cultural and historical expressions of a
transcendent one; otherwise there would be no
good reason for having dialogue at all. There
must be a certain tension by the very nature
of the case.[12]

Respect for the other while at the same time holding
firm to one's own views, then, is a characteristic of
interreligious dialogue. Dialogue does not mean that
differences between peoples of various faith commitments will be removed. In dialogue, one has to face up
to the fact that differences may persist.

2. The Theological Evaluation of
   the World's Religions

The theological evaluation of the world's religions that emerges from the remarks of the Secretariat's officials during this time follows the direction
of the themes outlined in the previous chapters. These
underlying themes are but given further emphasis and
clarification.

The view of religion and the religions of the

world is one element of the theology of religions one sees, then. A basic anthropological affirmation grounds this view, namely, that humankind is by nature religious. All men and women seek God who alone fulfills their deepest yearnings.[13] It is this essential human religiosity that is at the root of humankind's religions, because it is through the religion of a particular people that it is expressed institutionally and socially. The religions of humankind reflect the particular spirit of a people and its culture as that people attempts to express in a social way the religiosity inherent in its population.[14] Significantly, however, there is something more. The religions of the world may contain elements of God's self-revealing presence and so they not only reflect the human quest for God, but they may contain reflections of God's saving and revealing quest for human beings. Mgr. Rossano summed up this notion as follows:

> The Christian needs to recognize that "elements of truth and of grace" exist outside the Christian community, that the other religions "are all impregnated with innumerable seeds of the Word (**Evangelii Nuntiandi**, no. 53) and that Scripture and Christian tradition have always acknowledged a sapiential and salvific economy, beyond the confines of Israel and of the Church.[15]

The remarks of the Secretariat's officials, though, also indicate that the non-Christian religions of the world, grounded upon the human quest for God and possibly containing traces of God's revelatory presence, are incomplete without the fullness of revelation that comes in the person of Jesus Christ. Moreover, these religions also reflect the fallen condition of humankind and so the human tendency to pervert the good. They therefore distort the human quest for God that lies at their very base as well as any elements of God's revelatory presence they may contain.[16]

The above understanding of humankind's religious experience and the religions which result from it have to be understood along with another consistent feature of the Secretariat's reflections on dialogue which also can be seen in the remarks of its officials during this period, namely, the relationship between revelation and religion. As has been shown, a continual assertion in the Secretariat has been that revelation is both continuous and discontinuous with humankind's religious disposition and its concrete social manifestations. When God intervenes in human history, revealing the divine nature and making it possible for men and women to attain salvation, the religious aspirations they already have and the cultural forms these have taken are purified, raised, and transformed. This notion received considerable attention during this period, especially by Mgr. Rossano, because of his dealings with the World Council of Churches and its dialogue body. This was not an idea totally acceptable in Protestant circles, as has been mentioned already and as will become evident in the next section. A major Protestant view stressed the discontinuity between religion and revelation. Hence Mgr. Rossano insisted, in face of this, that revelation (sometimes described as the Gospel message) was not only a break or a scandal when facing religion, but also its real fulfillment. Humankind's religious nature, embodied socially in the religion of a culture, could thus be seen as a "stepping-stone" to or a "preparation" for the Gospel revelation.[17]

Mgr. Rossano did not want to suggest, however, that God's revelatory interventions did not add something fundamentally new and qualitatively different to the human quest for God which these interventions fulfilled. Fulfillment and break, continuity and discontinuity, as has been shown, sum up the understanding the Secretariat's officials had concerning the relationship between revelation and religion. It was through revelation that humankind came to a true knowledge of God and it was through revelation that humankind was granted a share in the divine life. These were beyond the ability of human beings to attain on their own. God's revelatory activity added something new and transcendent.[18]

It is now possible to comment on the idea of Christianity and its relationship to the other religions of the world that appears in the comments of the Secretariat's officials during this time. First of all, there is no systematic attempt to distinguish between such terms as the Church, Christianity, and Christian revelation. One has to be on guard lest confusion arise since all three are used interchangeably. Underneath this mingling of terms, though, it is clear that the Secretariat's officials want to affirm that it is in Christianity that God's saving revelation is embodied in a social way. It is Christianity that contains the social concretization of God's definitive self-revelation through Jesus Christ. It is Christianity that extends God's saving grace to all humankind in the normative way. As such, Christianity is transcendent and unique, and cannot be counted as merely one religion among others.[19]

There is, however, a rather more nuanced understanding of Christianity that emerges during this time

in the writings of Mgr. Rossano. Christianity, he indicates, cannot be equated purely and simply with
Christianity as it has developed in Europe. The Gospel
message, God's revelation in Christ, interacts with the
culture to which it is addressed and raises and transforms the goodness and spirituality of that culture.
The Christianity of a particular culture is the result,
yet other forms of Christianity are also possible in
other cultures. The Gospel transcends any particular
culture and can be expressed in different cultural
terms. Speaking at a colloquy in Kinshasa, Zaire, in
1978, Mgr. Rossano noted,

> The faith for the Christian cannot be iden-
> tified simply with his or her tradition or
> culture, but rather is a transcultural real-
> ity that has entered into that culture. Its
> communication does not at all imply a trans-
> fer or a communication of that culture. Thus,
> the Christian faith, although immersed in a
> culture and although it supports that cul-
> ture, spreads its roots beyond the culture
> and can be transmitted without there being at
> the same time an overflowing of the original
> culture and without supplanting or elimi-
> nating the cultural and religious tradition
> of those to whom it comes . . . . Thus the
> Christian belonging to the Latin culture must
> learn to communicate the Gospel message to
> the Bantu people without transplanting his or
> her culture.[20]

Moreover, while the cultural expression of Christianity may be open to change as God's revelation interacts
with the cultures of various parts of the world, these

cultural expressions may themselves suffer from the same defects as seen in other religions, chiefly defects resulting from humankind's sinful condition. Christianity itself, in other words, is not "pure" revelation. The implication is that any cultural expression of Christianity is subject to correction.[21]

A final consideration of the Secretariat's theological evaluation of the religions of the world as the officials of that body expressed it during this period concerns the role of the non-Christian religions in God's economy of salvation. As has been mentioned before, although there is the constant claim that God's salvation is extended to all through the Church, yet this salvific work is not restricted to the visible confines of the Church. God can indeed be present salvifically **in the religions of the world** other than Christianity. Mgr. Rossano, for example, remarked at the Kinshasa colloquy noted above,

> . . . I believe that the presence of a universal economy of Wisdom (see Ps. 8:15-36; Si. 17:1-12; Wis. 6:24, 7:23ff; Amos 9:6-7) is scripturally founded, even if it has to be elaborated further. This exists beside a particular economy of the Covenant which continues in the Church on a new and universal basis . . . . In this context I find the definition given in the "Guidelines for Inter-Religious Dialogue" published at Varanasi in 1977 by the Committee of the Bishops of India for dialogue to be perfect: "Dialogue is the response of Christian faith in **God's saving presence in other religious traditions** and the expression of firm hope of their fulfillment in Christ.[22]

Yet there is no move to consider these religions as
normative ways of salvation, equal to the Church. The
idea persists that they can be the occasion for opening
their followers up to God's extraordinary saving activity which is present everywhere, but the Christian way
is always superior, willed by God for all.[23]

II. Interreligious Dialogue Meetings

When Cardinal Pignedoli became President of the
Secretariat in 1973, the Secretariat's activity took a
new direction. There was a greater desire to sponsor
dialogue meetings. These meetings accordingly became a
major part of the Secretariat's activity between 1973
and 1978 and they are significant to note because they
show the real questions being faced and the actual issues being raised in concrete dialogue situations. In
order that this important aspect of the Secretariat's
work be brought to light, then, the following section
of this chapter will be devoted to a study of representative dialogue meetings involving the Secretariat's
four major dialogue partners: Muslims, Hindus, Buddhists, and those influenced by the African religions.
A noteworthy feature of these dialogue meetings is that
they are for the most part intra-Christian, that is,
they are meetings involving Christians concerned with
discussing and clarifying issues in dialogue among
themselves. Most are not, then, truly "interreligious."

1. Dialogue With Muslims

During the period here under consideration, the
Secretariat sponsored a number of dialogue meetings
dealing with Christian-Muslim relations.[24] Among these,
significantly, there was one truly interreligious encounter. It took place at Tripoli, February 1-5, 1976.

The other meetings were meetings in which Christians alone took part. In these dialogue meetings, a number of common concerns emerge, and certain aspects of the Secretariat's dialogue thinking already brought to light are emphasized. It is upon these that I want to focus some attention.

(a) Meetings Concerned With Muslims in Europe

The Secretariat organized meetings in Luxembourg, March 13-14, 1974 and in Vienna, November 19-21, 1976, to discuss the attitudes of Christians in Europe to the increasing Muslim presence in their midst and what practical steps they could take to improve relations between the followers of these two major religious traditions.[25] The presentations and discussions during both of these meetings centered on analyzing the sociological situation of Muslims in Europe, the responsibilities of the Church towards these Muslims, and suggestions as to how to cope with the problems posed.[26] Like most of the meetings the Secretariat sponsored, these two meetings were among Christians themselves, although in Vienna on the final day Muslim speakers presented their views on what they expected from Christians in the European context. Like most of the Secretariat's dialogue meetings there was a great deal of emphasis on gaining a better knowledge of the dialogue partner and his or her beliefs as a first step in coming to grips with the problem of living together in peace. Knowing the other better reveals itself as a necessary first step in many of these meetings.

The major recommendations emerging from both of these conferences have to do with how Christians in Europe can better show their love for the Muslim minority in their midst and how prejudices and hostility, so

long a feature of Muslim-Christian relations because of
a history of conflict between the two groups, could be
overcome. In the conferences, the participants recognized that there was a profound lack of knowledge and
understanding by Christians of their Muslim neighbours
and thought that more efforts had to be made to edu-
cate Christians. This included, one should note, teaching about Islam in Christian catechisms and revising
the books used in religious education to present more
accurately and with a greater degree of esteem the Muslim faith to Christians. They also called on Christians
to become more sensitive to the spiritual values in Islam. They hoped that local churches would become more
involved in making contacts with Muslims in their areas
and promote better relations between these Muslims and
the Christian majority. The conferences also recommended that members of the two religions be encouraged
to join together to try to resolve social problems that
threatened all of them. In short, the conferences
marked the beginning of the Christian task of being
sensitive to the problems of the Muslim minority and of
establishing friendly contacts with it.[27]

(b)The Meeting at Bamako, Mali

One of the most active years in the Secretariat's
sponsorship of dialogue activity was 1974 when it sponsored a series of regional dialogue meetings, each designed to encourage dialogue in a particular area. One
of these meetings took place at Bamako, Mali, June
18-20, 1974. Its general purpose was to discuss the
state of relations between Christians and Muslims in
East Africa. The delegates at this meeting attempted to
analyze the problems in this relationship, examine how
to encourage a more positive attitude on the part of

Christians towards Muslims, and study ways of training
Christian leaders to foster the improvement of relations between the followers of these two great traditions.[28]

Lack of knowledge by Christians of their Muslim
neighbours and their beliefs was one of the greatest
barriers towards improving Christian-Muslim relations
singled out by the participants.[29] Thus the Bamako conference called for a greater effort by Christians to
get to know Islam. It noted that this would require a
complete change of mentality on the part of Christians
towards Islam. The practical measures the conference
recommended included the establishment of courses in
Islam in seminaries and pastoral centers and the dis-
semination of information about Islam to Christians and
to those studying to become Christian. The conference
also urged individual Christians to make personal contacts with their Muslim neighbours.[30]

The state of dialogue in East Africa about which
this conference in Bamako gives witness is clearly dialogue in its very initial stages. The accent is very
much on gaining accurate knowledge of the other as a
start toward the breaking down of barriers of prejudice
and hostility. From the Christian side, there is the
insistence that Christians must begin to look upon Islam more favourably and to appreciate sincerely its
spiritual and moral values.

(c) The Tripoli Meeting

At the invitation of the Libyan government, the
Secretariat agreed to participate in an Islamic-Christian dialogue at Tripoli, February 1-5, 1976.[31] In contrast to most other dialogue meetings that the Secretariat held, this meeting was a truly interreligious

one. Its planning and execution were carried out jointly by the two sides taking part. At the end of the
meeting, a joint memorandum was issued, although not
without some tension and disagreement, as will be noted
below.

The general purpose of the Tripoli meeting was "to
create a new atmosphere of mutual confidence between
the Muslim world and the Christian world."[32] The delegates listened to presentations on and then discussed
four main topics: (1) the common ground between Christians and Muslims, (2) the relationship between faith
and politics, (3) social justice and faith in God, and
(4) the elimination of hostilities between Muslims and
Christians. The hope was that by bringing the two sides
together and exchanging ideas on these topics, Christians and Muslims could come to a better understanding
of each other. The text of the final memorandum accordingly notes,

> They [the two sides] have agreed that the aim
> of this dialogue is the exchange of knowledge
> and ideas that contribute to a better mutual
> knowledge of history and civilization between
> the participants of the two Religions, in or-
> der to clarify the convergences and differ-
> ences sincerely and objectively, allowing
> each party to cling to its beliefs, its obli-
> gations and its commitments in a spirit of
> concord and mutual respect.[33]

The resolutions that arose from the meeting and
which form part of the final memorandum contain a number of important theological considerations as well as
exemplify some of the problems in the Christian dialogue with Muslims in northern Africa and the mid-East

where Islam is the dominant religion. One of the more
important theological considerations is the agreement
to honour all of the prophets and messengers of the
"heavenly" religions, that is, the Jewish, Christian,
and Muslim religions which have a common revelatory
heritage. The text of the final declaration says,

> 2. The two parties honour all the Proph-
> ets and Messengers of the "heavenly Reli-
> gions." The two parties denounce all attempts
> to disparage or discredit the Prophets and
> Messengers, because that is against the will
> of God who sent them.[34]

This implies, significantly, that Christians should respect Mohammed, even honouring him as one sent by God,
for Mohammed is certainly the greatest messenger in the
Muslim religion.[35] Muslims, one should note, are called
on to have a similar respect for Jesus.

A second important element with theological implications is the insistence on religious freedom for the
followers of the two traditions[36] and the condemnation
of proselytism, the placing of undue pressure on members of one tradition to convert to the other. The inclusion of this condemnation reflects the bitter rivalry that has often been a feature of the relations between Christians and Muslims and testifies to the concern to ease tensions. It is all the more significant
when one considers the strong missionary thrust in both
traditions based on the conviction each has that it has
received God's definitive revelation. The memorandum of
the meeting says,

> 17. With a view to a real cooperation
> between the Moslem world and the Christian
> world, the two parties recommend ending all

pressure exerted by Christians on Moslems to
turn them away from their beliefs or by Moslems on Christians for the same purpose.[37]

Many of the recommendations in the memorandum of
this meeting deal with Christian-Muslim cooperation in
affirming the spiritual and religious dimension of reality over against secularism and materialism, a major
concern in many Christian-Muslim dialogues. Thus, the
memorandum insists that religion and belief in God
alone provide the ground for true morality and true
justice.[38] With this religious base, the memorandum
recommends more collaboration between Christians and
Muslims in pursuing humanitarian and social goals.
Thus, it urges the two sides to unite in trying to
solve the problems of world hunger and underdevelop-
ment,[39] in denouncing racial discrimination,[40] and in
promoting world peace.[41]

This meeting at Tripoli reflects in many ways the
state of Christian-Muslim relations in the mid-East.
The concern was primarily to begin to decrease feelings
of hostility and to come to a more positive appreciation of the other and of his or her religious tradition. There was great emphasis on what the two sides
had in common (especially belief in the same God and in
the Old Testament revelation). Yet the difficulties in
the relations between the two sides were also evident.
One of the Muslim papers turned out to be simply an
attack on the Crusades,[42] and the final memorandum became highly controversial. A last minute attempt by the
Muslim side to apply the condemnation of discrimination
and oppression to the state of Israel by inserting a
number of statements condemning Israel was completely
unacceptable to the Christian side which was totally
unprepared for this development. The meeting thus broke

off with less than amicable feelings between the two parties.[43]

2. The Traditional Religions in Africa

Dialogue meetings held to discuss the traditional religions in Africa were a major part of the Secretariat's dialogue activity during this period. Meetings took place at Abidjan, July 29-31, 1974, Kampala, August 5-7, 1974, Yaoundé July 8-11, 1976, and Kinshasa, January 1-14, 1978. These meetings show the special concerns and interests which were part of dialogue activity in the African context.

(a) Meetings in Africa in 1974

As part of a plan to hold regional meetings in 1974 to stimulate dialogue, the Secretariat organized two conferences in Africa to discuss the traditional religions in Africa. The first took place at Abidjan, July 29-31, 1974, to examine dialogue possibilities in western Africa where French was the major colonial language, while the second took place at Kampala, August 5-7, 1974, to examine dialogue in English speaking countries of eastern and southern Africa.[44] These meetings were primarily meetings of Christians discussing problems of integrating an African spiritual heritage into Christianity.

One of the dominant concerns that was present in both of these meetings, like that seen above in the discussion of dialogue with Muslims, was the concern of coming to a greater knowledge of the religious mentality of the dialogue partner. Thus, the recommendations made by the delegates of these conferences recognized that lack of such knowledge was one of the greatest barriers to dialogue and urged Christians to engage in

further research and study of African religious traditions.[45] The presentations at the conferences reveal
this concern also as a large amount of time was devoted
to the description of rites and ceremonies of the traditional religion of given areas and to an analysis of
major African religious symbols.[46]

One of the recurring features of the presentations
given during both of the conferences was that of pointing to similarities and points of compatibility between
the beliefs and symbols of a particular African religion and Christianity. In this regard, it is noticeable
that a deep desire to respect and esteem the values in
African religious traditions permeates the reflections
of the Christians attending these meetings and the
question of the compatibility of these traditions with
the Christian message receives a generally affirmative
response. What is at the base of this affirmative response is the notion that the values in these religions
are "preparations" for the Gospel, capable of being assumed and transformed by it.[47] The presupposition is
that the traditional African religions do indeed have
underlying values which, in spite of the "superstitious" or "bizarre" practices which Christians have
often seen in these religions, are nevertheless valid
expressions of the human quest for God which Christianity can build upon. The recommendations of both meetings, then, express the desire on the part of those
taking part that Christians be encouraged to change
their negative attitudes towards the African religions.
The Kampala recommendations, for example, say,

> The attempt must be made to inculcate a sin-
> cere respect for genuine religion as found in
> African Tradition. This is mainly a cateche-
> tical task . . . . It was noted that the sub-

ject of African Traditional Religion was already part of the two new religion syllabus-
es for the East African Certificate of Education, however, there was much Catholic cat-
echetical literature in circulation which employed opprobrious terms when speaking of
traditional religion, such as: witchcraft,
witch-doctor, paganism, devil-worship, superstition, primitive religions, etc. It was
strongly urged that such terms be deleted
from all publications. It was felt that
Christians must take a more sophisticated
view of Traditional Religion, seeing it, not
as a collection of bizarre or antiquated
practices, **but as a system of values, concepts and attitudes which demand respect.**[48]

(b) The Yaoundé Colloquy

The Secretariat organized another conference on
dialogue in Africa at Yaoundé in the Cameroons from July 8-11, 1976. The theme was "The Permanence of the
Traditional Cultural Patrimony in the Practice of the
Christian Life in Africa."[49] Like those that preceded
it, this meeting was among Christians. As the theme indicates, the primary concern of the conference was that
of the indigenization of Christianity.

This conference is another example of the recognition by the Roman Catholic Church through its dialogue body of the values inherent in African religious
traditions and it testifies to the desire on the part
of African Christians to retain their cultural and traditional identity by making Christianity truly African.
Indeed, this was becoming, for Africans, a major topic
for discussion. Like the presentations given at the Af-

rican meetings in 1974, the talks at this meeting centered around pointing out and analyzing selected themes
in the African religious inheritance.[50] The purpose of
this was to show that these themes, when properly understood, could be points of contact for dialogue worthy of serious attention by Christians and, further,
that they could be integrated into the African expression of Christianity.

The key theological consideration to note, therefore, about the remarks made at this conference is a
subject that has been constantly present in the reflections of the Secretariat, that is, the Gospel does not
simply denounce the religious inheritance it addresses
but rather builds upon those valuable and legitimate
aspects of this inheritance and transforms them. The
valid religious values of a culture are given the orientation that truly satisfies them by the Gospel message. There is a continuity (the values are taken up)
and a break (they are transformed, given a new orientation, raised to the supernatural level). In commenting on the Yaoundé colloquy, then, Mgr. Rossano made
the following remarks about the dynamics at work in the
relationship between the African religious heritage and
the message of the Gospel:

> The Gospel is for the African tradition, as
> it always is in the face of historical real-
> ity, at the same time a break, a new element,
> and a completion of its deepest aspirations.
> It does not impose pre-established uniform
> cultural categories, but uncovers new living
> interpersonal relationships . . . . Thus the
> Gospel will substantially enrich African
> spirituality in exalting its typical perma-
> nent expressions in order to elevate them to

a new life in the divine-human communion offered by the Church.[51]

The presentations at the Yaoundé conference attempted to go beyond the outward look of the rites and
ceremonies of particular African religious traditions
to illumine the underlying values present in them, values which could be associated with Christianity. One of
the speakers, Pierre Tchoaunga, accordingly spoke of
the strong sense of community present in the ancestor
worship of the Bamilek tribe.[52] Another speaker, Aloys
Tsaba, pointed out that at the base of the medical
practices in many African traditions, with their elements of magic and divination, lay a strong sense of
morality based upon the perception of a profound unity between illness and evil and a sense that a Supreme
Being was at the base of the moral order.[53] The tone
of the talks, in short, was one of respect and esteem
for these values and there was present an overall conviction that Christians could receive enrichment from
them.[54] This understanding of the goodness in the African religions, then, places emphasis in dialogue on
getting to know better the spiritual heritage in Africa so as to recognize those aspects of it which can
contribute to an African Christianity.

(c) The Kinshasa Colloquy

The development of a truly African Christianity
was also the principle theme of another dialogue meeting on African religions at Kinshasa, Zaire, January
9-14, 1978[55] co-sponsored by the Secretariat and the
Centre d'Etudes des Religions Africaines. As in the
other dialogue meetings in Africa, the dominant theological presupposition was that the Christian message
does not destroy the religious heritage of the culture

it confronts, but rather builds upon it and completes
it. Cardinal Malula of Kinshasa thus said in his opening address at the meeting,

> By its incarnation, the Incarnate Word
> has come to dwell among us, among the peoples
> of Africa, not to destroy the religion of our
> ancestors, but to bring it to its fullness,
> to its perfection . . . . What exists in Af-
> rica are certain moral and religious values
> of the African traditions. We consider these
> values deservedly as the pre-Gospel. It is
> these moral and religious values of our cul-
> tures which Christianity comes to complete,
> to elevate, and to carry to their justifica-
> tion.[56]

The Cardinal accordingly called upon African theologians to begin the task of making Christianity in Africa truly African. The debate over the principle of such
an enterprise, he noted, was over. The time had come to
begin the actual task in spite of the uncertainties
ahead.[57]

3. Dialogue in Asia

The third major area of dialogue activity in which
the Secretariat was engaged involved dialogue with people belonging to one of the great religions of Asia. At
first, this involved Hindus and Buddhists, but religious movements in Japan became part of the Secretariat's concern as well. The following section highlights
the Secretariat's dialogue meetings dealing with dialogue with the followers of these religious traditions.

(a) Meeting With Theravada Buddhists

As part of its series of regional meetings in 1974, the Secretariat sponsored a conference on dialogue at Bangkok, Thailand, May 17-19, 1974.[58] Its purpose was to encourage dialogue between Christians and Buddhists in Thailand and its deliberations were directed towards Christians with the intention of making them more aware of the possibilities for and the problems of dialogue in that country. There were three workshops held during the meeting, one discussing how Buddhists understood Christianity, another discussing the problems faced by Buddhists who had been converted to Christianity, and a third discussing the role of the laity in dialogue.

The deliberations of the workshops and the suggestions that they proposed show the questions being faced by those Christians attempting to dialogue with Buddhists in Thailand. The first workshop, discussing the theme, "Christianity seen by Buddhists," tried to outline some of those areas where Buddhists had misunderstood Christianity and how Christians could correct these misunderstandings. One of those areas identified by the participant in the workshop was the Buddhist perception of Christianity as a legalistic religion, emphasizing the following of rules rather than religious, mystical experience. Christians must counter this view, the members of the workshop said, by pointing to those many mystical elements in Christianity. This would not only present a more accurate understanding of Christianity, they felt, but it would also provide a point of contact upon which to build dialogue.[59]

The second workshop, dealing with the theme, "Buddhist and Christian," dealt with a very great problem for many converts in Buddhist countries. When they be-

came Christian, these former Buddhists found that they
became alienated from their friends and, most especially, from their own culture which was permeated by many
Buddhist rituals and with the Buddhist world-view.
These converts had to decide whether they could take
part in many cultural and civil ceremonies which had
Buddhist religious elements. The workshop mentions the
example of the expectation in Buddhist countries that
young men spend some time as Buddhist monks as part of
their normal growing up:

> . . . a Christian converted from Buddhism
> faces problems of religious beliefs and prac-
> tice--e.g. if his father wants him to be a
> monk when his mother dies, he wants to do his
> father's wish and thereby show his love and
> gratitude to his parents, but a Catholic can-
> not be a Buddhist monk . . . at least no one
> has done this yet.[60]

The desire to find points of contact between
Buddhism and Christianity, a common feature in the Secretariat's dialogue meetings, and the sensitivity to
the problems faced by Buddhist converts to Christianity did not at all mean that those taking part in this
dialogue meeting were willing to compromise in any way
what they considered to be essential to their faith.
Nor did they want to engage in a strategy which would
downplay the real differences between the two systems
of belief. The participant at the meeting acknowledged
that real, irreducible differences did exist between
Christian and Buddhist views of reality. Furthermore,
they insisted that the Christian revelation added something essential and new to the Buddhist way.[61] Yet,
there was still the prevailing sense, present in all of

the dialogue meetings the Secretariat sponsored, applied this time to Buddhism, that non-Christian religions do indeed contain real values and that God may be
present in them.[62] This sincere respect for the non-
Christian religious traditions continues as a characteristic feature of the Secretariat's dialogue efforts.

(b) The Nemi Meeting

A dialogue meeting of a different kind took place
at Nemi, near Rome, July 24-26, 1978. This meeting, co-
sponsored by the Secretariat for Non-Christians, the
Secretariat for Non-Believers, and the Pontifical Commission for Justice and Peace, met with a delegation
from the Japanese Religious Committee for World Feder-
ation, a coalition of Buddhist, Shinto, and even Roman
Catholic groups in Japan. It was, then, a truly interreligious dialogue meeting.[63]

There were four general topics discussed: (1) concrete ways of contributing to world peace, (2) harmony and collaboration among the world's religions, (3)
dialogue with atheists, and (4) ethics for the world of
today. The emphasis of the meeting was on promoting
harmony and collaboration among the religions of the
world, especially in facing crucial world problems such
as peace.[64] The participant expressed a desire to promote more study of the beliefs and practices of the
others so that better mutual understanding could be
possible.[65]

III. Important Meetings of the
Secretariat's Consultors

The Secretariat's dialogue meetings during the period of time under consideration included yearly Consultors' meetings. These show the concerns and issues

being raised internally by those most responsible for
the direction of the Secretariat's work. I want to
comment briefly on two of these meetings, one held at
Grottaferrata, near Rome, October 12-15, 1975, and the
other in Rome itself, April 24-26, 1979.

1. The Consultors' Meeting at Grottaferrata

During the Roman Catholic Holy Year of 1975, the
officials of the Secretariat decided not to engage in
activity outside of Rome, preferring instead to remain
in that city to receive any official representatives of
non-Christian religions that would come to Rome during
the course of this important year. The Secretariat did,
however, convene a general meeting of its Consultors,
October 12-15 at Grottaferrata, near Rome, taking ad-
vantage of the presence of many of its Consultors at a
major missionary conference being held at Rome at that
time.[66]

The general purpose of this Consultors' meeting
was to examine the then present state of dialogue between the Church and the followers of the major non-
Christian religions of the world. Consultors from different regions of the world gave presentations on the
problems encountered and the progress made in their
particular regions.[67] One of these, in particular,
given by Fr. Jesus Lopez-Gay, provides an excellent
glimpse into the sorts of concerns being raised about
dialogue. A preliminary questionnaire is also of note
because it, too, gives a valuable glimpse into the concerns the officials of the Secretariat had about their
activity.

(a) The Preliminary Questionnaire

As part of the preparatory activity for the Grottaferrata meeting, the Secretariat sent out to a number of Consultors and bishops a questionnaire which
asked about the dialogue activity in the particular
area to which the questionnaire was sent. The questionnaire asked about the content, the purpose and the nature of the dialogue activity. One rather interesting
question about the content of dialogue centered upon
the Secretariat's attempt to keep dialogue on the "religious" level. It asked for comments on whether topics dealing with social and ethical matters should be
considered.[68] With respect to the purpose of dialogue,
the questionnaire asked if dialogue was the same as
mission, if its goal was to present Christianity to
non-Christians, to indigenize Christianity, get to know
the other as a friend, or serve to help the dialogue
partners in their common quest for God.[69] As to the nature of dialogue, the questionnaire asked if persons
should be the focus of dialogue or if dialogue should
rather be a meeting of the Church with the culture and
religious values of a particular region. The Secretariat also wanted comments on the charge that dialogue
was incompatible with mission and if it was possible to
respect the religious conviction of others even if they
were inimical to Christianity.[70] Finally, in a specific vein, the questionnaire asked about the nature of
the dialogue in the area to which it had been sent. It
asked, in this regard, if dialogue was merely at the
stage of breaking down barriers, if Christians were
discussing common social problems with non-Christians
or if dialogue had reached a level at which Christians
and non-Christians were living and praying together,
exchanging spiritual insights.[71]

Accompanying the questions on dialogue were some
key theological questions. The most important of these
appear on the following list:

>--Which points of doctrine should be deepened
>for a more open and less hesitant dialogue:
>e.g. the **status theologicus** of the religious
>founders; theological values of rites and of
>the non-Christian religious practices; as-
>sumption of rites and of non-Christian cere-
>monies; inspiration and revelation in the
>non-Christian sacred books; relationship be-
>tween the Bible and the religions; methodol-
>ogy for reading the non-Christian sacred
>texts (e.g. is it legitimate to read them in
>a Christian sense? Is it allowed to apply the
>method which the N.T. practices upon the
>O.T., and which the O.T. does upon the sacred
>texts of the milieu?); the relationship be-
>tween revelation and religions, between faith
>and religion, can faith do without religion
>or do they coincide; or does it postulate an
>incarnation or an exodus from religion, and
>how?[72]

These were the issues and concerns, then, on which the
Secretariat wanted discussion so that it could carry
out more effectively a dialogue strategy and better
promote dialogue in the Church.

(b) The Presentation of Fr. Lopez-Gay

A presentation at the meeting by Fr. Jesus Lopez-
Gay entitled "Current Criticisms of the Theology and
Practice of 'Dialogue'" serves to illustrate many of
the concerns and difficulties faced in interreligious

dialogue.[73] Fr. Lopez-Gay pointed to the relationship between dialogue and mission as one of the major questions in the movement towards dialogue. Many missionaries, he noted, were uneasy with dialogue because of its emphasis on the respect for the religions of the non-Christians and its apparent downplaying of the effort to convert others. The missionary nature of the Church was being compromised, some thought.[74]

Another problem which Lopez-Gay pointed to was that of the theological foundation for dialogue. Many missionaries and theologians, he said, could not see any scriptural foundation for dialogue. In fact, they saw in the New Testament an emphasis on preaching, witness, and conversion with a call for non-Christians to leave their former ways in response to the call of Christ.[75] Dialogue seemed incompatible with these elements of scripture. Moreover, there were those who felt that dialogue was a step towards regarding all religions as essentially the same, thus denying the Christians claims of uniqueness, transcendence, and definitiveness for all.[76]

Lopez-Gay concluded his remarks by calling for more efforts in the Christian theological reflection on dialogue and its consequences. In particular, he noted that Christians had to consider seriously the questions of the relationship between dialogue and truth (for example, did all share in the truth in some way? was truth relative?), between dialogue and mission, and between dialogue and the universal presence of Christ (i.e., was Christ present in the non-Christian religions?).[77] These were all questions, one should note, to which the Secretariat's officials had already advanced some form of answer.

2. The Plenary Meeting at Rome in 1979

A plenary meeting of the Secretariat at Rome, April 24-27, 1979, provided an occasion for the Secretariat to evaluate its activity in a major way. During this meeting, the participants reviewed the work of the Secretariat,[78] listened to presentations on the state of dialogue in various parts of the world, approved some general recommendations about the direction in which the Secretariat's activity should proceed in its three major areas of concern (dialogue with Muslims, with the followers of the Asian religions, and with the traditional religions in Africa), and discussed a new set of dialogue guidelines. A large number of bishops interested in the Secretariat's work and three guests from the WCC joined the Consultors and the officials of the Secretariat for this meeting.[79]

The participants agreed that there was still much to do and that a good many problems still needed to be overcome in encouraging interreligious dialogue in the Church. Mgr. Rossano's opening address touched on this. He spoke of the slow, gradual attempts by the Secretariat to have dialogue accepted as a legitimate form of Christian activity, distinct from missionary work. These attempts, he admitted, were not yet successful. Dialogue was still not a major part of the Church's work.[80]

Two major areas of discussion during this meeting illustrate the problems the Secretariat faced as well as its reflection on dialogue after eighteen years of work. These centered on the state of interreligious dialogue in various parts of the world and on a new set of dialogue guidelines with suggestions for an acceptable theological framework.

(a) The Discussion on the State of Dialogue

The state of dialogue in the three areas of the Secretariat's special concern was the topic of discussion in workshops held during this meeting as well as in Mgr. Rossano's opening address. With respect to Christian-Muslim dialogue, Mgr. Rossano noted that among the chief difficulties were the Muslim refusal to accept an historical-critical analysis of the Koran, the view of Muslims that Islam was the definitive and universal religion superseding Judaism and Christianity, and Islam's lack of distinction between the religious and political levels of existence.[81] For its part, the workshop on Christian-Muslim dialogue noted that there was a resurgence of Islamic nationalism in Muslim countries which was leading to a sense of superiority on the part of the Muslim majority and, in places, the application of Islamic law to everyone in the society. There was even evidence of a rise in levels of intolerance to other views. These developments were causing Christians in these Muslim countries to mistrust their Muslim neighbours and increased the tension between these two groups.[82]

In most areas where Christian-Muslim dialogue had to be encouraged, the major concern, the workshop felt, was simply to encourage openness and friendliness on the part of Muslims and Christians towards one another. The workshop accordingly called upon Christians to make an effort to attain a better knowledge of Islam.[83] The workshop also felt that there was much confusion about the relationship between dialogue and mission on the part of many Christians. It called for a clarification of this relationship which would deal with the value of the non-Christian religions and the purpose of dialogue with their followers.[84]

When it came to dialogue with African religious
traditions, Mgr. Rossano remarked that the emphasis in
Africa had come to be placed on the indigenization of
the Gospel which was something "to be grafted on to,
while not destroying, the pre-existing substratum."[85]
The workshop discussing dialogue in Africa repeated
this same idea, noting that dialogue in Africa was different from dialogue elsewhere because of the absence
of direct contact with representatives of traditional
African religions. An "indirect" contact, through spe-
cialists in African religions, was usually the form
contact took. The workshop recommended that continuing
study of African religions be carried out in order to
pursue the many questions involved with indigenization.
As part of this process, the workshop recommended that
the Secretariat sponsor a conference with the theme
"African Religions and Catholicism." This conference
would have as one of its goals that of outlining systematically the positive values in African religions
which could be taken up, purified, and transformed by
Christianity, as well as pointing to those features
which were incompatible with the Gospel.[86]

In commenting on the Secretariat's dialogue efforts with followers of the Asian religions, Mgr. Rossano noted at first the problems of dialogue with Buddhists. There were fundamental differences between the
Christian and Buddhist mentality, he claimed, chiefly
when it came to the Christian affirmations of a personal God, the human person as the object of divine love,
and salvation as a gift. Points of contact could be
found, he suggested, in the Buddhist monastic experience and in its search for an Absolute.[87] He also
noted, with satisfaction, the desire on the part of
Buddhists (and Shintoists) in Japan to dialogue with

the Church. Concerning dialogue with Hindus, Mgr. Rossano felt that the main obstacle to dialogue was the Hindu affirmation of the equality of all religions: all were but different paths to and perceptions of the same divine Reality.[88] This attitude tended to blunt the desire on the part of Hindus to engage in "religious" dialogue because they saw little value in it.

The workshop report from the group discussing Asian religions made some remarks on the general problems of interreligious dialogue in Asia. The group felt that Christians in Asia were confused about the relationship between dialogue and mission and about the very purpose of dialogue. Some felt that dialogue betrayed the missionary mandate of the Church.[89] Others were afraid dialogue would lead to syncretism and erode the uniqueness and transcendence of the Christian message.[90] The group also noted that many outside the Church were suspicious, fearing that dialogue was but a missionary tactic.[91] As a result, the recommendations of the workshop included further emphasis on educating Christians as to the value and necessity of dialogue.[92]

(b) Discussion of New Dialogue Guidelines

During this plenary meeting, a draft copy of a proposed set of new guidelines for dialogue was discussed by the participants. This draft proposal was neither adopted nor rejected. Following the meeting, the Secretariat's officials began the task of revising it, making it more "theological." Aspects of this draft are worth looking at because they provide insights into the sorts of issues and concerns the Secretariat's officials faced.

The understanding of the nature of dialogue in the draft is in many ways the same as the understanding

that had earlier emerged in the Secretariat as its officials reflected on this issue. Dialogue is seen as an
interpersonal encounter, yet one which can also take
place between religions in the sense that "people live
in a context of traditions and socio-cultural organizations."[93] The draft guidelines insert the notion of
a certain progression in dialogue. It is an encounter
which should progress from an easing of tensions and a
development of friendly relations, to collaboration in
common human concerns, to discussion and sharing of religious experiences.[94] The Secretariat had by this time
clarified the subject matter of the interreligious dialogue it was concerned with: dialogue was not necessarily only about religious topics, but it could involve any topic discussed "from the point of view of
one's own faith and religious experience."[95]

The draft guidelines insist that dialogue demands
a sincere and total respect for the cultural and religious identity of the dialogue partner, the willingness
to let the other be free, and the desire to learn about
and listen to the other.[96] The prime motivation for all
of this is "evangelical Love." Thus, the draft notes
that it is actually a Christian duty to take the initiative in establishing dialogue.[97]

The goals of dialogue, according to the draft
guidelines, include, first of all, the mutual edification of the dialogue partners, both the Christian and
the non-Christian.[98] This continues the idea, already
present in the Secretariat's dialogue reflections, that
Christians can indeed learn from non-Christians. On a
very practical and increasingly important level, the
guidelines also see dialogue as a means of developing
ways of living together for people in religiously pluralistic societies.[99] Notable in these proposed guide-

lines, however, is the lack of any mention of dialogue as a form of pre-evangelization. There is, moreover, no development of the relationship between dialogue and mission beyond the mere assertion that dialogue can be considered an activity in its own right.[100]

Although there is no systematic development of the theological principles involved in interreligious dialogue, there are a number of theological judgments and presuppositions evident throughout this draft. First, the draft guidelines repeat the underlying anthropological understanding that is present throughout the Secretariat's work: humankind by nature seeks God. Moreover, there is the reiteration of the idea that God is present and active among **all** peoples. The draft guidelines state,

> . . . there must be: a theological appreciation of the "homo religiosus," in so far as expressing the "quaerere Deum" in consequence of creation and the action of God on men; respect for the mysterious design of God for history and for individual men: an awareness that the Spirit of God has been active and is still active among men of other religions.[101]

The familiar refrain about the continuity and discontinuity of the Gospel is yet another feature of the theological views present in these dialogue guidelines. There is no necessary radical antithesis between human religiosity, the world's religions and the Gospel. This Gospel, though, adds a radically new dimension to the already existing religious expressions. Hence, the Christian shares with all others the experience of the search for God, while at the same time being distinct

because of the novelty and transcendence of the revelation he or she has received.[102] Importantly, however,
there is the recognition in the guidelines that the
Gospel message always takes on the character of a particular cultural embodiment. It inevitably "bears the
stamp of the nation and culture to which the individual Christian belongs."[103]

IV. The 1984 Statement On Dialogue

The statement on dialogue discussed at the 1979
meeting of Consultors underwent a series of drafts that
led to a final statement approved during a plenary
meeting of Consultors held at Grottaferrata, Rome, 27
February--3 March 1984. This new statement on dialogue
marks the end of this examination of the Secretariat's
work. It is the fruit of some two decades of dialogue
activity and it shows not only the position reached but
also the problems that remained in the official Roman
Catholic reflection on interreligious dialogue. The
statement was officially proclaimed by Pope John Paul
II on Pentecost, June 10, 1984 under the title "The Attitude of the Church Towards the Followers of Other Religions: Reflections and Orientations on Dialogue and
Mission."[104] The following discussion well serve as a
kind of summary of the Secretariat's work to this
point.

The purpose of this statement, announced in the
opening remarks, is twofold. Firstly, it says that the
Church wants to offer a solution to the problem of the
relationship between dialogue and mission or evangelization. Secondly, it says that the Church wants to let
non-Christians know how the Church views them and how
it intends to behave towards them.[105] The focus of the
statement, though, is on the relationship between di-

alogue and mission. This had become the major question
in the Secretariat and in official Catholic reflection
on dialogue. There is no systematic treatment of the
religions of the world. Scattered comments that have a
bearing on a theology of religions are all there is to
be found.

1. Dialogue in the Statement

When it comes to understanding the nature of dialogue, the new statement insists that dialogue is a
way of acting and an attitude that implies respect for
others, concern for others, and hospitality. In a dialogical attitude, the dialogue partners must be allowed to retain their identity. This attitude must
characterize Christian dealings with others.[106]

The bases for dialogue, i.e., the reasons why
Christians should adopt an attitude of respect for others, are many. The new statement, firstly, repeats the
notion of the respect for human dignity that emerged in
Vatican II's discussion on religious freedom. Indeed,
this declaration is frequently quoted in the dialogue
statement. Human dignity demands that people freely,
without coercion, seek the truth. No force, then, is to
be exerted on others to have them change their religious views.[107]

The particular social context in which humankind
finds itself today also is a basis for a dialogical approach. The growing interdependence of all peoples, the
growing awareness that we must try to live together in
peace, necessitate an approach to others which must be
based on mutual respect and the desire to work together in harmony. Thus the statement says,

Socio-cultural changes in the world, with
their inherent tensions and difficulties, as

well as the growing interdependence in all
sectors of society necessary for living together, for human promotion, for pursuing the
demands of peace, all render a dialogical
style of human relationships today even more
urgent.[108]

A dialogical approach to others is also appropriate, in fact it is demanded, because of the dynamics of the Christian faith itself, the statement insists. Christians can, in dialogue with others, come to
appreciate God's omnipresent goodness.[109] Respect and
concern for others, among whom God is present, is then
a legitimate Christian activity.

The focus of the statement, though, is on mission
and how dialogue is related to it. The statement is,
first of all, uncompromising in its affirmation that
the Church has the duty of preaching the Gospel message
to all peoples, sharing with them its experience of God
and establishing the Church among peoples where it has
not yet been set up.[110] Yet this must be done in the
spirit of love and with tremendous respect for the
freedom of others to accept the Church's message or
reject it in good conscience[111].

The goal of the Church's missionary proclamation
is conversion, but the document has a view of conversion which allows for others to remain loyal to their
faith commitments at least until they come to recognize
the truth of the Christian claims. Conversion is first
and foremost a conversion towards God's will, a process
which may lead one out of one's present religious traditions to another. The statement reads,

> In biblical language and that of the
> Christian tradition, conversion is the humble

and penitent return of the heart to God in
the desire to submit one's life more gener-
ously to Him. . . . In the course of this
process, the decision may be made to leave
one's previous spiritual or religious situation in order to direct oneself toward another.[112]

2. Theological Reflections

The most disappointing aspect of this 1984 statement on dialogue is that it contributes little to the
discussion of a theology of religions. Absolutely critical questions, such as whether the religions are means
of salvation and how they may fit into the divine plan
of salvation, are not touched on. The statement does
nothing more than repeat the words of Vatican II that
the religions of the world contain "rays of truth which
illumines all mankind."[113] This comment simply reflects
the traditional Catholic view that it is in Jesus
Christ that one finds the fullness of the truth.

If there is anything to be said in a positive way
about the underlying ideas present in this statement,
it is that it reflects the humble attitude towards the
Church taken at Vatican II. The Church is a pilgrim
people, on its way towards the final goal of history,
the establishment of the Kingdom of God. It makes its
way along with other believers, and is called to seek
perfection with them. Yet, this humbleness is always
accompanied by an insistence that it is through Christ
that humans see God and it is through Christ that they
are ultimately brought to salvation. God may be present and active everywhere, but there is an unsurpassability and definitiveness in the divine saving work
through Jesus Christ.

3. A Note On Ecumenical Collaboration

During the period of time under review in this chapter, the World Council of Churches, through its "Sub-Unit for Dialogue With People of Other Faiths and Ideologies," began a series of interreligious dialogue meetings followed by reflection on them. The Secretariat for Non-Christians, represented by various appointed Consultors and especially by Mgr. Rossano, took part in this activity. One should keep in mind in the next major section of this study, then, that a Roman Catholic presence is always in the background in the WCC's work. The early reticence on the part of the Secretariat to cooperate with the WCC, due in part to the relative newness of true ecumenical collaboration, gave way to the sense that dialogue encounters with non-Christians should have an ecumenical face. One of the reasons for this willingness to collaborate, from the side of the Secretariat, was the perception that the WCC and the Secretariat were very close in their attitudes about dialogue.[114] This had not always been the case. There had been a fear within the Secretariat in the early years of ecumenical contacts that, on the theological level, the WCC's dialogue activity would reflect too much the theology of Karl Barth and his followers with its negative view of non-Christian religions. Once the Secretariat's officials perceived that this was not necessarily so, they felt more comfortable with ecumenical collaboration in the field of interreligious dialogue.

PART TWO
The Sub-Unit for Dialogue with People of Living Faiths and Ideologies

CHAPTER FOUR
TOWARDS THE ESTABLISHMENT
OF THE DFI

I. Antecedents of the Dialogue Debate

Within the World Council of Churches and particularly within one of the bodies that forms an important
part of its pre-history, namely, the International Missionary Council (the IMC), the theological problems associated with the Christian encounter with men and women of other religions has been the topic of a debate
that goes back to the beginnings of this century. The
debate has for the most part been carried on within the
context of the missionary activity of the "ecumenical"
movement as the member churches discussed their missionary effectiveness. This early debate has been the
subject of ample documentation and analysis,[1] so there
is no need to go into it in much detail here. There
are, however, some aspects of it that are worth noting
because they shed light on many of the difficulties the
WCC's dialogue activity faced as it began to pursue its
dialogue activity in the 1970's.

1. The Influence of Karl Barth
and Dialectical Theology

One of the major influences on Protestant thinking
about non-Christians and their religions in this century has been that school of theology called "dialectical" theology associated often with the name of Karl
Barth.[2] The significance of this theology in an assessment of the religions of the world is that it posits
an antithesis between the religious strivings of humankind and the supernatural Word of God revealed in Je-

sus Christ.[3] Dialectical theology carried through the
central theme of the Protestant Reformation that it is
God alone who justifies humankind, not the latter by
its works. Justification and hence salvation come as
gifts from the grace of God alone, and men and women
can do nothing to earn them.

Barth understood religion and the various forms of
religions throughout the world as essentially based on
the attempt by human beings to attain salvation and
come to know God by their own efforts. In other words,
the religions were human attempts to gain what God
alone could grant and so were examples of humankind's
folly and pride.

Barth's position rests ultimately on his view that
God is the Wholly Other, completely transcendent. By
its own powers, humankind cannot come to a knowledge of
what God is really like. There is an unbridgeable gap
between God and humankind, unbridgeable, that is, unless God intervene.[4] And this intervention has occurred, for Barth, in the person of Jesus Christ. Jesus is God's definitive inbreaking into human history,
God's definitive revelation. Outside of Jesus, there is
no other revelation.

Revelation, then, stands in sharp contrast to religion. It is only by God's grace, received through acceptance of God's revelation in faith, that justification and knowledge of God are possible. What about
Christianity? Christianity, in a sense, is a religion
like others, but with this fundamental difference: it
has been "justified" by God by being made the bearer of
divine revelation. Barth calls it "true" religion, as
opposed to the other religions which are "false." It is
the true religion only because God's grace shines
through it. It is not true because of anything human,

but solely because it has been accepted by God and is the religion in which God's revelatory Word is encountered.[5]

In Christianity, then, God's revealed Word is present. Only in this Word, Jesus Christ, is knowledge of God possible and thus insofar as Christianity preaches this Word, only in it is God's revelation found. For Barth, there was no revealed knowledge of God in the other religions of the world. This is extremely important to keep in mind. God's revelation is **not** found in other religions **at all**.[6] Moreover, God's revelation does not fulfill or complete the human strivings made concrete in the religions. These are the result of human attempts to attain knowledge of God and justification. God's revelation stands over against these attempts. Human beings must submit to God's revealed Word in faith. Their strivings are simply folly; God alone justifies. Humans can do nothing.

2. The Tambaram Conference: Continuity or Discontinuity.

The negative view of the human religious effort and the non-Christian religions of the world advanced by Karl Barth was by no means totally accepted within the missionary circles of the early ecumenical movement. More positive views were also present. An important clash between supporters of the two sides occurred at a major missionary conference held by the International Missionary Council in 1938 at Tambaram, Madras, India. This conference, discussing the Christian approach to non-Christians, was to establish the framework for the debate on this question within the ecumenical missionary movement for years following.

The debate centered around the question of whether

God's revelation, found in Christianity, was continuous
or discontinuous with respect to the values found in
other religious traditions. Hendrik Kraemer, in a book
which was the basis of much of the discussion at the
conference,[7] adopted a view which follows the general
thrust of Karl Barth's position outlined above. There
was, Kraemer insisted, a radical discontinuity between
divine revelation and human religiosity, between Christianity and other religions, in other words.[8] This view
led to considerable controversy, since there were many
at the conference who supported the view that God's revealing activity existed everywhere throughout the
world in some form, even in the non-Christian religions. For these, there were real points of contact and
common elements between Christianity and other religions. God's truth was not confined to Christianity,
although, of course, it was present there in its most
complete form.[9]

As it turned out, the participants at the Tambaram
Conference could not agree on this fundamental issue.
The question of whether the religions were simply the
product of human beings striving after God or whether
they also contained some form of revelation from God
remained unanswered. The most the participants could
agree on was that God has sought to reveal the divine
self and the divine will to humankind at all times, but
whether this revelation was present in the religious
experience and moral achievements of non-Christians was
left unsettled. The statement that came from this conference thus says,

> As to whether the non-Christian religions as
> total systems of thought and life may be re-
> garded as in some sense or to some degree
> manifesting God's revelation, Christians are

not agreed. This is a matter urgently demanding thought and united study . . . .[10]

3. The Aftermath of Tambaram and the
Emergence of the Idea of Dialogue

The result of the Tambaram Conference was that an
impasse was reached between those who favoured positions such as Barth's radical denial of humankind's religious strivings in the face of God's revelation and
those who favoured a certain amount of continuity between revelation and religion and who were more positive in their evaluation of religion in general and the
non-Christian religions in particular. Reflection on
this impasse resumed in earnest after the Second World
War, primarily under the impetus of new challenges to
the missionary task of the churches. Faced with the increasing rise of secularism and a revival of the traditional indigenous religions in Asia and Africa (a revival due partly to the sense of nationalism sweeping
through these continents which had so long been under
European colonial domination), missionary circles in
the ecumenical movement sought to re-examine their missionary approach.[11] Part of this re-examination involved the approval in 1962 by the IMC and the by-then
established WCC to set up a number of study centers in
those parts of the world where Christians were in the
minority. These were supposed to provide an opportunity for Christians to increase their knowledge of non-
Christians and their religions and to enable Christians
to study how to witness more effectively to their
faith. Another part of the re-examination was the establishment in 1955 of a long-term study entitled "The
Word of God and the Living Faiths of Men," a study undertaken jointly by the IMC and the WCC. This study had

as its goal that of coming to a new understanding of the relationship between Christians and people of other faiths beyond the continuity-discontinuity polarity that had been the focus of attention after the Tambaram Conference.[12]

While the ecumenical movement reflected on the proper Christian attitude to the followers of other religions and upon the value of these religions themselves, the idea of "dialogue" emerged as a way of approaching non-Christians. Dialogue appeared first as part of the missionary strategy of the ecumenical movement. This was the thrust of a statement on dialogue which surfaced at the general assembly of the WCC at New Delhi in 1969. Through dialogue, the statement said, the Christian can come to know the non-Christian better and thus be better able to preach the Gospel.[13] The question of interreligious dialogue surfaced also at the first meeting of the newly formed Commission of World Mission and Evangelism (formerly the IMC) at Mexico City in 1963. Intended primarily to examine the witness of Christians to their neighbours in a secular world, this meeting looked briefly at the relationship between dialogue and witness. It saw a dialogical approach in which the Christian was respectful of the other and sincerely sought to engage in a conversation with the other as a proper approach in the modern world where Christians everywhere were encountering men and women of other faiths and of various secular ideologies.[14] The emphasis on a more dialogical approach to non-Christians emerged, as well, in the statement of the assembly of the East Asian Christian Conference held at Bangkok in 1964. Its declaration, "Christian Encounter with Men of Other Beliefs,"[15] pointed to the tension existing in the idea of dialogue between the

sincere conversation with non-Christians, respecting
their beliefs, and the Christian mandate to witness and
to call others to recognize Christ. Yet, in spite of
this tension, there were factors making dialogue possible and desirable, the statement said. It singled out
the need to search for answers to fundamental human
needs and the concern to cooperate in the building up
of the human community. Christians were urged by the
assembly to approach others in a spirit of friendliness
and to be willing to collaborate with them.[16] This emphasis on collaboration was particularly strong, one
should note, in India, where Christians were examining
their role in the building up of their post-colonial
nation along with the Hindu majority in their country.[17]

In order to reflect more deeply on the relationship of Christians to men and women of other faiths and
on the idea of interreligious dialogue, Victor E.
Hayward, then Director of the CWME, convened a conference at Kandy in what is now Sri Lanka in 1967. It is
this conference that marks the beginnings of the WCC's
interest in dialogue in a major way.

II. From Kandy to Ajaltoun: On
the Way to Dialogue

1. The Kandy Consultation

The consultation convened at Kandy took place from
February 27 to March 6, 1967. There were three parts to
the consultation. First, the Directors of the various
study centers which had been set up to encourage research into the religious traditions of missionary areas of the world met to discuss the direction their
work should take. Second, the plans for the next stages

of the long-term study, "The Word of God and the Living Faiths of Men" were laid. Finally, there was a
meeting to discuss the specific theme of dialogue.
Three Consultors from the Secretariat for Non-Christians attended and statements from Vatican II, the decree **Nostra aetate** and parts of **Lumen gentium**, were included in the preparatory material.[18] The meeting on
dialogue is the most relevant to this study and so the
discussion which follows will focus on this aspect of
the Kandy consultation.

(a) Important Presentations and
     Preparatory Material

The position of Karl Barth which so influenced
many European theologians has been outlined briefly
above. It is necessary, at this time, to outline some
other positions which in their turn influenced the WCC
discussion on dialogue and its theological implications. The preparatory material given to the participants of the Kandy meeting and several of the presentations which they heard and discussed reflect tendencies very much opposed to that of dialectical theology and so provide a valuable look at various undercur-
rents of theological thinking present within the WCC.

One of the preparatory papers was by D. T. Niles
entitled "The Christian Claim for the Finality of
Christ."[19] In trying to point out a way by which
Christians could understand the life and death of
Christ as the definitive redeeming action of God for
all, Niles proposed a view which turned out to be quite
inclusive of other religions as well. His proposal centered upon a view of Christ which stressed the "cosmic"
or "universal" nature of the work of Christ. Using the
idea of the "cosmic" Christ that one sees in the let-

ter of Paul to the Colossians (1:16ff.), Niles described Christ as "he from whom all things proceed and
receive their vocation," "he in whom all things cohere
and work together," "he by whom all things are judged
and brought to judgement," and "he unto whom all things
must go."[20] Christ's work was not confined to the activity of the historical person, Jesus. The work of
Christ in saving humankind was ongoing, not finished
until the end of time, encompassing all people, all
communities, all generations. Although not everyone
recognized this active presence, Christ was nonetheless
active and present everywhere. There was no explanation, however, as to how.

The important thing about Niles' suggestions was
that he voiced a view which held that Christ was active
in a saving way among all peoples, even now. The Church
was not the only place where Christ's saving work was
present. Rather, the Church was a representative body
pointing to the final end to which all things were moving.[21]

What Niles' remarks implied with respect to the
non-Christian religions of the world, he thought, was
that Christ could be present in them, too. Christ was
not absent from the non-Christian religious world; he
was there, albeit unrecognized. It was the task of
Christians to point out the unknown Christ in the midst
of the non-Christian religions. Niles thus states that
Christians

> . . . are committed by the witness they bear
> both to believe in the presence of Jesus
> Christ in the history of all other faiths, as
> well as to accept their responsibility to de-
> clare to men of other faiths the identity of
> 'the unknown God' by whom each man's faith is

validated and their systems of faith are
judged (Acts 17:23).

To disclose the 'unknown God' is not to
rename the known gods. Instead, it is to
uncover a presence which has been there even
though unidentified. . . .[22]

In addition, Niles insisted that it was possible
to be saved without explicit faith in Christ. Using Mt.
25:37-39 as his scriptural backing, he argued in favour
of this idea as follows:

. . . when Jesus Christ makes his place and
time of appointment with men, he does not always give his name. I can imagine a man such
as Jawaharlal Nehru saying, "But when did I
see you naked or hungry or in prison?" (Matt.
25:37-39). The point is not that there are
alternatives to commitment to Christ, other
ways by which men can be saved; but that to
speak about the finality of Christ is not to
tie oneself to where his name is actually
pronounced. As he himself tells us, he deter-
mines the form and occasion of his presence,
and where and to whom he will come incogni-
to.[23]

An implication of Niles' theological views for dialogue was the idea that when Christians encountered
men and women of other faiths, they encountered people
among whom Christ was already present and active. One
of the purposes of dialogue, for Niles, was to discover
this.[24]

The affirmation in Niles' paper of the saving
presence of Christ in non-Christian religions was to be
seen as well in a declaration of a meeting of the Na-

tional Christian Conference in Nasrapur, India, entitled "The Mission of the Church in Contemporary India."[25] This declaration, part of the preparatory reading material for the Kandy meeting, asserted that
Christ was Lord of all history and of all of humankind.
God was at work in all cultures and religions[26] and so
Christians had to replace their negative attitudes towards non-Christian religions with a more positive appreciation.[27] While salvation was through Jesus Christ
alone, his saving work was universally present. The
declaration reads,

> In Christ all men have to be liberated
> from the bondage of sin. This saving work of
> Christ is not limited to the organized Chris-
> tian Church. He works where He wills. It is
> not for us to judge the manner and place of
> His working. The Christian should be sensi-
> tive in discerning His presence and His do-
> ing. Changes have taken place in the prac-
> tices and interpretations of India's old re-
> ligions, and people have been liberated in
> many instances from oppressive bondages, (**Sa-
> ti**, Untouchability, **Purday** etc.). Changes are
> still going on. Christ is at work here.[28]

As with Niles, a vision of a "cosmic" Christ, everywhere present and active, permeates this declaration's
view of God's saving activity. And, along the same line
as Niles had suggested as well, interreligious dialogue
could be an occasion for listening to what God had to
say in the religious experience of non-Christians. The
declaration remarks,

> Christian mission must be carried out in the
> spirit of dialogue, in which we are prepared

not only to speak but also to listen to what
God has to say to us through the other.[29]

The presentations given during the Kandy meeting
as well as the preparatory material noted above also
give evidence of theological views that differ consid-
erably from those of the dialectical theologians. One
of these presentations was by Kenneth Cragg, an expert
in Christian-Muslim relations. In a paper entitled "The
Credibility of Christianity,"[30] Cragg launched into a
criticism of Barth's emphasis on the complete transcendence of God's revelation and called upon his listners
to take more seriously the idea that nature and revelation were not antithetical. Rather, God's revelation
built upon the natural world. There was, in other
words, an affinity between nature and revelation. It
was the Incarnation, God's assumption of human nature
in the person of Jesus Christ, argued Cragg, that
grounded this point of view. He thus remarked,

> The revelatory feasibility of Incarnation
> presupposes the revelatory quality, in part,
> of all experience. Unless everything is in
> its own sense revelatory of God nothing can
> be. A world into which we believe God has
> been born is nowhere irrelevent either to Him
> or for Him. The 'new' or special sacredness
> which greets us in the Incarnate Lord employs
> the channels of natural sacredness.[31]

The assumption of that which was already present in the
natural world, an "incarnational" approach, was the direction in which Cragg's remarks thus pointed.

The Reverend Lynn de Silva, Director of the study
center at Colombo, presented another paper which illustrates a very different tendency to that of Barth and

his followers. His paper, "Non-Christian Religions and God's Plan of Salvation,"[32] insisted that salvation is indeed possible outside of the Christian Church, and it implied that other religions could be ways of salvation. The paper argued that the definitive salvation of the entire cosmos was in the future, when all things would be summed up in Christ. Until the end, however, there was a "progressive actualization of the positive elements in man in an intermediate period before the consummation."[33] God made use of all sorts of people and events in the meantime, de Silva argued, to bring men and women to salvation before the final time. He said,

> The Christ-event is the classic instance of salvation but not the exclusive event in history through which God has mediated his salvation to mankind. The other events, although they do not measure up to the classic event, are in no way insufficient means of salvation. Each event, like the Christ-event, is a promise and guarantee of the salvation that is to be in the end-time.[34]

In his remarks on mission, de Silva stated that the purpose of mission was not necessarily to bring non-Christians into the Church. The definitive salvation at the end-time involved an all-embracing unity and a harmony in Christ, he noted, and so mission should promote the unity and harmony that would characterize the end. It should, then, promote the breaking down of barriers that separated people from each other and from God. To separate people from their colleagues and friends by making them Christian ought not be mission. Everything that promoted harmony and rec-

onciliation, though, was what mission was really all
about.[35]

(b) Dialogue in the Kandy Statement

The statement that emerged from the Kandy meeting
was entitled "Christians in Dialogue With Men of Other
Faiths."[36] It saw dialogue as an encounter between the
followers of different religions in which the dialogue
partners respected their mutual differences and listened to what the other had to say. Dialogue thus involved a willingness to hear the other and to respect
the other's point of view. It was not geared towards
the winning over of the other to one's own position.[37]
The issues discussed could be many--questions of ultimate concern, religious experiences, how to solve common human problems--but whatever they were, true dialogue implied a sincere willingness to listen to the
other in respect.

There was more to dialogue than simple co-existence and the exchange of information, the declaration
went on to say. Through dialogue, both partners should
be able to come to a far greater understanding of the
truth, the truth about God, human nature, and human
destiny, for example.[38] The declaration insisted that
Christ was present whenever true dialogue occurred, so
that Christ could speak to the Christian through his or
her non-Christian partner. The declaration reads,

> We believe that Christ is present when-
> ever a Christian sincerely enters into dia-
> logue with another man; the Christian is con-
> fident that Christ can speak to him through
> the neighbour, as well as to his neighbour
> through him. Dialogue means a positive effort
> to attain a deeper understanding of the truth

through mutual awareness of one another's
convictions and witness. It involves an expectation of something new happening--a
readiness to be changed as well as to influence others.[39]

The declaration also briefly discussed the relationship between dialogue and proclamation. It defined
proclamation as "the sharing of the Good News about
God's action in history through Jesus Christ."[40] The
two, dialogue and proclamation, were not identical, although they could be very related. The concern that the
declaration addressed in this was one of the central
concerns that dialogue posed for many Christians: did
dialogue mean that Christians no longer had to proclaim
Jesus as the Lord and Saviour of all as they attempted
to respect the beliefs and practices of others? Was dialogue a betrayal of mission? On the other hand, there
was the question raised by non-Christians: was dialogue
a missionary tactic? The declaration, in reply to these
questions, only said that chances for proclamation
would occur in dialogue situations. The Christian had
good news to share and would be able to do so. This was
because dialogue allowed for mutual witness. The Christian in dialogue did not have to forget about his or
her beliefs.[41]

In its remarks on the bases for dialogue, the Kandy declaration first of all pointed to the essential
solidarity of all people everywhere. The declaration
saw all of humankind as being engaged in forging a common history as people everywhere were being faced with
common tasks and hopes. The underlying idea of the declaration is that humankind forms one race; the peoples
of the world are essentially one. On the theological
level, the declaration insisted that there were bases

in the Christian tradition for Christians to come together in mutual love and respect with others. All men
and women have been created by God, it noted, and
Christ had died for all. In addition, the Christian experience of a God who enters into communion with humankind was a reason for reaching out to others as a sort
of imitative response.[42]

(c) Theological Directions in the
Kandy Declaration

There are a number of interesting and even surprising statements in the Kandy declaration that bear
directly on a Christian evaluation of other religious
traditions. For example, the declaration affirms in its
opening lines that "God's love and purpose of salvation
extend to all mankind, of every century, country and
creed."[43] This saving will of God, the declaration insists, is accomplished through Jesus Christ alone, but,
significantly, the declaration points to a willingness
to admit that Christ's saving work does not necessarily occur within the confines of the historical Church
alone. The Kandy declaration understands the Church as
that body which "consciously responds to Christ in
trust and obedience," on the one hand, yet it says on
the other hand that the Church is an open fellowship,
existing for all, not "coterminous with the historical
community that openly bears [Christ's] name."[44] What is
more, all may be saved. Christ, through the Spirit, is
at work in the hearts of all, bringing grace and judgement to all. The declaration quotes with approval section 18 of **Lumen gentium** from the Second Vatican Council, admitting that even those outside the Church may
have access to God's saving work. This important part
of the Kandy declaration reads as follows:

Now and hereafter Christ brings grace
and judgment to all men. "God has no favour-
ites, but in every nation the man who is God-
fearing and does what is right is acceptable
to him" (Acts 10:34-35, cf. Romans 2:6-16).
We draw attention to the formulation of this
truth in the Vatican Council's Dogmatic Constitution on the Church: "Those also can attain to everlasting salvation who through no
fault of their own do not know the gospel of
Christ or His Church, yet sincerely seek God
and, moved by grace, strive by their deeds to
do His will as it is known to them through
the dictates of conscience.[45]

Although the tendency towards a universal or a
cosmic Christology is present in the Kandy statement's
understanding of God's saving work,[46] the question of
the implications of this on a Christian evaluation of
the non-Christian religions does not receive any development. Thus, there is no answer to the problem of the
place of non-Christian religions in the divine economy of salvation. The declaration says merely that
through dialogue greater insight may be possible. Yet,
in this, the Kandy declaration indicates an important
shift in reflection on this issue: theological reflection must take place in the context of actual dialogue.
Theoretical discussion alone is an inadmissable procedure. The declaration states,

As our dialogue with men of other faiths de-
velops, we may gain light regarding the place
held by other religious traditions in God's
purposes for them and for us; this is a question which cannot be answered a priori or

academically, but must continue to engage our earnest study and reflection.[47]

The Kandy consultation on dialogue reflected a movement within the WCC to consider more seriously the issue of dialogue and its implications in a major way. Such consideration was to be based on actual dialogue with the followers of other religions and not simply the result of Christians talking about them. The outcome was to be a greater emphasis on the sponsoring of interreligious dialogue meetings, a procedure that contrasted with the approach taken by the Secretariat for Non-Christians which preferred to engage in more theoretical work before entering into actual dialogue situations.

2. The Uppsala Assembly

Because there were so many unresolved theological issues still present, there was to be no discussion of interreligious encounters at the Fourth General Assembly of the WCC which took place at Uppsala, Sweden, July 4-20, 1968. The Central Committee of the WCC, that organization's governing body, decided that more consensus was needed before taking it up at a general assembly. Nonetheless, this important question of dialogue did emerge at the assembly during discussions on the renewal of the Church's missionary work, one of the major themes at Uppsala. As a result of these discussions, a section on dialogue was included in the assembly's final statement.[48]

The comments on dialogue that appear in the final report of the Uppsala assembly echo in many ways those of the Kandy declaration, although they are not as detailed. Thus the Uppsala report, for example, points to the common humanity which all share as being the basis

for dialogue. It understands dialogue in general terms
to be a friendly, respectful encounter between men and
women of differing religious traditions. It insists
that in dialogue both partners can witness to one
another as they share their respective insights into
and approaches to the important questions that face all
human beings. What is more, neither side is called upon
to renounce its own identity or uniqueness. The assembly's statement comments on the relationship between
dialogue and witness, saying that in dialogue the
Christian can witness to his or her faith. Finally, the
statement insists that dialogue can lead to mutual
growth between the dialogue partners as in their encounter with one another they encounter Christ who is
present as well. The statement reads,

> 6. The meeting with men of other faiths
> or of no faith must lead to dialogue. A
> Christian's dialogue with another implies
> neither a denial of the uniqueness of Christ,
> nor any loss of his own commitment to Christ,
> but rather that a genuinely Christian ap-
> proach must be human, personal, relevant and
> humble. In dialogue we share our common hu-
> manity, its dignity and fallenness, and ex-
> press our common concern for that humanity.
> It opens the possibility of sharing in new
> forms of community and common service. Each
> meets and challenges the other, witnessing
> from the depths of his existence to the ul-
> timate concerns that come to expression in
> word and action. As Christians we believe
> that Christ speaks in this dialogue, reveal-
> ing himself to those who do not know him and
> correcting the limited and distorted knowl-

edge of those who do. Dialogue and proclamation are not the same. The one complements
the other in a total witness.[49]

III. Gaining Practical Experience: The Ajaltoun Conference and Its Aftermath

1. The Increasing Concern for Dialogue

Increasing interest within the WCC concerning dialogue led to the sponsorship of a large multilateral
interreligious dialogue meeting at Ajaltoun, Lebanon,
in 1970. Evidence of this increasing interest can be
seen in the work of Dr. Stanley J. Samartha, head of
the already-mentioned "Word of God" long-term study.
For example, Dr. Samartha had written to the directors
of the various study centers that had been set up in
1955 and had asked them to consider dialogue and its
theological implications. Part of his letter asked,

> 1. What is the purpose of the dialogue? What
> is the relation between dialogue and procla-
> mation? What does it mean . . . to be total-
> ly committed to one's faith and radically
> open to that of the other? The experience of
> actual dialogues should be brought to bear on
> these questions . . . .
>
> 2. What is the basis on which these dialogues
> actually take place? . . .
>
> . . . .
>
> 4. What is the meaning and implication of an
> existence in dialogue for Christian mission
> in a religiously and secular pluralistic
> world?[50]

Further evidence of Dr. Samartha's concern for reflection on dialogue can be seen in a report he wrote
for the WCC's Division of Studies for Mission and Evangelism. In this report, Dr. Samartha outlined some of
the issues he thought the WCC faced in its approach to
people of other faiths and insisted that a more positive approach to these faiths was necessary. Among the
factors he identified as making it necessary to adopt
a more favourable attitude towards those of other
faiths were the following. Christians, especially in
newly independent countries, were being called on to
cooperate with others in the development of their respective countries. This meant that a new relationship
between peoples of various faiths was essential. Competition and lack of respect for the other were de-
structive elements in such circumstances. There were
also multi-religious societies increasingly being
formed. Christians were thus being drawn into daily
personal contact with people of other religious traditions and were living side by side with them. Finally,
the WCC itself was increasingly being called upon to
cooperate with other religious organizations in facing
up to world problems such as the search for world peace
and social justice. These factors all contributed towards the necessity on the part of the WCC to examine
the possibilities for new approaches to men and women
of other faiths and to engage in dialogue with them.
Samartha concluded, then,

> The cumulative effect of all these
> points . . . is to raise the fundamental
> question as to how the WCC's commitment to
> its basis of faith viz., the confession 'of
> the Lord Jesus Christ as God and Saviour'
> can, at the same time, be related to the fact

that all peoples, including those who profess
other faiths and ideologies, belong to one
humanity. The answer to this question cannot
be sought in isolation from, but together
with, men of other faiths.[51]

The insistence at the end of the above quotation,
that reflection had to be carried out together with
people of other faiths, led Samartha to suggest that
the WCC establish an agency to encourage interreligious
dialogue.[52] He urged the WCC to become involved with
peoples of other faiths even though this was something
new and needed further theological evaluation.[53]

2. The Approval for Interreligious Dialogue:
The Canterbury Meeting

Sensitive to the suggestions coming from the Division of World Mission and Evangelism as exemplified
in the above remarks of Stanley Samartha, the WCC's
Central Committee at its annual meeting in 1969 held at
Canterbury, England, approved the sponsorship of a multilateral dialogue meeting. The suggestion had come
from the Working Group of the DWME in an earlier Canterbury meeting, and the recommendation of this body
received enthusiastic approval from the Central Committee. The minutes of the Central Committee's Canterbury
meeting show this approval:

2. Believing that the Christian Mission and
faithfulness to the Gospel imply a respect
for men of all faiths and ideologies, the
Central Committee
welcomes the increased emphasis on dialogue
with men of other faiths and of secular ideologies;

encourages the Department [of World Mission
and Evangelism] to study further the relation
between dialogue and mission, as well as the
relation between our common humanity with
other men and our new humanity in Christ;
approves the plan for an Ecumenical Consultation in Dialogue with Men of Other Faiths in
March 1970 in Beirut . . . .[54]

The Central Committee's statement indicates that the
members of the Committee did not think that dialogue
was something foreign to Christianity or something incompatible with their faith. It was, their statement
shows, the Gospel itself that led Christians to respect
men and women of other faiths. Yet, as the statement
also shows, the interreligious encounter had implications that Christians had to work out. The two it notes
in particular are: 1) the relationship between dialogue
and mission, and 2) the relationship between God's work
in creation (the common humanity which all share) and
the redeeming activity in Christ (the new humanity).
These, it will be seen below, are questions that recur
throughout the WCC's dialogue work.

3. The Ajaltoun Meeting and Memorandum

The meeting in Ajaltoun, near Beirut, March 16-26,
1970, was the first multilateral interreligious dialogue conference sponsored officially by the WCC. There
were four Buddhist, three Hindu, and four Muslim participants, as well as twenty-eight participants from
various Christian denominations.[55] It did not include
participants from Judaism or from any of the African
religions. Christians, as the above numbers show, were
very much in the majority.

The purpose of the meeting was simply to engage in

an actual dialogue encounter and experience the problems as well as the successes that such an encounter
could bring. It was an attempt to follow through with
the call from Kandy, repeated by Dr. Samartha, that
Christian reflection on other religions and their followers should take place out of real dialogue with
those of other religions. This new context demanded renewed thinking on the part of Christians as they became
aware of and considered seriously the problems and
ideas of their dialogue partners in a spirit of friendliness. Dr. Samartha, who helped to organize the Ajaltoun meeting, discussed the new context in which Christian reflection would take place at Ajaltoun as follows:

> The character and purpose of the Beirut Con-
> sultation as modified by the thinking since
> Canterbury should be noted. Kandy 1967, (a)
> brought together for the first time Roman
> Catholic, Orthodox and Protestant scholars as
> full participants, (b) produced a statement
> on Christian dialogue with men of other
> faiths and (c) listed the priorities of the
> Church in a pluralistic world. Beirut 1970
> hopefully (a) will for the first time bring
> together men of different faiths in a context
> of 'we' rather than 'we-they', (b) give at-
> tention to issues arising out of living, per-
> sonal encounters, and (c) seek new and con-
> tinuing ways of reflection, relating and co-
> operative action in the world . . . . Some-
> thing new is being attempted here . . . .[56]

Since the participants were not official representatives of their respective traditions, they did not

issue a statement that could in any way be considered as being the position of their particular religion. The memorandum they agreed to was more a summary of impressions of the meeting on the part of those taking part. The real value of the meeting was simply to be the experience of living in dialogue.[57]

The memorandum of the Ajaltoun meeting is perhaps most noteworthy in that it indicates a consensus about the nature of dialogue as experienced by the participants. For example, the memorandum states,

> A keynote of the Consultation was the understanding that a full and loyal commitment to one's faith did not stand in the way of dialogue. On the contrary, it was our faith which was the very basis of, and driving force to, intensification of dialogue and a search for common action between members of different faiths in the various localities and situations in which they find themselves neighbours.[58]

The memorandum also calls for further promotion of interreligious dialogue. Among the topics it singles out for further discussion is that of the meaning, basis, and purpose of dialogue, always, though, in particular historical situations. Concrete dialogue, in living contexts, and not mere theoretical reflection on dialogue was thus seen as important. Finally, the memorandum notes the difficulties for interreligious dialogue posed by the question of missionary activity and suggests that the relationship between dialogue and mission be a matter of ongoing reflection.[59]

4. The Zurich Consultation: Reflecting
on Ajaltoun

Soon after the Ajaltoun meeting, the DWME organized an intra-Christian consultation at Zurich, May
20-23, 1970. This meeting was designed to be a follow-
up to the Ajaltoun experience so that the Christian
participants could discuss the theological implications
of that dialogue encounter as well as the nature and
purpose of interreligious dialogue in general.[60] Since
dialogue was to be one of the major themes of the upcoming meeting of the Central Committee in Addis Ababa in 1971 when a set of guidelines for dialogue was
to be issued, this meeting at Zurich was also designed
to produce a statement on dialogue which could be useful to the Central Committee in shaping a dialogue policy for the WCC.

The deliberations at Zurich resulted in the publication of a statement entitled "Christians in Dialogue with Men of Other Faiths," commonly referred to
as the "Zurich Aide-Mémoire."[61] It was the most comprehensive dialogue statement to appear in the WCC to that
time. Its importance lay not only in the influence it
had on the Central Committee's discussions the following year but also in the fact that it incorporated the
experience of the Ajaltoun consultation. Christians at
Zurich were not reflecting theoretically on dialogue
but were reflecting out of an actual dialogue experience and trying to verbalize what that experience
meant.

(a) Dialogue in the Zurich Aide-Mémoire

The Zurich Aide-Mémoire begins its discussion of
dialogue by saying that dialogue is "inevitable, urgent, and full of opportunity" in the present-day sit-

uation characterized, it notes, by the increasing emergence of pluralistic societies. Men and women of differing faiths must live together peacefully. Moreover, all face the challenge of cooperating in solving the great problems of contemporary human existence. Historical forces were drawing people together. The statement says,

> [Dialogue] is inevitable because everywhere
> in the world Christians are now living in a
> pluralistic society. It is urgent because all
> men are under common pressures in the search
> for justice, peace, and a hopeful future and
> all are faced with the challenge to live to-
> gether as human beings. It is full of oppor-
> tunity because Christians can now, as never
> before, discover the meaning of the Lordship
> of Christ and the implications for the mis-
> sion of the Church in a truly universal con-
> text of common living and common urgency.
> Men, whether Christian or not, must live to-
> gether and do live together. Dialogues, de-
> signed to get to the deepest levels of com-
> mitment and directed to the most serious ex-
> plorations of common action are, therefore, a
> clear human demand at this hour of human his-
> tory.[62]

The Zurich statement does not only see dialogue as inevitable because of the contemporary human situation, however. It also insists that dialogue is an authentic form of Christian activity, with roots in the Christian faith itself. It is not merely expedient, but also demanded by the Gospel. Dialogue is an imitative response to the divine activity in Jesus Christ who "assumed hu-

manity on behalf of all men of all ages and all cultures."[63] Dialogue is a form of reaching out to all, an
expression of the Christian desire to enter into positive relationships with people of other faiths.[64]

Like the Ajaltoun memorandum, the Zurich Aide-Mémoire insists that dialogue is an encounter between
persons committed to their respective faiths and that
the partners are free to witness to their particular
commitments.[65] One does not, then, disguise one's beliefs or try to minimize the differences between one's
own beliefs and those of another where such differences
exist. The statement also sees dialogue as a process
involving risk and vulnerability which can lead to a
transformation of one or both of the dialogue partners.
It sees all men and women as being led to the fullness
of truth by the Holy Spirit, and says that dialogue can
serve to further this.[66] Finally, dialogue is seen as
a living contact between people who respect one another and who share their experiences of life with one another. It is a "dynamic contact of life with life." It
is not something theoretical or academic in the negative sense of that term.[67]

There are a number of goals in dialogue to which
the Zurich Aide-Mémoire points, most of which flow from
the bases and nature of dialogue. In the first place,
dialogue is a means of breaking down barriers that impede harmony and cooperation between peoples of differing faiths.[68] It promotes the peaceful living together that the statement sees as so necessary in a world
of pluralistic societies and interdependent communities. On a more theological level, the Zurich statement
sees dialogue as a means for Christians to come to know
more about God's presence and activity in the world.
The statement, citing the story of the conversion of

the pagan, Cornelius, in Acts 10, states that God is active among all peoples.[69] Dialogue is thus a means of contact with others which may enable Christians to understand better the nature of God's activity among peoples of other faiths. The statement says,

> 12. Clearly, at present Christians have many different views about the significance of other religions (and, indeed, about the status of Christianity as a religion) in relation to the whole economy of God in Jesus Christ. One thing, however, is clear. All Christians believe that God is at work in the world and have expectations about the signs and effects of His work. The investigation, in dialogue with men of other faiths, into how we are to understand this economy can therefore be undertaken in faith and hope. We cannot hope to be shown how we are to see men of other faiths in relation to our Christian faith, and how our Christian faith is to approach men of other faiths unless we are in human and personal contact with these men.[70]

Certain tensions among the views of Christians concerning dialogue are in evidence in the Zurich Aide-Mémoire. As an approach to people of other religions, there were difficulties. One of these was the problem of syncretism. The Zurich statement remarks, "[M]any sincere and informed Christians are genuinely apprehensive that dialogue . . . may lead to syncretism."[71] What is at stake here is the fear that the uniqueness and transcendence of the Gospel revelation may be compromised as Christians start to treat other religious beliefs with esteem and genuine appreciation. It is not so much the mixing-up of elements of various religions to form a new religion that is the problem, but rather a suspicion that the Gospel challenge to other religions will be downplayed. The statement acknowledges this as a problem but goes on to say that it is perhaps overstated by those it calls "western" missionaries and theologians. It calls for freedom in different regions of the world, notably Asia and Africa, for Christians to make the Gospel indigenous, and this means adopting and transforming elements in the culture concerned, not simply denouncing them as evil or of no relevance to Christianity. Dialogue is seen as a means of furthering the process of indigenization.[72]

Another tension present in the Zurich statement is the relationship between dialogue and mission. The declaration notes, in this regard, that many Christians are indeed suspicious that dialogue is a betrayal of mission, while many non-Christians think that dialogue is but a missionary tactic.[73] The statement proposes a concept of mission, in response, that attempts to minimize the negative overtones of superiority and condescension in Christian missionary work but which at the same time alters the more traditional view of mission. There is no mention of conversion, of bringing non-Christians into the fold of the Church. Rather, it sees mission as a sharing of God's love as this has been revealed in Christ. It involves making Christ known, not to a world in which Christ is absent, but to a world where Christ is already present, holding all things together now and in whom all things will be summed up in the end. The Zurich statement here uses the model of the universal Christ drawn from the Pauline epistles to the Colossians and the Ephesians as a basis for its comments on mission.[74] It says,

10. The mission of the Church stems from and is concerned with the activity of God for the salvation of the whole world. This Christians understand to be an activity of the love of God which they see particularly embodied in Christ. It is in Christ that all things hold together (now--cf. Colossians) and it is [in] Christ that all things will be summed up (in the end--cf. Ephesians). Hence the mission of the Church . . . stems from and is a response to the mission of God (who sent the Son of His love). This mission, therefore, is concerned with discovering Christ where he already is, holding all things together, with making Christ known so that men may consciously receive and share in his work of moving all things to their fulfillment in his Kingdom, the Kingdom of love, and with receiving Christ as he makes himself known to us through his activity in, and through the followers of, other faiths and commitments.[75]

(b) Some Important Theological Issues in the Zurich Aide-Mémoire

There are a number of important theological issues which the Zurich statement raises as well as some problems to which it points. The discussion of syncretism is a case in point. As noted above, the underlying fear was that Christianity would lose its uniqueness and transcendence through a respectful dialogue with the followers of other religions. There would be a tendency to downplay the challenge and confrontational demand of God's revealed Word. This is a constant fear in the

ecumenical discussion on dialogue. On the other hand,
there was also the feeling, especially among Christians
in Asia, that this fear had made the introduction of
the Gospel very difficult because it was perceived as
something coming from a foreign culture. It was these
Christians who were demanding that the Asian churches
be free to adapt Christianity to their own culture. The
Zurich statement on dialogue captures some of this debate, and it favours those who wanted to go ahead in
spite of the uncertainties and attempt some sort of indigenous expression of the Christian message. Thus one
sees in the Zurich statement the assertion that "when
the Christian church becomes organized, it has always
to incarnate the Gospel through certain cultural and
intellectual forms."[76]

There is, by implication then, no "pure" revelation exempt from cultural conditioning in some way.
Very much in the same way as was being expressed in the
discussions in the Secretariat for Non-Christians, this
WCC document recognizes that the Christian revelation
interacts with the culture it confronts, enriching it
and transforming it. The document calls for further
consideration of this, and sees dialogue as a means of
discerning those aspects of a culture which can be useful in a new expression of Christianity outside of its
traditional context. It is thus critical of any attempt
to see the present forms of Christianity as the only
legitimate ones. The statement says,

> It is, presumably, as unChristian to be
> trapped in a particular form of a "Western"
> culture as it is to succumb overly to an
> "Eastern" or an "African" one. We have to
> discover how to make sure that the revelatory
> element lives creatively with and transforms

the cultural elements while taking from them all that truly enriches . . . . [W]e need dialogue to enable us to find out both what are the authentic changes which the Gospel demands and the authentic embodiment which the Gospel offers.[77]

The discussion of mission in the Zurich statement points to what is perhaps one of the major theological concepts that is present in the statement because of its implications. This is the idea of the "universal" Christ. As the statement explains this concept, Christ is present to all of creation now. Because of this presence, Christ can speak through the non-Christian to the Christian in a dialogue encounter.

There are key theological tensions that are evident in this dialogue statement. One of these is the problem of the relationship between God's presence and activity in the world at large, and therefore among peoples of other faiths, and this presence and activity in the mission and person of Jesus Christ. This problem affects the understanding of the relationship between dialogue and mission. The statement says,

11. A main topic for further and urgent theological consideration with regard to the proper connection between Mission and Dialogue may be stated as follows: What is the relation of God's economy in Jesus Christ to the economy of his presence and activity in the whole world, and in particular in the lives and traditions of men of other living faiths?[78]

The statement quite clearly presupposes that God is present and active in creation, but it cannot affirm

the nature of this activity. God has been present salvifically in Jesus Christ, but is God's presence and
activity in creation at large salvific? What about the
presence of the universal Christ? The statement does
not answer these crucial questions. However, as the
Kandy declaration on dialogue had done before, the Zurich statement for its part insists that it is only
through real contact with the followers of these religions that answers to these questions will be possible.
A new context for doing theological reflection is
called for.[79]

The question of the nature of the Church is a final key theological issue which the Zurich statement
identifies as important. Christians, it says, believe
that what has happened in Jesus has universal significance and the Church must reflect this universality in
some way. How, the statement asks, is this to be done
in a world in which the Church is no longer seen as the
center of history and in which many significant developments "are emerging outside the Christian tradition?"
In situations of dialogue, what meaning does the
Church's universality have?[80]

The Zurich statement on dialogue, then, reflects
the increasing concern seen in the WCC about interreligious dialogue as well as an awareness of key theological issues which affect the way Christians see
themselves and their Church. Important theological tensions are in evidence as a new context was arising in
which Christian thinking had to take place and the WCC
was struggling for appropriate answers.

IV. The Addis Ababa Meeting of
the Central Committee

The meeting of the Central Committee at Addis Ababa, Ethiopia, January 10-21, 1971, was a turning point
in the WCC's interreligious dialogue activity. The
meeting showed the WCC's willingness to face up to the
issues such dialogue posed. This meeting is important
for two reasons. First of all, the question of dialogue
was one of the main topics of discussion. As a result
of the discussions that took place, the WCC's Central
Committee issued a policy statement and guidelines on
dialogue for the consideration of the member churches.
Secondly, the Central Committee approved a new organizational structure for the operations of the WCC, a
structure which included a special unit responsible for
carrying out dialogue with people of other faiths and
for promoting WCC discussion of this dialogue. The name
of this dialogue body, as noted previously, was the
"Sub-Unit for Dialogue With People of Living Faiths and
Ideologies." The incorporation of a dialogue unit into
the WCC elevated dialogue to a new status, giving it
greater prominence. Dialogue was no longer an esoteric,
if interesting, endeavour. It was an official WCC activity.

1. Significant Contributions to the Dialogue
Discussions at Addis Ababa

There were two major presentations to the Central
Committee at this Addis Ababa meeting to help the Committee in its deliberations. One was by the Greek Orthodox Metropolitan of Mount Lebanon, Georges Khodr,
entitled "Christianity in a Pluralistic World--The
Economy of the Holy Spirit," and the other was by Dr.
Stanley Samartha entitled "Dialogue As a Continuing

Christian Concern."[81] Both of these presentations reflect some concerns being raised within WCC circles
over dialogue and over a theological evaluation of the
world's religions and so merit some attention.

(a) The Presentation of Georges Khodr

The presentation of Metropolitan Georges Khodr is
but another indication of theological opinion in the
WCC concerning the religious strivings of humankind and
God's saving activity that was quite at odds with the
neo-orthodox tendencies present among many European
theologians. The Metropolitan's way of understanding
God's saving work thus differed from the "Christomonism" of much Protestant European theology. This latter view in effect condemned all religious activity
outside of Christianity as ultimately meaningless. Only in Christianity was God present in a saving way.
Other religions were not loci of salvation.[82] Khodr's
presentation was a plea for the recognition of the revealing and saving work of God through the Holy Spirit (in what Khodr called the "economy of the Holy Spirit") throughout the world, including such activity
within the non-Christian religions. The Church, founded
upon the saving economy manifest in Jesus Christ, was
a witness to God's love for all, the sign of the fullness of God's redemptive power, he suggested, not the
exclusive locus of this saving power. Now, before the
end time, God should be considered as being active in
the Spirit even beyond the Church. Khodr noted,

> The Spirit operates and applies His energies
> in accordance with His own economy and we
> could, from this angle, regard the non-Chris-
> tian religions as points where His inspira-
> tion is at work.[83]

A significant difference, then, between Khodr's
view and that of the Christomonistic views he was trying to correct was that God was indeed present in a
salvific way in the non-Christian religions of the
world even if their followers were not conscious of
this. These religions were, then, not simply strivings
of a proud humanity vainly attempting to grasp salvation on its own. They were places where God was very
much active. Khodr does not, however, suggest ways by
which this activity could be recognized.

Khodr's view reflects very much a universalist and
inclusive understanding of God's work in the world, an
understanding he insists is present in the Christian
tradition. He refers to Paul's speech in Acts 17:22-34
at Areopagus: the Athenians worship the true God,
though they do not know it. He sees this tradition
carried on in Justin Martyr with his notion of the **logos spermatikos,** the scattered seeds of the Word (identified with the pre-existent Christ): there is truth
outside of Christianity because the divine Logos, the
ground of all truth, is present everywhere. Khodr also points to a similar strain in Clement of Alexandria:
God has spoken to all; the divine Logos is everywhere
present, a presence recognized especially by the great
Greek philosophers.[84] Khodr favours a universalistic
Christology. The Spirit is leading all people to the
fullness of truth and salvation at the end of time,
when all things will be recapitulated in Christ, but
Christ is present now, throughout the world. The non-
Christian religions, then, loci for the presence of
Christ, may be seen as "training schools" where God's
Spirit is at work drawing their followers to recognize
Christ who is there and who offers salvation and full-
ness of truth.[85] This implies, for Khodr, that non-

Christians may have something useful to say to Christians about God, and so Christians should treat them accordingly.[86]

   With the notion of a universal Christ who is the fulfillment of the promptings of the Spirit present among non-Christians, Khodr suggested that the mission of the Church should not be so much concerned with trying to add members to the Church by denouncing non-Christian religions as devoid of goodness. Rather, mission should be more a witness to Christ who fulfills the religions and who is present in them. This may be accomplished by establishing friendly contacts with non-Christians and making them comfortable with Christians and the Church. They will then, suggested Khodr, recognize that Christ fulfills their aspirations and "come in of their own accord once they begin to feel at home in it [the Church] as in the Father's home."[87]

(b) The Presentation of Stanley Samartha

   In his paper to the Central Committee, Stanley Samartha, who was to be named the Director of the dialogue unit, presented a brief overview of the dialogue activity in which the WCC had recently been engaged and commented upon what he felt were the theological reasons for dialogue. He started by noting that dialogue was no longer an activity foreign to and distant from the Christian West. Conditions for dialogue existed everywhere as migrant workers, students, and people connected with international organizations were creating societies which were increasingly pluralistic. In recent years, he pointed out, the number of interreligious encounters was increasing and the WCC was being called on more and more to take part in them.

   There were three important aspects of the WCC's

dialogue activity to date, Samartha said, which were
providing a new context for interreligious dialogue and
Christian reflection on it. First, Roman Catholics were
taking an active part in the WCC's dialogue activity.
This was the case at the Kandy, Ajaltoun, and Zurich
meetings. This meant that Christians were coming together and reflecting on dialogue activity in common,
providing the possibility for a more comprehensive
Christian discussion. Second, Christians from Asia and
Africa were taking part in this dialogue activity. What
had previously been a discussion about other religions
and their followers dominated by western theologians
was now more truly an ecumenical discussion. Finally,
the Christian reflection on other religions and their
followers was being informed by actual contacts with
these others. The context was not simply theoretical.[88]

The most important part of Samartha's presentation, however, dealt with what he thought to be the
theological reasons for dialogue. Dialogue was not simply an activity forced upon the Church because of the
contemporary world situation, he insisted, but rather
flowed from the very dynamics of the Christian faith
itself. He listed three theological reasons for dialogue. The first one centered around the action of God
on behalf of humankind, action which showed, especially in the life and death of Christ, the love of God for
all men and women. Christ became human and died for the
sake of all humanity, offering God's saving love to
all. The point here is that God's loving action is universal, knowing no boundaries. This universal aspect
becomes a paradigm, for Samartha, for the way Christians should act. Faith in Christ, he insisted, "draws
us out of our isolation into a closer relationship with
all."[89]

The second basis for dialogue in the Christian faith to which Samartha pointed derived from his understanding of the Christian life as a call to build up a loving and free community of human beings, a community symbolized by the Church. Christians are called on, then, to fight against anything that impeded the formation of such a community and hence against anything that impeded the establishment of loving relationships between people. Dialogue, that friendly encounter and discussion between people who respect one another, was a means of contributing to this.[90]

The final theological basis for dialogue in Samartha's address rested upon his view that Christians were being led to fullness of truth by the Spirit in accordance with the promise of Jesus to his disciples in John 15:13.[91] Samartha saw this as a process necessarily involving communion and dialogue. This is because he understood the Christian experience of discovering the truth in terms of the setting up of a series of alliances between God and chosen men and women and between human beings themselves. In other words, the growth in knowledge of the truth was furthered by dialogue between God and human beings and between human beings themselves. Samartha pointed to Jesus as one who was in a constant dialogue with his followers. He thus observed that "the way in which truth is revealed, understood and communicated in the Bible makes it clear that one should look for 'things that are to come' in the areas of personal relationships with God and our fellowmen."[92] Dialogue with others, then, was a means of attaining a greater understanding of the truth.

(c) The Central Committee's Discussion

The brief summaries in the minutes of the Addis Ababa meeting of the discussion concerning the above two presentations illustrate the sorts of concerns found within the WCC about dialogue.[93] Perhaps the most central objection to what Khodr and Samartha said centered on the traditional Christian affirmation of the uniqueness and transcendence of the Christian message. For example, the Rev. Raymond Buana Kibongi of the Evangelical Church of the Congo thought that dialogue presupposed that Christianity was but one religion among the others. He suggested that one should see Christianity not as a religion, but as God's answer to humankind's religions. Metropolitan Damaskinos Papandreou, the Patriarch of Constantinople, remarked that the truth, which he thought Dr. Samartha said was attainable through dialogue with non-Christians, was rather something revealed from God alone and could not be reached through any encounter with non-Christians. Bishop Juvenaly of the Russian Orthodox Church wondered how dialogue with other religions could contribute to Christian witness. Finally, Dr. W.A. Visser't Hooft of the Netherlands Reformed Church criticized the view of mission advanced by Metropolitan Khodr saying that recognition and acceptance of Jesus Christ as Saviour and Lord was essential. The summary in the minutes of the Addis Ababa meeting of this latter point is worth citing. It reads,

> Dr. W.A. Visser't Hooft (Netherlands Reformed Church) said he could be grateful for the address [of Metropolitan Khodr] only if it could be considered as a corrective. At this present time in history what was most needed was not the Alexandrian approach but the pro-

phetic word. If all missionaries from the
time of St. Paul had followed the line of the
paper would there be a world-wide Christian
Church today? He was glad that missionaries
had gone to all countries represented in the
Committee and had proclaimed the Christian
Gospel in all its fullness, asking for total
commitment to the Gospel.[94]

Despite these questions and any apprehensions over dialogue, however, the Central Committee decided to approve an interim policy statement and guidelines on dialogue, proposing them to the member churches of the
WCC for their study and comment.[95]

2. The Interim Policy Statement and Guidelines of the Addis Ababa Meeting

(a) Dialogue in the Policy Statement

The Addis Ababa statement on dialogue sees dialogue as a normal component of the encounter Christians
are having with people of other faiths today.[96] It emphasizes the necessary freedom that must be part of
such an encounter. The partners must be free to be committed to their faiths and to witness to them. Dialogue
ought not involve, then, any denial on the part of either dialogue partner of any element of his or her beliefs. It does require, though, a sincere respect for
the beliefs of the other.[97] Dialogue, moreover, is not
simply a talking together about one's faith or a witnessing to it. It is also a means of living and acting together, concerned with building up the human community.[98]

In its remarks on the basis for dialogue, the Addis Ababa interim policy statement first of all repeats

the words of the Zurich statement that dialogue is today "inevitable, urgent and full of opportunity."99
Christians are today living in pluralistic communities,
it says, making dialogue inevitable. Moreover, all men
and women are faced with common urgent pressures to
search for justice, peace, and a hopeful future. Christians in this situation are thus faced with new opportunities for their Christian witness and must consider
new implications of their Christian faith in this con-
text.100 Christians share, as well, a common humanity
with all others. They are fundamentally united to the
rest of humankind and are forging a common history with
all others. The Christian faith and practice must reflect this. The statement goes on to say, then,

> 6. Opportunities and occasions for dialogue
> are different in different situations. They
> are grounded in the humanity in which all
> share and which Christ redeems . . . . [I]n
> humanity as we experience it and as we look
> for its fulfillment in Christ, the "spiritu-
> al" and the "material" cannot be separated,
> but constantly impinge on each other in our
> common quest for the well-being of man. "In
> dialogue we share our common humanity, its
> dignity and fallenness, and express our com-
> mon concern for that humanity." (**Uppsala 68
> Report**, Geneva, p. 29).101

There are reasons in the Christian faith itself,
as well, which impell Christians towards dialogue. The
chief one to which the Addis Ababa interim policy
statement points is the example of Jesus who became human for the sake of all men and women everywhere. The
idea, as seen elsewhere, is that God has reached out to

all, that God's saving will is universal, and thus
Christians should display a universal concern.[102]

There are many purposes for dialogue. The Addis
Ababa statement notes that dialogue can take place to
foster common action in pluralistic societies, it can
foster mutual understanding between peoples of different faiths, and it can promote the indigenization of
Christianity in different cultures.[103] Dialogue can
also offer the opportunity for Christians to develop
new relationships with people of other faiths in a new
context and contribute to a new self-understanding on
the part of Christians themselves as they work out the
implications of this.[104]

(b) Theological Tensions in the
Interim Policy Statement

Theological implications and problems connected
with interreligious dialogue remained problematic for
the Central Committee. It identifies, in particular,
three general questions demanding further study. The
first of these concerns the fundamental issue of God's
saving presence in the world. Is God present in a saving way? What is the relationship between God's universal presence in the world and the divine saving activity in Jesus Christ?[105] There was no consensus in the
WCC as to how to answer this question and so the Central Committee recognized it as one needing further
study.

The second major question was that of the relationship between dialogue, mission and witness, another of the familiar questions being posed as Christians
engaged in thinking about dialogue. The interim statement points to the difference in opinion among Christians on this issue. For some, dialogue and its respect

for the beliefs of the other weakens the Christian witness to God's workings in Jesus Christ. For others, dialogue created a climate of love and respect which made
witness more possible.[106]

Finally, the interim policy statement takes up the
problem of indigenization and repeats the view expressed at Zurich: there is always an interplay between
culture and revelation. Christians must decide what is
the proper way to embody the Gospel in different cultures, knowing that the Gospel transforms, redeems, and
judges the culture it confronts. There is recognition
that the process of indigenization is uncertain, with
the risk that something important may be lost, but
there is equally the recognition that it must occur.[107]
Dialogue can play a part in this process.

(c) Recommendations in the Interim
Policy Statement

Part of the interim policy statement from the Addis Ababa meeting is a series of recommendations addressed to the member churches of the WCC. These recommendations serve to highlight the sort of attitude
the Central Committee was hoping to arouse among Christians with respect to the followers of other religious
traditions. For example, the recommendations urge member WCC churches to promote a greater understanding of
the people of other faiths through educational programmes.[108] They urge the churches to remove anything
in current material on other religions that fosters insensitivity or lack of respect.[109] They encourage the
sponsorship of bilateral dialogue meetings, especially
those dealing with a single specific topic.[110] Finally, they urge collaboration with the Roman Catholic
Church in interreligious dialogue initiatives.[111] The

way was therefore cleared for an intensification of dialogue activity within the WCC, with emphasis on the
holding of actual dialogue meetings and reflection on
them.

3. The Establishment of the Dialogue Sub-Unit

The meeting of the Central Committee in Addis Ababa did more than approve a WCC policy on dialogue. It
also approved a reorganization of the WCC's internal
operating structure to coordinate better that body's
activities. Part of this reorganization involved the
setting up of a special dialogue unit, the "Sub-Unit
for Dialogue With People of Living Faiths and Ideologies" (called generally the DFI). This move shows the
importance dialogue was beginning to assume in the
minds of those responsible for the work of the WCC.

By way of some background, a special committee had
been appointed before the Addis Ababa meeting to provide the plans for a new structure within the WCC. This
committee had recommended the establishment of three
major "programme units" which were to encompass relevant sub-units. The first of these major "units,"
called "Faith and Witness," was the general programme
unit within which the dialogue sub-unit was located.
The special committee thought that the dialogue sub-
unit should have the task of promoting dialogue with
people of other faiths and ideologies and of leading
the WCC churches in their deliberations on the meaning
and the implications of dialogue for the Christian
faith.[112] The sub-unit's task was further clarified
following its actual establishment by an ad hoc Working Group formed to set its activities in motion. Under the leadership of Dr. Stanley Samartha, the func-
tions of the dialogue sub-unit were to be as follows:

1. To assist the churches to engage in responsible dialogue with men of living faiths
and ideologies in local situations.

2. To promote dialogue with men of living
faiths and ideologies beyond the local level,
to foster wider relationships involved, and
to develop interdisciplinary and cross-cul-
tural studies on such dialogue.

3. To foster theological reflection in the
churches on the relation between dialogue and
witness and to bring out its implications for
the life and witness of Christians in a plural, yet single world.

4. To provide documentation and information
on ongoing dialogues in different parts of
the world and interdisciplinary and cross-
cultural studies on such dialogues.[113]

It is of interest to note that the Working Group
specifically identified the relationship between dialogue and mission as problematic. The perceived tension
between a respect for the religious beliefs of others
which is demanded by dialogue and the conviction that
Jesus is Lord and Saviour of all, thereby impelling one
to witness and mission, is ever present. This tension
is all the more important, the Working Group noted, in
the context of living in a world community in which
Christians and peoples of different beliefs live their
lives trying to maintain their specific identities (and
thus contributing to plurality) while at the same time
living in a world becoming increasingly united on many
different levels (this "plural, yet single world" to
which the Working Group refers).

The issue of the relationship between dialogue and

mission, however, was not the only theological problem with which this ad hoc Working Group was concerned. In a report in which it comments on the Addis Ababa statement, the Working Group acknowledged the three issues brought up in the statement and underlined the question of the nature of God's activity in the world at large. It accordingly called for further exploration of what it calls a "Trinitarian" understanding of God's activity in the world. By this it meant that Christians should consider ideas similar to those that have been discussed above in the presentation of Georges Khodr to the Central Committee at Addis Ababa. What is of most importance in these views is the affirmation that God is present to created reality in the divine Spirit in a saving way, transforming men and women everywhere, making them children of God. This takes place even in the religious history of humankind.[114] One sees in these remarks a desire to move away from the "Christomonism" so present in much European Protestant theology. The report of the ad hoc Working Group says,

> The working group of the sub-unit might follow up the questions of what are the fundamental theological implications of dialogue by going deeper into the issues cited in the Addis Ababa statement . . . and by locating other implications therein. The terms of reference of a salvation theology or of a Christian presence theology may be admirable starting points, but they need to be undergirded by a fully Trinitarian understanding of God's active initiatives in creation, reconciliation, and continuous transformation of mankind.[115]

4. A Short Excursus: The Evangelical Opposition of the Frankfurt Declaration

Within Protestant circles, a positive evaluation of religions such as that pointed to above was not un-opposed. A reaction against a positive evaluation of non-Christian religions and the fear that dialogue led to a betrayal of Christ's missionary mandate appear in the **Frankfurt Declaration** issued by a group of so-called "evangelical" theologians meeting in Frankfurt in 1971.[116] It is important to look at this declaration so that tensions within the WCC itself with respect to dialogue can be understood.

One of the major points of controversy was over the idea of the anonymous, saving presence of Christ in the history of humankind and, by extension, in its religious history. Christ is not present outside of a direct encounter with him made possible by the preaching of the Gospel, the Frankfurt declaration says. It emphatically asserts,

> We . . . oppose the false teaching (which is circulated in the ecumenical move-ment since the Third General Assembly of the World Council of Churches in New Delhi) that Christ himself is anonymously so evident in world religions, historical changes, and rev-olutions that man can encounter him and find salvation in him without the direct news of the Gospel.[117]

The true mission of the Church, the declaration goes on to say, is not to engage in social reforms, but rather to preach the Lordship of Jesus Christ.[118] Such preaching should lead to the establishment of the Church everywhere.[119] The men and women of other faiths

must be encouraged to leave their faiths and join the
Church since only by belief in Christ and baptism in
his name can one be saved.[120] The declaration says,

> The offer of salvation in Christ is di-
> rected without exception to all men who are
> not yet bound to him in conscious faith. The
> adherents to the non-Christian religions and
> world-views can receive this salvation only
> through participation in faith. They must let
> themselves be freed from their former ties
> and false hopes in order to be admitted by
> belief and baptism into the body of
> Christ.[121]

With respect to dialogue, the Frankfurt declaration expresses the fear that dialogue is being seen as
a replacement for mission. It denies that the presence
of Christ within non-Christian religions can be a basis for dialogue, because Christ is not present in
them. It sees the only purpose of dialogue as being
that of establishing points of contact with non-Christians so that the Gospel message may be more effectively communicated to them. Thus,

> We refute the idea that "Christian pres-
> ence" among the adherents to the world reli-
> gions and a give-and-take dialogue with them
> are substitutes for a proclamation of the
> Gospel **which aims at conversion.** Such dia-
> logues simply establish good points of con-
> tact for missionary communication.[122]

The Frankfurt declaration, then, represents the
opposition to the more positive attitudes towards non-
Christian religions and the spirit of dialogue that are
present among those who encouraged the establishment of

the DFI. The existence of these divergent tendencies is ever present both within the WCC and among its critics.

V. Summary Observations

With the Addis Ababa policy statement and guide-lines along with the establishment of the DFI sub-unit, the first part of this examination of the WCC's dia-logue activity comes to a close. In the years between the 1967 Kandy consultation and the Addis Ababa state-ment of the Central Committee, dialogue emerged as an appropriate way for Christians to interact with men and women of other faith commitments and had become part of the WCC's institutional response to Christian living in the world today.

There are a number of features of the dialogue statements that have been examined in this chapter upon which I would like to make some summary comments. First, there is a constant tension between those who supported what can be called a form of "Christomonism" and those who advocated a more universal way of under-standing God's saving activity. The question of wheth-er there is a real knowledge of God and whether there is divine saving activity outside of the bounds of Christianity is a real, unsolved issue. A corollary to this is that there is no consensus as to whether God is redemptively present in the non-Christian religions of the world.

Second, there is a constant questioning about the relationship between dialogue, mission, and witness. This problem reflects a certain confusion about the na-ture and goal of dialogue, and, indeed, its very legit-imacy. Dialogue by its very nature involves a respect for the beliefs of the other and a willingness to let the other remain in his or her faith. Dialogue is seen

as an encounter between those who are committed to
their respective faiths. In opposition to this, on the
other hand, is a strong evangelistic missionary tendency which emphasizes the demand to persuade others to
leave their religion and become Christian. There is the
underlying fear that dialogue betrays the Christian
duty to make disciples of all peoples. There is thus a
tension between those who want to respect the faith of
others and allow them to remain in their faith and
those who feel impelled to convert others.

A significant feature of the WCC's view of dialogue and theological reflection on its implications is
the insistence that a new context for such reflection
is made possible by dialogue. Although the various
statements on dialogue admit that there is no common
agreement within the WCC on such important matters as
whether God is salvifically present outside the Church,
there is a constant refrain that it is only through
actual dialogue that such issues can be resolved. Dialogue is seen as an adventure, then, undertaken in the
hope for answers to crucial problems that affect the
very self-understanding of Christians.

A final note of importance about these early dialogue statements centers on the perception of world
history that is present in them. The theme of a world
community is ever present. The statements presuppose
that there is a movement in the world today towards a
world community in which peoples are interdependently
united. This movement is seen as a challenge to Christians and indeed to men and women of all faiths to see
how their faiths can contribute to this process of coming together. Dialogue is seen as one of the primary
ways of easing tensions in this situation as well as
being a way of bringing people together to solve com-

mon problems they face. This focus became, indeed, the
major focus for dialogue in the WCC as the next chapter will show.

The major statements of dialogue which emerged
from the WCC during the time between Kandy and Addis
Ababa, in sum, show that organization entering into dialogue in a spirit of hope and excitement, but with major unresolved questions. The movement towards dialogue
reflects the awareness of some within the WCC of a new
context in which Christians had to live out their faith
commitment, something the WCC saw as "inevitable" and
"full of opportunity," affording Christians an occasion
for re-evaluating their self-understanding as they met
and lived with people of different religious convictions. The next chapter will start to examine the work
of the DFI sub-unit as it began to carry on the dialogue activity that had become a recommended way for
Christians to relate to other believers.

CHAPTER FIVE
THE WORK OF THE DFI
TO NAIROBI 1975

From its establishment in 1971 to the Fifth General Assembly of the WCC at Nairobi in 1975, where the
DFI's work was a major topic of discussion, the DFI
sub-unit sponsored a number of interreligious dialogue
encounters and promoted further reflection on the results. The idea of a "world community" became the major theme in this dialogue work. The DFI's work, however, did not remain without some question on the part
of some within the WCC. It is to an examination of the
DFI-sponsored dialogues and the theological concerns
they raised that this chapter will turn.

I. Beginnings of the Dialogue Work

1. The Muslim-Christian Consultation
at Broumana

The first major dialogue meeting sponsored by the
DFI took place at Broumana, Lebanon, July 12-18, 1972.
It was a meeting between Christians and Muslims and
considered the theme, "The Quest for Human Understanding and Cooperation--Christian and Muslim Contributions." Significantly, both sides were equally represented. The Secretariat for Non-Christians sent two
Consultors at the DFI's request.[1] The participants discussed papers presented on four topics: 1)religions,
nations and the search for a world community, 2) truth,
revelation and obedience, 3) community relationships
between Christians and Muslims, and 4) prayer and worship.[2]

The general purpose of the consultation, agreed to
at a preparatory meeting in Geneva the previous year
(December 1-2, 1971), was to seek ways of improving relations and cooperation between the two sides so that
they could better face up to common problems imposed by
modern society. The aide-mémoire from the Geneva preparatory meeting says,

> Acknowledging that Christians and Muslims
> both face the challenge of the secular world,
> the group decided they should deal with is-
> sues arising from encounters of living faiths
> with the problems of contemporary society.
> This does not mean that the members of the
> two faiths should join forces against people
> of other faiths and ideologies. But through a
> clearer understanding of their essential be-
> liefs it is hoped they will be able to widen
> the area of concerns and cooperation.[3]

In his opening address at the consultation, Dr.
Samartha identified some of these problems of contemporary society. He felt that modern technology and increasing secularism were powerful forces in the world
today which contributed to a loss of the sense of spiritual and religious concerns. It was thus imperative,
he said, that believers show the relevance of belief in
God in today's world. Dr. Samartha also pointed to the
difficulties that religious sectarianism brought in ag-
gravating tensions in the world. It was through common
reflection and working together, he hoped, that Christians and Muslims could begin to address these problems.[4]

(a) Dialogue in the Broumana Memorandum

The memorandum issued by the participants at this consultation, although rather general, does provide an insight into the expectations from and views of dialogue acceptable to both sides taking part. It outlines some of the reasons why dialogue is desirable. Chief among these is the increasing interdependence among nations today: peoples are being brought together as never before. Muslims and Christians, then, the memorandum states, must come to a wider vision of community in which narrow self-interest will not hamper the search for answers to common human concerns such as justice and peace.[5] Moreover, the memorandum points out, the secular world is challenging the two religious communities to foster peace and harmony and "never again prove to be the instruments of mutual hatred and division in society."[6] It is the contemporary world situation, then, bringing people together and driving humanity onwards toward a common history that makes dialogue important and necessary today.

The perception of a new situation in which men and women of the two religious traditions were being called to come together to struggle for justice, peace, and the transformation of society was a basis for dialogue that was not simply demanded by the present situation. The search for these goals was also demanded by the Muslim and Christian faiths, the participants felt. There were then theological reasons for peoples of the two faiths to come together and work for the common good of society.[7]

The nature of dialogue, as this memorandum describes it, is similar to that described in the WCC's dialogue statements that have been examined already. Genuine dialogue, the memorandum asserts, includes the

freedom to witness fully to one's own faith and the
need to respect the integrity and freedom of the faith
of the other.[8] Since dialogue presupposes freedom of
religious conviction, it precludes what the memorandum
calls "proselytism," the aggressive effort to convert
others to one's own faith. There is no suggestion that
the two sides refrain from welcoming converts into
their faiths, nor that they renounce all missionary efforts. The concern is over a polemic and aggressive
drive to convert others. The memorandum says,

> While we accept that both religious tradi-
> tions have a missionary vocation, proselytism
> should be avoided, whether by a majority in-
> tent upon pressing a minority to conform, or
> whether by a minority using economic or cul-
> tural inducements to swell its ranks.[9]

Witness, mutual respect, and religious freedom, then,
characterize the interreligious dialogue encounter as
the participants at the Broumana consultation understood it.

The type of dialogue that the Broumana memorandum
describes is the type of dialogue which aims primarily
at promoting collaboration and harmony between the members of the two religious communities involved. This
does not mean, however, that dialogue must lead to a
suppression of any differences between their beliefs.
The memorandum rejects any movement to back away from
principles simply to avoid tensions. True dialogue, according to the memorandum, is not free from tensions or
disagreement, but rather allows the participants to
come to a clearer understanding of the real differences
that separate the two communities as well as what
brings them together.[10] The emphasis throughout the

memorandum, in spite of the difficulties it admits must exist, is nonetheless on cooperation rather than competition. It represents the outcome of the desire on the part of the participants to struggle together in a spirit of concord to face up to the tensions that separated them. The memorandum thus testifies to the willingness on both sides to reflect from within a different context on what their respective faiths mean in today's world.

2. Continuing Evangelical Opposition: The Bangkok Assembly

Although not part of the DFI's dialogue programme, the meeting of the Commission on World Mission and Evangelism at Bangkok, December 31, 1972 to January 12, 1973, is relevant in understanding the context in which the DFI was carrying out its dialogue work. One can see in this meeting the tensions present within the WCC concerning the Christian approach to those outside the Church. During this assembly, the conflict between the so-called "ecumenicals" and "evangelicals" came out into the open, a conflict that is very much concerned with the proper Christian understanding of how God deals with humankind.[11] For this reason, it is a conflict which touches upon the most fundamental of issues. The following examination of the Bangkok assembly will have as its focus the evangelical critique of dialogue made by Dr. Peter Beyerhaus, a leading figure in that critique.

The discussion on dialogue at this assembly occurred within the context of a view of salvation that emphasized the overcoming of political and economic oppression in the world. For most of the participants, the inbreaking of God's Rule through Jesus Christ had

implications which affected humankind's social institutions as well as the individual's relationship with
God. Collaboration between Christians and those of
other faiths and secular ideologies in dealing with un-
just social institutions was seen as a way of participating in the salvific work of God. Dialogue was important because it was one of the means by which Christians could come together with others to face up to the
problems involved in the struggle for justice and
peace. The type of dialogue meant was not dialogue
about religious beliefs and practices but about cooperation in solving common human problems. Through dialogue the Christian could contribute his or her point
of view as well as learn from the other.[12]

The section of the assembly's final report which
talks about dialogue states plainly that the Christian
attitude to people of other faiths rests on the conviction that God wills the salvation of all.[13] It affirms,
likewise, that God is present and at work among the
people of other faiths making the divine saving love
available to them. It calls on Christians, then, to be
open to the workings of God throughout the world, even
beyond the boundaries of the Church, workings which are
manifest in the drive among all peoples for truly just
and humane communities. A key section of the report
reads,

> . . . we urge our member churches to go for-
> ward with eager faith, with greater love for
> our fellowmen, with prayer for guidance and
> with confidence that God is at work among all
> people to make his saving love available for
> all in every generation, and to build the
> Kingdom of His love, which we Christians see
> manifested in Jesus Christ.[14]

The discussions and working papers at the assembly show that there was tendency to see the religions of the world as loci for the active presence of God.[15] As a result, besides leading to cooperation in solving common human problems, dialogue was seen as a way of helping Christians to be more sensitive to the work of God through the Spirit which takes place everywhere in the world.[16]

It was the idea that God was redemptively present outside the Church that Dr. Peter Beyerhaus, a representative of the "evangelical" wing of European Protestantism, criticized. He opposed vigorously the claim that the Holy Spirit was active in the non-Christian religions or in the world's historical struggles for a more just world.[17] Any attempt to extend God's saving activity beyond the revelation of God in the historical events of the life of Jesus Christ was not in keeping with the biblical witness and was therefore not true to Christianity. He took up the theme of dialectical theology that the revelation of God was in opposition to the religious strivings of humankind. Rejecting any compromise on this principle in the face of apparent attempts by the "ecumenicals" to reach some form of accord with the evangelicals, Beyerhaus remarked, in terms which show the underlying differences between the two groups,

> The fundamental presupposition . . . for cooperation with the evangelicals is "that the Holy Spirit works in the world by various means"; but this assertion cannot be found in the Bible. Stanley Samartha of India sees this working of the Spirit as the basis for dialogue and cooperation with non-Christian religions and ideologies. Has Sa-

martha really forgotten that the history of
Hinduism presents an analogy to this? Hinduism concedes a relative place to every human
religion as long as it yields to its panthe-
istic presuppositions and to the inclusion
into the Hindu system. But according to the
Bible, the Holy Spirit speaks through the revealed Word of God and cannot contradict Himself. Christian theology is either purely
"evangelical," that is, in "conformity with
the evangel" or it is in fact not Christian.[18]

Connected with his criticism of the ecumenical
tendency to see the Spirit at work in creation in a
salvific way was Beyerhaus' criticisms of the WCC's
concern with the search for world community as well as
the WCC's tendency to align missionary work with social
movements and social progress. What Beyerhaus seems to
be most concerned with in these criticisms was the danger of compromising what he saw as the radical demands
and critique of the Gospel on human strivings by the
alignment of the WCC with other religions and secular
ideologies. The Gospel truth, he insisted, was opposed
to human striving and the quest for a mere human salvation such as one finds in other religions and secular ideologies. The Gospel called upon men and women to
accept the salvation God offers through Jesus Christ by
being baptized in his name. Christians had the duty to
preach Christ as the fullness of salvation and call on
them to be converted. They should not lead people to
suspect that they could achieve salvation outside of
faith in Jesus. They should especially not lead people
to suspect that their struggles on earth to achieve
better human conditions were signs of God's redemptive

presence in their midst.[19] Salvation was possible only
by belief in Jesus Christ.

The Bangkok assembly, then, is representative of
the major underlying tensions within the WCC which affected the DFI's dialogue work. The key tension involves the understanding of the nature of God's presence outside of Christianity. Is this salvific or not?

3. The First Meeting of the
Dialogue Working Group

In order to plan and examine the activities of the
DFI sub-unit, a regular dialogue Working Group was set
up and met for the first time at Pendeli, near Athens,
March 19-24, 1973.[20] The meeting discussed and approved
a conference for Ibadan, Nigeria, to deal with the
Christian encounter with African religious traditions.
It also approved a multi-lateral dialogue, at a loca-
tion to be determined, to discuss the theme of world
community and living together in a pluralistic world.
Finally, it discussed the contribution the DFI should
make towards preparations for the next general assembly, then planned for Jakarta in 1975.[21]

One of the dominant themes that appears in the reports and recommendations from the minutes of this
meeting is that of world community, the very theme of
the proposed multi-lateral dialogue meeting. Thus, a
principle goal of dialogue to which reference was made
during the meeting was that dialogue aims at encouraging the followers of different religious traditions to
discuss the role of their respective traditions in facing the problems and responsibilities in building up
the human community. In his report to this meeting,
Stanley Samartha said,

Along with our colleagues in the churches and
with the help and advice of members of the
Working Group we seek to assist the churches
to engage in responsible dialogue in local
situations, to promote dialogues on the ecumenical level, and to further theological reflection not only on the part of Christians
but also people of other living faiths on the
deeper implications of dialogue **in providing
resources to undergird the search for wider
community.**[22]

Dialogue, the Working Group hoped, would help generate
an atmosphere of friendliness and cooperation so that
this search could be advanced.[23]

The type of world community which the DFI Working
Group envisaged was not some form of uniform society in
which all differences would be suppressed. It was rather a world community that allowed for diversity and the
richness such diversity brings but without hostile com-
petitiveness. Dialogue, then, did not aim at the suppression of differences, but it promoted mutual respect
and the willingness to collaborate in spite of them.[24]

There are two underlying ideas that are essential
ingredients in the Working Group's reflections on seeking community. These are, first of all, the fundamental unity of all men and women, and, secondly, the
feeling that all people everywhere share a responsibility in the development of a just and peaceful world.
These ideas have underpinnings in the Christian faith
itself to which the Working Group's meeting points. For
example, humankind is one in that all peoples have God
as their creator. Moreover, God, through Jesus, is a
reconciling power, drawing all human beings towards
reconciliation with their divine source and with one

another. This is an historical task and so the Church
has the duty of promoting reconciliation. Such reconciliation is an aspect of the quest for a just and
peaceful human community. Moreover, there is present in
the Working Group's discussion a tendency to see God as
the active force behind the movement towards world community. Christians are thus united to all others in
that all share in this presence of God and are called
to respond to it. A report to the Working Group about
the proposed multilateral dialogue meeting says, for
example,

> Our conviction is that we are all children of
> the one God who has created mankind and the
> universe in which we live. We believe that
> the creator's concern and love for his cre-
> ation was shown in Jesus Christ, who recon-
> ciles us to God and to one another, and who
> calls his Church, still needing to be fully
> sanctified and united, to work for the unity
> of mankind in an order of justice, love and
> hope. At the same time, we believe that the
> Spirit of God is at work among all people,
> inspiring whatever is true and good in their
> experience and traditions, in their ideals
> and achievements in community, which can con-
> tribute towards the common purpose of living
> together in world community.[25]

This report clearly shows the presence of a tendency
within the WCC to see God as an active force behind the
search for a just and peaceful human community.

II. Increasing Dialogue Activity

1. The Ibadan Consultation

In accordance with the plans of the Working Group, the DFI sub-unit sponsored what it called an "exploratory" consultation at Ibadan, Nigeria, September 15-25, 1973, with the theme, "The Wholeness of Human Life: Christian Involvement in Mankind's Inner Dialogue With Primal World-Views." This consultation marked a new thrust in the WCC's dialogue activity as it began to turn its attention to traditional indigenous religious forms. The mainly negative attitude of many Christians towards these religions and their followers which regarded them as primitive and superstitious was being replaced by a more positive evaluation.[26]

The consultation itself was an intra-Christian affair, designed to explore the issues involved in dialogue of this sort and to seek the proper method of carrying it out. The final memorandum attempts to summarize the various discussions and it also outlines directions as to the nature, purpose, and basis for dialogue as well as indications of some of the theological presuppositions connected with it.

(a) Dialogue In the Ibadan Memorandum

One of the first things of importance concerning the nature of the sort of dialogue the participants hoped to encourage in Africa is that it is a dialogue with "primal world views." By using the expression "primal," the consultation wanted to draw attention to the fact that it was dealing with the most fundamental and basic elements in the religious expression of the people of Africa.[27] This expression, the participants at the consultation felt, was less objectionable than

other terms such as "tribal," "primitive," "animistic,"
and the like. Instead of calling the dialogue encounter
one between the followers of African "religions," moreover, the consultation referred to African "world
views." This was because it felt that in the face of
modern society the overt religious expressions of the
indigenous African peoples were dying away while the
world view that grounded them and its symbols continued
to influence in some way the lives of many Africans,
even those who did not practice the former traditional rites. The memorandum states,

> . . . many of the beliefs and values, the
> views about reality, man and the world, that
> prevailed in a primal society may survive the
> loss of its overt religious system and con-
> tinue to provide at least part of its terms
> of reference in a new and more complex sit-
> uation, even within a new religious faith and
> practice. It is this structure of beliefs and
> values, this way of life, that may be called
> a primal "world view."[28]

A second significant feature of the Ibadan consultation's understanding of dialogue with the African
primal "world views" is that dialogue in this context
takes on an "inner" as well as an "outer" dimension.
The outer dialogue is dialogue with a person of a different faith. Inner dialogue, as has been mentioned in
the previous section in the discussion of the dialogue
work of the Secretariat for Non-Christians in Africa,
involves dialogue with oneself, so to speak, that is,
dialogue with the underlying influences that have
shaped one's self-understanding and world view. It is
a process of self-awareness in which the Christian

comes to know more about him or herself and, by extension, about the others living in the same society,
shaped by the same influences. The memorandum says,

> As Christians we seek . . . to discover
> our own special part in a dialogue that may
> be outward with those engaged in the living
> primal traditions and their revived forms,
> but inward when we are concerned with the
> primal inheritance in ourselves. . . . In our
> dialogue as Christians with all these people
> [including Muslims, Buddhists, and those who
> espouse modern ideological systems such as
> Marxism] we must remember this further dimen-
> sion which we share with them, and perhaps
> may even assist each other to discover our
> common primal inheritance. Our Christian in-
> volvement in this dialogue may therefore be
> both intensely personal within ourselves, and
> also in a sense vicarious in relation to oth-
> ers.[29]

A third important feature of the DFI's attempt to
dialogue in the African context which can be seen in
the Ibadan memorandum concerns the identity of the dialogue partner. During the preliminary discussion at
the Pendeli Working Group meeting, this had been identified as a problem.[30] The Ibadan memorandum likewise
refers to it as a problem. The dialogue partner in Africa may be more difficult to discern and was certainly more varied than in other dialogue contexts. This
was because the primal world view affected more people
than those who actually practised the primal rites and
ceremonies and it was difficult to persuade the latter
to engage in dialogue. The Ibadan memorandum lists a

number of those who may be considered potential dialogue partners and who are likely to be influenced by
the primal traditions. These are: the actual followers
of some living primal religious system, especially the
leaders; the members of what are called "neo-primal"
religious movements who were attempting to reassert
their traditional world view in the face of what they
considered to be an alien, imposed western culture;
people of the African elite who, while not participating in any of the primal religious ceremonies, nonetheless were adopting aspects of the primal world views;
members of certain Afro-Judaic cults who sought to replace the primal religious system with a new form of
religion which integrated the traditional religious expressions with Old Testament religious symbols; Muslims
in Africa who were affected by the primal world views
of their ancestors despite their Muslim faith; independent African Churches; and finally, mainstream African
Christians themselves.[31] All of the above groups had
one thing in common: they shared a view of reality that
was in some way influenced by the primal world views of
their ancestors.

The goals of the dialogue encounter to which the
Ibadan memorandum points center around two themes:
building community and indigenization. With respect to
the first of these, the memorandum describes dialogue
as a means of contributing to the removal of fragmen-
tation, isolation and opposition among men and women of
different cultures. In this way, the memorandum notes,
there can be a movement towards "the wholeness of human life as set forth in the biblical witness to Jesus Christ."[32] Through dialogue, the partners can together face up to the challenges and problems of modern society and seek solutions to them, solutions which

were not the possession of any particular group or tradition but which must be sought out in common.33

Indigenization is a very prominent theme in the
Ibadan memorandum, and it is here that the idea of inner dialogue plays a prominent role. Through dialogue
of this inner sort, the African Christian may, the memorandum says, be able to confront his or her Christianity with the primal world view which is part of his or
her very being. Through this encounter, the Christian
may be able to integrate aspects of the primal tradition with the Christian faith and produce a truly African Christianity. The memorandum says, in commenting
on this process,

> There are many such issues [for example, the
> use of religious rites in civil ceremonies]
> between African culture and the Christian
> Church, and each of them should lead the
> Church into a fuller dialogue with the under-
> lying world-views. This may possibly lead
> Christians to rethink, re-express, and redis-
> cover certain fundamental Christian attitudes
> and theologies first formulated in other cul-
> tures.34

The memorandum also suggests that Christians in Africa read the Scriptures with categories drawn from their
primal understandings of reality. In this way, the Gospel message could truly become part of the local Christian self-understanding.35

(b) Theological Considerations in
the Ibadan Memorandum

There are a number of attitudes and presuppositions in the Ibadan memorandum that resemble the

theological views present in the dialogue work of the Secretariat for Non-Christians.[36] In the first place, the memorandum seems to presuppose an affinity between the values in the African primal world views and the Gospel message. It therefore distinguishes points of contact between the two, points of contact which have to do with their respective views of humanity, community and even healing. For example, the memorandum notes that there is a strong sense among Africans of the extreme inter-relatedness between human beings and the whole cosmos. Human beings do not stand aloof from the cosmos but are rather inseparately linked to it. This is somewhat compatible with the New Testament idea that the Christ-event has had cosmic effects, the memorandum says. The Christ-event has had an impact on the whole of creation, not just human beings. The entire cosmos has been healed and redeemed by Christ.[37] Another example of this attempt to show the compatibility between the African world view and Christianity is found in the way the memorandum discusses the strong sense of community solidarity present among Africans. There is present in the African world view, it claims, an emphasis on human beings as part of a community and not as isolated individuals. This was very compatible with the Christian sense of community and may even be a value Christians could reappropriate in the face of the loss of a sense of community among many today.[38]

The memorandum does not suggest, however, that the values in the African cultures can be simply taken over by Christians. The Gospel message confronts and challenges these values adding a new dimension to them. Commenting on the strong sense of community in the African world view (often involving the idea of a common blood ancestor) the memorandum states,

> This [sense of] solidarity can lend itself to being broadened into a universal sense of belonging to Christ, the common spiritual ancestor, and the source of common life and action which goes beyond a particular clan or tribal solidarity.
>
> In a common blood relationship all members treat each other as brothers and sisters who respect, love and help one another. The Christian vision of universal oneness in Christ can find an ally in this primal vision of human solidarity, as it is expanded to include a brotherhood of all Christians regardless of difference in origin, whether tribal, provincial, or national.[39]

Christianity, then, can open up a restricted, tribal view of community and make it all-inclusive and universal. There is a suggestion here, although it is not extensively developed, of the notion prevalent in the Roman Catholic thinking that the Gospel message assumes, purifies, and transforms the religious culture it confronts.

The Ibadan memorandum reflects a very positive attitude towards African religiosity. The Christians taking part in it, as the memorandum they issued shows, display a great esteem and respect for the underlying values of the African religious spirit. They sincerely feel that Christians can learn from these values. The interaction is thus not one-way. What is missing, however, is an explicit statement of the grounds for this positive evaluation in terms of the work of the Spirit among the peoples of the world. The entire thrust of the memorandum, though, is not hostile to such a view.

2. The Multilateral Consultation At Colombo

The second major consultation approved by the dialogue Working Group at its Pendeli meeting took place
at Colombo, Sri Lanka, April 17-25, 1974. It was a multilateral dialogue meeting, bringing together representatives from Hinduism, Buddhism, Islam, and Judaism as
well as representatives from various Christian denominations. Unlike the first WCC-sponsored multilateral
dialogue, however, this meeting was more truly a multilateral encounter. It did not have the great overbal-
ance of Christian representatives that the former had,
and spokespersons from other religious traditions
played a greater role in its planning and execution.40
The theme of the meeting was "Towards World Community:
Resources and Responsibilities for Living Together."

As the theme shows, the concern of this multilateral dialogue was that of fostering "world community."
This theme was becoming the major focus of attention in
the DFI's dialogue activity. The participants at the
meeting thus discussed the question of how the different religious traditions concerned could contribute to
the promotion of a wider community perspective that
transcended the narrow self-interests of each particular religious community.41 They admitted that religion
was often a divisive force which set up barriers among
peoples, but they hoped that they could draw out those
aspects of their respective traditions that could contribute towards harmony in an increasingly interdependent world.42

The concluding memorandum of this multilateral
meeting identifies dialogue as one of the primary means
of fostering world community. Dialogue, it states, is
a way of building up harmony and concord by leading to
an increasing knowledge of the other and sensitivity to

his or her views. Dialogue also promoted mutual tolerance and openness and provided a context in which to
face common problems. Dialogue thus is seen as a key
activity promoting peaceful living together. The memorandum says,

> Dialogue as a relation and interaction be-
> tween people could become a means for promot-
> ing co-operation, mutual respect and toler-
> ance of other communities. Dialogue offers to
> concerned people a method for working togeth-
> er to achieve practical goals.[43]

The type of world community which the participants
had in mind was a community composed of different
communities in which each respected the differences of
the others in a spirit of mutual respect and reconciliation.[44] It thus urges people throughout the world to
be open to the larger community of communities, going
beyond their own. This did not mean, with respect to
religious beliefs, that the members of a particular religious tradition had to give up any claims they may
have that their religion was ultimate, final, or universal. It did mean, though, that any such claim had to
be made while respecting the views and similar claims
of others. The memorandum condemns what it calls "dog-
matism," defined as an insensitivity to the claims of
the other, and "syncretism," defined as the attempt to
do away with the differences that exist in favour of
setting up some form of new religion. Both are inimical to the spirit of world community.[45]

The memorandum lists the following reasons why believers should engage in a quest for world community:
all people share a common humanity, human beings are
being seized by a sense of universal responsibility,

and there is increasing interdependence among all peoples.[46] Since the Colombo statement was one composed by people of different faith commitments, mention of any particular Christian basis for world community and dialogue would have been out of place.

Loyalty to one's own tradition, yet openness to and respect for that of others, then, characterize the dialogue of the Colombo multilateral consultation. The concern of the consultation was on the development of world community. It attempted to urge the followers of the religions represented at the consultation to search their traditions to discern those aspects in them which promoted unity with others. The consultation provides another example of the DFI's resolve to carry out Christian reflection within the context of actual dialogue.

3. Dialogue With African Muslims: Legon 1974

Recognizing the wide diversity of concrete situations in which Christians and Muslims lived together, the DFI began a series of regional Christian-Muslim meetings in 1974. The first one was held at Legon, Ghana, July 17-21, 1974. The theme of the meeting was "The Unity of God and the Community of Mankind: Cooperation Between African Muslims and African Christians in Work and Witness." Its purpose fitted into the more general framework of dialogue meetings sponsored by the DFI, that of "bringing together . . . concerned people from the major religious traditions as well as non-religious ideologies in a concerted effort to provide a wider basis for human collaboration and action."[47]

The memorandum from this regional dialogue meeting lists some of the things that Muslims and Christians share which provide a basis for dialogue. The common

humanity which men and women of both traditions shared
was one of the most important, a common humanity which
today had to be lived out in increasingly interdependent and pluralistic societies. But there were also
"religious" ties between the followers of the two traditions. The memorandum mentions the monotheistic view
that both share. Indeed, they worship the same God.
Both traditions have a common heritage including respect for Jesus, and they both cherish spiritual values and thus are sensitive to the challenge of materialism.[48]

The memorandum clearly emphasizes the need for
Christians and Muslims to work together in Africa and
not compete in a race for superiority. It urges members
of both communities to seek cooperative ways of dealing
with problems in society and to come together to serve
the wider interests of their communities.[49] This striving for mutual respect and cooperation, the memorandum
insists, is a demand of the religious faith that each
have. It is based on the command to love God and neighbour. Indeed, God is served and honoured when the
neighbour is loved. In today's context, this means fostering loving communal relationships.[50] The memorandum
sees dialogue as a way in which cooperation and mutual involvement for the sake of all can take place in
loyalty to the demands of the respective faiths. It
does not betray these faiths.

There is, however, something more to dialogue.
Through dialogue, not only do the participants gain mutual knowledge or strive to cooperate for the common
good, but they also hope to strengthen their knowledge
of "religious truth." This hope rests in the presupposition that God is present in the encounter. The memorandum thus describes dialogue as follows:

Dialogue is therefore concerned about personal meeting and encounter and cooperation in work and worship, as well as about sustained mutual involvement in local level contacts. It can lead to a common desire for a search for truth and a reciprocal exchange of information and insights with each other, thus deepening and strengthening our knowledge of each other and of religious truth . . . . Also dialogue as the meeting of persons is different from, and indeed critical of, conversion understood as a "numbers game" or a membership drive. That attitude, which sees conversion either as a piece of statistical manipulation or a triumphant band-waggoning, is contrary to the spirit of dialogue. **Dialogue sees conversion as a growing mutual awareness of the presence of God in an encounter in which each becomes responsible for the other and where both seek openness in witness before God.**[51]

A key issue for Christians, however, remains unanswered: What is the nature of this divine presence?

4. The Second Meeting of the DFI Working Group

A second meeting of the DFI Working Group took place at New Delhi, September 15-21, 1974.[52] The Director of the DFI, Stanley Samartha, considered the meeting an important one because he wanted to discuss the role of the dialogue sub-unit in preparing for the next general assembly of the WCC, especially since one of the topics at the assembly was going to be "Seeking Community: The Common Search of People of Various Faiths, Cultures and Ideologies." The meeting was also

important, however, because of its discussion of the
dialogue meetings that had taken place up to then, and
it is this aspect of the meeting upon which the following section will focus.

(a) Reflections on Dialogue at
the New Delhi Meeting

One of the most significant features of the DFI's
dialogue activity pointed to by members of the Working
Group was that the framework for dialogue had come to
be that of the search for world community. This search
was seen by one of the reports of the Working Group as
a responsibility Christians shared with the followers
of other religious traditions. Thus the group study on
"Dialogue--Community--Witness" that emerged from this
meeting notes,

> . . . we would like to draw attention to the
> fact that one emerging concern in present
> ventures in dialogue, such as the multilater-
> al dialogue in Colombo, is the common respon-
> sibility Christians share with the adherents
> of other religions for world community. Fur-
> thermore, neither mission nor dialogue are
> pursued in the air but in communities and
> they affect these communities.[53]

Dialogue is seen, in the discussions and reports
of this meeting, as an open attitude to peoples of other faiths, characterized by a desire to listen to them.
The Christian, too, must be able to witness to his or
her deepest convictions. The purpose of dialogue is
primarily to form positive relationships which will
contribute to understanding among peoples and promote
the search for community. A report presented at the

meeting, entitled "Styles of Dialogue," sums this up as follows:

> The main elements of dialogue are always turning away from mutual isolation or from one-way mission to encounter of each other in a spirit of mutual open-ness and with a desire to enter into relationships which include the search for community and the deepening of mutual understanding.[54]

(b) Some Theological Concerns in the New Delhi Meeting

Given the existence within WCC circles of conflicting views about how Christians should understand God's saving work ranging from the Christomonism of dialectical theology to an affirmation of God's saving presence everywhere, it is not surprising that the Working Group recommended ongoing reflection on this matter as Christians engaged in dialogue with the followers of other faiths. The Working Group also repeated the insistence that such reflection be carried on within the context of actual dialogue activity. Moreover, it pointed to the problem of the relationship between dialogue and mission, that is, between the desire to respect the other and his or her beliefs and the desire to convert the other. These issues needed ongoing study.[55]

If the New Delhi Working Group pointed to some of the theological problems connected with dialogue, there also is evident in its meeting a direction in which answers could be found to some of them. This direction can be summarized as the "imperative of love." This imperative, says the group report on "Dialogue--Witness

--Community," should dominate Christian action and reflection. With special reference to mission, the report
condemns mission which is "one-way," that is, mission
which does not respect the views of those to whom the
Gospel message is being preached. It also condemns a
closed mentality on the part of Christians as being
contrary to the imperative of love. Christians must go
out to others in a spirit of dialogue.[56]

A tendency to be open to the presence of the Spirit in all of creation and in the non-Christian religions of the world can also be seen in the discussions
at the New Delhi meeting. In a discussion of the nature of God's activity among the peoples of the world,
there is present a desire to move away from the teaching that God's saving will is realized only through explicit ackowledgement of Christ and only in the Church.
The notion of the Church as the sign of God's eschatological community to come, and not as the only locus
of salvation, and the idea that God's Spirit is at work
drawing all of humanity towards this final goal, were
two of the suggestions for a new theological framework
in which to evaluate the religious strivings of people
of other religious traditions. The observations of Paul
Verghese from India were the most forceful on this
point. He said,

> Here we come to the need for a re-exam-
> ination of the doctrine of the Holy Spirit as
> taught in the churches. If the Spirit of God
> who was already hovering upon the waters at
> the beginning of creation has been at work in
> all parts of creation at all times, we may
> need to specify more clearly the relation be-
> tween the special work of the Spirit who
> gives gifts to the community of faith for its

building up and the general work of the Spirit in creation.

Creation as a dynamic process moving towards an end (telos) seems to be the right
framework within which to understand the Incarnation of Jesus Christ as well as the reality of our fellow human beings of other
faiths and ideologies. This kind of an eschatological existence-ontology based on an
integration of the doctrines of Creation and
Incarnation, with a Trinitarian rather than a
simple Christ-monistic framework needs to be
developed by Christians.[57]

The Working Group decided to submit these ideas as part
of the preliminary discussion papers distributed to the
member churches of the WCC in preparation for the upcoming general assembly.

5. Dialogue With Asian Muslims, Hong Kong 1975

The final dialogue meeting sponsored by the DFI
before the Nairobi general assembly was a regional bilateral consultation between Christians and Muslims
held in Hong Kong, January 4-10, 1975. It fitted into
the DFI's plan to hold regional Christian-Muslim consultations, the meeting at Legon, Ghana, in 1974 being
the first. The theme, "Muslims and Christians in Society: Towards Goodwill, Consultation and Working Together in South-East Asia," again exemplifies the thrust of
the DFI's dialogue activity, namely, to concentrate on
dialogue as a means of building up good community relations. The memorandum of this meeting stresses the
notion of developing a "unity in diversity" in which
the followers of the two religious communities seek to

face together the problems of their particular community while remaining faithful to their respective traditions. The memorandum insists that mere coexistence
is not enough. Rather, good will and the desire to cooperate actively are required because of the serious
demands of the society in which they live to promote
the social, material, and spiritual welfare of all concerned.[58]

The memorandum of the Hong Kong meeting also outlines some of the theological grounds for dialogue and
cooperation between the followers of the two faiths involved. God is the creator of all men and women, it
says, and so all are brothers and sisters. Moreover,
God's love, a self-giving love, provides the example
for Christians to seek loving relations with others,
while God is understood by Muslims as the Compassion-
ate One demanding that believers likewise be compas-
sionate. The memorandum says,

> . . . our respective faiths, properly under-
> stood, enjoin on us a loving relationship
> with each other and with all human beings.
> The ground and impetus for this loving rela-
> tionship is no less than the One God Himself
> who has made all human beings brothers and
> sisters. Muslims emphasize that God the Com-
> passionate (**Al-Rahman**) and the Beloved (**Al-
> Habib**) commands the faithful to be merciful
> and compassionate and loving in their deal-
> ings with all people, and therefore they are
> able to be so. The Qur'an embodies this com-
> mand and specifies ways in which the faith-
> ful may obediently comply with it in various
> life situations. Christians, for their part,
> emphasize that God's love shown in his self-

giving in and through the person of Jesus Christ both inspires and enables their loving relationship with all humankind. Responding to God's love in Jesus Christ, Christians find the example and basis for love in their social dealings with all people. Thus, allowing for these differences in understanding, both Islam and Christianity find their ethical mandate in the All-Merciful God who loves and is loved.[59]

There is also a lot of common ground shared by the two faiths to which the memorandum points. They have a special relationship, in fact, because they share in the same spiritual heritage. This common ground, the memorandum says, should provide the basis for a new relationship between the two communities.[60]

An important part of the new relationship that the memorandum hopes will develop between the two communities, and one that has come up in other Christian-Muslim consultations already examined, is a willingness to allow religious freedom to be fostered and a desire to condemn "proselytism." The historical conflicts between the two communities made this an especially important concern. Thus, the memorandum notes,

Of special importance for our religious communities in some situations is the matter of proselytism. We are moved to call upon all religious bodies and individuals to refrain from proselytism, which we define as the compulsive, conscious, deliberate and tactical effort to draw people from one community of faith to another.[61]

III. The Fifth General Assembly of the World
Council of Churches, Nairobi 1975

As has been mentioned above in the discussion of
the two dialogue Working Group meetings, dialogue and
community were to be major themes at the Fifth General
Assembly of the WCC held at Nairobi, Kenya, November 25
to December 10, 1975. The discussion of these themes
took place under "Section III" of the Assembly's programme, with the general title of "Seeking Community:
The Common Search of People of Various Faiths, Cultures
and Ideologies." While this general assembly was not a
DFI-sponsored meeting, it was very important for the
dialogue sub-unit because it subjected the notion of
dialogue to general scrutiny and so provided a forum
for a general WCC discussion of dialogue activity.
Moreover, since these general assemblies were major
events in shaping the WCC's work, the DFI had to react to what took place at this Nairobi assembly in its
subsequent work.

1. Preparatory Questions Concerning Dialogue

The preparatory dossier to Section III of the Nairobi assembly, which the DFI staff had helped to prepare, outlined some of the theological problems that
the issue of dialogue was raising in the WCC. Consistent with the theme of Section III, the problems were
raised in such a way as to reflect the context in which
dialogue was taking place: the search for community in
an increasingly interdependent and pluralistic world.
Those problems the preparatory dossier singled out were
the following: 1) the basis in the Christian faith for
Christians to cooperate with others in the building up
of the human community; 2) the implications of dialogue
on the Christian self-understanding; and 3) the prop-

er theological framework for living in community.62 The "Work Book" issued to the assembly delegates pointed to other theological concerns. It asked about the relationship between God's presence in creation and the redemptive work of Jesus Christ. It asked about the relationship between dialogue and mission. It called for a "new theological framework" which would do justice to the universality of God's love. The "Work Book" asked these questions in the following way:

a) How is God's work as Creator and Saviour in Christ related to his work among people of all faiths, cultures and ideologies? How do we do Christology in the living context of Asian or African religions and within the struggles for a just society? Is Jesus Christ ahead of Christians in dialogue with people of living faiths?

b) What is the nature of Christian witness and what are its forms in the context of dialogue? Are "dialogue" and "mission" really valid alternatives? What is the shape of a fresh theological framework which can do justice to our faith in the universality of God's love and our experience of the particularity of Jesus Christ? Such a framework may throw fresh light on or even radically transform questions like: Does openness in dialogue betray Christ-centredness? Is dialogue a tool for mission or a betrayal of it? To what extent and by what criteria could we recognize any validity in the truth claims and even the "missions" of other faiths and ideologies?63

These questions, one might note, are questions that
have many serious implications for the very self-understanding of Christians and have, in various forms, been
present as the DFI carried out its dialogue activity.

2. The Debate Over Dialogue

The issue of dialogue with men and women of different faiths and ideologies turned out to be a contentious one at the Nairobi general assembly. The debate
it aroused serves to emphasize the deep difference of
opinion within the WCC about dialogue and a proper
Christian evaluation of other religions. These divi-
sions were noted in the report of the Moderator of the
Central Committee as he relayed to the general assembly delegates what had taken place in the WCC since the
last assembly at Uppsala. This report, in fact, singles
out as perhaps the most difficult problem facing the
WCC that of coming to some consensus on how to interpret God's presence and activity outside the Church.
This question, one must note, is one that the DFI was
indeed constantly facing. The report says,

> The presence of God and his Spirit outside
> the Church, his self-disclosure and the sav-
> ing work of Christ outside the Church, and
> the discernment of and response to these by
> the Church are theological issues of great
> importance. They have been raised in relation
> to the Christian theology of dialogue with
> people of living faiths and secular ideolo-
> gies. It is perhaps here that we have the
> deepest theological cleavage demanding fuller
> exploration. In fact, it is my impression
> that on the whole no group has formulated a
> theology of dialogue . . . . We are only at

the beginning of our reflection; it is not yet time to crystallize a theology of religion. Nevertheless, conversations with this aim in view must be continued.[64]

As examples of two radically different approaches, the Moderator's report pointed to two recent missionary conferences, one at Lausanne and the other at Bangkok, which had touched upon this issue. The former, a meeting of "evangelicals" in 1974, had denied that there was a saving knowledge of God outside the boundaries of the Church because of the corruption of all human capacities and drives. That meeting had also denied that the divine offer of salvation was made available in non-Christian religious traditions.[65] The Bangkok conference in 1975, on the other hand, had been open to the idea of God's saving presence in the religions of the world and throughout creation in general. The Moderator's report concluded by asking,

Is there any possibility of going beyond these tentative approaches? Any Christian theology of dialogue has to be Christ-centred . . . . But since we believe . . . that in spite of man's idolatrous rebellion against God, Christ holds all things together **now** (Col. 1) and will sum up all things in himself in the **end** (Eph. 1), should we not make greater efforts to discern how Christ is at work in other faiths . . . ? [66]

The greatest criticisms of dialogue came from the side of the so-called "evangelical" theologians whose criticisms at the Bangkok assembly have already been discussed. They had three basic concerns. First of all, they wanted to be sure that the saving uniqueness of

Christ and the Gospel would be upheld, and they were
suspicious that dialogue and any admission of salvific activity outside of the Church denied this uniqueness. Secondly, they felt that dialogue and openness to
the religious affirmations of others ran the risk of
syncretism, understood, it seems, as the denial of elements of God's transcendent revelation in Christ.
Truth came from Christ alone, not from the teachings of
any of the world's non-Christian religions. Finally,
they criticized dialogue as a betrayal of Christ's mandate to preach the Gospel to and make disciples of all
peoples. The duty of the Christian was to attempt to
convert others, not engage in a dialogue which was open
to and respectful of their beliefs.[67]

The theological grounds for the evangelical criticism of dialogue at Nairobi was essentially the following: Christ was present salvifically only in the
Word and in the sacraments of the Church. Thus, the divine presence in creation at large was not salvific.
Only through Christ did one truly come to know God.
Only by faith in Christ did one receive the Father's
saving justification.[68]

Among the strongest proponents of dialogue and the
most forceful critics of the views mentioned above were
a number of Asian theologians who argued in favour of
dialogue and more openness to the religious faith of
non-Christians. The arguments of Russell Chandran of
India and Rev. Lynn de Silva, a Methodist minister from
Sri Lanka, are captured in the official report of the
assembly and illustrate some of the concerns of this
group. Chandran's views are worth noting, for he provides an example of a positive approach to non-Christian religions and insists that dialogue is a proper
Christian activity. Chandran thus noted that recent Ro-

man Catholic and WCC-sponsored dialogue consultations
had begun to deepen reflection among Christians on the
presence and activity of Christ and the Holy Spirit in
other religions and cultures. Chandran implied in his
remarks that God must be thought of as present and active everywhere in creation in a saving way. He remarked,

> The theology of creation affirms the presence
> and the work of God in all cultures. Our con-
> fession of Christ as Lord is an affirmation
> that he is Lord, not only of Christians, but
> of all peoples. He is the Logos who holds all
> things together. He is the light which en-
> lightens everyone. It is in him all things
> and all peoples are united.[69]

The idea of the "cosmic" Christ, holding all
things together now and in whom all things will be recapitulated in the end, is the Christology which underpins Chandran's remarks. The idea of Christ as the all-
pervading Logos, enlightening everyone in the world
meant, for Chandran, that Christ is experienced even
outside the boundaries of the Church. Thus, non-Christians can witness to Christians about him. Witnessing
to Christ is a two-way movement: the Christian witnessing to the non-Christian, the latter to the former.
Dialogue with peoples of other religious traditions,
then, with its inherent respect for the other and willingness to learn from the other, was an appropriate
approach for Christians to take. Chandran explained as
follows:

> [Christ] possesses us and all peoples. Dis-
> cerning and making manifest his presence in
> the faith and experience of others is also

part of the process of witnessing to him.
Therefore those who preach Christ to people
of other faiths should also be willing and
expectant to learn about the fullness of the
reality of Christ by listening to what they
have to say in witness of their faith. Only
through such dialogue can we grow into the
presence of Christ and deepen and enlarge the
catholicity of the Church.[70]

The Reverend Lynn de Silva, for his part, argued that
dialogue was needed to overcome the effects of long
years of Christian triumphalism and aggression. This
triumphalism had given Christianity a negative image.
He assured the audience that dialogue did not lead to
syncretism or to a lessening of one's faith. Rather, he
thought that dialogue actually sharpened one's faith
because it was always being tested in comparison to the
faith assertions of the dialogue partners. Moreover,
dialogue was necessary to come to a greater understanding and appreciation of the faith of others so that
Christians could discover the "Asian" face of Jesus, a
remark that shows de Silva's view that Christ is, indeed, present among these others.[71]

One of the major criticisms by the so-called
"Asian" theologians of some of the critical remarks
about dialogue coming mainly from western theologians
was that the latter were advancing theological arguments without having engaged in any actual interreligious dialogues. The "Asians" argued that theology had
to arise out of life experiences; it was not a theoretical enterprise. Thus, Russell Chandran complained
that those who were critical of dialogue and of new understandings of the relationships among followers of
different religions were not being open to the experi-

ence of committed Christians living in different cultural settings. He claimed that for Christians living
in situations where they were in a minority and where
dialogue was actually practiced all the time, different and new insights into the Gospel message were being perceived.[72] Christian theology, he insisted, had
to develop new insights into God's activity in the
world from the context of real interreligious encounters.[73]

3. The Assembly's Declaration on
   Dialogue in Community

     As can be expected from the theme of Section III,
"Seeking Community," the declaration agreed upon at the
assembly dealt with the meaning of community and the
Christian responsibility for fostering good community
relations. Dialogue was seen as one of the key activities in this process. The delegates at the assembly
did not agree easily, however, on the shape the assembly's declaration on community and dialogue should
take. As the record of the deliberations, shows, many
delegates felt that the first draft of a declaration on
these matters did not satisfy questions centering on
syncretism and mission. There was still the fear that
dialogue and respect for and openness to others led to
a betrayal of the Church's responsibility to preach the
Gospel or to a watering-down of the radical demands the
Gospel made. The first draft of the declaration was rejected as a result.[74] However, from the continuing discussions, a preamble was added to meet these objections. The preamble specifically states that the WCC is
opposed to syncretism, meaning by it any attempt to
create a new religion composed of elements taken from
many different religions.[75] It affirms, likewise, that

Christians must not compromise in any way Christ's command to preach the Gospel to the ends of the earth. In
this regard, the declaration notes that dialogue can be
a way of witnessing to one's faith as well as listening to others.[76]

(a) Dialogue and the Search for Community

The assembly's declaration on seeking community
outlines a number of reasons why such an activity is
part of the Christian life today. Christians are called
upon, it says, to form a wider community beyond their
own smaller community for the following reasons. First
of all, there are the usual "human" reasons. Christians
are part of a common search being undertaken by men and
women today for peace and justice, a search for human
welfare and even survival in an interdependent world.[77]
In such a situation, Christians must not allow their
faith to add to the tensions and hatreds that are already present in the world and which are the cause of
so much scandal.[78]

The declaration goes on to list the reasons for
this search for a wider community that exist within the
very dynamics of the Christian faith itself. For in-
stance, the declaration notes that Christians are
joined to all others as fellow creatures of the same
God who has created everyone.[79] It says that some
Christians see in the Incarnation a basis for seeking
wider community, for in the Incarnation God has reached
out to human beings to start a movement towards reconciliation and the restoration of creation to wholeness.
Others, it says, see the trinitarian understanding of
God as the grounds for seeking community because the
Trinity is the perfect community and shows that at its
most fundamental level, reality is community oriented.

Finally, the declaration points to those who see the historical forces at work in the world breaking down barriers as having a basis in the very activity of God who is the ground for the search for community.[80]

Dialogue, in the assembly's declaration, is one of the ways of fostering the wider community. Whether dialogue involves discussing ways to overcome common problems in society or discussing theological issues, it is a means of bringing people together in openness and mutual respect. For this reason, dialogue is a Christian activity in its own right. It does not replace mission, however, nor does it necessarily lead to a lessening of one's faith commitments. The declaration had to insert this to allay the fears of many Christians who were uneasy with this new form of activity. The declaration states,

> Many stressed the importance of dialogue in view of the necessity of co-operation of all people in order to establish a righteous and peaceful society. Dialogue helps people in their search for community. Authentic dialogue is a human and a Christian undertaking in its own right. It should not be seen as an alternative for mission and it should not compromise our faith.[81]

(b) Theological Issues in the Nairobi Declaration

The most contentious theological concerns surrounding the Nairobi statement on dialogue and on community were those noted above, namely, syncretism and mission. There are, however, some other theological concerns present in this declaration. It raises, for example, some important considerations with respect to

the relationship between Christianity, the revelation
of Christ, and the culture to which the Gospel message
is addressed. The declaration thus points out that
there is no one culture better suited to Christianity
than another. The relationship between the revelation
of Christ and the culture it faces is always one of
both affirmation and judgement. Jesus restores, the
declaration states, what is "truly human" in any culture, and the Church, that Body of Christ, is called
accordingly to relate itself "critically, creatively,
redemptively" to every culture.[82] The declaration calls
on Christians to respect the experience and the expressions of faith in Christ that emerge in cultures alien
to their own. The recognition of these different forms
of Christianity it calls part of the Church's catholicity.[83] What is of great importance in these remarks is
that they exemplify a theological perspective which
recognizes valid understandings of Christ in the cultures of all peoples, understandings which may result
in the emergence of new forms of Christianity.

The Nairobi declaration also dealt with the question of the Christian evaluation of other religions and
continued to reflect the opposing views held within the
ranks of the WCC members. While some delegates were
willing to admit that there was a saving presence of
God in the non-Christian religions, others were not.
The relationship between God's redemptive work in
Christ and the divine activity throughout all of creation remained a point at issue. The declaration summarizes the various points of view as follows:

> The question was discussed whether we
> can posit that Jesus Christ is at work among
> people of other faiths. Here opinions dif-
> fered. Some stated as their conviction that

Jesus Christ as Saviour is not present in the religions, although they accepted the idea of a natural knowledge of God. Others acknowledged the presence of [the] **logoi spermatikoi** (scattered seeds of truth) in other religions but stressed that only in Jesus Christ do we receive the fullness of truth and life. Others gave first-hand testimony that their own faith in Jesus Christ had been greatly deepened and strengthened through encountering him in dialogue with those of other faiths. The point was also made that the Spirit works among people outside Israel and outside the Church, and that the Spirit is one with the Father and with the Son.[84]

IV. Summary Reflections

During the first few years of its existence, from its establishment in 1971 to the Nairobi assembly in 1975, the DFI sub-unit attempted to carry out its task of promoting interreligious dialogue and leading the WCC's reflections on the implications and results. A number of features of this activity are worth noting. First of all, the emphasis in the DFI was upon theological reflection based on actual dialogue experiences. Christians were no longer evaluating non-Christians and their religions without informed contact with them. Secondly, there emerged a clear context for dialogue: dialogue in and for community. Whether on a regional or a worldwide level, dialogue and the Christian reflection on it was carried out from within this definite quest.

In its theological reflections, the DFI could not expound an official theological evaluation of the non-

Christian religions as the Secretariat for Non-Christians had done. This was simply because of the fact
that no consensus on such a theology was possible given
the strong differences within the WCC on the nature of
God's saving presence in the world. Thus, while there
is evidence of views which see the Spirit of God at
work in the world at large, drawing all people to their
final goal, the Kingdom of God, or views which see a
"cosmic" Christ present among the various non-Christian
religions of the world, there is also the strong
"Christomonism" evident in "evangelical" theology.

One of the recurring problems with dialogue during this time was that of the relationship between dialogue and mission. The statements coming from the DFI
dialogue activity and from the official WCC declarations on dialogue all attempt to assert, when they address this issue, that the two need not be rigorously
opposed. While dialogue does not aim directly at mission, it does not mean that the Christian must hide his
or her faith commitment either. Christians in dialogue
can proclaim to others that Christ is the ultimate revelation of the Father and the one who brings salvation
to human beings. The Christian can indeed witness to
his or her faith.

CHAPTER SIX
FROM NAIROBI TO KINGSTON
THE EMERGENCE OF NEW GUIDELINES

The final chapter of this study of the dialogue activity of the DFI covers the years following the Nairobi assembly to the Central Committee's promulgation of a second set of guidelines for dialogue in 1979 (the first set of guidelines had been issued at Addis Ababa in 1971). Before this important set of guidelines was issued, however, the DFI held a number of dialogue consultations, including a major one at Chiang Mai, Thailand, in 1977. It was at this consultation that a theological statement on dialogue emerged, a statement which grew out of the previous dialogue experiences and which formed the basis for the 1979 guidelines. The focus of attention of this chapter will be on the meetings leading up to the Chiang Mai consultation, that consultation itself, and the dialogue guidelines which followed it two years later.

I. Preparations for Further Dialogue:
The Aftermath of Nairobi

Following the Nairobi assembly, a special "Core Group" of the DFI was formed to evaluate the Nairobi debate on dialogue and plan the next stages of the DFI's activity. This Core Group was to act until the Central Committee could appoint a full Working Group.[1] The Core Group held two meetings, one at Chambésy, Switzerland, in May 1976 and the other at Glion, Switzerland, in January 1977. The reports of these meetings

not only show what activities the DFI planned to undertake, they also show some of the issues and questions
those concerned with its work thought to be important.[2]

1. The Chambésy Meeting of the Core Group

The Core Group's meeting in Chambésy in 1976 which
followed the Nairobi assembly discussed the theme,
"Where Are We After Nairobi?" and identified a number
of issues in connection with dialogue which it felt
needed attention. Perhaps the most important of these
concerned the question of dialogue in community. The
members of the Core Group felt that this issue had not
really been adequately dealt with at Nairobi, although
it was supposed to have been the major focus of attention in Section III of that assembly. The Core Group
members felt that the assembly had paid too much attention to other issues and so the question of the Christian role in the search for community remained largely unexplored.[3] Although the report of the meeting does
not identify these "other" issues, they must have been
the assembly's concern over mission and syncretism
which proved to be the cause of much heated controversy at the Nairobi assembly and the root of the opposition to dialogue.

In these discussions, one can see the continuing
presence of the concern that dialogue be carried out in
the context of a search for a better human community on
the local, national, or world-wide level. The Chambésy
report notes that this search for community is natural
and inevitable in today's world and demands a dialogical approach between the followers of different religious traditions, an approach that stresses mutual respect and the desire to cooperate.[4] Because of the
great importance it thus attaches to dialogue in com-

munity and because it thought that the Nairobi assembly had not dealt adequately with this theme, the Core Group recommended that the DFI sponsor a consultation with this particular theme in mind. It was to be an intra-Christian consultation in which Christians could reflect on the implications of the search for community and how it affected their faith commitment.

In its report, the Core Group identified a number of specific questions it felt the proposed consultation should discuss. These included questions on the Christian basis for seeking community in the first place, the type of community desirable, and the relationship of the Christian community to the human community at large. Other questions concerning the nature and purpose of dialogue and the Christian evaluation of other religions within this context of dialogue in community would also be part of the discussion. The report said, then,

a) What is the nature of the community Christians are committed to seek? What are the impediments to seek community and what are the insights from within the Christian faith that help them to relate themselves as a "serving community" to their neighbours?

b) How do Christians understand and practice dialogue--its nature, its purpose, its variations in different contexts. Is dialogue part of the Christian ministry in a pluralistic world?

c) What is the theological significance of people of other faiths and cultures in the Christian perspective? Is God at work among people of other faiths?[5]

The latter above mentioned sets of issues are substantially the same ones that had emerged in the DFI's
dialogue activity before Nairobi. There was still no
agreement on any answers to them that were acceptable
within the WCC as a whole. The Core Group members hoped
that in its planned consultation these issues would receive the consideration they needed so that guidelines
for future dialogue could be provided to the WCC member churches.[6]

Other problems connected with the quest for dialogue are also in evidence in the Chambésy meeting,
problems which the Core Group felt needed more consideration. For example, the Core Group pointed to the
need for a "rationale" for dialogue. Its report suggests a number of theological reasons why dialogue has
been considered by some Christians as a legitimate
Christian activity. Dialogue with people of other religious traditions, for some, could be a way of deepening the Christian's relationship with the "cosmic" yet
personal Christ. It could be an expression of the
Church's mission in a pluralistic world. Or, significantly, it could be a witness to Christ within the to-
tality of God's creating and saving work. The report
states,

> . . . it could be said that the salient point
> [concerning dialogue] is openness and the
> challenge or the possibility to live from the
> Source, from Christ Himself, a deeper life of
> relationship to our cosmic yet personal Lord.
> Again, a re-awakening to the Presence of
> Christ and life in him as the heart of the
> Christian community could be seen as the very
> essence of Dialogue with People of Other
> Faiths and Ideologies. Or it could be seen as

participation in the duty and joy of the mission of the Church in a pluralistic world. Finally, it may be that our witness to Christ should be seen more consciously as part of the total work of God's creative, sustaining and saving work and plan.[7]

There was, as well, the Core Group's report noted, need for a clarification of the nature, purpose and variations of dialogue activity. One purpose which dialogue definitely does **not** have, it insisted, is that of mission. Dialogue is not part of a missionary strategy.[8]

Some of the programme proposals recommended by the Core Group exemplify the desire that dialogue be concerned with specific topics. In addition to the consultation on dialogue in community, then, the Core Group recommended a number of other consultations. For example, it recommended that a Christian-Muslim planning meeting be held to explore the direction dialogue should take between the members of these two religious traditions. One of the themes that seemed to be of interest to both sides was, the Core Group felt, that of the relationship between faith and science.[9] The Core Group also recommended that steps be taken to see if Buddhists or Hindus would likewise be interested in holding consultations on a similar topic.[10] To complete the plans, the Core Group recommended the exploration of possibilities for meetings dealing with traditional religions and cultures in Africa, East Asia, and the Pacific.[11]

A final major topic of discussion which the Core Group singled out was that of syncretism. Connected to this topic were those of the indigenization of Christianity and the relationship between Christianity and

culture. The fear expressed at Nairobi that dialogue
led to syncretism with its loss of the Christian message, and the reply by the "Asian" theologians that
western Christians were imposing a western form of
Christianity on them, were behind the Core Group's concern for an examination of what syncretism really was.
This problem, like that of the relationship between
mission and dialogue, continued to be a constant one in
the DFI's dialogue work. The Core Group hoped that a
small consultation could be held to discuss this issue.
It outlined the problems such a consultation would discuss as follows:

   a) What is syncretism? How does it express itself in particular cultural situations today? Is Christianity in the West syncretistic in its roots? What are the criteria to evaluate the phenomenon of contemporary syncretism?

   b) What are the ideological/cultural
components of syncretism in Europe? Is syn-
cretism-indigenization a threat or an opportunity for the Christian search for community with their neighbours? Is the term "wider
ecumenism" syncretistic?

   c) What is the relationship between Gospel and culture today? How can the primacy of
the Gospel and the identity of the Church be
maintained in the midst of contemporary cultural phenomena such as secular humanism,
Eastern spiritual movements in the West,
youth culture etc.12

2. The Glion Meeting of the Core Group

Meeting again at Glion, Switzerland, January 24-28, 1977, the DFI Core Group dealt with the theme, "Where Do We Go From Nairobi?" In essence, it continued the discussion of programmes suggested at Chambésy and by now approved by the Central Committee. Among the topics on the agenda was that of the upcoming consultation at Chiang Mai on dialogue in community to be held later that year. This Core Group meeting added nothing to the plans already under way. It simply expressed the hope that the consultation would lay the groundwork for a new set of dialogue guidelines to replace those issued at Addis Ababa in 1971.[13]

It was at this meeting that the Core Group approved a Christian-Muslim consultation to be held after the Chiang Mai consultation dealing with the theme of the relation between faith, science and technology. This consultation had been one of the suggestions of the Chambésy meeting. Its plans had been finalized at a meeting of Christians and Muslims at Cartigny, Switzerland, following that Chambésy meeting. Official representatives from the Organization of the Islamic Conference of Jeddah, the World Muslim League, and the World Muslim Conference had met with the DFI staff at Cartigny.[14] The Glion meeting of the Core Group recommended that the DFI respond to other local regional meetings between Christians and Muslims, saying further that the "DFI needs to be in touch with the situation in Lebanon" where Christians and Muslims were engaged in a civil war.[15] The Core Group also thought the DFI should include in its programme a consultation on traditional religions and cultures, repeating in this what the Chambésy meeting had suggested, and a consultation involving representatives from Eastern religions on the

theme of the religious dimension of humankind's relation to nature.[16]

II. The Chiang Mai Consultation

Following the plans of the Core Group meetings in
Chambésy and in Glion, and approved by the Central Committee in its 1976 meeting at Geneva, the DFI organized
a theological consultation on the theme, "Dialogue in
Community," April 18-27, 1977, at Chiang Mai, Thailand.[17] It was a consultation among Christians to reflect upon dialogue in community, an issue the DFI felt
had not received adequate treatment at the Nairobi assembly. The participants heard papers presented on four
themes: 1) the nature of the community Christians were
called upon to seek, 2) whether their dialogue was part
of the Christian ministry in a pluralistic world, 3)
whether God was at work among people of other faiths
and ideologies, and 4) the biblical foundation for dialogue and openness to peoples of other faiths. In his
opening address, Dr. Samartha summarized the purpose of
the consultation as follows:

> a) to clarify the Christian basis for
> seeking community by focussing theological
> reflection on specific issues and particular
> contexts;
> b) to indicate the nature of the Chris-
> tian community within the human community in
> a pluralistic world; and
> c) to suggest "guidelines" to Christian
> communities in pluralistic situations to be
> communities of service and witness without
> diluting their faith or compromising their
> commitment to Christ.[18]

The statement that resulted from the deliberations was not meant to be a definitive and final statement on dialogue.[19] Rather, it was to be sent to the member churches of the WCC for their reactions and then used as a basis for a more definitive set of dialogue guidelines later. As an attempt to resolve the problems raised at Nairobi and because of its use as a basis for the future guidelines, the Chiang Mai statement on dialogue ranks as a pivotal dialogue statement.

1. Dialogue in the Chiang Mai Statement

The primary focus of attention in the Chiang Mai consultation was, as has been mentioned already, dialogue in community. As such, the consultation's considerations of dialogue fit into the pattern that had developed in the DFI's work. The emphasis was not on discussing religious differences as such, but rather on examining them in a definite context, that of the search for a better community by people of different living faiths. Because of this particular context, the understanding of community that one sees at Chiang Mai is an important one.

The very notion of a search for a better human community with the followers of other religious traditions was one which had been greeted with suspicion by the "evangelical" wing of the WCC, as has been noted above.[20] This was not because they were opposed to bettering the human condition. The concern was grounded on a fear that the attempt to create friendly relations would lead to a minimizing of the radical Gospel demand for faith in Jesus Christ by all men and women everywhere if they are to receive God's salvation. There was even a fear that the search for community would lead to a form of "syncretism" in which elements of other re-

ligions would make their way into the Gospel message as
Christians attempted to minimize the Gospel demands to
establish a peaceful community.[21] The statement tries
to allay this fear by insisting on the legitimacy of
differences within communities. Diversity, the statement insists, is a good, willed by God. It provides the
earth with a valuable richness. It is not something in-
herently evil, although it may certainly become so.[22]

The type of community the statement envisages,
then, is a type of world-wide community of communities
where each individual community is allowed to retain
its own identity, including its religious identity. The
presupposition is, of course, that in retaining their
own identities, the different communities (in the context of the statement, the different faith communities)
examine their traditions so as to find resources allowing them to contribute to the good of all and not allow their distinctive natures to set up barriers or
hostile competition. The statement says,

> Because of the divisive role to which
> all religions and ideologies are so easily
> prone, we believe that they are each called
> to look upon themselves anew, so as to con-
> tribute from their resources to the good of
> the community of humankind in its wholeness.
> . . . As workers for peace, liberation, and
> justice, the way to which often makes con-
> flict necessary and reconciliation costly, we
> feel ourselves called to share with others in
> the community of humankind in search for new
> experiences in the evolution of our communi-
> ties, where we may affirm our interdependence
> as much as our respect for our distinctive
> identities. The vision of a worldwide "commu-

nity of communities" commended itself to us
as a means of seeking community in a pluralistic world. The vision is not one of homogeneous unity or totalitarian uniformity . .
. . 23

Another of the perennial and controversial problems concerning dialogue, debated at Nairobi, was that
of the place of dialogue in the Christian life, in particular, how dialogue was compatible with the ideas of
witness and mission. The Chiang Mai consultation tried
to address this question by saying that dialogue was,
indeed, a valid Christian activity because it was a way
for Christians to express their love for others in the
common search for a better human community.[24] But this
serving, the statement goes on to say, is not done in
a way which hides the truth that Christians have seen
in the revelation of Christ. Dialogue does not aim at
converting the other and so is not mission, but it is
a way for Christians to witness to their faith and give
testimony to what God has done in Jesus Christ. The
statement asserts,

          . . . we do not see dialogue and the
     giving of witness as standing in any contra-
     diction to one another. Indeed, as we enter
     dialogue with our commitment to Jesus Christ,
     time and again the relationship of dialogue
     gives   opportunity   for   authentic   witness.
     Thus, to the member churches of the WCC we
     feel able with integrity to commend the way
     of dialogue as one in which Jesus Christ can
     be confessed in the world today 25

The grounds for dialogue to which the Chiang Mai
statement points are similar to those that can be found

in previous DFI-related statements. There is first of
all the very practical basis for dialogue as a response
by Christians to the situation in which they find themselves today. This situation involves the growth of
pluralistic communities and the increasing sense of interdependence among all peoples. The need to live together in peace and to solve common problems together,
along with the idea that a human community with one
common history is being formed, constitute, then, a human basis upon which to ground the Christian dialogue
with people of other religious traditions.[26]

The Chiang Mai statement also attempts to ground
dialogue and the search for community in the Christian
faith itself. One of the chief theological reasons for
dialogue arises from the Christian understanding of
God. The statement sees God as the creator of all who
calls all of humankind to relationship both with one
another and with the creator. This means that Christians are called to develop friendly relations, even
community, with all others, an activity in which dialogue can play an essential role.[27] Dialogue is also
grounded in the Christian faith in that it is a form
of Christian service to others, a means of responding
to the divine command to love one's neighbour inasmuch
as through dialogue Christians strive to help others
build up the human community in which they both live.[28]

The above comments on the nature of dialogue and
the various grounds on which it is based point to the
purpose of dialogue as it emerges in the Chiang Mai
statement. The predominant goal of dialogue is to foster better relationships both within one's own society
and between different societies. Dialogue in this sense
is a way of responding to the Christian call to serve
others. It moreover allows Christians to witness to

their faith to others. In addition to these, however, dialogue provides new conditions for theological reflection. It allows the Christian to reflect upon his or her faith from within a new framework, one which stresses sympathetic understanding of people of other faiths and a working with them towards the formation of better human communities. Dialogue is therefore a way of coming to a new understanding of Christianity itself.[29]

2. Theological Issues and Concerns in the Chiang Mai Statement

The Chiang Mai statement, like other dialogue statements of DFI-sponsored consultations, contains no developed theological evaluation of the world's religions. In fact, like the other statements, it ultimately poses a number of key questions which it hopes will be the basis for further reflection by the member churches of the WCC. The delegates at the consultation, though, did not draw back from discussing the theological issues connected with dialogue, in spite of their inability to come to an agreed-upon set of principles. They recognized that as Christians engaged in dialogue, they could not avoid asking important questions about such things as the place of other religions and their followers in God's plan.[30]

The outstanding questions which the consultation singled out as needing further reflection really center on the question of the nature of God's activity beyond the boundaries of the Church and beyond the divine explicit self-disclosure and activity in Jesus Christ. Does such activity bring about salvation? Can God really be known outside of contact with Jesus Christ? What indications are there in the Bible for answers to these questions? The Chiang Mai statement lists the questions in the following way:

> There were . . . questions where we found agreement more difficult and sometimes impossible, but these also we would commend for further theological attention:
>
> What is the relationship between God's universal action in creation and his redemptive action in Jesus Christ?
>
> Are we to speak of God's work in the lives of all men and women only in tentative terms of hope that they may experience something of him, or more positively in terms of God's self-disclosure to people of living faiths and in the struggle of human life and ideology?
>
> How are we to find from the Bible criteria in our approach to people of other faiths and ideologies, recognizing as we must, both the authority accorded to the Bible by Christians of all centuries, particular questions concerning the authority of the Old Testament for the Christian Church, and the fact that our partners in dialogue have other starting points and resources, both in holy books and traditions of teaching?
>
> What is the biblical view and Christian experience of the operation of the Holy spirit [sic], and is it right and helpful to understand the work of God outside the Church in terms of the doctrine of the Holy Spirit?[31]

The issue of syncretism which had aroused some controversy at Nairobi also received attention at Chiang Mai. The statement of this latter consultation first of all explicitly rejects the notion that the mingling of elements of various religions to form some form of "super" religion is a goal or a necessary result of dialogue.[32] It reassures Christians that they do not have to relinquish the integrity of their faith. Yet the Chiang Mai consultation was also sensitive to the objections of many non-European theologians that the fear of syncretism was preventing non-Western Christians from developing a truly indigenous Christianity. The consultation's statement, therefore, also insists that Christianity cannot be reduced to a particular cultural expression, especially an European one. It urges more tolerance and understanding as churches in various parts of the world attempt to translate the Gospel into the cultural categories of their particular social context.[33]

3. The Group Reports on Dialogue

The Chiang Mai statement concludes with a number of "Group Reports" which deal with the existing state of dialogue between the DFI and particular dialogue partners. These reports show the types of dialogue being carried on by the DFI and the great variety that existed in the various concrete dialogical relationships that were developing. The reports also indicate the concerns of the various dialogue partners, as the DFI understood them, and their willingness to engage in dialogue. Finally, they provide more indications of the theological tensions present in the DFI's dialogue work.

(a) The Group Report on Dialogue With Muslims

One of the important sets of relations the DFI had been fostering was that between Christians and Muslims.[34] The group report on Christian-Muslim relations in the Chiang Mai statement points out the difficulties that had arisen in this endeavour. The group report mentions, for example, that although the two faiths share a common heritage, they are often separated by different views of Christ, Mohammed, and the Scriptures.[35] Moreover, the historically-based mistrust and rivalry between the two faiths has greatly hampered dialogue.[36] Consistent with the DFI's understanding of dialogue, however, the report recommends not a downplaying of the differences, but an honest recognition of them and a sincere respect for the views of the other by members of each side. It calls on both faith communities to continue efforts to overcome mutual suspicion and hostility.[37] Furthermore, the report says that it is through continual efforts to live together in the world and develop good community relations with Muslims that Christians may come to a deeper understanding of God's work in the world and the responsibilities this implies.[38] In the actual dialogue between Christians and Muslims, then, God's work may be discerned.

(b) The Group Report on Dialogue With Buddhists and Hindus

A second major set of relationships dealt with by a group report is that between Christians and Buddhists and Hindus. The great variety of situations in which Christians met with members of these two faiths is mentioned: Christians are at times in the majority (in Western countries) and at times Buddhists or Hindus are in the majority; there are places where one of these

great Asian faiths is on the resurgence (the report
points to India and Sri Lanka) when once Christians
thought they were declining. Because of the varying
contexts, dialogue takes on, the report notes, a different aspect in each case. A rather important feature
of the report is the insistence that Christians adopt
a positive view of these religions and that they come
to know more about them.[39] Consistent with the theme of
the consultation, the report also urges cooperation between the followers of these traditions and Christians
in overcoming problems faced by the society they share.
The report ends with the remark that for some Christians, it is the Holy Spirit that is leading them to
develop better relations with people of other faiths,
an activity whose implications on Christianity are yet
to be worked out. The report says,

> . . . we are convinced that . . . Christians
> are being led in our present time to a new
> way of relating to and living with peoples of
> other faiths. We do not yet fully understand
> all the implications, opportunities and re-
> sponsibilities of living in dialogue. But
> many of us can say that the Spirit Himself
> has brought us here and that we must be ready
> to explore with His help the still unchar-
> tered road that lies ahead of us.[40]

(c) The Group Report on Dialogue Involving
Traditional Religions

A third group report deals with the DFI's dialogue
relations with traditional religions.[41] The report
deals mainly with experiences in Africa, although it
does say that dialogue in other primal cultures is desirable, too. The report reflects the emphasis that had

emerged in this area of dialogue, namely, the relationship between the Gospel and culture. It asserts
that the Gospel of Christ does not only bring judgment
upon human cultures (and their religions), but also
fulfills them. Thus, while recognizing that the Gospel
has to be critical of any culture and its religious
forms, the report at the same time notes that there are
many positive aspects of these cultures and of the religious spirit prevalent in them which provide concepts
that Christians can use and which may become part of
any indigenous form of Christianity.[42] As an example,
the report comments on the strong theme running through
many traditional cultures in Africa that one's identity is closely tied up with one's community. To be human is to be in relation to others, both past as well
as present. The notion of "blood relationship," then,
tying all the peoples of a community together, is a
feature of many "primal" African cultures. This could
become, says the report, part of the African character
of Christianity--Christianity as a gathering not of individuals but of a community, under Christ, the common
"blood ancestor."[43]

This report on "traditional" religions and cultures stresses the theme of adaptation and fulfillment.
It reflects a positive and appreciative evaluation of
traditional cultures. The traditional values are not to
be disparaged. Rather, they can be the grounds (indeed,
the mood of the report is that they must be the
grounds) for an enculturation of Christianity. The report therefore encourages continuing study and evaluation of traditional values and customs so that these
may be assumed and renewed. The following passage sums
up the general attitude of the report:

A study of beliefs and practices out of primal world-views which need to be transformed into something new when traditional peoples participate in the life of Christian communities will need careful attention--and in this respect we need reports from the many different continents of our world where the Christian community and traditional peoples are already engaged in entering upon or, sometimes, resisting a meaningful and constructive dialogue.[44]

4. An Assessment of the Chiang Mai Consultation

What was the importance of the Chiang Mai consultation in furthering the WCC's reflection on dialogue and on the Christian evaluation of non-Christian religions? That the consultation was seen as an important step forward by the staff of the DFI can hardly be in doubt. The Director of the sub-unit, Stanley Samartha, called it a "landmark in the development of the dialogue debate in the ecumenical context."[45] He confidently asserted that it had both overcome the confusion and controversy of the Nairobi debate and that it had provided a theological framework within which discussion of dialogue could proceed.[46] It was crucially important for the deliberations of the Central Committee meeting two years after, for it became the foundation of a new official WCC dialogue statement replacing that of Addis Ababa.

The overcoming of the confusion and controversy of Nairobi seems to center around three main points. First of all, the Chiang Mai consultation clarified the idea of "community." What was at the bottom of fears over the search for "world community" was the fear that this

implied a uniformity which negated differences, differences which could be negated only at the expense of denying one's Christian faith and thereby "watering" it
down. At the Chiang Mai consultation, however, what was
envisaged was a search for a world **community of communities.** This notion was intended to preserve the existing legitimate and unresolvable differences among the
various faith communities (or any other type of community, for that matter), while at the same time insisting that they live together in peace and harmony. The
Chiang Mai consultation, then, acknowledged that all
could, and should, maintain the integrity of their respective beliefs. The only prohibiting factor was if
these beliefs involved hostility towards other groups.
In the context of the Nairobi debate, this meant that
the search for world community did not have to imply
that Christians had to give up essential aspects of
their faith.

The second important point of clarification that
emerged from Chiang Mai concerned the relationship between dialogue and witness. Just as the search for
world community did not mean that Christians had to relinquish distinctive elements of their faith, so too,
dialogue itself did not mean that Christians had to refrain from witnessing to their experience of God in Jesus Christ. Such witness could extend even to the proclamation of Jesus as the one who truly mediates salvation to human beings. Indeed, dialogue includes witness
in the consultation's view. Through dialogue, the
Christian is able to share his or her faith with others. This same right is also recognized for the followers of other religions, one must note. Dialogue is not
a one-way communication.

The third important clarification at Chiang Mai

concerned the issue of syncretism. Fears that dialogue led to syncretism and loss of essential parts of the Christian faith had emerged at Nairobi and had persisted. One of the "evangelical" participants at the Chiang Mai consultation, bishop Per Lonning of Norway, expressed this fear as follows:

> The danger, as I see it, is not so much a possibility of some conscious mixing of elements from different religions but that the uniqueness of the Gospel may be pushed to one side so that we more or less smooth over the offence of the Cross of Christ. That tendency is always there--anywhere--I mean, it is essentially the same thing that happens if the Church preaches the uniqueness of the ecclesiastical establishment or of Christendom instead of the uniqueness of Christ. That is certainly wrong. An important truth for me is the recognition of Christianity as the religion of the empty hands. I made several references here to Rom. 3.23: "For all have sinned, and come short of the glory of God"--this involves a full understanding of man's complete failure to cope with God's will. It is essential to see the Gospel in this perspective. What I fear is that in some way the Gospel may be made so temperate, so reasonable, that it just becomes some good and nice theory of God's love to nice people --in our own religion and in other people's religions. It is precisely here that the threat of syncretism is real, and not in any conscious blending of religions about which Nairobi spoke.[47]

At Chiang Mai, it was clear that the participants did not see dialogue as an impediment to holding firmly onto one's religious convictions, and further, it was clear that dialogue did not at all involve the mixing up of elements from different religions. Dialogue did not lead to a diminution of Christianity.

With respect to the theological framework within which the discussion on dialogue by the DFI should proceed, the Chiang Mai statement shows, once again, the emphasis on theological reflection taking place within the context of the search for community. In spite of the theological problems and tensions within the WCC community about a theological evaluation of the religions of the world, which the Chiang Mai statement clearly admits, there is a commitment to engaging in dialogical relationships first, encouraging a friendly and positive encounter, and then reflecting on the results from a Christian perspective to see what theological implications could be discerned. Thus Dr. Samartha remarked in an article in which he assessed what had taken place at Chiang Mai,

> . . . on the theological significance of people of other faiths and ideologies, although some of the (old) issues remain, there is a perceptible change in the framework in which theological questions are formulated and the mood in which Christians approach people of other faiths and ideologies. The process of reflection has to be continued by Christians as they share life in the community with their neighbours.[48]

The Chiang Mai consultation on dialogue in community epitomizes the new attitude towards dialogue and towards the religious traditions of other peoples that had been gradually developing during the course of the DFI's work. Dialogue had by this time become an activity in its own right. It was not simply part of the missionary enterprise. Dialogue was a legitimate response to the present world situation in which Christians found themselves. It denoted a new attitude on the part of Christians towards men and women of other faiths and towards these faiths themselves. The negative attitudes evident in twentieth century Protestant thinking in the theology of Karl Barth and his followers were clearly being challenged. There was a real desire to know more about the persons belonging to other religious traditions, to appreciate their views, and to respect them sincerely. There was clear emphasis on witness and less on conversion, as dialogue was seen as an opportunity for giving witness to what God had done in Jesus Christ. It was an approach which called on Christians to discern God's work among peoples who did not follow Christ and it invited Christians to reflect on the nature and implications of this work.

III. Continuing Dialogue Between Chiang Mai and Kingston

Between the Chiang Mai consultation and the new set of dialogue guidelines issued by the Central Committee at Kingston, Jamaica, in 1979, there were three DFI-sponsored dialogue consultations of concern to this study, all of which had been suggested by the DFI Core Group meetings following the Nairobi assembly. The first was a Christian-Muslim dialogue at Beirut, Lebanon, the second a Christian-Buddhist dialogue at Colombo, Sri Lanka, and the third a consultation involving Christians responding to the so called "tradition-

al" cultures, at Yaoundé, Camaroon. The memoranda that
these consultations issued will be the focus of attention of this section of the present chapter. The DFI
also held a Working Group meeting which evaluated the
dialogue activity in which it had been involved. Important parts of this meeting will also be examined.

1. The Christian-Muslim Meeting at Beirut, 1977

The Christian-Muslim consultation on the theme
"Faith, Science and Technology and the Future of Humanity" at Beirut, Lebanon, November 14-18, 1977, fell
within the DFI plans to hold a series of bilateral
meetings on this theme.[49] The participants discussed
the relationship between faith and science, the understanding of nature in the respective faiths, humankind's role in caring for nature, the dangers as well
as the promise of technological developments, socio-political influences on science, and some theological
concerns, for example, creation and evolution. As in
other consultations, the participants proclaimed their
willingness to work together, in this case in order to
face up to problems caused by science and technology.
They agreed that their commitment to the one God led
them also to a commitment to use the resources of the
world for the good of all of humankind, since God had
made human beings responsible for the earth. They
agreed, as well, that the spiritual and moral implications of science and technology needed to be stressed
more in today's world. Thus the memorandum says,

> . . . we felt that Christians and Muslims
> should try to work together actively in order
> to sustain the natural world, to rebuild so-
> ciety and [also] to give meaning to life and
> death.[50]

An example of the mutual enrichment that can result from dialogue, in the view of the participants, appears in the memorandum's brief remarks on the suffering of Christ and certain directives in the Qur'an. Muslims, it says, can look to the figure of Christ and his sufferings for the sake of justice as an example in their fight for social justice in the proper use of technology and the earth's resources. Christians can see in the Qur'an the insistence on corporate justice. Thus the fundamental components of each tradition--the Cross and the Qur'an--can enrich followers of the other tradition. Dialogue is truly a two-way affair.[51]

2. The Buddhist-Christian Dialogue at Colombo

Following the general topic of the problems to religious faith posed by science and technology, the DFI co-sponsored (with the Ecumenical Institute for Study and Dialogue at Colombo) another dialogue meeting, this time with a group of Buddhists at Colombo, Sri Lanka, February 22-25, 1978. The theme of the meeting was "Religious Dimension in Humanity's Relation to Nature."[52] The meeting was designed to allow the participants to examine critically the religious resources of each side to see if there were aspects in either which would help in the human struggle to use nature wisely and justly. Thus while the participants discussed religious concepts in each tradition that had to do with the problems at hand--their respective beliefs about the nature of ultimate reality and humankind's relation to it, humankind's place in the world, the meaning of history, for example--they also discussed the ethical dimensions of these ideas as well. The two could not be separated.[53]

Mutual enrichment was a prime characteristic and

goal of this dialogue meeting, a meeting which, it was
hoped, would begin a series of such meetings to continue the discussion on this issue of humankind's response
to and use of science and technology. Thus, Dr. Samartha remarked in his opening address,

> We must avoid polite generalities and mutual
> praise, above all claims of superiority one
> over the other. We need to be rigorously
> self-critical and also critical of each oth-
> er. Otherwise fresh insights are unlikely to
> emerge. In any case, I believe that strug-
> gling together with these questions is worth-
> while not only because of the reward of mu-
> tual enrichment but also because of its pos-
> sible outcome in initiating a process of re-
> flection that should be continued in the
> years to come.[54]

Both traditions, then, could help the other. Neither
had a monopoly on answers to solve the problems at
hand.[55]

The meeting, concerned with the problems caused by
science and technology, is an example of a dialogue
having to do with a definite topic and attempting to
find practical solutions so that a better community can
be formed. The participants agreed on a number of values that they felt could act as a basis for solving the
problems they face. These values, which show that cooperation, mutual respect, and mutual enrichment are at
work in the dialogue, are described in the memorandum
as follows:

> "A cluster of values" was suggested as form-
> ing a basis for working together as "a com-
> munity of the concerned." These are:

(i) A presumption against the taking of life, since loss of life deprives a person of any further opportunity in this life for personal and social fulfillment.

(ii) A presumption against causing pain.

(iii) A presumption in favour of benevolence (e.g., **agape** and **karuna**).

(iv) A presumption in favour of providing conditions of positive freedom and minimising encroachments on such freedom, either for contemporaries or future generations, and

(v) A presumption in favour of creating a truly human and fulfilling community.[56]

In spite of the religious differences between the two sides, then, they could both find common ground on which to base a quest for solutions to the problems facing their society.

3. The Third Meeting of the Working Group

For the first time since the Nairobi assembly, the full DFI Working Group met at St. Benedict, Trinidad, May 17-24, 1978. The most important task of this meeting was to prepare a draft statement on dialogue and to make recommendations for the continuing dialogue activity of the DFI. These were to be submitted to the Central Committee for discussion and approval at its meeting in Kingston, Jamaica, in 1979, a meeting which had as one of its main concerns that of publishing a new set of dialogue guidelines and recommendations. Since the draft statement on dialogue proposed by this Working Group is substantially the same as the one the Central Committee adopted, detailed examination of it will be deferred. What is noteworthy at this point is the evaluation of the DFI's dialogue activity to date that

occurred at this meeting and the recommendations it
made concerning the future work of the DFI in the three
areas of dialogue which had developed: dialogue with
Muslims, dialogue with Hindus and Buddhists, and dialogue with primal cultures.

(a) Dialogue With Muslims

One of the major characteristics of the Christian
dialogue with Muslims was the great variety of dialogue
situations that existed. Dr. Samartha, in his report to
the Working Group, remarked that the Muslim world extended beyond the Middle East. Large communities of
Muslims existed also in Africa, Indonesia, and Pakistan.[57] The relations between Christians and Muslims,
and hence the type of dialogue they could pursue, varied greatly throughout the world, then. John Taylor,
Dr. Samartha's assistant, pointed to some of this variety and the difficulties it caused in Africa. In his
presentation to the Working Group, he said,

> The overall climate of Christian-Muslim rela-
> tions has suffered from the excesses in Ugan-
> da, from some self-conscious introduction of
> Islamic institutions in Nigeria and from po-
> litical tensions between Ethiopia, Eritrea,
> Somalia, and Kenya. Religion may no longer be
> as blatantly invoked by both sides as during
> the Biafra or Sudan wars, but tensions con-
> tinue and there are too few signs of Chris-
> tians and Muslims bringing reconciliation by
> virtue of their respective faiths. However,
> there are more promising signs where Chris-
> tians and Muslims work together in nation-
> building as in Tanzania or in relief work as
> in the drought-stricken zone south of the Sa-

hara. Youth camps in Senegal over the last
few years have regularly brought Christian
and Muslim students together to work and reflect on common spiritual and social concerns.[58]

The great variety of Christian-Muslim relations
made it necessary, Dr. Samartha thought, to reflect
more on the priorities the DFI should emphasize in promoting these relations. Much of the DFI's activity up
to now, he said, had involved consultations in which
experience was shared mainly by the reading of papers.
He thought that the time had come to explore different
ways of sharing experiences.[59]

Recommendations about Christian-Muslim dialogue
activity came from a sub-group within the larger Working Group. It repeated earlier recommendations that the
DFI continue to encourage friendly relations between
Christians and Muslims whenever the opportunity arose,
responding even to initiatives from Muslims. The "Muslim group" also pointed to the continuing need to
spread information among the member churches of the WCC
about what had already taken place between Christians
and Muslims. Finally, it recommended the gathering together of a large group of Muslims and Christians within the following two years to discuss the existing
state of relations between members of the two faiths,
the tensions that existed, and the respective theological understandings they had of each other. The recommendations of this group, then, show the importance the
DFI placed on simply creating a peaceful and an harmonious climate among members of the two faiths.[60]

(b) Dialogue With Hindus and Buddhists

Dr. Samartha's remarks on dialogue with Hindus and Buddhists summarized for the Working Group a number of features of this dialogue. He noted that it was diffi- cult to find "official" representatives for formal di- alogues because neither of these two religious tradi- tions had an hierarchically-organized structure with officially constituted spokespersons. But even more im- portantly, Dr. Samartha drew attention to the emphasis on inward spirituality and contemplation rather than social action that was in many respects the most impor- tant part of the Hindu and Buddhist religious life. This dimension of these two religions needed, he felt, further exploration by the DFI which did not have much experience in them. Samartha felt that the Roman Cath- olic Church could contribute insights gained through its monastic tradition which made it more open to this aspect of the Hindu-Buddhist-Christian encounter.[61]

The group making recommendations on Hindu-Bud- dhist-Christian dialogue picked up on Dr. Samartha's remarks about the contemplative tradition of these great Asian religions and suggested that the DFI ex- plore possibilities for a dialogue which would empha- size it. It was not to be a study, but rather a real "live-in."[62] The group also recommended a continuation of the theme of the relation between humankind and na- ture and the proper use of science and technology, and accordingly it suggested a Christian-Hindu dialogue along the lines of the Christian-Buddhist dialogue held at Colombo earlier that year.[63]

A rather important feature of the discussions of Christian encounters with Buddhists and Hindus that can be seen in the remarks of the group concerned with Christian-Buddhist-Hindu dialogue was the emphasis on the mutual enrichment possible in these encounters. As an example, the group felt that the contemplative aspect of Hindu and Buddhist spirituality might be useful to Christians in facing the problems and pressures of technology by its attitude of tranquillity before and respect of nature and because it showed another approach to nature besides that of domination and control. The report from this group says,

> It looks as if the Protestant tradition in particular lacks patterns for solving [the problems of technology] through providing contemplative communities to face the pressures of technology. Here dialogue with Hindus and Buddhists might be of some help to:
>   (a) pursue a sense of tranquillity, respect and veneration for nature;
>   (b) face the question whether one can intelligently control nature without being in control of one's nature; and
>   (c) find out in what sense science is also a mode of knowing and an approach to truth and how this could be seen in relation to perhaps more intuitive ways of knowing.[64]

(c) Dialogue With Primal Cultures

The DFI had not given much attention to the dialogue with "primal cultures," and what attention it had given to it, for example, the Ibadan consultation in 1973, had stressed the inner dialogue of Christians with their own cultural roots. Dr. Samartha cited the lack of real dialogue partners as one of the main reasons for this lack of attention.[65] As part of the DFI's plans to hold bilateral meetings on the question of faith and science, though, the Working Group approved

the plans underway to hold a meeting at Yaoundé, Cameroon, under the theme, "Religious Experience in Humankind's Relation With Nature," with special reference to
what primal religions could contribute to this theme.
The Working Group also hoped that this consultation
would make some suggestions on specific guidelines for
dialogue with the primal faiths and cultures.[66]

4. The Yaoundé Meeting

The third meeting dealing with the general theme
of humankind's relation to nature and the problems of
science and technology planned by the DFI involved a
discussion of the "primal" world-views and values. It
was held at Yaoundé, Cameroon, September 15-23, 1978.[67]
Unlike the other two meetings held on this theme, this
meeting was primarily an intra-Christian meeting, and
although there were Christians from Asia, Oceania,
North and South America, and Europe, most of the discussions centered around primal religious experiences
and world-views in Africa. There were papers presented
on three main topics: (1) the origin and destiny of the
world (myths of cosmogony),[68] (2) the human person in
relation with nature (anthropological reflections),[69]
and (3) the Church and local culture.[70] The papers, as
the accompanying notes show, dealt mainly with convey-
ing information about the customs, beliefs, and symbols
in primal African cultures.

The reports of the discussions and the recommendations that were made at this meeting exemplify a
basic feature of dialogue as it was attempted with primal world-views, namely, a sincere respect for and a
positive evaluation of the values inherent in these
world views. For example, referring to the way traditional cultures deal with views of life and death, the

consultation made the following recommendation to the WCC churches:

> [Christians should] make every effort to identify, respect, renew and assimilate the positive values of traditional societies and, in particular, their reverence for life, their reverence for the dead, the continuity between this life and the hereafter, the belief that this earthly life conditions the future life and that there is justice after death . . . . [71]

The recommendations also exemplify the sincere desire to assimilate the values of traditional cultures into a truly indigenous form of Christianity. Thus the churches are urged, among other things,

> 2. To do all they can to ensure that the Christian rites match the daily needs of Christians in their specific society and environment, by interpreting certain traditional rites and symbols in a Christian sense.

> 3. With this object in view, to revise the traditional rituals of the churches, enriching them in the process with the spiritual experiences of the younger churches.

> 4. To encourage the communities of religious orders to embody in their community life the values of traditional spirituality and to interpret them in terms of their Christian religious vocation. [72]

IV. The Kingston Guidelines

The final statement on dialogue which this study
will examine is the statement approved by the Central
Committee of the WCC at its meeting in Kingston, Jamaica, in 1979, the "Guidelines on Dialogue With People of
Living Faiths and Ideologies." Although it is not a DFI
statement, the DFI played a major role in determining
its shape. In fact, with exceptions which will be
brought out, the Kingston guidelines on dialogue repeat
almost verbatim the Chiang Mai declaration, "Dialogue
in Community." Moreover, since the Central Committee is
the WCC's governing body, its directives determine the
course of action taken by the various units that make
up the WCC, including, in this case, the DFI.

1. Dialogue in the Kingston Guidelines

In accordance with the context for dialogue that
the DFI had emphasized, namely, dialogue in community,
the Kingston guidelines first of all sketch out what is
meant by community. The guidelines follow Chiang Mai
very closely. It is part of human nature and the divine
plan, the guidelines say, that men and women live in
communities. But it is a feature of the world that
there are a great many communities. Moreover, in today's world as never before, people from different communities with their different cultures are being thrust
together. Formerly isolated communities are having to
face up to the challenges of contact with other communities and cultural interaction is thus a common phenomenon. It is in this situation that Christians, along
with all other men and women in the world, must rethink
their identities.[73]

The Kingston guidelines, as the Chiang Mai statement before them, stress the positive aspects of the

religious and cultural diversity that characterizes the
world. While not unmindful of the tensions and problems
such diversity can cause, the guidelines see this diversity as a richness "created and sustained by God."[74]
They call for a creative, non-hostile, non-competitive
encounter of the various religions and ideologies of
the world for the good of humankind as a whole. They
call for all religions and ideologies to cooperate, to
use their resources to build up, not only their own
communities, but the entire human community. The guidelines do not want to imply that each distinctive religious or ideological community give up its own distinct
identity, but rather that each contribute from its dis-
tinctiveness to the good of all. Thus the idea envisaged is a "community of communities." In a way which
insists on the role of individual communities in contributing to the good of the whole in a manner more em-
phatic than at Chiang Mai, the Kingston guidelines say,

> At the Colombo consultation of 1974 the vi-
> sion of a worldwide "community of communi-
> ties" was discussed. Such a vision may be
> helpful in the search for community in a plu-
> ralistic world; it is not one of homogeneous
> unity or totalitarian uniformity, nor does it
> envisage self-contained communities, simply
> co-existing. Rather it emphasizes the posi-
> tive part which existing communities may play
> in developing the community of humankind.[75]

It is in the context of the search for community,
world community especially, but also community at the
local level, that the Kingston guidelines discuss dialogue. There is, one must note, no simple definition
of dialogue. The guidelines from Kingston, as most of

the DFI statements before them, do however indicate
that dialogue involves a sharing on the deepest level
of one's convictions and beliefs. Through dialogue, one
comes to know the other truly. It presupposes mutual
respect and openness to the other. Dialogue involves
more than the holding of formal meetings, as well. It
is in essence a **style of life** characterized by cooperation, the willingness to listen and learn, and a sincere esteem for the other's position. The Kingston
guidelines thus say,

> No more than "community" can "dialogue"
> be precisely defined. Rather it has to be de-
> scribed, experienced and developed as a life-
> style. As human beings we have learned to
> speak; we talk, chatter, give and receive in-
> formation, have discussions--all this is not
> yet dialogue. Now and then it happens that
> out of our talking and our relationships
> arises a deeper encounter, an opening up, in
> more than intellectual terms, of each to the
> concerns of the other. . . . Dialogue helps
> us not to disfigure the image of our neigh-
> bours of different faiths and ideologies. It
> has been the experience of many Christians
> that this dialogue is indeed possible on the
> basis of a mutual trust and a respect for the
> integrity of each participant's identity.[76]

In order to allay persistent fears that dialogue
is a betrayal of the Christian mission to preach Jesus
as Lord and Saviour of all and the view that it is an
esoteric concern of a few Christians, the Kingston
guidelines repeat the insistence seen throughout the
DFI's work that dialogue is, in fact, a legitimate

Christian activity in today's world. The guidelines describe dialogue as a means of expressing the commitment
Christians have to love all people. Dialogue is a form
of service within the community in which Christians
live, a way for Christians to participate in the building up of a better human community, thereby showing
their loving concern.[77] Moreover, through dialogue, the
Christian is able to witness to his or her deepest convictions and thus witness to Christ. Dialogue is not a
betrayal, then, of the Christian duty to witness to
Christ. The introductory section of the Kingston guidelines therefore repeat the words of Chiang Mai,

> The words "mission" and "evangelism" are not
> often used in this statement. This is not be-
> cause of any desire to escape the Christian
> responsibility, re-emphasized in the Nairobi
> Assembly, to confess Christ today, but in or-
> der to explore other ways of making plain the
> intentions of Christian witness and service.
> Christian integrity includes an integrity of
> response to the call of the risen Christ to
> be witnesses to Him in all the world.[78]

2. Theological Reflections and Concerns
in the Kingston Guidelines

Much as the comments on dialogue in the Kingston
guidelines repeat in essence those that had emerged at
Chiang Mai, so too the underlying theological tensions
of the Chiang Mai statement reappear in these later
guidelines. A rather surprising statement, though, does
emerge in the Kingston guidelines in their identifica-
tion of questions needing further reflection: whereas
the Chiang Mai statement had said that Christians had
to reflect upon the relationship between the universal

action of God in creation and the redemptive action of
God in Jesus Christ, the Kingston guidelines, following the draft of the DFI's Trinidad Working Group meeting, phrase this question as follows:

> What is the relation between the universal
> creative/**redemptive** activity of God towards
> all humankind and the particular creative/re-
> demptive activity of God in the history of
> Israel and in the person and work of Jesus
> Christ?[79]

As they stand, the Kingston guidelines seem to affirm
that God's universal creative work in the world **is** redemptive, and the problem remaining is simply how to
relate this redemptive work to the redemptive work that
takes place with the person and mission of Jesus
Christ. Yet this question--is God's presence and activity in creation at large redemptive?--is one that has
not before been answered affirmatively on the official
level.

On the other hand, the theological question which
follows the above affirmation in the guidelines serves
to mitigate this seemingly radical statement. It asks
whether there is any real self-disclosure of God in the
lives of other peoples, that is, is there an extra-
Christian divine revelation?[80] Since in the Christian
understanding, God's self-revelation is a necessary
prerequisite for human salvation, the apparent affirmation of God's saving work everywhere in creation and
the question of the presence of divine revelatory activity everywhere seem to be at odds. Because of this
unresolved question within the ranks of the WCC
churches over the locus of God's revelatory work, the
question of the divine saving work of God among people

of non-Christian faiths remains, it seems to me, up in the air. The Kingston guidelines reflect the uncertainty within the ranks of the WCC.

In the rest of its theological considerations, the Kingston guidelines repeat in substance the ideas of the Chiang Mai statement. Thus while saying that the Bible must be the basis for the Church's reflections on interreligious dialogue, the guidelines also admit the difficulty in this: all sides use the Bible to ground their affirmations, yet there continue to be very different approaches and criteria employed. The guidelines also ask whether the symbol of the Holy Spirit is a useful one in understanding God's extra-ecclesial work, a reference to what Dr. Samartha had identified as the "Orthodox" approach to this question.[81] Finally, the guidelines note the question of syncretism with its fear that the Gospel message will somehow be mitigated. They take, however, the often repeated approach to this latter question, namely, it is necessary to move out into the unchartered, dangerous waters of dialogue. Not to engage in it is to fail to respond to the needs of the time.[82]

V. Summary Observations

The new guidelines which the Central Committee issued in 1979 reflect very much the underlying tensions within the WCC community, tensions which have been in fact present throughout the entire period of the DFI's activity up to 1979. There is quite simply a lack of full consensus on the basic understanding Christians should have of their non-Christian neighbours and their religious traditions. The question of God's revealing presence outside of the Christian community clearly remains an unresolved question, as does the question of

the nature and locus of the divine saving activity.
Very closely connected with these questions is the
question of the view of Christ that informs the positions seen. An exclusive Christ has been contrasted to
an anonymous "cosmic" Christ, for example. Thus the
fundamental issues of the revealing presence of God,
the saving work of God, and the person and mission of
Jesus Christ, so important in any theological evaluation of religions, have remained contested. There is no
consistent theological evaluation of the world's religions evident in the DFI's work. Even dialogue itself,
which the officials of the DFI hoped would serve to
settle some of these questions, remained a controversial activity since the fear persisted that it was un-
dercutting the missionary mandate of the Church. Nonetheless, there was progress concerning the charge that
dialogue was a betrayal of Christian commitment.
Through dialogue, Christians could witness to their
faith. Dialogue did not necessarily result in any lessening of the integrity of one's faith commitment.

The new guidelines also demonstrate that the insistence by the DFI that dialogue be geared towards the
bettering of the communities in which Christians and
their neighbours of other faiths live has been accepted. Dialogue is a style of life which is directed
towards living in community, fostering cooperation, understanding, and mutual respect with men and women who
do not share the Christian faith. It is this emphasis
that is perhaps the most important aspect of the DFI's
dialogue activity in the preceding chapters. In an increasingly interdependent world, living in dialogue has
become a way for Christians to witness to and make real
their love for all by their lives.

PART THREE
**Dialogue and the Development
of an Adequate Theology of Religions**

CHAPTER SEVEN
DIALOGUE AND ITS THEOLOGICAL IMPLICATIONS
A SUMMARY AND CRITICAL REFLECTIONS

In the preceding chapters of this study, I have attempted to examine the dialogue activity of the Roman Catholic Church's Secretariat for Non-Christians and the World Council of Churches' Sub-Unit for Dialogue With People of Living Faiths and Ideologies. I have concentrated on major statements and publications emerging as a result of the work of these two organizations, important meetings they have held, and reflections by some of their key personnel. My intent has been to document what these two groups have been able to say about dialogue as an approach in interreligious relations and to discern the theological problems that have accompanied their activity. In this concluding section, I intend to summarize and critique some of the significant features of the dialogue work and the theological reflection accompanying it that I have examined, comparing and contrasting the work and thought of the two organizations studied when appropriate. I will end by outlining the directions I think Christian theology can and should take in the question of interreligious relations and their theological implications.

I. Features of Interreligious Dialogue

1. The Multivalent Nature of Dialogue

Dialogue, with its emphasis on respect for the religious affirmations of the other and its willingness to learn from the other, is a new way for Christians

to interact with the men and women of other religious
traditions. The World Council of Churches has called it
a "common adventure" to be undertaken by its member
churches and has referred to the movement into dialogue
as a movement into "unchartered waters." Both the Vatican's Secretariat for Non-Christians and the WCC's dialogue sub-unit have had to justify dialogue as a legitimate form of Christian activity. It is readily apparent from the preceding chapters of this study,
though, that dialogue is a multivalent activity. It assumes a number of forms and has a variety of objectives
depending on the social milieu in which the prospective
dialogue partners live and the history of interreligious relations that has pertained in that milieu. I
would like to point out and comment on four types of
dialogue that I think can be discerned in the activity of the dialogue groups examined in the previous
chapters.

(a) Informational Dialogue

One of the most basic types of dialogue that has
been promoted by the dialogue agencies studied is dialogue aimed simply at getting to know people of other religious traditions and the religious world view
they have. In this form of dialogue, each participant
makes an effort to come to an unbiased and accurate
knowledge of what the other actually believes. Knowledge of the other is, of course, a necessary first step
in any relationship, and it is especially important in
areas where interreligious rivalry has been prominent.
The hope expressed by the two dialogue groups examined
has been that harmful misinformation and prejudices can
be dispelled and, through personal contact, an atmosphere of cordiality be promoted.

In the work of the Secretariat for Non-Christians and that of the DFI, there has indeed been an effort to promote this type of dialogue. It has been perhaps most emphasized in the work of the Secretariat. In the case of this agency, much activity has been spent in efforts to prepare those planning to engage in inter-religious dialogue by means of dialogue guidebooks which are largely concerned with providing an accurate picture of the major religious traditions of the world. These efforts to encourage better understanding by Christians of the religious affirmations of others have been complemented to some extent by the participation by members of the Secretariat in actual interreligious dialogues, most of them being sponsored by the DFI. The DFI, for its part, has the task of implementing the WCC guidelines on dialogue which recommend that Christians learn more about the religious affirmations of others, although as an agency, it has not itself published and distributed information about them.

This type of dialogue is absolutely fundamental. Any attempt to make statements about others from the Christian perspective must begin with a true knowledge of the "what" of the situation. What are we talking about when it comes to a particular religious tradition that has not developed in our cultural setting? What sort of people are those "others" whom we meet? What ideals, hopes, fears, world-view do they have? Without this basic information, it is impossible to formulate adequate theological positions about the world's religions and their followers simply because basic data is missing.

Such dialogue, however, is not enough. It is a minimal first step. It is quite possible that this kind of dialogue simply leads to interesting discussions

with the participants going on their separate ways once
it is over. Yet, it is a necessary step, and perhaps
an easy one to take at the beginning of any attempt to
establish harmonious relations. It does provide a context for people to come together and actually think
about, even meet, others whose religious convictions
are different. It may be a catalyst for establishing an
harmonious mood in interreligious relations, and mood,
as I shall argue below, is an important factor in the
development of religious positions.

(b) Solving Common Problems

A second major type of dialogue that has received
mention by the two dialogue groups examined has been
dialogue aimed at resolving problems faced by members
of a local community or the world community at large.
This is a type of dialogue which the emergence of pluralistic societies and the awareness of the interdependence of all people everywhere has made possible and
necessary. Christians are called upon to cooperate with
others, not close themselves off from others, and in so
doing demonstrate their loving concern for the well-be-
ing of all.

In this type of dialogue, one sees a call to the
various religious communities to see what their particular religious traditions can contribute towards resolving problems. The DFI dialogue meetings on the
question of science and technology examined in the last
chapter are examples. In these dialogue meetings, the
participants were asked to look at their respective
traditions to see if there are directions indicated in
them for answers as to how humanity can best use science and technology and live in harmony with nature.
One can see this type of dialogue in the work and

thought of the Secretariat for Non-Christians, too, in
what the Secretariat calls dialogue on the "human"
level.

Dialogue for the purpose of solving common human
problems has been a major focus of attention in the dialogue activity of the DFI. The theme of "dialogue in
community" that one sees in its work involves the
search for resources in the religious traditions involved that aid in the building up of the community in
which the participants in the dialogue live.

Dialogue geared towards resolving common problems
presupposes that the followers of the world's religious
traditions should be actively involved in promoting
peace, justice, and good will in their local community and in the larger global community. This dialogue
calls for more than furthering peaceful coexistence
among the parties concerned. It is a dialogue demanding a common search for resources and answers in building up a better world in which all participants have a
real stake and an equal share.

Dialogue investigating how to cooperate in solving
pressing human problems is, I think, the most important
type of dialogue going on today. There is little doubt
that solutions to the major problems of the world demand international cooperation. Even solutions in individual nations require cooperation among peoples of
different religious traditions because of the increasingly pluralistic nature of many countries. What this
type of dialogue will show, I rather suspect, however,
is that there are tremendous differences not primarily between religious communities but between groups
within those communities adopting different social, political, and economic perspectives. What may very well
emerge, then, are groups that may be religiously di-

verse, yet which share social and political views that
conflict with those of others in their own religious
tradition. Religion will be seen to be of secondary importance, and socio-political analysis will occupy the
primary place. Interestingly, this type of dialogue may
further friendly relations between people of different
religious perspectives and contribute to tensions among
people sharing the same religious tradition.

(c) Seeking Truth

There is a third type of dialogue that can be
loosely called a mutual search for truth. It aims at
mutual enrichment and edification as the dialogue partners share their respective insights into the nature of
reality. It is dialogue, then, which goes beyond the
mere understanding of the views of the dialogue partner. Since the sort of dialogue discussed in this study
is dialogue among believers committed to religious traditions, a central place in this type of dialogue is
discussion about God or the Ultimate or the transcendent dimension of reality and how humankind is related
to it.

Insofar as the Secretariat for Non-Christians is
concerned, this type of dialogue rests first of all on
the recognition of the natural goodness and virtue
which are present in creation and which are present in
the religious traditions that have developed in human
history. Both dialogue partners can, it is hoped, come
to a fuller understanding of this natural goodness
through their dialogue. There is, however, another dimension to this type of dialogue in the reflections of
the Secretariat. In the theological views seen in this
body, there has been present the view that God has revealed the divine Self in a "supernatural" way and is

salvifically present everywhere, even, perhaps, in the
religions of humanity. Christians, through dialogue,
then, may discover something of this ubiquitous presence and activity and thus discover something more fully about God and the divine dealings with humankind. On
the part of non-Christians, one should note, this type
of dialogue involves a coming to the awareness of the
truth that has been revealed in Jesus Christ. The Secretariat's officials assume in everything they say that
it is in Jesus Christ that the fullness of God's self-
revelation to humankind has occurred.

For its part, while the DFI could not unequivocal-
ly say that God is present in a "supernatural" and
salvific way in the religions of the world, one can
also see in its work this notion that dialogue can
bring about a mutual enrichment of the dialogue partners. This idea is expressed more in terms of a hope,
though. Christians may be able to enlarge their understanding of God by becoming sensitive, through dialogue, to the divine presence to people of other religious traditions, should such a presence in fact exist.
There are indications of where some of those engaged in
dialogue want to find this presence: it is in the reconciliation and transformation of human beings as they
struggle to build up more loving communities. Christians can become more aware of God's transforming presence through their dialogue.

(d) Indigenization

A fourth type of dialogue that has emerged in the
work of the two organizations examined is dialogue
aimed at the indigenization of Christianity. In the actual dialogues studied, this form of dialogue has taken
place particularly in Africa and has involved primar-

ily Christians engaged in what is termed an "inner" dialogue. African Christians, in this dialogue, have been
seen attempting to come to grips with their traditional
spiritual resources so that they can express Christianity in an African and not a European way. This dialogue
presupposes some real good in the African religious
traditions. It is based upon the recognition that
Christianity is an historically and culturally conditioned religion, like all other religions, and so is
open to cultural transformations. The outcome of this
form of dialogue is unclear, at present, since what
shape a non-Western Christianity would take is impossible to determine in advance. The attempt is being
made, however, in theory, a movement away from a western dominated Christianity has begun.

The concerns and presuppositions of this type of
dialogue have profound implications on all religious
traditions. There is manifest in this sort of dialogue
a movement away from seeing religious writings and doctrines as kinds of immutable truths which have dropped
down from heaven, as it were. Rather, it reflects a
growing awareness that what religious traditions say
about God and about reality involves the cultural situation of the human beings involved. Religious writings
and doctrines seem to be human attempts to express insights into reality. Christians, and many other religious people, would say that these insights are a result of an experience of that ultimate reality, God,
but nonetheless this experience is understood and
talked about by human beings who must rely on the categories, symbols, and language of their culture to say
anything at all. This understanding of things has not
really been seriously thought out by any religious tradition, it seems to me. The desire for some form of

"indigenization" is a step towards working out what it actually involves.

2. The Inevitable Tension in Dialogue

In all of the reflections and statements on dialogue that have been seen in the course of this book, there is a crucial feature of dialogue that is constantly present: dialogue involves a certain and necessary tension. By this I mean that a dialogical approach to people affirming religious world views other than one's own implies that one respects these other positions while at the same time affirming the truth of one's own. Mgr. Rossano has perhaps best expressed this when he said in a statement worth repeating,

> Each of the parties has the right of adhering to his absolute, of feeling basically sure of his own position. He has the right (and the duty, if he is a Christian) to think that the other is not achieving human and religious fullness as willed by God. A Christian cannot place his own faith and other religions on the same level. He cannot hold that the Holy Spirit dwells equally in the Church, in Hinduism and in the dar-es-Islam. There cannot be agreement that each party in the dialogue is equally in the truth, or that different religions are only cultural and historical expressions of a transcendent one; otherwise there would be no good reason for having dialogue at all. There must be a certain tension by the very nature of the case.[1]

Dialogue, then, does not necessitate any watering-down of one's own position or that of the dialogue partner.

This refrain is constantly present as well in the dialogue statements of the DFI. In fact, one of the consequences of dialogue seems to be that the real differences that separate the dialogue partners are brought
to light in all their starkness. The intention is not
to arrive at some lowest common denominator in the hope
of reaching an irenic common ground in religious affirmations.

     This attitude of respect for differences in reli-
gious perspectives on the part of those engaged in interreligious dialogue may simply be a practical attitude taken by people who, in a pluralistic world, want
to live in peace and harmony with those who do not
share their religious perspectives. On the other hand,
it can also give rise to a genuine appreciation of the
value of plurality and the view that the best community is a community of communities. This appreciation has
indeed emerged in the statements coming from the WCC.
The Chiang Mai consultation and, following it, the 1979
Kingston guidelines specifically praise plurality as a
good thing. The model of human community that informs
this view is that of an organic body in which the various parts retain their identities, yet contribute in
a special way to the good of the whole. This attitude
presupposes that religious communities act in a cooperative, respectful way towards one another, contributing from their own particular resources and perspectives towards the building up of the human community.
It presupposes that the building up of just and loving
human communities is the proper way for one to serve
God.

     Both the DFI and the Secretariat for Non-Chris-
tians have taken great pains to insist on the tension
inherent in dialogue because of the continual fears

that dialogue leads to what has been called "syncretism." Openness to the religious convictions of non-
Christians has been seen as a tendency that leads to a
loss of the transcendent and judging truth of the Gospel message of Jesus Christ.[2] This objection has been
especially pronounced in WCC circles and surfaced in a
major way during the 1975 general assembly at Nairobi.
Thus both the Vatican's Secretariat and the DFI, for
the sake of their Christian audiences, have been quick
to emphasize that all partners in dialogue, including
then the Christian partner, have the right to remain
firmly committed to their perspective faiths in all
their integrity.

3. The Persistent Problem of Mission

The insistence that the dialogue partners be allowed to remain firmly committed to their respective
faiths has played a role in what has been the most persistent problem faced by the DFI and the Secretariat
for Non-Christians, namely, the problem of mission. The
problem can be summarized as follows. For much of its
history, Christianity has been a missionary religious
movement geared towards persuading non-Christians to
becoming followers of Jesus Christ by being baptized in
his name, thereby becoming members of the Christian
Church. Dialogue with the followers of other religious
traditions seems to be a shift in this in that dialogue
does not aim at conversion. The fear that dialogue actually downplays conversion has been apparent as the
DFI and the Secretariat have pursued their activity. On
the other hand, one must note, there is the underlying
suspicion by prospective dialogue partners that dialogue is a new strategy now employed by Christians to
convert them, other methods no longer being effective.[3]

The position that emerges from the documents of
the Secretariat for Non-Christians and from the statements of its officials, notably Mgr. Rossano, concerning the relationship between dialogue and mission has
been fairly consistent. These have insisted that dialogue and mission are separate activities, yet they also show that in the minds of those running the Secretariat dialogue is an activity carried on in the context of a Church which is essentially missionary. Thus
one sees statements which affirm that dialogue is a
means of contacting people who would be closed to missionary activity properly speaking. Dialogue becomes a
way of sowing the "seeds" of the Gospel message. Those
engaged in dialogue are those who plant the seeds,
while others, missionary workers in the true sense,
will reap the harvest. The "harvest" is the conversion
of the non-Christian to the Christian faith. Dialogue
is, in this line of thinking, a form of pre-evangelism.
It is a step in the ongoing process of spreading the
Christian message. The hope, and indeed the expectation, is that those who hear the message will eventually be converted and so fulfilled by it. Yet, as Mgr.
Rossano's remarks show about letting the other retain
his or her absolute, and as the earlier insistence that
dialogue and mission are separate activities indicates,
the Christian in dialogue is willing to allow the other to remain in his or her religion and respect that
other's convictions.

There are, in fact, explicit denunciations of aggressive, militant attempts by Christians to convert
others. These attempts at "proselytism" which do not
respect the freedom of the other to retain his or her
absolute receive such denunciation, for example, in
Christian-Muslim dialogues. The Vatican's 1984 state-

ment on dialogue insists that the search for religious truth must be carried out freely. Intense rivalry and animosity have characterized Christian-Muslim relations in the past and so one of the first steps in setting up friendly relations has been that of condemning overt, militant missionary pressure.

A view of dialogue which allows the other to retain his or her faith commitment is understandable if one recognizes the saving presence of God outside the boundaries of the visible Church, as the Secretariat indeed does. The motive for wanting to convert the other is not to save them from certain damnation, then, but to share with them the good news Christians perceive in the message of Jesus Christ. Dialogue does not rule out a desire to convert the other, but it does rule out the desire to do so in an aggressive way that does not respect the faith of the other.

In the work of the DFI, the major term that dominates the issue of dialogue and mission is that of "witness." While there is no condemnation of conversion, neither is there any mention of conversion even as a future hope in the process of dialogue. The DFI shares with the Secretariat, however, the view that there should be no aggressive proselytism. Whatever form missionary activity takes, it must not impede the search for a better human community and must not lead to division and rivalry.

4. Some Final Comments on Dialogue

The dialogue activity as it has actually been practiced by the agencies examined in this study has involved primarily the followers of humankind's major religious traditions. There is nothing about the notion of dialogue, however, to restrict it in this way, and

neither the DFI nor the Secretariat for Non-Christians
has discouraged dialogue with all interested parties.
It remains to be seen if their respective activity will
begin to embrace religions such as the Ba'hai faith,
for example.

There are, however, difficulties in the quest for
increasing dialogue encounters. The most serious is the
willingness on the part of followers of even major religious traditions to engage in dialogue. Dialogue demands respect for the other and the willingness to allow the other to remain committed to his or her faith
position. This is not an attitude that has been too apparent in the religious history of humankind, especially in the West. One can seriously raise the question as
to whether the movement towards dialogue reflects only
the attitude of a few, the majority of the followers of
the religions of the world remaining largely uncon-
cerned.

II. Dialogue and a Theological Evaluation of
Religions: Observations and Critique

1. Observations on the Theology of Religions
in the Secretariat for Non-Christians

The dialogue activity of the Secretariat for Non-
Christians has been accompanied by a rather consistent
theological evaluation of humankind's religions. Since
I have already discussed the major elements of this
evaluation in some detail in the first major section of
this study, I will not go into it in great detail here.
There are, though, some important features of it that
are worth repeating for purposes of evaluation. Perhaps
the most important, because it contrasts with a tendency to deny it in some of the Protestant theology stud-

ied and because it grounds an openness to the positions of other religious traditions, is the willingness to affirm the effective saving and revealing presence of God beyond the explicit boundaries of Christianity. This is coupled with the understanding of humankind as essentially religious, that is, as naturally seeking after some transcendent God or Absolute. The religious traditions of humankind, then, represent the social expressions of the quest for God and (here is where the views seen in the Secretariat are important) they may (and probably do) capture something of the divine revealing outreach to all men and women. The religious history of humankind is not, in other words, merely a "natural" history, representing only humankind's drive for the Absolute. It is a history that embodies the human quest for God **and** the divine outreach to humankind.

The acknowledgement that God is salvifically present beyond the confines of the Church and that there can be genuine revelatory experiences of God in the religious traditions of humankind that do not recognize Christ provides an important theological basis for interreligious dialogue and gives to such dialogue the possibility for enrichment on the part of the dialogue partners. Given this view, then, whenever Christians meet with men and women of other religious traditions, they are encountering people whose lives are touched by God and who perceive (although perhaps dimly) and make thematic (however imperfectly) this divine presence.

In spite of the affirmations that the religious history of humankind everywhere can reflect God's revelatory presence, however, the theological evaluation of this history which accompanies the Secretariat's dialogue activity separates Christianity, or the Church, from other religious traditions in a way that makes

Christianity superior. There is a constant affirmation
that only Christianity is based upon the fullness of
God's revelation, the revelation of God in the person
and life of Jesus Christ. Other religious traditions
have at best "traces" of God's revelatory activity.
Moreover, there is in the Secretariat a continued insistence on the superiority of Christianity in mediating the divine saving grace to humankind. The Church
has the means of salvation which mediate God's grace.
These means are primarily the preaching of the Word and
the administration of the sacraments. The Church is the
ordinary means of salvation for all. While it is possible for those outside the Church to be saved, there
is extreme reluctance to admit that they can be saved
by means of their particular religious traditions.[4]

This latter aspect of the views found in the Secretariat deserves further comment. It does not mean
that other religions play no part at all in God's saving work. There is repeated insistence that non-Christian religious traditions can be the **occasions** for
their followers to be open to God's saving grace. Yet
these religions do not, by their rites and beliefs, mediate this grace. Those who are saved outside of the
Church are saved by God's extraordinary presence, in a
mysterious way.

The dominant view of the non-Christian religions
that one sees in the theological reflection accompanying the Secretariat's work is that they are "preparations" for the Gospel and for the salvation mediated in
the Church. They remain ambiguous, reflecting both the
"traces" of God's supernatural presence as well as the
sinful opposition of humankind to God. What these religions teach and the way of life they promote must be
purified, elevated, and transformed by an encounter

with Christ. This does not mean, it is important to
note, that all peoples of the world are called upon to
copy a model of Christianity that is European. The dialogue activity in Africa studied in the preceding
chapters shows an openness towards an indigenization of
the Gospel, at least in principle. Yet what is hoped
for is an African **Christianity** (and, by extension, an
Indian or a Japanese Christianity). There is no notion
that it may be a good thing to allow the other religious traditions to persist in their integrity.

2. Some Critical Reflections on the Theology
   in the Secretariat for Non-Christians

One of the recurring questions that can be seen in
the theological reflections of the Secretariat's official publications and in the comments of its key personnel, especially Mgr. Rossano, is the question of
whether non-Christian religions can be considered "ways
of salvation." That is, can the followers of these religions be saved and thus fulfilled by means of the
truths these religions propose, the morality they promote, and the rituals they celebrate? Do these things
mediate God's saving grace? What strikes one on reading the remarks on this matter in the Secretariat is
that there is a real hesitancy to answer this question
affirmatively. The early answer of the 1965 Consultors'
meeting was that the non-Christian religions "in themselves" do not mediate God's salvation although God can
and probably does use the "good" elements in these religions to arouse an implicit faith on the part of
their followers. This same general view appears in the
Secretariat's dialogue guidebooks and in the remarks of
Mgr. Rossano.

What these remarks mean is that non-Christian re-

ligions are not what the Secretariat calls the "ordinary" means of salvation willed by God to mediate the
divine saving offer to humankind. They can be, though,
the occasion for "extraordinary" means of salvation.
Yet these remarks seen in the Secretariat are, I think,
too hesitant and negative. As an example of what I
would call the overly hesitant statements one sees in
the Secretariat on this matter, I would like to recall
a quotation from Mgr. Rossano that I think captures
this view:

> . . . the hypothesis which considers the non-
> Christian religions as positive and parallel
> ways of salvation, instituted by God, even if
> of an inferior quality to the Church, seems
> . . . irreconcilable with the biblical per-
> spective.[5]

Mgr. Rossano does not at all deny that the non-Christian religions can, in a sense, mediate God's salvation. They can to the extent that they make an implicit faith in Christ possible. Why not, then, call them
positive "ways of salvation," even if only provisional ones? Why cannot the divine saving and revealing activity be considered as part of their fundamental
structure and as standing at their base and so, in that
sense, why cannot they be seen as "instituted" and
"willed" by God?

    This reluctance to say that the non-Christian re-
ligions can be "positive" ways of salvation, even
willed by God, is unnecessary and even somewhat contrary to tendencies in the thinking seen in the Secretariat itself. There are indeed many aspects of the theology seen in the Secretariat that would lend themselves to what I would see as a legitimately more pos-

itive and less hesitant view of the non-Christian religions. Chief among these is the affirmation that God
is salvifically present everywhere, even possibly in
the religions of the world. The Secretariat has also
affirmed the social nature of human existence and has
praised the non-Christian religions as social expressions of humankind's response to God's presence and activity. These ideas lend themselves to a more positive
view of the world's religions, a view that one can see
in the remarks of, for example, Karl Rahner. I would
like to highlight something of Rahner's view again
briefly as a critique of the Secretariat's hesitant and
ambiguous view of the non-Christian religions of the
world.

Rahner takes very seriously the notion that God
wills the salvation of all men and women and accordingly asserts that all people, everywhere, must live in a
situation where they can be open to and respond to the
divine saving presence. However, because men and women
are essentially social beings, Rahner goes on to argue,
the divine offer and the human response inevitably take
on a social, institutional character. The experience of
a particular person of God and God's saving presence is
never without some form of social mediation. Among the
social institutions in which this experience happens,
says Rahner, one must consider the religious traditions
of the society in which a person happens to be raised.
That religion ought to be considered a "legitimate" way
of salvation because in it a person encounters and responds to God. In a statement that summarizes this
view, Rahner writes,

> . . . by the fact that man as he really is
> can live his proffered relationship to God
> only in society, man must have had the right

and indeed the duty to live this his relationship to God within the religious and social realities offered to him in his particular historical situation.[6]

Such a view, one should note, need not at all imply that Christianity and other religions are equal, a
view that Mgr. Rossano, especially, reacts against. It
only affirms that the religion of a society can be a
legitimate and positive way of salvation, willed by
God, providing the social structures by which the divine saving grace is encountered and responded to.

3. Observations on the Theological Reflections
in the Work of the DFI

Whereas there is a rather consistent and singular
vision of humankind's religious history and the value
of non-Christian religions in the dialogue activity of
the Secretariat for Non-Christians, this is not the
case in that of the DFI. A coherent theological evaluation of the religions of the world has remained impossible throughout its work. The reason for this, of
course, lies in the great diversity of theological positions within the WCC which the DFI has to take into
account. As a result, key questions pertinent to a theology of religions remain continually unanswered, one
of the most important being the nature of the relationship between God's activity and presence in creation in
general and this activity and presence in the Christ-
event in particular. The question is made all the more
serious because there is no consensus on the issue of
whether the divine presence in creation at large is
salvific or grounds any significant revelatory experience. The persistence of these questions shows the influence that "neo-orthodox" tendencies continue to have

in WCC circles, tendencies based on views found in the
Christian scriptures themselves.

4. Some Critical Reflections on the Theological Problems Seen in the Work of the DFI

The problem within the ranks of the WCC that makes
it impossible for the DFI to articulate a consistent
theology rests on the extreme Christomonism held within the ranks of the WCC, reference to which has been
made in the course of this book. This Christomonism
results in a very exclusivist view of God's dealings
with humankind that in effect relegates those who do
not have explicit contact with the Gospel message of
Christ to a position of ignorance about God, in effect
placing them beyond the pale of salvation. Such a
Christomonistic view, while it may have been understandable in times when Christians thought that all
people everywhere had effectively heard the Gospel message and could respond to it, is surely unacceptable
today.[7] We are increasingly aware of the powerful influence of culture and social institutions in shaping
and reinforcing human consciousness, including one's
religious perspectives, and we are aware of the cultur-
ally-conditioned manner in which the Gospel message is
couched. This message, then, is often seen as alien,
and one cannot claim that it has such an immediate appeal that it necessitates a decision for or against
Christ such that to reject it is to reject God.[8] The
majority of people in the world, if they are to receive
and respond to God's offer of salvation, must do so
without any significant reference to Christ and to the
Christian Church. It is an offence to the Christian
view of a loving God who desires that all people be
saved to have a theological perspective which condemns

most of the human race. In a summary of this problem,
written from a perspective that shows an association
with an exclusivist position, John Hick, a contemporary philosopher of religion, says,

> We say as Christians that God is the God of
> universal love, that he is the creator and
> Father of all mankind, that he wills the ultimate good and salvation of all men. But we
> also say, traditionally, that the only way to
> salvation is the Christian way. And yet we
> know, when we stop to think about it, that
> the large majority of the human race who have
> lived and died up to the present moment, have
> lived either before Christ or outside the
> borders of Christendom. Can we then accept
> the conclusion that the God of love who seeks
> to save all mankind has nevertheless ordained
> that men must be saved in such a way that
> only a small minority can in fact receive
> this salvation? It is the weight of this moral contradiction that has driven Christian
> thinkers in modern times to explore other
> ways of understanding the human religious
> situation.[9]

A critique of an exclusivist Christianity need not
come only from moral abhorrence at the consequences
that it seems to entail. There are, I believe, openings
in the Christian scriptures and in the tradition of
Christianity which do, indeed, extend the saving and
revealing work of God well beyond the boundaries of explicit Christendom and beyond explicit acknowledgement
of Christ. Since most of this has been documented elsewhere, I will simply briefly summarize a number of im-

portant considerations in this regard.[10] These scriptural openings are especially crucial because of the
long tradition in Christianity to argue from Scripture.

There is no doubt that there are texts in the biblical writings which do lead to an exclusivist position. Paul, in his writings, insists on the necessity
of faith in Jesus Christ for salvation, for example,[11]
and Luke has Peter say before the gathered Sanhedrin in
Acts that only in the name of Jesus is salvation to be
found.[12] It is this exclusivist strain that grounds the
Christomonism that has appeared in the course of my examination of the work of the DFI. However, there are
also a few opposing strains in the Christian scriptures
and these have been used in the Christian tradition to
ground a more universal view of God's presence and saving activity. For example, the Wisdom tradition of the
Books of Proverbs, Wisdom, and Sirach, although extremely complex, talks about a personified figure of
Wisdom, the Wisdom of God, who is God's agent in creation[13] and who, significantly, has been poured out
over all creation and who is in creation.[14] The Gospel
of John has taken up the idea of Wisdom which by John's
time has been identified with the Word of God[15] and describes the pre-existent Word/Wisdom as one who was
with God at the beginning, through whom God creates,
and who enlightens everyone who comes into the world.
This Word/Wisdom becomes the historical figure of Jesus.[16] Jesus is God's Word, then, a Word that has already been given to all people. Jesus, who comes from
God and who witnesses to God, is thus continuous with
that which is universally already present.

The idea that God's revelatory presence extends
beyond its historical expression in Jesus Christ and
can be found among all men and women appears very early

among some Christian thinkers. The great second century apologist, Justin, is perhaps the most well known exponent of a form of universal revelation. For Justin, the ability of human beings to enunciate the truth rested on their being in touch with the scattered "seeds" of the divine Logos which, in his middle Platonic world view, permeated all of reality. Thus for Justin the divine Logos was present everywhere and the great pagan philosophers and figures of the Old Testament had given expression to their awareness of this, albeit in an incomplete way. It was in the figure of Jesus that the Logos was completely historically manifest, but all those who had given expression to the Logos in their teachings could be considered Christians before the time of Christ. Justin wrote,

> We have been taught that Christ was First-Begotten of God and . . . that He is the Word [the Logos] of whom all mankind partakes. Those who lived by reason are Christians even though they have been considered atheists: such as, among the Greeks, Socrates, Heraclitus, and others like them; and among the foreigners, Abraham, Elias, Ananias, Azarias, Misael, and many others. . . . So also, they who lived before Christ and did not live by reason were useless men, enemies of Christ, and murderers of those who did live by reason. But those who have lived reasonably, and still do, are Christians, and are fearless and untroubled.[17]

One also sees in Scripture limited references to God's saving activity that have been interpreted as allowing for what in the Roman Catholic tradition has

been called "implicit faith," that is, saving faith
that does not recognize Christ explicitly. An example
of this is reflection on the quotation from Hebrews
11:6: ". . . anyone who comes to God must believe that
he exists and that he rewards those who search for
him." This scriptural quotation was used by such medieval theologians as Peter Lombard and Thomas Aquinas to
talk about the implicit redemptive faith of those who
lived before the time of Christ.[18] The quote does not
mention that one must believe explicitly in Christ to
be rewarded by God, that is, to attain salvation. The
notion of implicit faith came to be a dominant one in
the Roman Catholic tradition about this question and
was extended to include those who, even after Christ,
in good faith do not recognize him as the Saviour.[19]
Another important scriptural affirmation that can
ground the extension of God's saving activity beyond
explicit faith in Jesus Christ is 1 Timothy 2:4 which
says God wills "that all men should find salvation and
come to know the truth." Faced with the fact that all
human beings cannot yet realistically come to know Jesus Christ as Lord and Saviour, this quotation from 1
Timothy serves as a basis for mitigating the harsh demand for explicit faith in Christ. If God wills that
all be saved, God must make it possible for them to be
saved. The idea of an implicit faith is one answer to
the problem.

    It is the latter scriptural quotation about God's
universal saving will and the corresponding idea that
God is a God of love that must, I think, counterbalance
the harshness of other scriptural references that would
make explicit faith in Christ a necessary prerequisite
for salvation. This causes a problem, though. What does
one do with those harsh, exclusivist affirmations? The

answer lies in one's view of Scripture. I want to comment on this more below, but at this time I would like to suggest the following. Scripture must be recognized as written by human beings, human beings responding to their experience of God, but written by human beings nonetheless. Thus Scripture will reflect the limitations that human beings have. There will be exaggerations, mistakes, partial insights, historically-conditioned insights, and the like. This need not deny the idea of "inspiration." It may be useful to see inspiration as a way of expressing the confidence that Christians have that the Scriptures, despite their limitations and their historically-conditioned nature, are authentic witnesses to God and capture, albeit incompletely, saving truth. Rather than looking at Scripture as containing absolute, infallible truths, then, one should see Scripture as containing the "relatively adequate" human responses to God's presence and activity accepted by the early Church as normative.[20] The harsh, exclusivist statements have to be judged in light of the affirmations of God's loving concern for all and of the state of the human condition including the realistic ability for people to encounter Christ in a meaningful way. The Christian communities, in whom God is still present and active, will then have to make further relatively adequate judgments, in the case at hand about the universality of God's saving presence. In this process, of course, Christians believe that the Holy Spirit keeps the Church "on the right track" as it struggles to find adequate ways of expressing its faith in the context of a pluralistic and interdependent world.

III. Towards an Adequate Theology of Religions

The preceding analysis of the dialogue activity of the DFI and the Secretariat for Non-Christians illustrates the concerns of the mainstream Christian communities as they reflect on their own religious affirmations and self-understanding from within the context of an interdependent yet pluralistic world. As I have shown, the Secretariat for Non-Christians does have a consistent theological position; the DFI does not. I would now like to advance a number of suggestions concerning the development of an adequate theology of religions, picking up some of the directions indicated by the dialogue agencies examined and proposing some directions of my own which I think are fruitful.

1. The Important Change in Context and Mood

I want to preface my remarks on the development of an adequate theology of religions by commenting on the new context within which Christian theology must now operate and the resulting new mood such a context helps to foster. The new context is the result of a shift in the awareness Christians are beginning to have, a shift that is both reflected and intensified by the interreligious dialogue activity of the two groups examined in this book. This shift centers around an awareness of the interdependence and essential unity of all humankind. The shift can be detected in the tendency to speak of history in universal terms: humankind, all men and women, are forging a common history. Particular groups and nations, in this perspective, are beginning to define themselves in terms of a developing global community. This view may have scarcely begun to take hold, but with the improvements in communications and transportation technologies along with the establishment of international economic and political structures (for example, the United Nations), it may plausibly be argued that it has begun to take hold of the human consciousness.

Those connected with the DFI, as I have shown, as well as those connected with the Secretariat for Non-Christians, presume this perspective in all of their work. Hence, cooperation with the men and women of other religious traditions in the building up of the human community and the idea that all are creatures of the same God who desires the welfare of all men and women is a consistent theme. The Second Vatican Council in its **Pastoral Constitution on the Church in the Modern World** has very precisely described this state of affairs in the following way:

> The destiny of the human community has become
> all of a piece, where once the various groups
> of men had a kind of private history of their
> own.[21]

The great importance of this vision and of the practical activity which flows from it is that it furnishes a new context within which theological reflection takes place. Thus, a new perspective in which men and women of other religious traditions are seen as co-workers and companion pilgrims has become a real option for the understanding of the human situation. This perspective has the result of altering the mood within which Christians and people of other faiths articulate their religious affirmations.

I think that this idea of "mood" needs further explanation. By "mood" I mean a way of being related to one's environment such that the nature of that environment is illuminated in a particular way.[22] The open-

ness that one has towards God and the divine presence,
and the manner in which this is articulated, in other
words, is in part, at least, a function of the mood or
"feeling" generated within a particular context.[23] Just
as one's openness to, say, a piece of music or a paint-
ing is a function of one's feeling or mood, so, too,
one's openness to God's presence is a function of one's
mood.

What is happening as a result of actually living
together and dialoguing on the part of men and women of
differing religious traditions is that it is becoming
more and more possible for a mood of friendliness and
openness to be generated. When theological reflection
begins by talking about "us," not "us" versus "them,"
then a new mood is generated. It becomes much more difficult, if not impossible, to deny the goodness found
in others and it becomes much more difficult, if not
impossible, to relegate them to the fires of hell. The
sort of friendly dialogue promoted by the two agencies
examined in this study has, I think, the inevitable effect of mitigating harsh, exclusivist stances that are
still present among men and women of all traditions. It
will, I suspect, serve to make Christians rethink their
views and make them more open to the possibility of
God's loving, saving presence among all people.

2. The Inherent Superiority of Christianity?

Despite the positive mood generated by dialogue,
however, even in the inclusive understandings of God's
work that have emerged within the Roman Catholic and
the WCC traditions, there has been an open or implied
tendency to regard the Christian view of reality as in
some sense superior to that of other religious traditions. The Christian claims about Jesus Christ, that

Jesus is the historical embodiment of the one in whom
all things hold together, or the one who truly reveals
the Father, or the one through whom God's salvation is
mediated to all, or, finally, the one in whom all
things will be recapitulated in the end--these claims
assert a superiority in terms of the recognition of
what reality is really like. When Christians therefore
dialogue with the followers of other religious traditions, they inevitably witness to an understanding of
God in which the figure of Jesus Christ is in some way
decisive and unsurpassable for all, even if only in an
eschatological way (that is, at the end of time beyond
history). The Christian vision is at least implicitly
affirmed as, if not absolutely correct in its historical form, then more appropriate to reality in its recognition of God's activity. God's activity through the
person of Jesus is superior to that in Moses or Mohammed or the Buddha.[24]

The Christian evaluation of all religious traditions and the attitude Christians have towards their
followers, then, is determined by a view which centers
human history ultimately on the figure of Christ. The
alternative is to make Jesus but one of many mediators
of God's saving presence to humankind. He may be universally relevant and, indeed, the best such mediator,
but not the only effective one.[25]

There are indeed Christians who are arguing for
this latter view. In a recently published book, Paul
Knitter, for example, argues that it is possible to
hold that Jesus is a mediator of God's revelation and
grace, yet not the only such mediator. It is possible,
indeed, necessary, says Knitter, for Christians to
insist that the insights they have received in their
encounter with God through Jesus are relevant for all

people, and determinative for Christians, yet it is also possible that others have encountered God through
other mediators. Knitter thus says,

> A confessional approach, then, will be
> both certain and open-ended. It will enable
> Christians to take a firm position; but it
> will also require them to be more open to and
> possibly learn from other positions. It will
> allow them to affirm the **uniqueness** and the
> universal significance of what God has done
> in Jesus; but at the same time it will re-
> quire them to recognize and be challenged by
> the **uniqueness** and universal significance of
> what the divine mystery may have revealed
> through others. In boldly proclaiming that
> God has indeed been defined in Jesus, Chris-
> tians will also humbly admit that God has not
> been confined to Jesus.[26]

The Christian tradition,then, insists that God is
"defined" and active in an unsurpassable way in Jesus,
yet this traditional Christian claim is undergoing increasing scrutiny today, as the above quotation shows.
One of the catalysts for this scrutiny has been the new
approach to Scripture that has dominated Scripture
scholarship this century along with a renewed look at
Christian doctrine. Scripture, then, is seen increasingly as very much the product of humans attempting,
from their culturally conditioned, finite perspective,
to express an experience of God's saving presence, an
experience mediated through the life and person of Jesus of Nazareth. In order to understand Scripture, one
must understand it in the context of its human authors.
Scripture is not a body of truths dropped down from

heaven. The experience of God's saving presence is understood and articulated in a very human way in Scripture.

   If that is true of Scripture, it is also true of
Christian doctrine. The dogmatic statements concerning
Jesus are statements that have emerged in particular
historical contexts as Christians in those contexts
have tried to articulate their understanding of what
God has and is doing for them. Christian statements
about Jesus' divinity must be seen in this light. It
may be that Christians will have to modify some of
their statements, even in the radical way suggested by
Paul Knitter and John Hick who argue that Jesus is one
of the many humans through whom people have encountered
God's presence and will. It is this Christological
question that stands at the heart of the Christian attempt to formulate a theology of religions. Christians
can no longer easily claim that Jesus was some sort of
"divine" man walking around Palestine performing count-
less miracles to prove his divinity. The most recent
mainstream Christian biblical scholarship, Catholic,
Anglican, and Protestant, presents us with a very human Jesus.[27] It is indeed the divinity that is the
question today. What do we mean by it? Is this fundamental Christian affirmation, which is at the root of
Christian claims to inherent superiority, the product
of a particular cultural context that Christians will
begin to modify? The Christian tradition is just beginning, at this time, to think about this more seriously, and the direction it takes remains to be seen. I
would argue, in this light, that the Christian evaluation of other religious traditions will be a provisional, tentative one until this question of the person of Jesus is sorted out more adequately.

3. The Exclusivist Statements in the Bible

Yet another fundamental question related to the development of an adequate understanding of the religions centers on the exclusivist statements that one sees in the New Testament, statements which insist that the only way to salvation is through Jesus Christ. I have already touched upon this above, but I would like to comment further. Such language, it seems to me, can best be seen as the sort of language which emerges from a personal relationship, language which expresses real commitment. It is personal, rhetorical language. It is not necessarily metaphysical language, although it may have for centuries been thought to be so. It is the sort of language a husband uses when he tells his wife that she is the most beautiful woman in the world or when a wife tells her husband that he is the only one for her. It is, if you will, love language. Is it an objective, metaphysical truth that the wife could not love another man? Not at all. The authors of the New Testament were enthusiastic and committed because they had experienced God's love and saving power in the life and person of Jesus. The exclusive language they used expresses this. I do not want to suggest that there is nothing "true" about rhetorical love language. It is not purely and simply emotive, with no basis in or understanding of reality. It does capture a dimension of the truth about one's existential situation, yet it does not capture everything about that situation.

This view of the exclusivist language of the New Testament recognizes the profoundly human dimension of Scriptural language. I do not think that one can over-emphasize this. It may indeed be the case that Jesus is the definitive revealer of God's will and God's nature, but it is quite simply offensive to the basic Christian

understanding of God as a God of love who desires all
to be saved to continue to hold that those who do not
believe in Christ cannot be saved. It is, moreover, too
artificial to continue to insist that all are saved
through Christ, even if they do not know it. There must
be other "paths" to salvation if Christians are to
avoid the moral contradiction or artificial concept involved in the idea that only in the name of Jesus is
salvation possible.

4. Towards An Adequate Theology of Religions

A theological evaluation of the world's religious
traditions that would satisfactorily ground the movement towards interreligious dialogue taking place today
is still in the process of being worked out by the various Christian communities. The preceding study of the
dialogue movement by the World Council of Churches and
the Roman Catholic Church indicates something of the
questions Christians are raising in their attempts to
formulate an adequate response to a world which gives
every evidence of remaining religiously pluralistic. If
they are to hold firm to a world view that stays within the recognized boundaries of traditional Christianity, the evaluation of humankind's religious history
will include recognition of Christ as the center of human history and as universally significant for humankind's relationship to God and for the relationship between men and women all over the earth. In other words,
a theology of religions in which all religions are but
cultural expressions of the religious genius of a people, arising from the insights of one or a few gifted
individuals who are responding to the inbreaking presence of God, Jesus being but one of many of these
gifted prophets, is a theology which Christians, at

this time, are unlikely to accept and which, if accepted, would significantly change the Christian tradition. Yet, it may be the eventual route taken. In the
meantime, there are certain directions Christians may
be able to follow in their reflections on the religious
history of humankind which would allow them to stay
within the boundaries of their traditional insights and
which would at the same time allow for a more positive
approach to other religious perceptions.

(a) Revelation, Salvation, and Religion

The directions that I would like to suggest as appropriate and, indeed, necessary at this time are by no
means novel, but they should, I think, be taken seriously and made part of the reflections of the two dialogue organizations whose activity I have examined.
One of the places where they can be found is in the
theological reflections of John Macquarrie. I would
like to sketch out his position briefly because I think
he provides insights which are useful for consideration
in the question at hand.

The key to Macquarrie's position is his concept of
the God-humankind relationship. In short, Macquarrie
sees God as present to human existence, continually im-
pinging upon this existence, enabling men and women to
actualize what it means "to be" and thereby allowing
them to attain what traditionally has been called "salvation." This view of the divine-human relationship is
very similar to that of the theology in the Secretariat for Non-Christians and to that of another theologian whose name has appeared in this book, Karl Rahner.
The human response to this divine presence takes on
various forms, suggests Macquarrie, among them the social, communal responses which constitute the many re-

ligions of the world. Thus the religious traditions of
humankind can be seen as responses to God's presence,
and this gives to all of these traditions a kind of
fundamental unity. The differences in the various religions is a function of such things as variations in
the symbols available in a culture to express and understand the divine impress, the psychology of a particular people, and even the manner by the God has "decided" to make the divine Self known.

What is important about the above view is that it
posits a form of universal revelation and a form of
universal divine activity on behalf of all of humankind. Insofar as Christianity is concerned, it, too, is
similar to all other religions in that it is a social
response to the divine activity, but it differs in that
it has sprung up as the response to God's presence and
activity such as these things are perceived in the life
and death of Jesus of Nazareth. Jesus, for Macquarrie,
is in fact the highest "symbol" of God, and in his reflections on Jesus, Macquarrie takes a traditional
stance. It is in Jesus that God (or "Being," as Macquarrie prefers to call God) becomes fully manifest in
concrete human form. Jesus manifests God particularly
in his self-giving, the supreme example of which was
his death when he utterly surrendered himself. It is
self-giving that Macquarrie understands as characteristic of divine being. Macquarrie summarizes his understanding of Jesus as the symbol of God as follows:

> God is absolute letting-be, and letting-
> be is the ontological foundation of love.
> Letting-be is also self-giving or self-spend-
> ing, so that God's creative work is a work of
> love and self-giving, into which he has put
> himself. In so far as created beings them-

selves manifest creativity, love, self-giving, they tend to be like God. This self-giving is supremely manifest in the particular
being, Jesus Christ. Just as there is self-
emptying, or **kenosis**, of God as he pours out
Being, so Christ empties himself in the life
that is portrayed in the gospels.[28]

Jesus, then, is definitive for all in that he defines the nature of what it is to be and hence reveals
the divine nature. Macquarrie recognizes, however, that
this is a judgement made from within the Christian
faith community. There is no absolute vantage point
above history which allows one to make it and from
there call on all to recognize it in turn. Moreover,
this faith affirmation is expressed in limited, cultural terms which make it always inadequate and subject to
reform and enlargement and which give it a character
that reflects a particular cultural base.[29]

(b) Witness and Ministry

What, then, is the proper attitude for Christians
to have towards themselves and others? Macquarrie's
view of this can be summed up best in terms of witness
and ministry. The Church must be that community which
gives witness to God and to what is "most important."
It does this by proclaiming and promoting the values it
has seen in the life of Jesus, the prime one being
self-giving love. Ministry to others in loving action
and furthering self-giving love are what should dominate all Christian reflection and action. This is to be
done without any sense of superiority, realizing that
God is present and at work everywhere, enabling others
to actualize likewise the values Christians see in the
life of Jesus, thereby attaining fulfillment.

(c) Minimal Directions?

The minimal direction Christian thinking on the religious situation of humankind should go, then, is to affirm that God is indeed present in a revelatory and saving way to all. The denial of this leads to an unacceptable view of God. The exclusivist statements in the New Testament can be seen, as I have suggested above, as examples of rhetorical love language expressed by finite, limited humans who have had an intense experience of God's saving presence. The inclusivist tendencies present in the New Testament indicate the more fruitful direction to follow because they are more consistent with the central insight of Christianity: God is love.

Christians must go further, however. The denial of other religious traditions as ways of salvation is unnecessary and harmful and it does not consider seriously enough what Karl Rahner calls the communal dimension of divine grace. We may experience God as a constant presence to all human life, but our understanding of God, our very experience of God, and our response always takes on a communal dimension. It is through the "filters" of our cultural institutions, in other words, that we experience reality, including that ultimate reality, God. Religious traditions are powerful, dominant factors which channel the way people experience and understand reality. It is not too much to consider them, as John Macquarrie does, responses to God's presence and activity. There is no way, of course, that one can "prove" this, yet it seems a reasonable attitude to adopt. This is all the more so because the major religious traditions of the world have contributed to the development of good persons whose religious concerns and devotion cannot be denied. Christianity has no monopoly on the people who can best be described as "saints." Can one really say, for example, that Mohatmas Ghandi or Martin Buber would have been better had they been Christians?[30] Can one deny that they are "good" people? Religious traditions have been very important in raising the consciousness of people to a transcendent dimension to reality and in promoting morally upright lives. This existential fact should play a role in the Christian assessment of non-Christian religions.

I do not want to suggest, however, that one regard all religions as of equal value and usefullness in promoting spiritual and moral living. There is much ideology and human sinfulness in all religions, including, I might add, Christianity (and here Karl Barth's insight is useful). Yet, this ought not lead one away from the presumption that God does act in and through humankind's religions. It will perhaps be through mutual witness and dialogue that the sinful dimension of all religions will be challenged and corrected.

What ought the Christian attitude towards the religions of the world be, then? John Macquarrie, I think, sums it up best of all when he says that this attitude must be one of openness and commitment[31]: openness to the religious traditions of the world as places where God is encountered in a meaningful way and commitment to one's own religious tradition as that religion where, for oneself, God is encountered and responded to. It will be through friendly, respectful dialogue that the rivalry and bitterness, so long characteristic of interreligious relations, will be overcome and a more "Christian" understanding of God's presence and activity encouraged.

IV. Final Remarks

Christians are, because of the historical circumstances in which they find themselves, beginning to realize that they are involved in a common history with men and women of other religious traditions. The dialogue movement that has emerged within the Roman Catholic Church and the World Council of Churches reflects the beginnings of this understanding in an official way by mainstream Christians. My study of this dialogue activity has shown that dialogue has many levels and many objectives, all of them being necessary features of an attitude and activity that is quite different from previous attitudes and activities as peoples of all faiths start to live out of an awareness that they should talk of others and themselves as "we" rather than as "we" versus "them."

Theological reflection has accompanied this dialogue activity. An important aspect for theological thinking in this regard is the generation of a new mood for reflection. Given this new mood, Christians are searching through their tradition to see if there are insights there for developing new theological articulations. Such insights, I have suggested, exist and point in the direction of an inclusive understanding of God's saving and revealing presence. While this direction is not new, it is time that it be more prominent. Thus, a recognition that God is working salvifically in other religious traditions which have so profoundly affected human history, along with a view of the Christian community which emphasizes its witness and service are, it seems to me, the minimum elements of an adequate theology of religions today. Only such a theology can ground a sincere and fruitful dialogue between Christians and persons of other living faiths.

NOTES

NOTES TO CHAPTER ONE

[1]In this letter the Pope remarked, ". . . ex re Nobis visum est sollicitudines conferre ad Secretariatum opportuno tempore constituendum etiam pro iis, quorum religio inter christianas professiones non recensetur." Quoted from _Acta Apostolicae Sedis_ 55 (1963): 743. The Pope's interest in the followers of other religions appeared also in his opening address at the beginning of the second session of the Council. He said, "Ultra igitur christiana castra oculos suos dirigit [Ecclesia], et ad alias religiones respicit, quae servant sensum et notionem Dei, unius, creatoris, providentis, summi et rerum naturam transcendentis; quae Dei cultum exercent sincerae pietatis actibus; quaeque ex iis usibus et opinionibus morum et socialis vitae praecepta derivant." Ibid., p. 858.

[2]For an introduction to and analysis of this debate, see John M. Oesterreicher, "Declaration on the Relationship of the Church to Non-Christian Religions. Introduction and Commentary," in _Commentary on the Documents of Vatican II_, vol. 3, gen. ed. Herbert Vorgrimler, various translators (New York: Herder, 1968), pp. 1-154.

[3]The announcement occurred within the context of a sermon whose main theme was the Church's catholicity. The Pope urged Catholics to demonstrate the universal concern of the Church by making contacts with men and women of other religions, even on simply the "human" level of everyday problems. To promote this, the Pope announced his desire to set up a Secretariat charged with this task: ". . . come tempo fa annunciamo, Noi istituiremo, e proprio in questi giorni, qui a Roma il 'Segretariato per i non-Cristiani', organo che avrà funzioni ben diverse, ma analoga struttura a quello per i Cristiani separati." Quoted from _Acta Apostolicae Sedis_ 56 (1964): 433.

[4]The official proclamation reads as follows: "Ad futuram rei memoriam. Progrediente Concilio Oecumenico Vaticano Secundo, expedire visum est peculiarem Coetum seu Secretariatum institui, cuius esset eos salubriter attingere, qui christianae religiones sunt expertes, scilicet in quos etiam haec verba Domini nostri cadere videntur: 'et alias oves habeo, quae non sunt ex hoc ovili; et illas oportet me adducere' (_Io._ 10,16). Hic vero ardor caritatis divinae Ecclesiam, quae opus Christi persequitur, urgeat oportet, his praesertim temporibus, quibus inter homines cuiusvis generis, lin-

guae, religionis multiplices intercedunt rationes. Ita-
que, motu proprio, certa scientia ac matura delibera-
tione Nostra deque Apostolicae potestatis plenitudine,
harum Litterarum vi peculiarem Coetum seu Secretariatum
de non Christianis erigimus et constituimus, cuius
Praesidem Dilectum Filium Nostrum Paulum Sanctae Roma-
nae Ecclesiae Presbyterum Cardinalem Marella, prudentia
admodum commendatum et in doctrina religionum peritis-
simum, eligimus et renuntiamus, tribuentes ei faculta-
tes omnes necessarias et opportunas ad id officium
fructuose in Domino implendum. Contrariis quibusvis non
obstantibus." Quoted from Acta Apostolicae Sedis 56
(1964): 560. One reason Cardinal Marella was chosen was
because of his experience as the Apostolic Delegate to
Japan in the 1930's. While there, in fact, he had written a letter to the clergy in which he recommended
openness to a dialogue with the religious culture of
Japan. A reprint of this letter appears as the fourth
supplement to Secretariatus pro non Christianis, Bulletin, printed in 1967. This latter publication will
hereafter simply be referred to as the Bulletin.

⁵See the remarks of Paul VI in a speech to the
College of Cardinals on June 23, 1964 in Acta Apostolicae Sedis 56 (1964): 584.

⁶See Pietro Rossano, "Il Segretariato per i non
cristiani e la missione," Euntes Docete 19 (1966): 267.
In the speech to the Cardinals noted above, the Pope
mentioned this concern that the Church take a more
openly "catholic" attitude in comments on his decision
to set up the Secretariat for Non-Christians. He said,
"Con queste e con altre simili iniziative Noi pensiamo
di dare una chiara dimostrazione della dimensione cat-
tolica della Chiesa, che in questo tempo e clima con-
ciliare non soltanti si stringe in vincoli interiori di
intese, di amicizie, e di fraterna collaborazione, ma
cerca anche al di fuori un piano di colloquio e di in-
contro con tutte le anime de buona volontà." Quoted
from Acta Apostolicae Sedis 56 (1964): 584.

⁷Ibid. The Pope said, ". . . Noi abbiamo determi-
nato di istituire anche un distinto Segretariato per i
non cristiani, che sia mezzo per venire a qualche leale
e rispettoso dialogo con quanti 'credono ancora in Dio
e lo adorano', per usare le parole del Nostro predeces-
sore Pio XI de felice memoria, nella Enciclica Domini
Redemptoris."

⁸The Secretariat for Promoting Christian Unity
handled the Church's relations with Jews, while a mixed
Commission composed of representatives from the Sacred
Congregation for the Propagation of the Faith and the

Sacred Congregation for the Oriental Church looked after relations with Muslims.

[9]An informational pamphlet given to the bishops
attending Vatican II by the Secretariat entitled Information for the Most Reverend Conciliar Fathers (Vatican City: Polyglot Press, 1964) says on p. 4, ". . .
the Secretariat turns its attention to all men who
raise their hearts above this world in an effort to
reach the spiritual, if not the supernatural."

[10]A list of the members of the Secretariat in
these early years appears in Bulletin 1 (1966): 6-8.

[11]For the first few years, the Bulletin was kept
confidential. From 1968, however, it was made available
to anyone interested in seeing it.

[12]For a survey of the Roman Catholic tradition on
this question, see Louis Capéran, Le problème du salut
des infidèles. Essai historique (Toulouse: Grand Séminaire, 1934). See also "Letter of the Holy Office to
Archbishop Cushing of Boston, 1949," The Church
Teaches. Documents of the Church in English Translation, ed. and trans. John F. Clarkson et al. (Rockford,
Ill.: Tan, 1973), pp. 118-121.

[13]Among Daniélou's works on this subject are: The
Advent of Salvation. A Comparative Study of Non-Christian Religions and Christianity, trans. Rosemary Sheed
(New York: Paulist, 1962); "Christianity and the Non-
Christian Religions," in Introduction to the Great Religions, trans. Albert J. LaMothe (Notre Dame, Ind.:
Fides, 1964), pp. 7-28; "Christianisme et religions
non-chrétiennes," Etudes 321 (1964): 323-336; "Father
Daniélou's Comments," in "Concerning Evangelization and
the Salvation of Non-Christians: Disturbing State-
ments," Christ to the World 10 (1965): 130-131; Dieu et
nous (Paris: Grasset, 1956); "Is It the Purpose of the
Mission to Bring Salvation? In Connection With the
Theological Seminar in Bombay," Christ to the World 10
(1965): 221-231; The Lord of History. Reflections on
the Inner Meaning of History, trans. Nigel Abercrombie
(London: Longmans, 1958); "Missionary Nature of the
Church," Christ to the World 12 (1967): 336-345; Le
mystère du salut des nations (Paris: Le Seuil, 1948);
"Non-Christians and Christ," The Month 223 (1967):
137-144; Les saints paiens de l'Ancien Testament (Paris: Le Seuil, 1956). For an article which examines the
main thrusts of Daniélou's position and which links
this position to other Roman Catholic contemporaries of
Daniélou, see Raphael Esteban Verastegui, "Christianisme et religions non-chrétiennes: Analyse de la 'ten-

dance Daniélou'," Euntes Docete 23 (1970): 227-279.
Among those discussed as falling into the Daniélou
"camp" are Pierre Humbertclaude and Pietro Rossano, the
Secretary and Under-Secretary, respectively, of the
Secretariat for Non-Christians when it was first
formed.

[14]See, for example, Le mystère du salut, pp.
12-17.

[15]See especially Dieu et nous, pp. 13-51.

[16]See, among other places, "Christianity and the
Non-Christian Religions," pp. 17-19.

[17]See, for example, The Lord of History, pp.
112-113.

[18]The following sums up Daniélou's position on
this matter: "This is the heart and core of the irreducible originality of Christianity, that the Son of
God came among us to reveal these two intimately related truths: that there is within God himself a mysterious living love, called the Trinity of Persons; and
that in and through the Son we men are called to share
this life of love. The mystery of the Holy Trinity,
known to us through the Word made flesh, and the mystery of the deification of man in him--that is the
whole of our religion, summed up in one person, the
person of Jesus Christ, God made man, in whom is everything we need to know." Ibid., p. 118.

[19]See, for example, "Christianisme et religions
non-chrétiennes, pp. 328-331.

[20]Ibid., p. 330.

[21]Ibid., p. 331. The text reads, "Si le feu expri-
mait sa puissance purifiante, l'eau sa vertu unifiante,
le souffle sa force créatrice, toutes ces images vont
maintenant désigner l'action des personnes divines.
L'Esprit est le feu que le Christ est venu allumer sur
la terre, le souffle divin qui soulève les Apôtres,
l'eau vive qui jaillit du thrône de Dieu et de l'A-
gneau."

[22]See, for example, "Christianity and the Non-
Christian Religions," pp. 22-23. Cf. Michel Sales, "La
théologie des religions non-chrétiennes," in Jean Daniélou 1905-1974, ed. Marie-Joseph Rondeau (Paris: Editions du Cerf/Axes, 1975), p. 46.

[23]Thus Daniélou critically remarks on certain
ideas on mission coming from a seminar on world religions and Christianity held at Bombay in 1965: "I criticized the idea that 'salvation can be obtained through

the world religions'. Certainly the author did not say that salvation could be obtained <u>by</u> the world religions, which would of course be false. But even so, the expression seems to me to be ambiguous. For pagan religions . . . are always ambiguous on the religious plane itself. To be exact, it would therefore be necessary to say that it is at once through them and in spite of them that pagans can be saved." Quoted from "Is It the Purpose of the Mission to Bring Salvation?" p. 229. See also "Disturbing Statements on Evangelization," p. 130 and "Missionary Nature of the Church," pp. 340-345. Cf. Verastegui, "Analyse de la 'tendance Daniélou'," pp. 259-263.

[24]For this and the above, see Karl Rahner, "Christianity and the Non-Christian Religions," in <u>Theological Investigations</u>, vol. 5: <u>Later Writings</u>, trans. Karl-H. Kruger (London: Darton, Longman & Todd, 1966), pp. 123-131. Other important essays in which Rahner's theology of religions appears are: "Anonymous Christianity and the Missionary Task of the Church," in <u>TI</u> 12: <u>Confrontations</u> <u>2</u>, trans. David Bourke (London: Darton, Longman & Todd, 1974), pp. 161-180; "Anonymous Christians," in <u>TI</u> 6: <u>Concerning Vatican Council II</u>, trans. Karl-H. and Boniface Kruger (London: Darton, Longman & Todd, 1969), pp. 390-398; "History of the World and Salvation History," in <u>TI</u> 5, pp. 97-114; "Observations on the Problem of the Anonymous Christian'," in <u>TI</u> 14: <u>Ecclesiology, Questions on the Church, The Church in the World</u>, trans. David Bourke (New York: Seabury; Crossroad, 1976), pp. 280-294; and "The One Christ and the Universality of Salvation," in <u>TI</u> 16: <u>Experience of the Spirit: Source of Theology</u>, trans. David Norland (New York: Seabury; Crossroad, 1979), pp. 199-225.

[25]See especially Rahner's discussion in "Anonymous Christians," pp. 390-398 and "History of the World and Salvation History," pp. 104-106. As an example, in the latter essay, Rahner argues (pp. 104-106) that all men and women operate out of a dynamic orientation to infinite Mystery (God) and take stances towards this Mystery (eg., appreciation or resentment). This stance is one way of accepting or rejecting God.

[26]See especially "Christianity and the Non-Christian Religions," pp. 118-131.

[27]Heinz Robert Schlette, <u>Die Religionen als Thema der Theologie: Uberlegungen zu einer 'Theologie der Religionen'</u>, Quaestiones Disputatae 22 (Freiburg: Herder, 1964), p. 39. Kung's remarks appear in an address he gave at Bombay in 1964. They are reprinted in "The

World's Religions in God's Plan of Salvation," in *Christian Revelation and World Religions*, ed. Joseph Neuner (London: Burns & Oates, 1967), pp. 25-66.

[28]Commenting on the importance of this encyclical, Mgr. Pietro Rossano, the first Under-Secretary of the Secretariat, noted that it could be considered as the "Magna Carta" of the three Secretariats formed to promote dialogue. These were the Secretariat for Non-Christians, the Secretariat for Non-Believers, and the Secretariat for Promoting Christian Unity. For Mgr. Rossano's remarks, see "Il Segretariato per i non cristiani e la missione," *Euntes Docete* 19 (1966): 267. An English text of the encyclical, issued on August 6, 1964, appears in *The Pope Speaks* 10 (1964): 253-292.

[29]*Ecclesiam suam*, nos. 93-113.

[30]Ibid., nos. 70-72.

[31]Note the following statements from the encyclical: "If, in our desire to respect a man's freedom and dignity, his conversion to the true faith is not the immediate object of our dialogue with him, we nevertheless try to help him and to dispose him for a fuller sharing of ideas and convictions" (no. 79); "The very nature of the gifts which Christ has given the Church demands that they be extended to others and shared with others. . . . To this internal drive of charity which seeks expression in the external gift of charity, we will apply the word 'dialogue'" (no. 64); and, "The Church must enter into dialogue with the world in which it lives. It has something to say, a message to give, a communication to make" (no. 65).

[32]Ibid., nos. 80 and 83.

[33]Ibid., no. 70.

[34]Ibid., no. 77.

[35]Ibid., no. 107.

[36]Ibid., no. 88. The Pope comments as follows: "Honesty compels us to declare openly our conviction that the Christian religion is the one and only true religion, and it is our hope that it will be acknowledged as such by all who look for God and worship Him."

[37]I will hereafter refer to this declaration as *Nostra aetate*, from the first two Latin words of the original text. An English version of this declaration can be found in *The Documents of Vatican II*, ed. Walter M. Abbott, trans. ed. Joseph Gallagher (New York: America Press, 1966), pp. 660-668.

[38]Nostra aetate, no. 1.

[39]Nostra aetate, no. 2. Cf. Carl F. Hallencreutz, Dialogue and Community: Ecumenical Issues in Inter-Religious Relationships (Geneva: WCC, 1977), pp. 41-46.

[40]Nostra aetate, no. 1.

[41]See the comments in ibid., no. 2.

[42]Cf. Hallencreutz, Dialogue in Community, p. 45. Hallencreutz points to the presence of this salvation history model in the Second Vatican Council's declaration on the nature of the Church, as well. It is evident in Nostra aetate in nos. 3 and 4.

[43]Nostra aetate, no. 2. The declaration here notes that the Church "proclaims and must ever proclaim Christ 'the way, the truth and the life' (John 14:6), in whom men find the fullness of religious life and in whom God has reconciled all things to Himself (cf. 2 Cor. 5:18-19)."

[44]Ibid., nos. 2-4.

[45]The decree on the Church, Lumen gentium, can be found in Abbott, Documents of Vatican II, pp. 14-101. The missionary decree, Ad gentes, can be found in ibid., pp. 584-630.

[46]Lumen gentium, no. 16. The Council Fathers probably have in mind the traditional notions of implicit faith and implicit desire to be a member of the Church. See below, n. 75, for a further explanation of these ideas. For an analysis of the Council's discussion of salvation for those outside the Church, see Jerome Theisen, The Ultimate Church and the Promise of Salvation (Collegeville, MN: St. John's University Press, 1976), pp. 37-64.

[47]Ad gentes, nos. 8, 9, and 21; Nostra aetate, no. 2; Lumen gentium, no. 16.

[48]Lumen gentium, no. 17; Ad gentes, no. 3.

[49]Ad gentes, no. 9.

[50]Ibid., no. 12.

[51]Ibid., no. 11.

[52]Ibid., nos. 8 and 13.

[53]Ibid., no. 22.

[54]The Secretariat for Non-Christians collected some of the Pope's remarks about non-Christians in a pamphlet, intending them to serve as guidelines for its members and for those engaged in interreligious dia-

logue. See Secretariat for Non-Christians, <u>Raccolta di</u>
<u>testi di S.S. Paolo VI concernenti i rapporti con le</u>
<u>religione non cristiane</u> (Vatican City: Polyglot Press,
1965).

[55]See, for example, ibid., pp. 21 and 26.

[56]Ibid., p. 29.

[57]Ibid., pp. 19, 24, 28, and 31.

[58]Ibid., p. 27.

[59]Ibid., p. 23. The text reads, "Ogni religione ha
in sé bagliori di luce, che non bisogna né disprezzare
né spegnere, anche se essi non sono sufficienti a dare
all'uomo la chiarezza di cui ha bisogno, e non valgo-
no a raggiungere il miracolo della luce cristiana, che
fa coincidere la verità con la vita; ma ogni religione
ci solleva alla trascendenza dell'Essere, senza di cui
non è ragione per l'esistere, per il ragione, per l'o-
perare responsabile, per lo sperare senza illusione. O-
gni religione è alba di fede; e noi l'attendiamo a mi-
gliore aurora, all'ottimo splendore della sapienza
christiana."

[60]Secretariat for Non-Christians, <u>Information for</u>
<u>the Most Reverend Conciliar Fathers</u> (Vatican City:
Polyglot Press, 1964).

[61]Ibid., p. 4.

[62]Ibid., pp. 4-5.

[63]Ibid., p. 8. The pamphlet says, "Perhaps you
have been struck by the fact that the words 'conversion' and 'entry into the Church' have scarcely been
hinted at in the course of this paper. It is by design
that we have omitted them. Our goal is to have frank
and sincere relations of sympathy and of charity with
our brothers, and to see them as they are, that is, believers in religions other than Christian. This does
not mean that by doing this we renounce the mission received from Christ to preach the Gospel. In taking upon
ourselves the ungrateful task of preparing the way for
others and of creating little by little an atmosphere
of understanding and cooperation, we at least are aware
that we are sowers even if we can never take part in
the harvest; and we know that these two tasks of sowing and reaping are going to be done by different persons. Moreover, we intend to sow in those areas of the
soil where any other kind of penetration would be impossible."

[64]For a short overview of the Roman Catholic concept of natural law, see <u>Sacramentum Mundi, An Encyclo-</u>

pedia of Theology, s.v. "Natural Law," by Rupert Lay.
See also Josef Fuchs, Natural Law: A Theological Inves-
tigation, trans. Helmut Recktes and John A. Dowling
(New York: Sheed and Ward, 1965).

[65]Information, p. 5. The pamphlet states, "Through
such knowledge [that is, the knowledge of other reli-
gions], we will be able to perceive in . . . the soul
of the non-Christian the vestiges of the natural law,
that seal of the divine Potter who has molded both of
us, leaving in each a sign of universal fraternity and
thus making it possible for everyone human contacts in
the best sense of the word."

[66]The author was able to read this letter in the
archives of the Secretariat.

[67]Thus the letter says, "Qui travaille dans la
ligne du Sécretariat ne doit pas regarder la conversion
comme chose qui relève de lui; il doit comprendre qu'il
ne verra les fruits de son travail ni dans sa généra-
tion ni même dans les premières qui suivront. Sa satisfaction sera d'avoir aimé son frère, de lui avoir dis-
pensé ce qu'il pouvait porter pour le moment, l'amenant
ainsi d'autant plus près de la Verité qui est Dieu.
D'autres viendront après lui dans la moisson qu'ils
n'ont pas semée pour recueillir les épis."

[68]The letter says, "Tous devront savoir que les
non-chrétiens ont une âme comme la leur pour laquelle
Jésus est mort comme il est mort pour nous . . . . Ils
apprendrons que Jésus a trouvé hors du peuple de Dieu
une foi vainement cherchée par Lui en Israêl et qu'à
cette foi il a accordé des miracles."

[69]See especially the comments above on Jean Daniélou and Karl Rahner.

[70]These concerns appear in an article published by
the Secretariat entitled "A propos du salut des non-
chrétiens." Written by Pierre Humbertclaude, it is a
summary of the conclusions from the 1965 Consultors'
meeting. The author of this study obtained a copy in
the Secretariat's archives. The article notes the problem: "Ces dernières années, une énorme quantité de
livres et d'articles ont paru sur le sujet, mais les
opinions exprimées y sont si diverses et parfois si
éloignées des principes communément recus qu'il en est
résulté plus de confusion que de clarté dans les es-
prits. L'optimisme exagéré d'un bon nombre de ces
écrits au sujet du salut en dehors de l'Eglise a déjà même fortement démoralisé par endroits les mis-
sionaires qui en sont venus à se demander si leurs efforts pour la conversion avaient encore un sens et

s'ils ne feraient pas mieux de se choisir une autre
forme de ministère" (p. 1).

[71]Ibid., p. 9. The text reads, "Les aides, ou les
moyens par lesquels Dieu parle à l'homme, c'est d'abord
la nature et la conscience, que l'on ne saurait sépa-
rer l'une de l'autre . . . . Ces deux maîtres jumelés
nous enseignent l'existence, la grandeur et la bonté de
Dieu créateur et providence. Ces notions sont à l'ori-
gine de toute vraie élévation religieuse. Mais même
chez les hommes les plus doués, cette connaissance de
Dieu par la création et la conscience est encore limi-
tée et non exempte d'incertitudes, surtout par suite
des passions et des préoccupations matérielles."

[72]Ibid. The text reads, "Y a-t-il eu, outre celà,
une intervention directe de Dieu auprès des hommes en
dehors des Testaments dont parle l'Ecriture? Il est
difficile de le nier d'emblée devant certain passages
de l'Ecriture comme ceux concernant Melchisedech, devant le concert des assertions des Pères et des Doc-
teurs pour ce qui regarde un certain prophétisme chez
les non-chrétiens. Reste qu'il est impossible de loca-
liser de facon sûre les traces d'un tel prophétisme
dans les religions existantes." A note attached to this
text mentions Saints Basil and Thomas Aquinas as discussing the role of angels in the spreading of this
special revelation. For a discussion of this tradition
of revelation outside the Church, see Capéran, Le problème du salut des infidèles, pp. 170-218.

[73]"A propos du salut," pp. 2-8.

[74]This demand for faith is discussed in ibid., p.
2 where different levels of faith are mentioned. The
text reads, "La doctrine de l'Eglise est que ni la nature ni même la Loi ne sont capables de justifier
l'homme (Denz. 1521); que c'est la raison pour laquelle
Dieu, Père miséricorde, envoya son Fils Jésus-Christ en
ce monde pour sauver les hommes, les Juifs comme les
Gentils, en s'incarnant et mourant pour eux. L'application de ses mérites se fait par la foi et par le baptême qui rend ceux qui le reçoivent membres de l'Eglise
dans laquelle seule est le salut. Telle est la voie du
salut fixée par Dieu, le plan unique par lui arrêté et
disposé." Later, on the same page, implicit faith is
defined as follows: "Mais même ce désir explicite [de
croire] est impossible à ceux qui vivent en des lieux
où le christianisme n'est pas connu ou ne l'est pas
suffisamment pour qu'on puisse le goûter. Alors inter-
vient la séconde suppléance, celle du désir implicite,
qui est l'intention bonne de faire ce que Dieu veut,
acceptation implicite aussi du plan de salut établi par

lui. C'est le cas d'un grand nombre de personnes vivant dans la pratique des religions non-chrétiennes."

[75]Ibid., pp. 6-7. The text on p. 6 reads as follows: "Si mention (des hommes non-juifs comme Job et Melchisédech) a été faite dans l'histoire du peuple de Dieu auquel ils n'appartenaient pas, c'est afin de nous montrer que bien d'autres cas analogues ont pu avoir lieu et que Dieu a pu inspirer certains philosophes ou penseurs religieux et éclairer ainsi leurs disciples au cours de l'histoire."

[76]Ibid., p. 10.

[77]Ibid., p. 3. The text reads as follows: "En somme, on peut dire encore aujourd'hui, comme déjà au temps de saint Prosper, que le tempus gratiae revelatae ne commence pas à date fixe et universel: celle de la naissance ou de la Passion du Sauveur; c'est un événement qui se réalise graduellement dans les divers pays et des divers communautés humaines."

[78]Ibid., p. 8. The text reads, "Il est bon d'abord de noter que tous les justifiés n'aboutiront pas nécessairement à la religion catholique, soit qu'ils soient dans l'impossibilité de la connaître, soit que la connaissance qui leur en est donnée s'accompagne de préjugés et de déformations qui les empêchent de la recevoir. Ils resteront donc jusqu'au bout chrétiens implicites tandis que d'autres plus heureux deviendront chrétiens explicites."

[79]Ibid.

[80]Ibid., p. 9. The text reads, "[Une religion non-chrétienne], l'hinduisme par exemple, pourra constituer un obstacle sérieux au passage au christianisme, et cependant ses valeurs morales plus hautes et la formation plus poussée donnée par elles à l'âme pourront la préparer à répondre plus aisément, plus généreusement aussi à l'appel de la grâce."

[81]Compare this with the views of the Roman Catholic theologians examined above.

[82]"A propos du salut," p. 12. The text reads, "On ne saurait donc dire au sens plein et absolu du mot que le non-chrétien est sauvé par sa religion, tout en admettant qu'il lui aurait été bien plus difficile de se sauver sans elle, à moins d'une grâce spéciale de Dieu . . . . [I]l arrive souvent qu'un homme soit sauvé dans sa religion et que Dieu se serve, pour l'attirer à Lui, de ce qu'il y a de bon ou d'indifférent dans sa croyance. Il ne faut pas cependant oublier que le bouddhiste ou hindouiste justifié est devenu en fait un

chrétien implicite, qu'il appartient de ce chef à la
vraie Eglise et reçoit à ce titre les signes qui lui
sont conférés. Il peut être--et il sera souvent--plus
ardent dans son culte ancien qu'il ne l'était aupara-
vant, mais il n'en est pas moins un membre de la vraie
Eglise."

[83]Ibid., p. 10. The text says that it is especially the philosophies and the religions of humankind that
can act as preparations for the Gospel for the following reason: "Les sages y ont enregistré les trou-
vailles et réactions de leur conscience devant la nature, y ont codifié les arrêts de la loi naturelle et,
s'il y eut des révélations, le contenu de ces communications divines." Emphasis added.

[84]Ibid., pp. 10-11.

[85]Ibid. The text reads, "Ainsi on ne peut que dire
du bien de la religion, mais il faut avoir des réserves
pour telle ou telle religion. Dans l'ensemble nous devons avec le Saint-Père Paul VI faire des voeux pour le
maintien de ce qu'elles ont de bon, désirer combler
leurs lacunes et redresser leurs erreurs: c'est un des
buts du dialogue, but qu'il faut réaliser en en parlant
le moins possible."

[86]The axiom can be found, among other places, in
"The Decree for the Jacobites," in The Church Teaches,
p. 78.

[87]For a reaction to this meeting, see Daniélou,
"Is It the Purpose of the Mission to Bring Salvation?"
For a collection of addresses presented at the meeting,
see Neuner, Christian Revelation and World Religions.

[88]See Kung, "The World Religions in God's Plan of
Salvation," p. 25.

[89]"A propos du salut," p. 13. The text reads as
follows: "Reste que nous devons l'employer [l'axiome]
le moins possible dans la tâche qui nous est spéciale,
et quand nous devons le faire, le présenter sous son
aspect positif: l'Eglise unique arche du salut et le
proposant à tous; l'offrant même par le moyen de la foi
implicite, à ceux qui restent en dehors d'elle sans
qu'il y ait de leur faute."

[90]These concerns can be seen in the remarks made
by the editor in "Concerning Evangelization and the
Salvation of Non-Christians," Christ to the World 10
(1965): 125-130.

[91]"A propos du salut," p. 13. Commenting on the
need for missionary work, the summary article of the

Consultors' meeting says, "Ayant sous les yeux [viz., les non-chrétiens] nobles et généreux efforts d'une part, bien aptes à leur concilier notre sympathie et notre estime, et de l'autre, les dangers énormes auxquels il leur faut faire face avec un bagage de grâce bien plus réduits que celui du baptisé, nous nous sentirons doublement poussées à leur venir en aide par une plus intensive propagation de notre foi."

NOTES TO CHAPTER TWO

[1]Secretariat for Non-Christians, Towards the Meeting of Religions. Suggestions for Dialogue: General Section, 3rd Supplement to the Bulletin (Vatican City: Polyglot Press, 1967), p. 1.

[2]In order of publication, these guidebooks are: Guidelines for a Dialogue Between Muslims and Christians (Rome: Ancora, 1969); Meeting the African Religions (Rome: Ancora, 1969); Towards the Meeting With Buddhism, vols. 1 and 2 (Rome: Ancora, 1970); For A Dialogue With Hinduism (Rome: Ancora, 1970).

[3]See, for example, Towards the Meeting of Religions, pp. 15 and 46-47, and For A Dialogue With Hinduism, p. 97.

[4]See especially Dialogue Between Muslims and Christians, pp. 7-8. This guidebook says, ". . . dialogue is first and foremost an encounter with other people whereby we seek to enter into personal relations with them in spite of our ideological differences. Dialogue can only be said to be producing all the good which it is capable of when we come to know and welcome the other person as he really and truly is."

[5]See especially Towards the Meeting of Religions, p. 33 and Dialogue Between Muslims and Christians, p. 29.

[6]See Meeting the African Religions, p. 157 and Dialogue Between Muslims and Christians, p. 101. See also below in the discussion of the purpose of dialogue. In none of the guidebooks is conversion seen as a direct goal of dialogue.

[7]See, for example, Dialogue With Hinduism, p. 97, where the guidebook says that dialogue on the "religious" level "prepares and disposes the non-Christian to receive the Gospel message and thus to benefit by the missionary apostolate." In this regard see also:

Towards the Meeting of Religions, p. 9; Dialogue Between Muslims and Christians, pp. 9-10; and Meeting the
African Religions, pp. 126-127.

[8]Dialogue Between Muslims and Christians, pp.
33-34. See also: Towards the Meeting of Religions, p.
12; Dialogue With Hinduism, pp. 109 and 121; Meeting
With Buddhism, vol. 2, p. 111.

[9]Meeting With Buddhism, vol. 2, p. 111; Dialogue
With Hinduism, p. 109; Dialogue Between Muslims and
Christians, p. 132; Towards the Meeting of Religions,
p. 9.

[10]See especially Towards the Meeting of Religions,
p. 37.

[11]Meeting the African Religions, pp. 124-125. See
also the following: Towards the Meeting of Religions,
p. 8; Dialogue Between Muslims and Christians, p. 136.
See the discussion of God's presence in the religions
of the world below.

[12]Towards the Meeting of Religions, pp. 46-47;
Meeting With Buddhism, vol. 2, p. 85; Dialogue Between
Muslims and Christians, pp. 9-10, 117; Dialogue With
Hinduism, p. 97.

[13]Towards the Meeting of Religions, p. 9; Dialogue
Between Muslims and Christians, p. 132; Dialogue With
Hinduism, p. 121.

[14]Meeting the African Religions, p. 128; Towards
the Meeting of Religions, pp. 13-14; Meeting With Buddhism, vol. 2, p. 81.

[15]Meeting the African Religions, p. 126. The text
says, "Instead of stopping at the exterior religious
forms, it will be more useful to get on to the deeper aspirations and intuitions [of the African reli-
gions]. Then a dialogue can be opened up, because it
will be found that the Christian can produce a valid
answer to these aspirations which are often unsatisfied
at the failure of the 'pagan mysteries'." See also the
discussion of the "good" in the religions in Towards
the Meeting of Religions, pp. 14-23 and in Dialogue Between Muslims and Christians, pp. 140-158.

[16]Dialogue With Hinduism, p. 109.

[17]Ibid., p. 124. See also Meeting the African Religions, p. 159 and Meeting With Buddhism, vol. 2, pp.
82-83.

[18]This anthropological basis is developed most extensively in Pietro Rossano, "Man and Religion," the

first chapter of Religions: Fundamental Themes for a
Dialogistic Understanding (Rome: Ancora, 1970), pp.
9-86.

[19]Religions, pp. 30 and 34. See also Towards the
Meeting of Religions, pp. 11-12 which says, ". . . man
is intrinsically open to the supernatural and tends toward it, and everything in his environment testifies to
a transcendent reality . . . . This religious nature
was bestowed by God on man from the first moment of his
creation in order that he might seek God and thus
achieve his end and his salvation."

[20]Religions, pp. 59-60. See also Towards the Meeting of Religions, pp. 8-9.

[21]See, for example, Dialogue Between Muslims and
Christians, p. 136 which says, "Our own personal history fits into the framework and follows the laws of
the history of salvation of the whole human race, that
divine pedagogy, which in mysterious ways causes such
different sorts of people to progress towards the fullness of God's gift to man."

[22]Meeting the African Religions, p. 125. Later, on
p. 129, the following statement is made: "Before its
incarnation in Jesus Christ, the word [sic] never
ceased to act on men since the beginning of time, especially on the 'Majores'. The founders of the African
religions, their thinkers and their wise men--are they
not the 'Majores' of whom St. Thomas spoke? On his return from India, did not Pope Paul VI declare: 'They
also have their prophets'? The values of the African
religions are more than valuable intuitions. In paganism we must see the Redemption at work." Emphasis added. Note also the remarks made in Meeting With Buddhism, vol. 2, p. 78: "We agree that with Amidism [a
form of Buddhism that stresses divine grace] especially, 'rarely has human yearning been expressed in a
purer dream; rarely has man seemed to experience his
wretchedness more clearly and to approach a religion of
grace more closely' . . . . [H]ow can we fail to recognize in these generous flights the meeting of human
experience and God's saving action?" Latter emphasis
added. This same idea appears in Dialogue Between Muslims and Christians, p. 136: "The early Fathers were
very much aware of the age-long story of the action of
God's grace throughout man's history as well as in the
hearts of Christian men and women. Perhaps we have
somewhat lost sight, especially after a long period of
apologetics in recent times, of this active presence of
God at the heart of nations and cultures. We need to
re-read certain of the Fathers, such as Justin, Clem-

ent of Alexandria and Irenaeus, who can help us recover
an awareness of the mysterious workings of grace outside the visible limits of the Church."

23I might point out again that the Secretariat
often uses the term "Church" instead of Christianity.

24Towards the Meeting of Religions, p. 9. Further,
on p. 34, this guidebook says, "The human moral law, at
least on its theoretical precepts, is more or less the
same in one religion and another. The essential difference in the pursuit of good and of virtue is that in
the human religions this tendency is anthropocentric,
aiming essentially at culture, at the elevation of man,
and on the other hand seeking to achieve its goal
through human effort and human resources. With us, on
the contrary, all is centered in Christ. From him pro-
ceeds the law, but a law which is none other than the
one which he has imprinted on our nature. This law also undoubtedly causes us to grow and in some way div-
inizes us. But the principle and ultimate aim of our
observance does not lie in this. We act for God and for
his glory, and all the rest is merely a corollary.
Likewise, we apply all our strength and all our attention to this fidelity to the law, but always admitting
that it is God who produces within us both the will and
the performance (Cfr. Phil. 2,13) and that without his
help our efforts, willed by him, would be vain." See
also the following: Dialogue With Hinduism, p. 107: "In
the face of the claim of equality of all religions or
the subtle claim to Hinduism's superiority, it is not
easy for the Christian to show the transcendence and
uniqueness of the Christian message. For the Christian,
what has happened in and through Christ is the centre
and source of all truths of revelation. A genuine
Christian dialogue has to be based on the conviction
that God has spoken and acted uniquely and decisively
in Jesus Christ. This claim of Christianity comes to it
because of the supreme historical reality of Jesus
Christ"; and Towards the Meeting With Buddhism, vol. 2,
p. 78: "Every Christian recognizes clearly the essential difference between God's direct intervention
through revelation and the noble effort man makes to
reach the Absolute guided by the light of his conscience and by the interior call from Him 'who enlightens every man' (John 1,9)."

25Towards the Meeting of Religions, p. 9. On the
previous page, one sees the following remarks: "The
'good and just', the 'true and holy' things to be found
in non-Christian religions can be at the same time the
fruit and occasion of grace and consequently can be re-

garded as 'seed of the Word' and 'preparation for the Gospel', providentially arranged by God." See also the following: Meeting the African Religions, pp. 10-11, 127-128 and Dialogue Between Muslims and Christians, p. 32.

[26]Mgr. Rossano makes the following critical remark in Religions, p. 16: "Others, of Christian origin, subjected to the influence of Luther and Calvin regarding the intrinsic corruption of Man and the absolute inaccessibility of God, consider religions as the expression of human corruption, condemn their theoretical and ritual manifestations as aberrations, interpreting Christian faith as the antithesis of religion."

[27]Towards the Meeting of Religions, p. 8. Cf. Dialogue With Hinduism, p. 127 and Meeting the African Religions, pp. 128-129.

[28]Note the following from Meeting the African Religions, p. 128: "The traditional African religions can help with their sense of the majesty of God, their cults, their offerings and their moral rules, in this justification by God which depends on the human dispositions. On the level of these dispositions, these religions are certainly useful." See also Dialogue Between Muslims and Christians, pp. 32-33.

[29]See, for example, the remarks in Dialogue Between Muslims and Christians, p. 33: "Islam is a means which, in given circumstances, helps men to draw nearer to God. We must respect the belief of men, who see no other way in which to approach God."

[30]The major writings of concern are the following: (1) by Paolo Marella: "L'Eglise et les non-chrétiens. Dialogue et mission," Bulletin 10 (1969): 3-19; (2) by Pierre Humbertclaude: "Role spécifique du Secrétariat pour les non-chrétiens et sa place dans l'Eglise," Bulletin 4 (1967): 29-39; "Clarification of the Nature and Role of the Secretariat for Non-Christians," Bulletin 11 (1969): 77-96; "Taking a Right View of the Founders of Religions," Bulletin 17 (1971): 99-102; (3) by Mgr. Pietro Rossano: "La Bible et les religions non-chrétiennes," Bulletin 4 (1967): 18-28; "Dialogue," Bulletin 6 (1967): 134-135; "Two Lines of Thought on the Non-Christian Religions," Bulletin 7 (1968): 35-38; "Is There Authentic Revelation Outside of the Judaeo-Christian Revelation?" Bulletin 8 (1968): 84-87; "Christianity and the Religions," Bulletin 11 (1969): 97-101; "L'Eglise catholique et les religions non chrétiennes," address presented at the Joint Working Group meeting at Gwatt in 1969, found in the archives of the Secretar-

iat for Non-Christians; "Dialogue, Maieutic and Kerygma in St. Paul," Bulletin 13 (1970): 46-51; "God, Israel and the Peoples: Theological Meditation on JEPD," Bulletin 14 (1970): 93-101; "Presentation of the Volume 'Religions' Published by the Secretariat," Bulletin 16 (1971): 36-40; "Dialogue With Non-Christian Religions," Bulletin 17 (1971): 103-108.

[31]See, for example, the following: Humbertclaude, "Clarification," p. 80; Marella, "L'Eglise et les non-chrétiens," p. 10; Rossano, "Dialogue with the Non-Christian Religions," p. 106.

[32]Humbertclaude's remarks in "Role spécifique du Secrétariat," p. 35 are typical: "Il s'agit de la préparation du terrain des âmes pour le rendre susceptible de recevoir la semence et de la laisser heureusement germer." See also the following: Rossano, "Dialogue With Non-Christian Religions," p. 106; Marella, "L'Eglise et les non-chrétiens," p. 11.

[33]See the following remarks: (1) by Marella: "L'Eglise et les non-chrétiens," pp. 14-15; (2) by Humbertclaude: "Clarification," pp. 106-107; (3) by Rossano: "Dialogue With Non-Christian Religions," pp. 106-107. In the latter Rossano writes, ". . . in dialogue the Christian must not be ready to let himself change, to renounce his faith; . . . the Christian does not forget he is the depository of a gift received and he must put all his powers to work in order to preserve it . . . . [T]he Christian knows one truth and all the searchings and all the progress which he is obliged to make must not be allowed to harm, far less eliminate, the true certainties . . . which lie at the foundation of this faith."

[34]See the following: Humbertclaude, "Role spécifique du Secrétariat," pp. 36-37; idem, "Clarification," pp. 82-83; Marella, "L'Eglise et les non-chrétiens," pp. 12-13; Rossano, "Dialogue With Non-Christian Religions," p. 104.

[35]Humbertclaude, "Clarification," p. 80. See also the remarks of Cardinal Marella in "L'Eglise et les non-chrétiens," p. 7, where he indicates that humankind's non-Christian religious traditions contain traces of God's revelation: "Vatican II a fait un pas en avant dans la grande voie de la Révélation et de la Tradition, en affirmant l'existence d'une réelle connaissance de Dieu, d'une authentique expérience religieuse, de vraies valeurs de la grâce, même si elles sont partielles et limitées, dans la contexture de l'histoire religieuse de l'humanité." See also the fol-

lowing by Pietro Rossano: "Dialogue," p. 139; "Christianity and the Religions," p. 98; "Dialogue With Non-
Christian Religions," p. 175.

[36]See Marella, "L'Eglise et les non-chrétiens," p.
5 and Humbertclaude, "Clarification," p. 96.

[37]See, for example, the following: Marella,
"L'Eglise et les non-chétiens," p. 4; Humbertclaude,
"Role spécifique du Secrétariat," pp. 36 and 38; Ros-
sano, "Dialogue," p. 135.

[38]For Mgr. Rossano's discussion of the "maieutic"
nature of dialogue, see the following: "L'Eglise catholique et les religions non-chrétiennes," p. 3; "Dialogue, Maieutic and Kerygma," p. 51; "Presentation of
the Volume 'Religions'," pp. 39-40. Mgr. Rossano makes
the following remark in the first above-mentioned article: "[L'Eglise] entend par là [dialogue] une acti-
vité visant à se mieux connaître et comprendre réci-
proquement, à se rapprocher dans la charité, à s'édi-
fier mutuellement dans la recherche du vrai et du bien
dans la 'decision' pour le vrai et le bien dans la
marche avec Dieu. Dans ce sens on pourrait peut-être
assigner au dialogue une fonction 'koenopoietique' et
'maieutique'. . . ."

[39]See, for example, Rossano, "Dialogue With the
Non-Christian Religions," p. 104.

[40]Rossano, "Presentation of the Volume 'Religions'," pp. 39-40. Cf. the following remarks to this
effect by Pierre Humbertclaude in "Clarifications," p.
85: ". . . our relations with the other religions
should enrich them, just as this contact ought to enrich us. Our humility and our zeal for perfection will
increase when we observe the virtues which God's action
produces in the souls of these brethren in spite of the
great differences in the graces and aids received. For
our part we can awaken and sensitize them to many
points of the natural law which the education they have
received prevents them from recognizing. This cannot
but make them better, even if they persist in the religions which they consider best at least for themselves. But this is not exactly our intention. What we
mean to do is to help these people advance with God,
to follow his inspirations (Acts 17:27) with greater
and ever fuller fidelity."

[41]See, for example, the following: Rossano, "La
Bible et les religions non-chrétiennes," p. 19; idem,
"Christianity and the Religions," p. 98; Marella,
"L'Eglise et les non-chrétiens," pp. 3-4.

[42]See, for example, the following: Humbertclaude, "Clarification," p. 85; idem, "Taking a Right View of the Founders of Religions," p. 102; Rossano, "Christianity and the Religions," p. 100.

[43]Rossano, "Christianity and the Religions," p. 98. See also Marella, "L'Eglise et les non-chrétiens," p. 7.

[44]See, for example, Rossano, "Dialogue," p. 138 and "Dialogue With the Non-Christian Religions," p. 105. Rossano remarks in the latter, "Catholic theology recognizes and maintains the universal action of God, of Christ and of the Spirit in individuals and, by reflection, in the culture and the religions; but it recognizes and maintains a special and unique action in the Church--in the order of knowledge (the word of God, revelation), in the order of structures (sacraments, teaching), and in the order of life (new life in the Spirit)." Emphasis added.

[45]This receives further treatment in chapter 4.

[46]Rossano, "La Bible et les religions non-chrétiens," pp. 27-28. The text reads, "Avant tout, que l'alternative Bible ou religion, foi ou religion, révélation ou religion, introduite d'une manière polémique par Barth et appuyée avec des nuances diverses par ses successeurs, se révèle devant la preuve des faits, antihistorique et anti-scientifique. Dans toute la Bible, l'histoire du salut et la révélation sont entrelacées avec la religion et ses formes; elles rejoignent l'homme et réagissent en lui à travers les formes et les catégories connaturelles au religieux. . . . Pour se limiter au Nouveau Testament, il apparaît que le don divin de la foi (pistis) se greffe sur les dispositions préliminaires de 'la crainte de Dieu' et de la soumission à lui; que la fraternité et la communion chrétiennes (philadelphia, koinonia) perfectionnent les aspirations à la solidarité et à l'association communes aux religions. Et de même la sacramentalité des actes sacrés (baptême, eucharistie) répond à la recherche universelle de moyens efficaces de contact avec le divin." See also Marella, "L'Eglise et les non-chrétiens," pp. 18-19.

[47]Cf. the discussion of Jean Daniélou's theology of religions above. Daniélou's position here is essentially identical to that of the officials of the Secretariat. Mgr. Rossano illustrates this view as follows: "Not only does [St. Paul] take on [the values of the Greek religion] so as to direct them, expanding them, towards the Christian fullness, but he uses el-

ements from it to integrate and enrich the Biblical image of God, in the belief that God 'has not left himself without witnesses' among the Greeks. It must not be forgotten that in this assumption he is purifying the Greek conceptions from the uncertainties and ambiguities with which they are overlaid, and in integrating them in the Christian vision he frees them and guarantees them against the deviations and repressions to which they were exposed (cf. Rom 1,18)." From "Dialogue, Maieutic and Kerygma in St. Paul," p. 50. Mgr. Rossano is here discussing the speech of St. Paul at Areopagus (Acts 17:22-31).

48Rossano, "Dialogue, Maieutic and Kerygma in St. Paul," p. 51. See also the following: Rossano, "La Bible et les religions non-chrétiennes," pp. 25-26; idem, "Two Lines of Thought," pp. 36-37; idem, "Christianity and the Religions," p. 100; idem, "Dialogue With the Non-Christian Religions," p. 105; Marella, "Taking a Right View of the Founders of Religions," p. 102.

49See, for example, the remarks of Mgr. Rossano in "Christianity and the Religions," p. 100: ". . . [some] prefer to think of the relationship [between Christianity and the non-Christian religions] in terms of coming, of preparation, of providential pedagogy: the religions are supposed to represent for the people what the Old Testament was for the Christians. But we must not forget that the Council applies the qualification of 'evangelical preparation', certainly not to the non-Christian religions in toto, but rather to the 'elements of truth and good' to be found in them, and in the decree Ad gentes (n. 3) (the Council) declares that the religious undertakings of the non-Christians can 'sometimes (aliquando) be considered pedagogy towards God or evangelical preparation'." See also the following: Rossano, "La Bible et les religions non-chrétiennes," p. 28; idem, "Presentation of the Volume 'Religions'," pp. 27-28; Humbertclaude, "Clarification," p. 85.

50See, for example, the remarks of Fr. Humbertclaude criticizing the notion that the non-Christian religions can be considered as the ordinary ways of salvation in "Role spécifique du Secrétariat," pp. 30-31.

51Ibid. The text reads, ". . . on prétend . . . [que] puisque l'homme a été créé social, les moyens du salut doivent être sociaux, ils doivent par suite se trouver dans les religions mêmes qui deviennent ainsi sacrements et transforment à leur insu bouddhistes, hindous, ou animistes, en autant de 'chrétiens anonymes'. Il faut cependant bien reconnaître que ni l'Ecriture, ni les Pêres, ni les textes conciliaires ne permettent d'accorder un tel role aux religions. Le salut des non-chrétiens n'est présenté que dans un dialogue secret entre Dieu qui appelle et l'individu, la conscience, qui accepte ou rejette."

[52]See Humbertclaude, "Role spécifique du Secrétariat," p. 31, n. 2: ". . . puisque les chrétiens ont déjà dès leur naissance le sacrement du baptême et l'appartenance à l'Eglise du salut, il est à plus forte raison inutile de leur prodiguer encore l'intense pastoration qui retient près d'eux la presque totalité du clergé. Celui-ci emploierait mieux son temps dans les missions où les gens, mêmes 'chrétiens anonymes', sont bien moins favorisés que les catholiques. Si au contraire il est vrai que les chrétiens baptisés risquent fort de se perdre sans le secours des prêtres et des sacrements dont le sacerdoce a le clef, combien plus les non-chrétiens ne restent-ils pas exposés au sein de tant de difficultés qui les entourent et avec un bagage de grâces malgré tout bien restreint."

[53]Rossano, "La Bible et les religions," pp. 24-25. The text reads, ". . . l'hypothèse qui considère les religions non-chrétiennes comme des voies positives du salut, instituées par Dieu et parallèles, même si elles sont de qualité inférieure à l'Eglise, semble également inconciliable avec la perspective biblique." See also "L'Eglise catholique et les religions non-chrétiennes," p. 2, where Rossano writes, ". . . le Concile ne doute pas qu'il y ait, par la grâce de Dieu, des anticipations, des prémisses, des valeurs, qui sans être des moyens du salut peuvent orienter vers lui, en dépit des déviations et des obscurités qui pèsent sur les religions qui, de ce fait, apparaîssent au regard du chrétien comme un fait ambigu."

[54]See, for example, Rossano, "Presentation of the Volume 'Religions'," pp. 37-38 where this is forcefully and clearly stated as follows: ". . . the Christian position on all the subjects dealt with [in the book, Religions] is shown briefly in each chapter of the book in a distinct and parallel study. In this way we obtain a documentary and, for certain aspects, exemplicative basis of the rapport 'fullness-fragment', 'light-glimmer', in which the Council Fathers considered the economy of Christian revelation and the theological stature of the non-Christian religions. A rapport which is not static but dynamic, and implies a tending, an 'ordering' (ordinantur diversis rationi-

bus), according to the famous expression of the dogmatic constitution <u>Lumen Gentium</u> (n. 16), of the non-Christians towards the Church of Christ."

[55]For a brief summary of the discussions, see "Réunion générale des Consulteurs," <u>Bulletin</u> 9 (1968): 126-128.

[56]Ibid., pp. 129-130. The summary account of the meeting lists the variety of views within Christian ranks as follows (p. 130): ". . . il est des chrétiens pour qui les religions sont détentrices de la révélation au même titre que l'Evangile (Heiler, Bleeker, Benz); pour autres, une même révélation s'exprime dans le <u>mythe</u> qui est à la base de toutes les religions; d'autres parlent du mystère du Christ <u>inconnu</u> ou du Christ <u>cosmique</u> s'exprimant selon des formes nationales différentes et ne saurait par suite être méconnu par le dialogue interreligieux, malgré la différence des expressions et formules culturelles ou conceptuelles [R. Panikkar?]; tels partent de la présupposition d'un surnaturel existentiel trascendant [sic] et non thématique qui se diversifierait selon les différences religions et d'une manière simplement priviligiée dans l'Eglise [K. Rahner?]; d'autres restant dans la ligne des enseignements du Concile, reconnaissent la présence d'éléments vrais et sains, de valeurs authentiques, dans les diverses religions, qui n'en restent par moins des complexes ambigus; certains enfin nient toute réalité de valeurs religieuses dans l'histoire de l'humanité et parlent volontiers de la mort des religions et de la religion."

[57]Ibid. On p. 130, the summary account of the meeting lists the practical consequences of some of the views on the religions in the following way: "Chacune de ces doctrines commande des attitudes pratiques auxquelles le Secrétariat se trouve confronté à chaque pas: tel propose d'introduire dans la liturgie, ou du moins dans la précélébration, des mystères, des textes tirés des livres sacrés du bouddhisme ou de l'hindouisme: tel souhaite qu'à la Messe, on fasse mention élogieuse des fondateurs d'autres religions; tel autre parle de dégrécisation de la Christologie; on propose comme voie d'un repensement de la théologie le schème de la Brahmavydya; d'autres déclarent tout net qu'aujourd'hui le but de la Mission n'est plus la prédiction de l'Evangile, mais bien la promotion des valeurs contenues dans les religions (viser par exemple à ce qu'un bouddhiste devienne meilleur, plus parfait bouddhiste). Comme chacun tient à avoir les coudées franches dans le système qu'il s'est construit, l'accord ne se réalise

que pour protester contre les inquiétudes doctrinales
de Rome qui gêneraient la parfaite indigénisation au
fil poussées de la vie."

[58]Ibid., p. 130.

[59]The entire issue of Bulletin 18 (1971) is devoted to this general Consultors' meeting. The major
presentations published in this Bulletin are the following: H. Dumoulin, "Buddhist Spirituality and Mysti-
cism," pp. 136-148; J. Jomier, "The Idea of the Proph-
et in Islam," pp. 149-163; V. Mulago, "Symbolism in the
Traditional African Religions and Sacramentalism," pp.
164-198; A. Camps, "The Person and Function of Christ
in Hinduism and in Hindu-Christian Theology," pp.
199-211.

[60]Dumoulin, "Buddhist Spirituality," p. 141.

[61]Mulago, "Symbolism in the Traditional African
Religions," pp. 184-198. An example of the sort of
thing Mulago does can be seen in the following compari-
sons between being born into the Bantu community and
being baptized into the Church: "Among the Bantus, the
fact of being born into a community plunges a man into
a vital specific current, 'ontologically' modifying his
whole being and orientating him towards living in the
manner of that community. There is a common unity of
blood, of life and of interests. Every member is a part
of the whole which is the family, the clan or the
tribe. And the duty is incumbent on each member and on
the whole community to safeguard, maintain, develop,
and perpetuate the communal life of the parents and the
ancestors. All those who partake of the same vital
source form an 'ontological' unity and are called aban-
guma (among the Bashi), abanwe (among the Banyarwanda),
that is to say the one." Quoted from ibid., pp.
186-187. He continues as follows: "Baptism makes all
the baptized into children of God, who form a supernatural community in Christ, in whose Death and Resurrec-
tion Baptism plunges us. Thus we participate in His divine Life and, because of the unity of supernatural
life, we form a community of 'supernatural associates
in life'. This new life should impregnate the whole man
and unite him, in his being and in his actions, with
his brothers in Christ."

[62]Ibid., p. 184. Mulago is here quoting from M.J.
Scheeben, The Mysteries of Christianity (Paris: Declée
de Brouwer, 1947), p. 570.

[63]In his article, "La Bible et les religions non-
chrétiennes" Mgr. Rossano explains the general theory
of indigenization as follows: "La rencontre du divin et

de l'humain se réalise sur la plateforme de 'l'homo religiosus', dont les formes d'expressions sont assumées,
purifiées, élevées et perfectionnées par la Révélation.
Ainsi se trouvent intégrés dans l'unité de l'histoire
du salut les charismes spirituels de chaque nation et
les produits des saisons successives de l'histoire."
Quoted from p. 26. Emphasis added.

[64]Mulago, "Symbolism in the Traditional African
Religions," pp. 197-198.

[65]The public summary of this meeting appears in
"Statement of a Conference, Domus Mariae 1972," Bulletin 21 (1972): 8-44. Only two of the presentations are
reproduced: Ugo Bianchi, "Religion and Religions," pp.
15-24 and A. Nambiaparambil, "Hinduism--Self-Under-
standing," pp. 25-44. The summary of the meeting says
that there were also presentations by Mgr. Tshibangu,
"Christianity and African Religions," professors Talbi
and Caspar on the way Islam and Christianity were con-
fronting the modern world, and a Fr. Pieris on Buddhism.

[66]Three non-Christian representatives were invited, Dr. Malalasekaera from Sri Lanka, Prof. Sivara-
man of Benares, and Prof. Talbi from Tunis. Only the
latter was able to attend.

[67]See the comments in "Statement of a Conference,"
p. 13: ". . . as far as regards the initiatives promoted by the Secretariat, the need is felt of moving in
its specific framework, that is, on the basis of religious premises, so as not to risk confusing or dilut-
ing the religious in the political and in the social
and therefore depriving it of its true and efficacious
action."

[68]The development of this dialogue program will be
the focus of attention in Part II of this study.

[69]Mgr. Rossano's remarks went as follows: "[L'E-
glise] s'interroge sur le rapport entre l'économie du
salut et les religions, entre l'action universelle de
Dieu envers les gentils . . . et envers son peuple .
. . ; elle cherche à saisir les liens entre la disposition religieuses de l'homme . . . et les religions,
entre la parole de Dieu et ses interventions dans la
Bible et la phénoménologie religieuse du milieu; elle
s'interroge sur la 'nouveauté' du christianisme . . .
et sur les éléments de révélation et de grâce qui lui
préexistent, sur la souveraineté universelle du Christ
et sur les voies par lesquelles la grâce atteint
l'homme, et comment celui-ci répond à l'appel de Dieu
. . . . La théologie de l'après-Concile a poursuivi la

recherche: elle s'interroge sur l'existence et la nature de la révélation et de la grâce données aux non-
chrétiens, sur la disposition religieuses de l'homme et
sur la valeur et la légitimité (voire même la nécessité) des religions pour la réalisation du salut, sur les
relations profondes qui existent entre les religions et
l'Eglise du Christ, et sur les fondements théologiques
des religions." Quoted from Rossano, "L'Eglise catholique et les religions non-chrétiennes."

[70]Ibid. The text reads, "La doctrine catholique
est moins absolue sur la corruption de la nature et par
conséquent son jugement sur les religions non-chrétiennes est moins négatif; la doctrine catholique se
méfie des antithèses trop radicales (religion et foi).
. . mais sur les points capitaux ici en question les
pensées sont convergeantes."

NOTES TO CHAPTER THREE

[1]The articles, presentations, and letters examined
in this section are as follows (in chronological order): (1) by Mgr. Rossano: "Inter-Religious Dialogue,"
talk given at Bombay, January 21, 1973, found in the
archives of the Secretariat for Non-Christians; "The
Spirit of Dialogue," keynote address given at the Shan-
tivanam Ashram, India, during a Hindu-Christian "live-
together," January 17, 1974, found in the archives of
the Secretariat for Non-Christians; "Clarifications,"
talk given during a visit to the WCC headquarters in
Geneva, February 13, 1974, Bulletin 26 (1974): 137-139;
"The Theological Problem of the Religions," Bulletin 27
(1974): 164-175; "Our Programme and Method," Bulletin
26 (1974): 143-144; "Dialogue avec les religions non-
chrétiennes: contenu, finalité, conditions, limites,"
talk given at the Abidjan colloquy, July 29, 1974, Bulletin 28-29 (1975): 26-28; "Opening Address," talk
given at the Kampala colloquy, August 5, 1974, Bulletin 28-29 (1975): 108-110; "Introductory Address," talk
given at the general meeting of Consultors at Grottaferrata, Rome, October 12, 1975, Bulletin 30 (1975):
211-213; "Guiding Rule and Methodology of the Secretariat," talk given at a meeting with WCC officials in
Rome, May 28, 1976, found in the archives of the Secretariat for Non-Christians; "Mgr. Rossano's Remarks at
the Closing Session," address presented at the Chiang
Mai consultation, April 27, 1977, Bulletin 36 (1977):
140-141; "Problème théologique du dialogue entre le
christianisme et les religions non-chrétiennes," talk

given at Kinshasa, Zaire, January 9, 1978, Bulletin 38
(1978): 87-93; "Interfaith, Its Importance and Implications," Bulletin 37 (1978): 29-39; "Convergences spirituelles et humanistes entre l'Islam et le christianisme," Bulletin 40 (1979): 15-19; "The Secretariat for
Non-Christian Religions From the Beginnings to the
Present Day: History, Ideas, Problems," address given
at the plenary meeting of Consultors in Rome, April 24,
1979, Bulletin 41-42 (1979): 88-109; (2) by Cardinal
Pignedoli: "Letter from the New President," Bulletin 22
(1973): 12-16; "Perspectives of the Secretariat," Bulletin 23-24 (1973): 84-86; "Pentecostal Letter of the
President of the Secretariat," Bulletin 26 (1974):
91-94; "Relation de S. E. le cardinal Sergio Pignedoli," address presented at the closing of the Bamako,
Mali, conference, June 29, 1974, Bulletin 28-29 (1975):
12-15; "A Japanese Encounter," report of Cardinal Pignedoli's visit to Japan from July 28 to August 8,
1974, Bulletin 28-29 (1975): 186-191; "Letter of Cardinal President of the Secretariat to the Bishops,"
Bulletin 36 (1977): 89-92; "Message to the Muslim World
at the End of Ramadan 1977," Bulletin 39 (1978):
179-180; "Introductory Address," talk given at the plenary meeting of Consultors at Rome, April 24, 1979,
Bulletin 41-42 (1979): 85-87.

[2]Views on the Secretariat's understanding of the
person with whom it was called to dialogue appear in
the following: Rossano, "The Spirit of Dialogue;" idem,
"The Secretariat for Non-Christian Religions," p. 142;
Pignedoli, "Perspectives of the Secretariat," p. 84;
idem, "Pentecostal Letter," p. 92.

[3]Rossano, "Introductory Address," pp. 212-213. The
text reads, "Comment comprendre et juger notre limita-
tion programmatique à l'homo religiosus? On touche ici
la connection délicate entre la religion et l'ordre des
choses temporelles. Chaque religion a sa façon de voir
cette connexion. Notre Secrétariat se tient à la position classique selon laquelle 'l'ordre du religieux',
c'est la sphère des interrogations suprêmes ('ultimate
concerns'), communes à tous les hommes transcendant
l'empirique quotidien, et de laquelle dérive un comportement éthico-social nouveau, qui dans la spécifici-
té chrétienne se dit 'fides quae per caritatem opera-
tur'. Mais nous restons plutôt sur la réserve quant
à nous engager dans la discussion sur la concrétisation
pragmatique de cette conduite nouvelle; il y a d'autres
compétences dans ce domaine. D'autres religions, par
exemple l'Islam, ont une structure différente, et nous
sommes sollicités par des organismes de dialogue et par
les exigences du monde d'aujourd'hui, à nous confronter

avec des problématiques non religieuses, par exemple la crise de l'énergie et des aliments, la communauté mondiale, etc. Comment envisager notre action? Comment la délimiter?"

[4]Thus, see Mgr. Rossano's remarks during the plenary meeting of the Secretariat at Rome in April 1979: "Inter-religious dialogue does not mean that one speaks only about religious experiences, but that religiously committed persons consider questions of common interest, shedding on these the light of one's own religious faith and thus bearing witness to it and to its fruitfulness. From this one passes easily to the level of concrete collaboration, at which Christians and non-Christians set out to work together for the good of their brothers (e.g. for justice, for morality, for peace etc.), putting together the inspiration and strength that drive from their respective religious faiths." Quotation from "The Secretariat for Non-Christian Religions," p. 103.

[5]Hence Mgr. Rossano's remarks: "When we speak of dialogue it is obvious we do so in the context of the Church, a prophetic, missionary, evangelizing community. All activities of the Church move towards the transmitting of what it has received, namely, the love of Christ and the word of Christ. Dialogue therefore takes place in the ambit of the evangelizing mission of the Church." Quoted from ibid., p. 100.

[6]See, for example, the remarks of Cardinal Pignedoli in a letter to the bishops of the world written when he assumed the presidency of the Secretariat: ". . . we participate in the love of Christ for all men and, therefore, we go towards them with our open hearts. It is becoming more and more evident that dialogue is the most suitable form of action for the Church in the world today, to say nothing of the fact that in various countries and in many environments the presence of dialogue seems to be the only way to bear witness to and share with men 'the hope which is in us' (1 Pet. 3,15). . . . The Secretariat for Non-Christians sets before itself the promotion of this ideal, intra Ecclesiam et extra Ecclesiam, aiming on one hand at the introduction of the evangelical leaven into the non-Christian cultures and religions, and on the other at a resolute process of incarnation and Catholicization of the Church in the various socio-religious areas of the earth (cf. AG 22; GS 58)." Quoted from "Letter From the New President," p. 13. See also the following: idem, "Letter of Cardinal President to the Bishops," p. 91; Rossano, "Remarks at the Closing Session," pp.

140-141; idem, "The Secretariat for Non-Christian Religions," p. 103.

[7]See the section on dialogue in Africa below.

[8]Quoted from a transcript of a radio interview given by Mgr. Rossano to Vatican Radio on July 6, 1976. The actual transcript reads, "Qui il dialogo asume, direi, un aspetto singolare che oggi viene chiamato negli ambiente anglofono l''inner dialogue', il dialogo interiore, ed è quella discussione, quel confronto che un cristiano singolo o meglio una comunità fa con il suo ambiente culturale, con il suo patrimonio culturale, religioso, spirituale, atavico." See also Rossano, "Opening Address," p. 109.

[9]See, for example, ibid., p. 103.

[10]Thus Mgr. Rossano remarks, ". . . we must always bear in mind that the Christian message . . . is a Word-Life, presented from the very beginning as seed, graft, salt, leaven, energy, regeneration (not judgment, not condemnation, cf. Jn 3,17). . . . [The recipient of the Christian message] must be enriched, lifted up, purified and perfected in his basic identity by the Christian message." Quoted from "The Secretariat for Non-Christian Religions," p. 105. See also ibid., p. 108 and idem, "Problème théologique du dialogue," pp. 91-92.

[11]See, for example, Pignedoli, "Letter From the New President," p. 103 where the Cardinal says that the goals of dialogue can come about "if the fundamental presuppositions of dialogue are respected: love for the non-Christians and recognition of their religious and cultural identity and of their sacred right to express themselves . . . ."

[12]Rossano, "The Secretariat for Non-Christian Religions," p. 104.

[13]See, for example, Rossano, "Contents of Dialogue With Non-Christians," p. 143: "This option of the 'homo religiosus' [with whom to dialogue] has been done on the base of a definite theological evaluation of religiosity and a positive estimation of the fundamental religious experience, originated in the creation of man as 'Imago Dei'. As created by God in and for Christ, man is basically in quest of God (zetein ton theon, Act 17,27) and oriented to God, even though he is wounded by sin. His quest of an Absolute is in fact the expression of the 'menschliche Kreaturlichkeit und Fraglichkeit'." See also the following: idem, "Theological Problem of the Religions," pp. 167-168; idem, "Dialogue

avec les religions non-chrétiennes," p. 27; idem,
"Problème théologique du dialogue," p. 88; Pignedoli,
"Perspectives of the Secretariat," p. 85.

[14]See, for example, Rossano, "Theological Problem
of the Religions," p. 168 and "Interfaith," p. 33.

[15]Rossano, "Secretariat for Non-Christian Religions," p. 105. See also Mgr. Rossano's illuminating
remarks in the following passage from "Problème théologique du dialogue," pp. 89-90: ". . . Dieu se mani-
feste également à ceux qui ne portent pas le nom de
chrétien. La Bible ne laisse aucun doute à ce sujet:
Dieu parle dans l'univers, dans l'histoire, dans la
conscience de chaque homme; la Sagesse de Dieu se ré-
pand sur tous les peuples et sur toutes les nations;
Dieu incite tous les peuples et tous les hommes indi-
viduellement à le chercher et à tous il donne témoi-
gnage de lui-même (cf. Ac 14,17; 17,27; Si 17,7-8;
24,6; Ps 19,4-5). C'est toujours avec surprise que je
note dans l'épître aux Romains que Saint Paul y désigne
par le même verbe grec pantou, 'manifester', à la fois
la manifestation de Dieu dans la Sainte Ecriture et
dans l'événement du Christ et celle opérée à travers la
raison et la nature (cf. Rom 1,19; 16,26). Il s'agit
d'une 'révélation' multiforme qui va au-delà de la
simple 'possibilité naturelle de connaître Dieu' mais
sans rejoindre encore l'ordre de la révélation historique qui existe dans l'Ancien et le Nouveau Testaments." Emphasis added.

[16]See, for example, Rossano, "Theological Problem
of the Religions," pp. 169-170: "As far as being the
expression of Man's creatureliness subject to the saving action of God, the religions must be considered as
depositaries of real, salvific values, objectivations
of deeply human propulsions sustained by the grace of
the Creator. But since God's image is obscured by Man
and the human psyche is in the mortifying grip of re-
actionary forces (laziness, egoism, self-complaisance
[sic], sensuality, pride, etc.), we must regard all the
religions as inevitably marked by this human negative-
ness, with all the ambiguities it implies. Whence the
contradictions, the alienations, the distortions with
which the variegated world of the religions is strewn."
See also idem, "Interfaith," p. 35.

[17]See, for example, Rossano, "Contents of Dialogue With Non-Christians," p. 144.

[18]The transcendence of Christianity is illustrated
by Mgr. Rossano in the following criticism he makes of
certain trends in Roman Catholic thinking on the reli-

gions (note his understanding of "anonymous Christianity"): "Some hold that a substantial identity exists
between Christian revelation, with its ecclesiastical
and sacramental economy, and the communication of God
present in the non-Christian religions. It is the the-
sis of 'anonymous Christianity', which, in the two
fields, Christian and non-Christian, marks a simple
difference of awareness and of knowledge. There are
also those who, in presenting us with this basic identity, do not hesitate to state a parallel identity,
which is equivalent to saying a plurality of fundamentally equivalent revelations. It is clear that whoever
continues in this direction can hardly avoid the danger of relativism, with the equipollence [sic] of the
ways that lead to salvation." Quoted from "Theological
Problem of the Religions," pp. 171-172.

[19]See, for example, the remarks of Cardinal Pignedoli in "Perspectives of the Secretariat," pp. 84-85.
See also the remarks of Mgr. Rossano in "Interfaith,"
p. 36: "God's historical intervention in Israel brought
into the religious history of mankind a certain dual-
ity destined to last as long as history itself. The
Jewish people's prerogative is that of having been
chosen as mediator of a promise and blessing of God to
all nations, and its mission continues on new foundations and with new horizons in the Church, who defines
herself 'sacramentum universale salutis'. This distinction between Israel and peoples, between Church and
mankind is, therefore, a permanent note in the economy of salvation and requires from the Christian a dialectical relationship with the religions."

[20]Rossano, "Problème théologique du dialogue," p.
89. The text reads, "La foi, chez le chrétien, ne
s'identifie pas simplement pas avec sa tradition et sa
culture, mais elle est une réalité transculturelle en-
trée dans la culture, dont la communication n'implique
aucumement le transfert et la communication de la culture. En résulte que la foi chrétienne, bien qu'immer-
gée dans la culture et promotrice de culture, pousse
ses rameaux au-dessus de la culture et peut être trans-
mise sans que s'opère en même temps un transbordement
de la culture de départ, et sans supplanter ni élimi-
ner la tradition culturelle et religieuse des destina-
taires auxquels elle parvient. . . . Ainsi, le chrétien
de culture latine devra apprendre à communiquer la Parole évangélique à celui qui est de culture bantoue
sans procéder à des transplantations culturelles. . .
." Elsewhere, in "Theological Problem of the Religions," pp. 174-175, Mgr. Rossano writes in a similar
vein, ". . . Revelation needs the categories of human

religion, but being transcendent it must not allow itself to be imprisoned or diverted by them. Hence the
fundamental dialectic of the Christian economy which is
the incarnation and exodus, the continuity and the
break, the acceptance and the surpassing of the human
religious categories. . . . Every incarnation of the
faith in culture and in the religious traditions of a
people must be accompanied necessarily by a surpassing
of them." See also Mgr. Rossano's remarks in "The Secretariat for Non-Christian Religions," p. 104.

[21]See, for example, Rossano, "The Secretariat for
Non-Christian Religions," p. 105: "[The Christian] must
realize that he is imperfect and perfectible both in
his knowledge of and in the cultural and practical ap-
plications of his faith, and that he does not understand all its aspects and values." He states this even
more forcefully in "Theological Problem of the Religions," p. 170 as follows: ". . . this ambiguity [the
good and evil that are part of humankind's religious
history], it is well to note, has to be acknowledged
even in the historical realizations of Christianity. We
well know that no historical objectivation of Christian
existence is perfect. . . . All Man's objectivations
are subject to Man's limit and carry a more or less
considerable margin of ambiguity. This is essential for
the theological evaluation of the religions." See also
Rossano's comments in "Interfaith," p. 37.

[22]Rossano, "Problème théologique du dialogue," pp.
89-90. The text reads, ". . . je crois fondé, s'il y
a nécessité d'approfondissement, de lire dans l'Ecriture la présence d'une économie universelle de la Sagesse (cf. Ps 8, 15-36; Si 17, 1-12; Sg 6, 24; 7,23ss;
Am 9, 6-7) à côté d'une économie particulière de l'Al-
liance, qui continue dans l'Eglise sur des bases nou-
velles et universelles . . . . Dans ce contexte, je
trouve parfaite la définition donnée dans les Guidelines for Inter-Religious Dialogue publiés à Varanasi
en 1977 par la Commission épiscopale indienne pour le
dialogue: 'Dialogue is the response of Christian faith
in God's saving presence in other religious traditions
and the expression of firm hope of their fulfillment in
Christ." Emphasis added. See also idem, "The Secretariat for Non-Christian Religions," p. 105.

[23]See the rather ambiguous statement by Mgr. Rossano in "Theological Problem of the Religions," pp.
170-171: ". . . those theologians who regard the non-
Christian religions as ways of salvation and the instruments of self-fulfillment for their followers are
not in the right. If it is undeniable that in many as-

pects the religions [that is, the non-Christian reli-
gions] are the objectivation of Man's response to the
instinctus Dei invitantis, it is no less true that this
response appears historically ambiguous, limited, frequently negative, so that the religions may also be the
experience of Man's insufficiency, of his Titanism and
of a mysterious refusal of grace. Perhaps we might say
that in these conditions the religions can be considered ways of salvation to the degree in which they are
a manifestation of the divine image of Man, of his
creatureliness enlightened by Christ."

24These were held at Luxembourg, March 13-14,
1974, Bamako, Mali, June 18-20, 1974, Tripoli, February 1-5, 1976, and Vienna, November 19-21, 1976.

25For a summary and discussion of what occurred at
these meetings, see Bulletin 26 (1974): 145-147 (Luxembourg) and Bulletin 33 (1976): 337-340 (Vienna).

26The comments in the Bulletin account of the 1974
meeting sum up the general tone of both meetings as
follows: "Il y eut . . . un cadre différencié où de
gros phénomènes de fond ont surgi: une présence massive
de travailleurs musulmans dans de nombreuses villes
d'Europe et une intense pénétration religieuse de
souche asiastique dans les grandes villes européennes
surtout parmi les jeunes et les intellectuels. La recherche s'est orientée dans une triple direction: analyse sociologique de la situation selon les données ac-
cessibles à chaque nation, responsabilité et sensibili-
té des chrétiens face aux nouveaux problèmes, indications opératives de nature pastorale et d'aide. Il a
paru trés clair . . . que les Eglises chrétiennes d'Europe . . . doivent profiter de ce moment privilégié de
leur histoire pour donner à ces frères un véritable té-
moignage de foi, d'amour effectif et d'appréciation
pour les valeurs humaines et religieuses qu'ils pos-
sèdent." Quoted from "Luxembourg: Les non-chrétiens en
Europe--Brève relation sur la rencontre au Luxembourg
(13-14 mars 1974)," Bulletin 26 (1974): 145-146.

27See ibid., p. 147 and "Les musulmans en Europe
(rencontre de Vienne: 19-21 novembre 1976)," Bulletin
33 (1976): 338-341.

28For a summary analysis of this meeting, along
with some of the talks given during it, see Bulletin
28-29 (1975): 3-15.

29The summary account of the Bamako meeting notes,
"Le regard porté sur les relations entre chrétiens et
musulmans fait surgir de partout une constatation una-
nime: 'Nous ne connaissons pas les musulmans.' Si 'la

première étape du dialogue consiste à connaître l'autre
et à se faire connaître de lui' (card. Pignedoli), le
dialogue entre chrétiens et musulmans est à peine
amorcé et seulement d'une manière sporadique." Quoted
from "Compte rendu: L'Eglise d'Afrique Occidentale en
dialogue avec les musulmans," Bulletin 28-29 (1975): 6.

[30]Ibid., p. 8

[31]See "Report on the 'Seminar on Islamic-Christian
Dialogue', in Tripoli (1st-5th February 1976)," Bulletin 31 (1976): 5-13 and "Text of the Final Declaration
of the Tripoli Seminar on the Islamic-Christian Dialogue," ibid., pp. 14-21.

[32]"Text of the Final Declaration of the Tripoli
Seminar," p. 14.

[33]Ibid., p. 20.

[34]Ibid., p. 17.

[35]In his presentation at the Tripoli meeting, Fr.
Jacques Lanfry, speaking on the removal of prejudices
between Christians and Muslims, asked for the forgiveness of the Muslim peoples for injurious remarks made
against Mohammed by Christians in the past. This new
attitude called for with respect to Mohammed represents
a major change in the direction of Christian thinking
about the leaders of other religious traditions and is
totally consistent with the policies and tendencies of
the Secretariat. See "Report on Islamic-Christian Dialogue," p. 9.

[36]The memorandum ("Text of the Final Declaration
of the Tripoli Seminar") states, "8. The two parties
affirm the necessity of freedom of religious beliefs
and the exercise of religious practice, as well as the
right of families to give their children a religious
education. They denounce religious persecution in all
its forms; they consider that the regimes and ideologies that persecute believers are inhuman."

[37]Ibid., p. 19. In an article in which he comments
on the reason for and the spirit of this remark by the
memorandum, Mgr. Rossano notes, "Tout le monde sait que
le monde islamique se préoccupe de la mission chrétienne, et du côté chrétien on a des appréhensions pour
la mission (dawa) musulmane . . . . Me référant à l'esprit et aux conclusions du Séminaire de Tripoli, à par-
tir des convergences spirituelles des deux religions,
dans le respect de nos différences, ne peut-on faire un
pas en avant pour l'élimination progressive de ces
craintes, en reconnaissant, par exemple, à chaque chrétien et à chaque musulman, le droit fundamental de pro-

fesser et de manifester sa foi sans discrimination aucune?" He goes on to say, "Nos religions sont essen-
tiellement missionnaires et ont le devoir de rester
telles, dans le respect total de la conscience des uns
et des autres, dans l'émulation pour la réalisation du
bien et dans la collaboration pour le primat du spiri-
tuel entre les hommes et les peuples." Quoted from
"Convergences spirituelles et humanistes entre l'Islam
et le christianisme," p. 19.

[38]See, for example, "Text of the Final Declaration
of the Tripoli Seminar," no. 3, p. 17: "The two parties affirm that Religion, in its essence, is the
source of moral commitment and that it is the fundamental guide of the conduct of individuals, communities
and States." See also ibid., nos. 4 and 5, and no. 10,
p. 18.

[39]Ibid., no. 7, p. 17.

[40]Ibid., no. 6.

[41]Ibid., no. 8.

[42]"Report on the 'Seminar on Islamic-Christian Dialogue'," p. 9.

[43]For the Secretariat's version of this incident,
see ibid., pp. 11-13. The disputed statements are reproduced with a disclaimer in "Text of the Final Declaration of the Tripoli Seminar," nos. 20 and 21, p.
21.

[44]The summary accounts, final recommendations, and
some of the presentations of these two conferences make
up most of Bulletin 28-29 (1975).

[45]See Mushete Ngindu, "Rapport général sur le colloque," Bulletin 28-29 (1975): 25 and Aylwood Shorter,
"Final Statement," ibid., pp. 106-107.

[46]The talks reprinted in Bulletin 28-29 (1975)
are: (1) from the Abidjan colloquy: P. Rossano, "Dialogue avec les religions non-chrétiennes," pp. 26-28;
Mgr. Christophe Adimou, "Vodu et christianisme," pp.
29-39; Fr. Léon Diouf, "Religions traditionelles et
christianisme au Sénégal," pp. 40-65; Fr. Mushete Ngindu, "Le propos du recours à l'authenticité et le christianisme au Zâire," pp. 66-86; Fr. Anselme Sanon, "Religions traditionnelles et christianisme en Haute-Vol-
ta," pp. 87-100; (2) from the Kampala colloquy: P. Rossano, "Opening Address," pp. 108-110; Fr. Aylwood
Shorter, "Problems and Possibilities for the Church's
Dialogue with African Traditional Religion," pp.
111-121; Fr. Alex Chima, "Dialogue With Traditional Re-

ligions in Malawi," pp. 122-131; Rev. Joseph Mawinza, "Possibility of Dialogue Between the Church and African Traditional Religions in Tanzania," pp. 132-158; M.B. Nsimbi, "Traditional Religion in Bugunda," pp. 159-163; Fr. Patrick Whooley, "Dialogue With African Cultures (South Africa)," pp. 164-173.

[47]Typical of the remarks to this effect are those of Mgr. Christophe Adimou in his talk, "Vodù et christianisme," pp. 37-38: "On peut même dire que le Vodù favorise d'une certaine manière le Christianisme en mettant en honneur certaines valeurs humaines et spirituelles que le Christianisme a assumées ou peut assumer très volontiers--telles que:
"La souveraine autorité de Dieu dont nous devons faire la volonté ici-bas.
"Les normes de la moralité qui ne sont pas dictée par chaque conscience individuelle . . . mais viennent de la volonté des ancêtres, de la volonté des Vodù et par déductions, de Dieu Lui-même qui a placé à la tête de la famille, du clan: ancêtre et Vodù.
"La notion du péché, de l'offense, qui exige pardon, purification.
"La grande solidarité des membres de la famille, l'unité fondamentale de la famille symbolisée pour l'ancêtre fondateur.
"La survie de l'âme.
"Le bonheur dans l'au-delà.
"Il y a tout un ensemble plus ou moins épais que l'on peut considérer comme des éléments positifs qu'il suffira de rectifier, de compléter pour que le Christianisme puisse les accueillir et les intégrer."

[48]"Recommendations," in "Final Statement," pp. 106-107. Emphasis added. Cf. "Voeux et recommendations," (Abidjan) in "Rapport général sur le colloque," p. 25: "Soulignons l'urgente nécessité de réviser certaines attitudes négatives et même méprisantes à l'égard des religions traditionnelles, qui véhiculent des valeurs humaines et spirituelles dignes de considération."

[49]A summary account of this meeting with some of the presentations given appear in Bulletin 33 (1976): 211-318.

[50]The presentations reprinted in Bulletin 33 (1976) are: Pierre Tchouanga, "La vérité du culte des ancêtres en Afrique chez les Bamiléké," pp. 219-253; Aloys Tsala, "L'éthique et la thérapeutique dans les traditions africaines," pp. 254-260; Nicolas Godian, "Actualité de la croyance à des agents mystiques maléfiques en Afrique Centrale," pp. 261-310; Pietro Ros-

sano, "Evangile et culture africaine," pp. 311-318. The main theme of these talks centered on the points of contact between Christianity and these African religions.

[51]Rossano, "Evangile et culture africaine," p. 314. The text reads: "Il est bien certain que l'Evangile représente pour la tradition africaine, comme c'est d'ailleurs toujours le cas face à la réalité de l'histoire, à la fois une rupture, une nouveauté et un achèvement des aspirations les plus profondes. Il n'impose pas des contenus culturels préétablis et uniformes, mais dévoiles de nouveaux rapports vitaux, interpersonnels, . . . Ainsi l'Evangile enrichira substantiellement la spiritualité africaine en exaltant ses expressions typiques permanentes pour les élever à une vie nouvelle dans la communion théandrique offerte par l'Eglise."

[52]See, for example, Pierre Tchouanga, "La vérité du culte des ancêtres en Afrique chez les Bamiléké," p. 225: ". . . la 'tête ancestrale' n'est pas une futilité, c'est le signe sensible du disparu, de celui par qui les présents et les hommes à venir se rattachent entre eux-mêmes, à l'humanité entière, au Créateur, se fondant en une communion de vie très réelle."

[53]See Aloys Tsala, "L'éthique et la thérapeutique dans les traditions africaines," p. 260.

[54]Thus Pierre Tchouanga remarked about his experience, ". . . c'est en toute sincérité, avec joie et émotion que je pouvais dire à l'homme bantou: 'Au fond de moi-même, je découvre également cette triple aspiration à la vie totale, pleine et intense, à une paternité profonde et totalement humaine, à l'union et à la communion avec des autres êtres.' Je pouvais ajouter que l'homme bantou m'aidait à me découvrir moi-même, et qu'il m'engendrait à la vie." Quoted from "La vérité du culte des ancêtres," p. 248.

[55]A summary of this meeting and the major presentations given appear in Bulletin 38 (1978): 65-123. The presentations reprinted are: Cardinal Joseph Malula, "Discours d'ouverture," pp. 83-86; Pietro Rossano, "Problème théologique du dialogue entre le christianisme et les religions non-chrétiennes," pp. 87-93; Médard Kayitakibga, "Le Saint-Siège et les religions africaines," pp. 94-113; T.K.M. Buakasa, "L'impact de la religion africaine sur l'Afrique d'aujourd'hui. Latence et patience," pp. 114-123.

[56]Malula, "Discours d'ouverture," p. 85. The text reads as follows: "Par son incarnation, le Verbe Incar-

né est venu habiter parmi nous, peuples africains, non pour détruire la religion de nos ancêtres mais pour la porter à son plénitude, à sa perfection. . . . Et ce qui existe en Afrique, ce sont certaines valeurs morales et religieuses des traditions africaines. Ces valeurs nous les considérons à juste titre comme le pro-évangile. Ce sont ces valeurs morales et religieuses de nos cultures que le Christianisme vient compléter, élever et porter à leur justification." Commenting on this colloquy, one of the Secretariat's Consultors, Fr. Henri Gravrand, repeated this theme: "Le devenir d'une religion non-chrétienne, c'est la 'continuatio', c'est-à-dire, la continuité entre Religion africaine et Evangélisation. Ce que la première commence, la seconde va l'achever. Ce que la seconde réalise, la première y aspirait. Ce passage se fait dans le peuple, d'abord formé dans la religion africaine et qui apporte ses valeurs spirituelles dans la communauté des disciples du Christ." Quoted from "Colloque de Kinshasa--pour un christianisme africaine," Bulletin 38 (1978): 127.

[57]See, for example, Malula, "Discours d'ouverture," p. 86: "Partant du vécu et du sens chrétien de nos populations, le théologien africain aboutira sans doute à des solutions neuves, inédites, peut-être, mais pertinentes à notre contexte. Il fera de la vraie théologie. Une théologie fidèle au message essentiel de Jésus Christ et respectueuse de notre histoire africaine. Tel est notre souhait."

[58]Bulletin 27 (1974) contains the opening addresses of Mgr. Moretti, the Apostolic Nuncio to Bangkok, Mgr. Rossano, and Mgr. Michai, archbishop of Bangkok at this meeting, along with the reports of its three workshops, pp. 225-232. Also found is one of the addresses given during the meeting, an address by Fr. E. Pezet, "Reflections On My Personal Experience In A Buddhist Country," pp. 176-185.

[59]"Report of Workshops. Group I: Christianity Seen By Buddhists," Bulletin 27 (1974): 227-228.

[60]"Report of Workshops. Group II: Buddhist and Christian," Bulletin 27 (1974): 230.

[61]The report of the second workshop says, "At the deepest level, connected with the Christian originality (personal relationship with God and with men in Jesus Christ, who invites and offers his Father's love), the identity [between Buddhist and Christian spirituality and religious experience] is not possible and we see the great difference of the two 'belongings'. . .

This Christian originality will change the spirit of all other different levels of possible communion and identity." Quoted from ibid., p. 231.

[62]Note the following remark in the report of the first workshop: "In Buddhism, which is a human reality, man's search is sustained by God. Therefore the Word of God is already present in this search." Quoted from "Christianity Seen By Buddhists," p. 229.

[63]A summary of this meeting, some of the presentations, and the final communiqué appear in Bulletin 39 (1978): 171-191.

[64]Thus the final communiqué makes the following remark: "We intend to collaborate actively with religious men to sustain those international institutions which seek to promote human rights, peace and progress among all nations." Quoted from "Final Communiqué of the Nemi Meeting," in "Report of the Nemi Meeting (24th-26th July, 1978)," Bulletin 39 (1978): 174.

[65]The final communiqué therefore recommends exchanges of lecturers and graduate students and the "twinning" of universities run by the different religions, as well as studying together the ethical positions of the different religions involved in the dialogue. See ibid., p. 174.

[66]The entire issue of Bulletin 30 (1975) is devoted to this meeting.

[67]Presentations on this theme can be found in Bulletin 30 (1975): Fr. Michael Fitzgerald, "Christian-Muslim Dialogue in Indonesia and the Philippines," pp. 214-217; Abbé Achilles de Souza, "Christian-Muslim Dialogue With Reference to Pakistan," pp. 218-222; Fr. Abou Mokh, "Le dialogue dans le monde arabe," pp. 223-226; Fr. Georges Anawati, "Le dialogue islamo-chrétien en Egypte aujourd'hui," pp. 227-232; Fr. Michel Lelong, "La communauté chrétienne et les musulmans en Tunisie," pp. 237-240; Fr. Maurice Borrmans, "Quelques informations sur la Libye et l'Eglise," p. 241; idem, "Les Journées Romaines 1975," pp. 242-244; Fr. Ary Roest Crollius, "Four Notes on Dialogue (Especially Regarding Islam)," pp. 245-248; Fr. Michel Lelong, "Le Secrétariat de l'Eglise de France pour les relations avec l'Islam," pp. 249-252; Fr. Albert Nambiaparambil, "Dialogue in India: An Analysis of the Situation, A Reflection on Experience," pp. 253-268; Abbé Paul Phichit, "Dialogue Situation in Thailand," pp. 269-276; Fr. Marcello Zago, "Le dialogue avec les Buddhistes au Laos," pp. 277-291;Fr. John Bosco Shirieda, "Dialogue Situation in Japan and Korea," pp. 292-295; Fr. Joseph

Shih, "Dialogue Situation in Taiwan and Hong Kong," pp. 296-297; Fr. Giuseppe Butturini, "De la participation des religions traditionnelles africaines au dialogue interreligieux: possibilités et limites," pp. 298-310; Fr. Joseph Masson, "Le dialogue avec les syncrétistes," pp. 311-314.

[68]The questionnaire (found in the archives of the Secretariat) reads as follows:
"--What do you think of dialogue if it is contained within a strictly religious context or in one of private morality? Is it possible? Credible? To what extent is it possible?"--What about, instead, strictly social themes (e.g., development, economics, health, education, social welfare, human rights, liberation, etc.)?
"--What about a dialogue on actual problems of the epoch in which we live, e.g., population problem, abortion, violence, economical crisis, impotence of religions, world hunger, violation of rights?"

[69]Thus the questionnaire asks (p.4), "In dialogue with the non-Christian, what are the problems which in a more particular way arouse the conscience of your churches? The desire to present Christianity? . . . Enculturation of the Christian life and of the liturgy in the national context? . . . [T]o develop mission? To know other participants? To reveal the face of Christianity? To exchange stimuli and spiritual experiences? To make friends? To build up each other spiritually?"

[70]Ibid., pp. 3 and 5.

[71]Ibid., p. 3.

[72]Ibid., p. 4.

[73]This article appears in Bulletin 30 (1975): 328-339.

[74]Lopez-Gay, "Current Criticism," pp. 337-338.

[75]Lopez-Gay thus noted the opposition to dialogue in the following comment: "The present post-Barthian school of thought rejects dialogue, starting off from the idea of witness; witness means to preach with authority, invested with full powers. The Biblical concept of conversion, they say, carries with it the decision to change one's life, giving up one's (own) religion. It is a fundamental option, the act of faith, with a conversion of the heart and of the mind. The Fathers (Clement of Rome, Justin, Hermas, Theophilus) join to conversion the idea of epistrophe, a Platonic idea which signifies a turning of the soul towards the supreme realities and a despising of the world of

sense; in the Fathers this term accentuates the convert's situation of tragedy or of struggle with the pagan type of environment. In the Acts, in fact, there is no account of any conversion through dialogue." Quoted from ibid., p. 330.

[76]Ibid., pp. 332-333.

[77]Ibid., p.339.

[78]Mgr. Rossano's opening address, "The Secretariat for Non-Christian Religions," was in fact a summary of the Secretariat's work from its beginnings.

[79]Some of the presentations appear in Bulletin 41-42 (1979), an issue of the Bulletin devoted entirely to this plenary meeting. The following presentations are reprinted: Cardinal Sergio Pignedoli, "Introduction to the Plenary Meeting," pp. 79-84; Mgr. Pietro Rossano, "The Secretariat for Non-Christian Religions From the Beginnings to the Present Day: History, Ideas, Problems," pp. 88-109; Stanley J. Samartha, "Guidelines on Dialogue," pp. 130-138; Mgr. Henri Teissier, "Possibilités et éléments d'un Directoire pour le dialogue," pp. 131-161; Mgr. Patrick D'Souza, "Contents of the Directory on Dialogue With Men of Other Religions," pp. 162-167; Mgr. Francis Arinze, "Means Necessary for Developing Dialogue with Non-Christians," pp. 168-170; Cardinal Joseph Parecattil, "Monasticism in Dialogue," pp. 176-182. A list of the participants appears on pp. 195-196 of this issue of the Bulletin.

[80]Rossano, "The Secretariat for Non-Christian Religions," pp. 105-106.

[81]Ibid., p. 106.

[82]"Rapport du groupe 'Islam'," Bulletin 41-42 (1979): 183-184.

[83]Ibid., pp. 184-185.

[84]Ibid., p. 185.

[85]Rossano, "The Secretariat for Non-Christian Religions," p. 108.

[86]The workshop ("Rapport du groupe des religions traditionnelles africaines," Bulletin 41-42 ((1979)): 189) thus recommended that the Secretariat should "Prévoir l'organisation d'une grande 'Conférence Générale' ayant pour objet: Religions Africaines et Catholicisme:
>   --à tenir dans les 2 ou 3 ans à venir;
>   --elle serait préparée par un questionnaire, à établir par le Secrétariat en consultation avec des experts dans les diffé-

rentes parties de l'Afrique;
--des réunions au plan national précéde-
raient la Conférence;
--celle-ci aurait pour objet:
a) d'établir un Bilan général des études
depuis la création du Secrétariat,
b) de déterminer systématiquement les
Valeurs positives des Religions africaines,
c) d'indiquer nettement les valeurs négatives ou éléments incompatibles avec la foi
ou la pratique chrétienne;
d) de contribuer par une critique scien-
tifique et philosophique à la structuration
positive des éléments religieux et spirituels
de la culture et de la civilisation africaine."

[87]Rossano, "The Secretariat for Non-Christian Religions," p. 107.

[88]Ibid.

[89]The report of this workshop says, "Among Christians there was often no clear understanding of the relationship between dialogue and evangelization, and
lack of understanding of the nature and scope of dialogue was considered a basic difficulty by the group.
Central to this point is the question asked by those
within the Church: is dialogue a betrayal of mission?
Does dialogue compromise our integrity as Christians or
prevent us from discharging the obligation of preaching the Good News of Christ to all mankind?" Quoted
from "Report of the Group for Asian Religions," Bulletin 41-42 (1979): 191.

[90]Ibid., p. 192.

[91]Ibid., p. 191.

[92]Ibid., pp. 192 and 193.

[93]Secretariat for Non-Christians, "Project Regarding General Guidelines for Dialogue With Non-Christians," Part I, no. 1. A copy of this proposal was
given to the author by the Under-Secretary of the Secretariat, Fr. John Bosco Shirieda.

[94]Thus the draft proposal reads, "There is normal-
ly a certain progression in the process of dialogue:
from a 'thawing' of hostility to relations of friendship, from a gradual elimination of the tensions and
hostilities accumulated in history to a deeper knowledge, to collaboration for common human objectives, to
search for and development of points held in common, to

the communication of respective religious experience."
Quoted from ibid., Part II, no. 16.

[95]Ibid., no. 33.

[96]Ibid., nos. 1, 9 and 10. See also no. 31 which
reads, "Catholic scholastic institutions and aid agencies should, in principle, seek to ensure that non-
Christians may have the possibility of exercising their
religious faith and of being educated in it."

[97]Ibid., no. 15.

[98]Thus the guidelines say, "[Dialogue's] aim is to
set out on a common road with the partner in dialogue
in order to communicate something to him and to receive
something oneself; in this sense dialogue will enrich
the Christian's experience." Quoted from ibid., no. 12.

[99]This was the major focus of attention in the
WCC's dialogue activity, as will become evident below.
The Secretariat's draft guidelines say, "Among the
tasks of Christian dialogue with other religions there
is that of developing rules of conduct for coexistence
in a society that is religiously plural. This is the
objective of the DIALOGUE between COMMUNITIES." Quoted
from ibid., no. 32.

[100]Ibid., no. 12.

[101]Ibid., no. 3.

[102]Thus the draft guidelines say, "The religious
dimension common to the Christian and to the Non-Christian offers the possibility of moving forward together to reciprocal enrichment and mutual understanding.
When, however, the Christian reaches the threshold of
the Gospel message, he knows he is presenting something
radically new, relating to an historical event and
something he personally has received." Quoted from
ibid., no. 7.

[103]Ibid., no. 6.

[104]The text of this statement can be found in Bulletin 56 (1984): 126-141. It can also be found in The
Pope Speaks 29 (1984): 253-264. References in this
study are to the version in the Bulletin.

[105]See "Attitude of the Church," no. 7.

[106]See ibid., no. 29.

[107]See ibid., nos. 18, 19, and 21.

[108]Ibid., no. 21.

[109]See ibid., no. 22.

[110]See ibid., no. 10.

[111]See ibid., no. 18.

[112]See ibid., no. 37.

[113]See ibid., no. 26.

[114]Thus in a letter to bishops explaining the Secretariat's work, Cardinal Pignedoli stated, "I should
like to add one word more regarding ecumenical collaboration: the division in the Church is well-known to
non-Christians and represents for them a cause for
amazement and scandal: on the other hand, we must take
note of the fact that the positions adopted by the Ecumenical Council of Churches as regards dialogue are
now seen to be nearer those of the Catholic Church, as
was seen clearly in the recent 'Theological Convention
on Dialogue in Community' held at Chiang Mai (Thailand)
from 18th to 27th April, 1977. For this reason, we have
committed ourselves, together with the Sub-Unit of Geneva 'Dialogue With People of Living Faiths and Ideologies', to giving an ecumenical aspect to all initiatives of dialogue with non-Christians, on every occasion that this seems to be possible and fruitful."
Quoted from "Letter of Cardinal President to the
Bishops," pp. 91-92. The draft for the new guidelines
presented to the plenary meeting of the Secretariat in
1979 also contains this idea. It says, "Every initiative of dialogue undertaken by the Roman Secretariat,
by local Churches, or by particular groups will always
be concerned to develop an ecumenical spirit among
Christians. For this reason every public initiative of
dialogue where the Christian party presents itself as
Christian, sic et simpliciter, should take the ecumenical dimension into account. Where, and as far as, it
is possible, dialogue should always be carried out with
ecumenical participation." Quoted from "Project Regarding General Guidelines," Part II, no. 25.

NOTES TO CHAPTER FOUR

[1]See especially Gérard Vallée, Mouvement oecuménique et religions non-chrétiennes. Un débat oecuménique sur la rencontre interreligieuse de Tambaram
à Uppsala (1938-1968) (Montréal: Bellarmine, 1975), and
Carl F. Hallencreutz, New Approaches to Men of Other
Faiths, 1938-1968: A Theological Discussion (Geneva:
WCC, 1970).

[2]For an analysis of Barth's influence on Protestant views of the religions, see Johannes Aagard, "Revelation and Religion. The Influence of Dialectical Theology on the Understanding of the Relationship Between Christianity and Other Religions," Studia Theologica 14 (1960): 148-185.

[3]For an analysis of Barth's views, see Aagard, "Revelation and Religion," whole article, and Paul Knitter, Towards a Protestant Theology of Religions. A Case Study of Paul Althaus and Contemporary Attitudes. Marburger theologische Studien, II (Marburg: Elwert, 1974), pp. 20-36. Barth's position appears in its classical form in "The Revelation of God as the Abolition of Religion," Section 17, Church Dogmatics, vol. 1, part 2: The Doctrine of the Word of God, trans. George T. Thomson and Harold Knight (Edinburgh: T. & T. Clark, 1956), pp. 280-361.

[4]Thus Knitter, for example, remarks as follows: "Barth's starting point is a theme which he heralded throughout his entire theological career: the transcendence of God and the finiteness of man, man's inability to find--even search for--God in and by himself, the necessity of God 'doing all', the impossibility of beginning with anything human when speaking of the divine." Quoted from Knitter, Towards a Protestant Theology of Religions, p. 24.

[5]Barth says, for example, ". . . the true and essential difference of the Christian religion from the non-Christian, and with it its character of the religion of truth over against the religions of error, can be demonstrated only in the fact, or event, that taught by Holy Scripture the Church listens to Jesus Christ and no one else as grace and truth . . . ." Quoted from "The Revelation of God as the Abolition of Religion," p. 349. Later Barth notes, "In the relationship between the name of Jesus Christ and the Christian religion we have to do with an act of divine justification or forgiveness of sins. We have already stated that the Christian religion as such has no worthiness of its own, to equip it specially to be the true religion. We must now aver even more clearly that in itself and as such it is absolutely unworthy to be the true religion. If it is so, it is so by election, we said. . . . It is not justified in itself. It is sinful both in form and also in its human origin. It is no less so than can be said of the story of Buddhism or of Islam. The hands into which God has delivered Himself up in His revelation are thoroughly unclean (pp. 352-353)."

[6]See the description by Paul Knitter of Barth's view in Towards a Protestant Theology of Religions, p. 35. Knitter writes, "The non-Christians are those who 'ohne ihn (Christ), ohne das Licht des Lebens, ohne das Wort vom Gnadenbunde verloren gehen, und bleiben mussten' ([Kirchliche Dogmatik, I/2]421). They are in a condition of 'verhangnisvollen Selbstmissverstandnis und Selbstwiderspruch'; the non-Christian is the 'im Tiefsten verwirrte, angefochtene, der tief geplagte, ratlose und betrobte Mensch' (923f.). Because the non-Christians do not have Christ and therefore cannot respond to God's universal salvific call, they fall into 'Not und Angst', . . ."

[7]Hendrik Kraemer, The Christian Message in a Non-Christian World (London: Edinburgh House Press, 1938; reprint ed., London: James Clark & Co., 1961).

[8]For an analysis of Kraemer's position at Tambaram and the debate it sparked, see especially Hallencreutz, New Approaches, pp. 21-39, and Vallée, Mouvement oecuménique et religions non-chrétiennes, pp. 36-82.

[9]In his discussion of this controversy, Gérard Vallée quotes from a letter of H.P. van Dusen to Kraemer dated July 28, 1938: ". . . the break is neither so absolute nor drastic, the preparations for Christ are not so non-existent nor inconsequential as the convert honestly believes. Do not dismiss this as a 'surrender of the absolute character of God's revelation in Christ to naturalistic relativism'. It is, rather, vigorous loyalty to 'truth'--a recognition that God's self-disclosure, while climactic, unique and absolutely authoritative in Christ, has not, in His wise provision, been confined to Christ." Quoted from Vallée, Mouvement oecuménique et religions non-chrétiennes, p. 57. For other examples of positions which opposed Kraemer's and which are part of the debate sparked by Tambaram or which form part of its pre-history, see the following: John N. Farquhar, The Crown of Hinduism (London: Oxford University Press, 1913); William E. Hocking et al., Re-Thinking Missions. A Layman's Inquiry After One Hundred Years (London: SCM, 1932); A.G. Hogg, The Christian Message to the Hindu (London: SCM, 1947).

[10]Tambaram-Madras Series. International Missionary Council Meeting at Tambaram, Madras, December 12th to 29th, 1938, vol. 1 (Oxford: Oxford University Press, 1939), pp. 210-211.

[11]Remarks in the statement issued by the second general assembly of the WCC at Evanston in 1955 illustrate this. The statement says, "The renaissance of non-Christian religions and the spread of new ideologies necessitate a new approach to our evangelistic task. In many countries, especially in Asia and Africa, these religious revivals are reinforced by nationalism and often present themselves as an effective basis for social reforms. It is not so much the truth of these systems of thought and feeling which makes appeal, but rather the present determination to interpret and change oppressive conditions of life. Therefore they confront us not only as reformulated creeds but also as foundations for universal hope." Quoted from W. A. Visser't Hooft, ed., The Evanston Report. The Second Assembly of the WCC (London: SCM, 1955), p. 106.

[12]This study is the major theme of Vallée's work cited above. For an overview of the work of this study see Vallée, "'The Word of God and the Living Faiths of Men': Chronology and Bibliography of a Study Process," in Stanley J. Samartha, Living Faiths and the Ecumenical Movement (London: SCM, 1971), pp. 165-182.

[13]The assembly's statement thus said, "Dialogue is a form of evangelization which is often effective today . . . . [T]he communication of the Gospel today consists in the listening first and then showing how the Gospel meets the need of the times as we have learned to understand it." Quoted from W. A. Visser't Hooft, ed., The New Delhi Report. The Third Assembly of the WCC (London: SCM, 1961), no. 23, p. 84.

[14]Thus the final declaration of this meeting notes, "While the basic need of all men, including Christians, is for the Gospel in all its fullness, the individually felt need of any man under his particular circumstances at any given moment also requires sympathetic and informed understanding on the part of the man who will speak to him of the Gospel. Dialogue requires a transparent willingness to listen to what the other is saying and to recognize whatever truth be in it." Quoted from "The Witness of Christians to Men of Other Faiths," in R.K. Orchard, ed., Witness in Six Continents. Records of the Meeting of the CWME of the WCC Held in Mexico City, Dec. 8th to 19th, 1963 (London: SCM, 1964), p. 144. Cf. Vallée, Mouvement oecuménique et religions non-chrétiennes, pp. 172-180.

[15]Reprinted in The Ecumenical Review 16 (1964): 451-455.

[16]See "Christian Encounter With Men of Other Faiths," p. 453.

[17]See for example Devanandan and Thomas, Christian Participation in Nation-Building.

[18]For the comments of Victor Hayward, reprints of some of the papers, and the text of the final declaration, see Study Encounter 3 (1967): 51-80. For further analysis of this meeting, see Vallée, Mouvement oecuménique et religions non-chrétiennes, pp. 191-201, and "Consultation de Kandy sur le dialogue entre chrétiens et non-chrétiennes," Bulletin 4 (1967): 118-119. The Consultors from the Secretariat who attended the Kandy consultation were Prof. Olivier Lacombe, Fr. Joseph Spae, and Fr. Klaus Klostermaier.

[19]Published in Dow Kirkpatrick, ed., The Finality of Christ (New York: Abingdon, 1966), pp. 13-31.

[20]Niles, "The Finality of Christ," pp. 21-24.

[21]Ibid., pp. 25-26.

[22]Ibid., pp. 27-28.

[23]Ibid., p. 28.

[24]Ibid., p. 29.

[25]The author found a copy of this declaration in the DFI archives.

[26]"The Mission of the Church in Contemporary India," no. 2.

[27]Ibid. The text reads, "We must admit that in the past Christians have tended to regard other religions as wholly hostile to the purpose of God, and hence Christian mission has often been associated with the idea of conquest. This attitude is not in keeping with the Christian Gospel of love and redemption; it needs to be replaced by an understanding of the positive values expressed in them. Under the guidance of the Spirit of Jesus Christ, we have to discern God's working in them and through them."

[28]Ibid., no. 3.

[29]Ibid., no. 5.

[30]Kenneth Cragg, "The Credibility of Christianity," Study Encounter 3/2 (1967): 56-61.

[31]Ibid., pp. 58-59.

[32]Lynn de Silva, "Non-Christian Religions and God's Plan of Salvation," Study Encounter 3/2 (1967): 61-67.

[33]Ibid., p. 65.

[34]Ibid., p. 64.

[35]Ibid., p. 66.

[36]"Christians in Dialogue With Men of Other Faiths," Study Encounter 3/2 (1967): 52-56.

[37]The text reads, "His [the Christian's] intercourse takes the form of dialogue, since he respects the differences between him and others, and because he wishes to hear as well as to speak. The fundamental nature of dialogue is this genuine readiness to listen to the man with whom we wish to communicate. Our concern should not be to win arguments." Quoted from ibid., p. 53.

[38]Ibid., p. 53.

[39]Ibid., pp. 53-54.

[40]Ibid., p. 55.

[41]Ibid., p. 53. In the issue of Study Encounter in which one finds this declaration, the editor, Victor Hayward, comments on p. 73, "We cannot place any formal precedence upon proclamation before dialogue, but we recognize that dialogue must include proclamation; we must reassure conservative evangelicals on this point, without assuming that dialogue is thereby debased to the level of evangelistic tactic or preparation."

[42]The declaration says on p. 53, "All mankind is furthermore being caught up into one universal history, and made increasingly aware of common tasks and common hopes. For the Christian, a deep sense of community is given by his belief that all men are created in the image of God, by his realization that Christ died for every man, and by the expectation of His coming kingdom. Here is the foundation of the Christian's approach to any human being. . . . Love always seeks to communicate. Our experience of God's communion with us constrains us to communion with men of other beliefs."

[43]Ibid.

[44]Ibid.

[45]Ibid.

[46]Cf. the remarks of Paul Knitter in Towards a Protestant Theology of Religions, p. 259, n. 51. For an analysis of the impact of the notion of the "cosmic" Christ within ecumenical circles in the early period of the WCC's existence, see Horst Burkle, "Die Frage nach

dem 'kosmischen Christus' als Beispiel einer okumenisch orientierten Theologie," _Kerygma und Dogma_ 11 (1965): 103-115.

[47]"Christians in Dialogue," p. 53. The problem of the place of the non-Christian religions in the divine economy of salvation appears also in "Study Consider- ations" listed by Victor Hayward in the _Study Encoun- ter_ devoted to the Kandy meeting [3/2 (1967)]. Included among the "theological tensions" in these study consid- erations was the following (from p. 73): "We are not unanimous that God's economy _must_ include other reli- gious _traditions_, but we must insist that the question should be raised, not presuming to know the mind of God, but being open to learn more of it." In his re- marks introducing the Kandy meeting in this issue of _Study Encounter_, Hayward noted on pp. 51-52, "There is . . . great need that theologians working within their confessional traditions should take up afresh questions relating to the place of other religious systems, and the place of other religious communities, in the econ- omy of God's purposes for mankind."

[48]This part of the assembly's report appears in "Renewal in Mission," "Section II of the Fourth Assem- bly, Uppsala," paragraph 6. It is reprinted in _The Ec- umenical Review_ 21 (1969): 368.

[49]Ibid.

[50]Stanley J. Samartha, "The Word of God and the Living Faiths of Men. Plans for Future Study," made available to the author from the archives of the DFI.

[51]Samartha, "The World Council of Churches and Men of Other Faiths and Ideologies," p. 3, made available to the author from the archives of the DFI.

[52]Ibid., p. 4.

[53]Samartha's final remarks in this report are, "Living in a world of cultural and religious pluralism and at a time when people everywhere, sharing the bur- den and mystery of human existence, are becoming in- creasingly aware of the common problems of the surviv- al or extinction of humankind, has'nt [sic] the time come for the ecumenical ship to move out of the safe waters of the Mediterranean into the unchartered ocean of the world?"

[54]_Central Committee of the World Council of Churches. Minutes and Reports of the Twenty-Third Meet- ing. University of Kent at Canterbury, August 12-22, 1969_ (Geneva: WCC, 1969), p. 29.

[55]The Secretariat for Non-Christians was represented by Fr. Georges Anawati, Fr. Klaus Klostermaier,
and Fr. Jesus Lopez-Gay. The latter wrote up a summary and analysis of the meeting for the Secretariat,
published in Bulletin 14 (1970): 77-84.

[56]Samartha, "Memo No. 2," October 10, 1969, made
available to the author from the archives of the DFI.

[57]The papers presented at this meeting along with
the concluding memorandum appear in Stanley J. Samartha, ed., Dialogue Between Men of Living Faiths. Papers
Presented at a Consultation Held at Ajaltoun, Lebanon,
March 1970 (Geneva: WCC, 1971).

[58]"Dialogue Between Men of Living Faiths--The
Ajaltoun Memorandum," in Samartha, Dialogue Between Men
of Living Faiths, p. 108.

[59]Ibid., p. 117.

[60]Mgr. Rossano and Fr. Jean Masson represented the
Secretariat for Non-Christians at this consultation.

[61]"Christians in Dialogue With Men of Other
Faiths," International Review of Mission 59 (1970):
382-391.

[62]"Christians in Dialogue," no. 1. The aide-mémoire repeats this idea in its final section saying,
"All the circumstances of human life on the globe at
this present stage force upon us the search for a world
community in which men can share and act together."
Quoted from ibid., no. 24.

[63]Ibid., no. 2.

[64]Ibid., no. 8.

[65]Ibid., nos. 3 and 8.

[66]Ibid., no. 4.

[67]Ibid., no. 6.

[68]Ibid.

[69]Ibid., no. 4. The text says, "Peter's words to
Cornelius are significant: 'Truly I perceive that God
shows no partiality, but in every nation anyone who
fears him and does what is right is acceptable to him'
(Acts 10-34-35). God is at work among all men and he
speaks to a Cyrus or a Cornelius and bids them to do
his will. By opening ourselves to other men we may be
enabled better to understand what God is saying to us
in Christ."

[70]Ibid.

[71]Ibid., no. 18.

[72]Ibid.

[73]Ibid., no. 9.

[74]See Col. 1:17 and Eph. 1:9-10.

[75]"Christians in Dialogue," no. 10.

[76]Ibid., no. 18.

[77]Ibid.

[78]Ibid., no. 11.

[79]Ibid., no. 12.

[80]Ibid., no. 22.

[81]Georges Khodr, "Christianity in a Pluralistic World--The Economy of the Holy Spirit," The Ecumenical Review 23 (1971): 118-128 and Stanley J. Samartha, "Dialogue As A Continuing Christian Concern," The Ecumenical Review (1971): 129-142.

[82]See a discussion of this idea of "Christomonism" in Paul Knitter, Towards a Protestant Theology of Religions, pp. 20-32 and idem, "Christomonism in Karl Barth's Evaluation of the Non-Christian Religions," Neue Zeitschrift fur systematische Theologie und Religionsphilosophie 13 (1971): 99-121.

[83]Khodr, "Christianity in a Pluralistic World," p. 123.

[84]Ibid., p. 122.

[85]Thus Khodr remarks in ibid., pp. 126-127, "The Christian who knows that, within God's plan, the great religions constitute training schools of the Divine mercy will have an attitude of profound peace and gentle patience. There will be an obedience to this plan being carried out by the Holy Spirit, an expectant hope of the Lord's coming, a longing to eat the Paschal meal, and a secret form of communion with all men in the economy of the Mystery whereby we are being gradually led towards the final consummation, the recapitulation of all things in Christ."

[86]Ibid., p. 127.

[87]Ibid., p. 128. Khodr goes on to say on this same page, "The task of the witness in a non-Christian context will be to name him whom others have already recognized as the Beloved. Once they have become the friends of the Bridegroom (the Church) it will be easy

to name him. The entire missionary activity of the Church will be directed towards awakening the Christ who sleeps in the night of the religions."

[88]Samartha, "Dialogue As A Continuing Christian Concern," pp. 135-137.

[89]Ibid., p. 140.

[90]Ibid., p. 141.

[91]The passage reads, ". . . when he comes who is the Spirit of truth, he will guide you into all truth . . . ."

[92]Samartha, "Dialogue As A Continuing Christian Concern," p. 141.

[93]See the summary of the discussion in Central Committee of the World Council of Churches. Minutes and Reports of the Twenty-Fourth Meeting of the Central Committee, Addis Ababa, Ethiopia, January 10-21, 1971 (Geneva: WCC, 1971), pp. 18-20.

[94]Ibid., p. 19.

[95]The text of this policy statement and guidelines appears in The Ecumenical Review 24 (1971): 47-54. I will hereafter refer to it as the "Interim Policy Statement."

[96]"Interim Policy Statement," no. 1.

[97]Thus the "Interim Policy Statement," no. 10 says, "Dialogue must take place in freedom. Each partner must be understood as he understands himself, and his freedom to be committed to his faith must be fully respected. Without this freedom to be committed, to be open, to witness, to change and to be changed, genuine dialogue is impossible."

[98]Ibid., no. 7.

[99]Ibid., no. 1.

[100]The statement reads (no. 1), "At the present time, [dialogue] is inevitable because everywhere in the world Christians are now living in pluralistic societies. It is urgent because all men are under common pressures in the search for justice, peace and a hopeful future. It is full of opportunity because Christians can now in new ways discover new aspects of the servanthood and lordship of Christ and new implications for the witness of the Church in the context of moving towards a common human community." Cf. "Christians in Dialogue" (the Zurich statement), no. 1.

101"Interim Policy Statement," no. 6.

102Ibid., no. 2.

103Ibid., no. 9b.

104Ibid., no. 8.

105Ibid., no. 12.

106Thus the statement says (no. 13), "There is .
. . acute difference among ourselves and in our
churches whether the emphasis on dialogue will blunt
the cutting edge of this mission [namely, the mission
to witness to Jesus Christ] or whether the community of
human and spiritual discourse created by dialogue will
further it."

107Ibid., no. 14.

108Ibid., no. 17(i).

109Ibid., no. 17(ii).

110Ibid., no. 19.

111Ibid., no. 18.

112The committee's report describes the general
aim of the "Faith and Witness" Programme Unit as follows: "To seek God's will for the unity of the Church,
to assist the churches to explore the context and meaning of the Gospel for their faith and mission, to encourage dialogue with men of other faiths and ideologies, and to enquire into the bearing of Christian belief on the spiritual and ethical issues posed for
society by science and technology." Quoted from "Report
of the Structure Committee," Appendix III, Minutes, Addis Ababa, p. 162. Emphasis added. The other sub-units
in this Programme Unit were: i) The Commission of Faith
and Order, ii) The Commission on World Mission and
Evangelism, and iii) The Working Group on Church and
Society.

113"Report on the Meeting of the Ad Hoc Working
Group on 'Dialogue With Men of Living Faiths and Ideologies'," p. 3. This report was presented at a meeting of the Division of Studies in Mission and Evangelism at Jogny, Switzerland, June 1-5, 1971. A copy was
made available to the author from the archives of the
DFI.

114Thus a few years later in 1973, Stanley Samartha was to say in a lecture at the Oxford Institute of
Methodist Studies, "A more sensitive recognition of the
wider work of the Holy Spirit may also help us to
broaden our understanding of God's saving activity,

thus correcting what our Orthodox friends describe as a Christomonistic tendency that seems to dominate Protestant theology and also preventing our conception of God from becoming too small and static." Quoted from "The Holy Spirit and Peoples of Various Faiths, Cultures and Ideologies," in Samartha, Courage for Dialogue. Ecumenical Issues in Inter-Religious Relationships (Geneva: WCC, 1981), p. 64. Samartha continues on p. 65, "There are others, however, for example in the Orthodox tradition, who refuse to limit the work of the Holy Spirit in the area of rational beings only but would include all creation within the scope of his presence and activity. This would, by implication, have a more generous attitude towards recognizing the work of the Holy Spirit among people of other religions."

115"Report on the Meeting of the Ad Hoc Working Group," p. 3.

116A text of this declaration appears, with an introductory comment, in Christ To the World 17 (1971): 73-78. A list of the signatories appears on p. 78. Among these is Dr. Peter Beyerhaus whose reaction to a universal, inclusive attitude towards the saving activity of God will be discussed further below.

117"The Frankfurt Declaration," no. 3.

118Ibid., no. 2.

119Ibid., no. 5.

120Thus, "We . . . reject the false teaching that the non-Christian religions and world views are also ways of salvation similar to belief in Christ." Quoted from ibid., no. 6.

121Ibid. In introducing this declaration, a Roman Catholic missionary writer, Fr. Domenico Grasso, says, "We would just like to point out that on [this] one point we are not in full agreement with the document . . . . Catholic doctrine, we would like to point out, though requiring explicit faith in Christ and baptism for all those who know about it, requires only an implicit faith in Christ and baptism 'in voto' for all those who, through no fault of their own, have not been able to listen to the announcement of the Gospel, the ordinary vehicle of faith, the premises to baptism, but do 'what is in their power' to live in accordance with the dictates of conscience." Quoted from ibid., p. 72. It is interesting to note that the Frankfurt declaration does not address the question of the salvation of those who are not able to hear the preaching of the Gospel.

122Ibid., no. 6. Emphasis added.

NOTES TO CHAPTER FIVE

1For a summary and analysis by one of these Consultors, Fr. M.L. Fitzgerald, see "Lebanon-Broumana: Muslim-Christian Consultation (July 1972)," Bulletin 21 (1972): 58-62.

2The major papers and concluding memorandum of the consultation appear in S.J. Samartha and John B. Taylor, eds., Christian-Muslim Dialogue. Papers Presented at the Broumana Consultation, 12-18 July 1972 (Geneva: WCC, 1973).

3"Aide-Mémoire. Christian-Muslim Consultation, December 1-2, 1971, Geneva, Switzerland." A copy of this aide-mémoire was made available to the author from the DFI archives.

4Samartha, "Christian-Muslim Dialogue in the Perspective of Recent History," in Samartha and Taylor, Christian-Muslim Dialogue, p. 12.

5"In Search of Understanding and Cooperation: Christian and Muslim Contributions," the Broumana memorandum, in Samartha and Taylor, Christian-Muslim Dialogue, no. 4(a).

6Ibid., no. 2.

7Ibid., no. 4(c).

8Ibid., no. 3.

9Ibid., no. 3(c).

10Ibid., no. 2.

11The two terms, "evangelical" and "ecumenical," are commonplace within the WCC and can be seen in the writings of Dr. Peter Beyerhaus, for example, in his comments on the Bangkok assembly. See Peter Beyerhaus, Bangkok '73. The Beginning or End of World Mission? (Grand Rapids, Michigan: Zondervan, 1974). The "evangelical" group holds to a "Christomonistic" view of God's saving work in the world at large.

12The assembly's statement on dialogue, "On Dialogue With People of Living Faiths," appears in Bangkok Assembly 1973. Minutes and Reports of the Commission on World Mission and Evangelism of the World Council of Churches, December 31, 1972 and January 9-12, 1973 (Geneva: WCC, 1973), pp. 78-80.

[13]Ibid., no. 11. The report states, "We have already said that our attitude to people of other faiths
arises out of our understanding of God's will that all
man [sic] shall be saved."

[14]Ibid. See also no. 4 which reads as follows: "We
are conscious of God's movement towards men as Creator
and Saviour, bringing man to wholeness and leading him
to wider community. We see in the Bible the record of
his saving acts among the people of the Sinai covenant,
in the incarnate life of our Lord and in the world mission given to the Church. Our eyes will be keenly open
to discuss what He is doing among people of other
faiths."

[15]See the remarks of Peter Beyerhaus in Bangkok
'73, pp. 71-72. It is interesting to note that Mgr.
Rossano commented with satisfaction that at this assembly "an optimistic vision of the religions emerged, in
antithesis to that of Tambaram (1938)." See "Report of
the Under-Secretary's Journey in Asia," Bulletin 22
(1973): 57.

[16]See Beyerhaus, Bangkok '73 p. 71. See also the
remarks of Stanley Samartha in "Die Grenzen geraten in
Unruhe. Im Dialog mit den Religionen und Ideologien,"
Evangelische Kommentare 10 (1972): 593.

[17]Thus he remarks, "The ecumenical program of education has here, it seems to me, betrayed its most pre-
cipitous aspect: the goal [of dialogue] is to make the
Christian sensitive for a work of the Spirit in the
very place where He, according to Holy Scripture, is
never at work (2 Cor. 6:14-17)." Quoted from Beyerhaus,
Bangkok '73, p. 71.

[18]Ibid., p. 103.

[19]See Beyerhaus' comments in "Growing Churches and
Renewal," Addendum II in Bangkok Reports, p. 109: "Newness in the biblical sense is not the gradual development or amendment of an old thing towards a better
quality. It must be understood ontologically as the
substitution of one kind of life by a completely different one. The Uppsala theme was taken from Revelations 21:5: 'Behold I make all things new'. In my understanding, the way in which this verse was made use
of [in Bangkok] in describing the participation of the
Church in the present socio-political quests to bring
about better conditions for human life was a misinter-
pretation of the word. For in Revelations 21:5, it
clearly means the totally new creation of Heaven and
Earth as a sovereign act of God himself at the end."

[20]For a list of the members of this Working Group, as well as the minutes and reports presented, see DFI, Minutes of the Meeting of the Working Group, Pendeli near Athens, March 1973 (Geneva: WCC, 1973).

[21]The meeting also dealt with dialogue with people of secular ideologies and dialogue with Jews, both of which remain beyond the scope this study but which were also part of the DFI's work.

[22]Stanley J. Samartha, "Director's Report to the Working Group," Minutes, Pendeli, p. 19.

[23]See, for example, "Report of the Sub-Group on Multilateral Dialogue," in Minutes, Pendeli, p. 19: "It's [namely, the planned multilateral dialogue] exploratory responsibility will include reflection on local and regional follow-up for promotion of multilateral and bilateral mutual understanding at the local level, for the removal of tensions and hostilities, for the promotion of racial and social justice, for liberation and human growth, for the generation of an atmosphere in which people of differing religious convictions can witness to each other and live and work together in openness and mutual respect."

[24]Ibid., pp. 17-18.

[25]Ibid., p. 20.

[26]The concluding memorandum, entitled "The Wholeness of Human Life: Christian Involvement in Mankind's Inner Dialogue With Primal World-Views," can be found in Study Encounter 9/4 (1973): 1-20. On p. 1, it says, "[These] fellow human beings, and the contribution the primal traditions and cultures have made to the rest of mankind, have too often been ignored, or regarded as worthy of serious attention only as possible subjects of conversion. Christians have seldom turned to listen to them, and if possible to learn from them . . . ."

[27]The memorandum notes on p. 3, "'Primal' is used in the sense of 'basic' or 'fundamental', and to refer to those forms of society or religion, or those forms of comprehensive reference systems, which are associated with what are commonly called tribal peoples or cultures. It is not meant to suggest that these are more fundamental, authentic or 'pure' than other religious systems, but simply that in historical fact they have been widely distributed across all continents and have preceded and contributed to all other known religious systems of mankind." Note here the difference between the DFI and the Secretariat for Non-Christians. The latter used the term "traditional" instead of "pri-

mal" to refer to these traditions. In rejecting that former term, the Ibadan memorandum notes, on p. 3, "Although . . . 'traditional' is often used of indigenous African forms, it applies to all known religions, and especially to both Islam and Christianity, and is not distinctive of the religions of African origin to which it is being applied . . . ."

[28]Ibid., p. 4.

[29]Ibid., p. 2.

[30]See Minutes, Pendeli, pp. 12-13.

[31]"The Wholeness of Human Life," pp. 5-8.

[32]Ibid., p. 2.

[33]Ibid., pp. 5-6.

[34]Ibid., p. 6.

[35]Ibid., p. 18.

[36]See the section on dialogue in Africa in chapter 3 above.

[37]"The Wholeness of Human Life," p. 12.

[38]Ibid., pp. 11 and 14.

[39]Ibid., p. 14.

[40]See the comments of Stanley J. Samartha in "Reflection on a Multi-Lateral Dialogue," The Church and the Jewish People, newsletter no. 2/1974, p. 21. Dr. Samartha lists the number of participants as follows: 8 Hindus, 8 Buddhists, 4 Jews, 10 Muslims, and 17 Christians. The names of the participants appear in Samartha, ed., Towards World Community: The Colombo Papers (Geneva: WCC, 1975), pp. 161-163.

[41]The papers and concluding memorandum of this meeting appear in ibid. The memorandum and list of participants also appear in Study Encounter 10/3 (1974): 1-14. References to the memorandum, "Towards World Community: Resources and Responsibilities for Living Together," in this study will be to version found in Towards World Community.

[42]The memorandum thus states, ". . . we must seek out in our respective traditions the resources which will further cooperation, the recognition of the equality of all men, their right to equal justice and to an equal share in material welfare. We must then seek to coordinate our particular efforts based on the moral and spiritual values of religions, with other endeavours to achieve world-community from whatever premise

they arise, not to compete with them or to counteract
them." Quoted from "Towards World Community," p. 120.

[43]Ibid., p. 126. Earlier, the memorandum notes
(pp. 123-124), "Dialogue involves the sharing of understanding and experience and as such is a significant
method of building community. It is also a means for
expanding self-knowledge and self-transcending knowledge. . . . We see in dialogue a means of sensitizing
people of various backgrounds to each other and through
this to the common concerns of mankind."

[44]Ibid., p. 120.

[45]Ibid., p. 125.

[46]Ibid.

[47]"The Unity of God and the Community of Mankind:
Cooperation Between African Muslims and African Chris-
tians in Work and Witness," (the Legon memorandum)
Study Encounter 11/1 (1975): 1.

[48]Ibid., p. 2. The text says, "Muslims and Christians in Africa, as in many other parts of the world,
live in a pluralistic society where their status as religious people has provided the opportunity for personal contact at work and in society. Both groups, in
their recognition and adoration of One God, share a
monotheistic tradition. They also recognize many points
of theological and spiritual convergence, including
reverence for Jesus. The adherents of both religions
therefore have cause and ground for mutual recognition,
respect and cooperation. They are particularly united
in their common cherishing of the religious and moral
values for which their respective traditions are dis-
tinguished. Furthermore, they are one in their common
experience of the challenge with which materialism and
modernism have faced religious and moral values."

[49]Ibid. The text reads as follows: "By sharing together our understanding, we should aim at trying to
put into practice our mutual understanding. A greater
degree of mutual sharing of resources should characterize our relations in society. . . . Both communities
need to be particularly alert to the danger of assuming attitudes of superiority or haughtiness in those
situations where, for whatever reasons, the resources
of society are unevenly or even unfairly distributed
among them."

[50]Ibid., p. 5. The text reads as follows: "Dialogue . . . forms part of the realization that the way
in which we recognize and adore God should be intimately connected with the way in which we cherish each oth-

er. The God of mercy and the God of love whom we honour and uphold is the same God we seek when we honour
and uphold our common brotherhood."

[51]Ibid. Emphasis added.

[52]For a list of the participants, the reports, and
the minutes of this meeting, see Minutes of the Second
Meeting of the Working Group, New Delhi, September 1974
(Geneva: WCC, 1974). Mgr. Rossano from the Secretariat for Non-Christians was present at this meeting.

[53]"Report of Group 1 on Dialogue--Community--Wit-
ness," in Minutes, New Delhi, p. 41.

[54]"Report of Group 3 on 'Styles of Dialogue'," in
Minutes, New Delhi, p. 47. The group report on "Dia-
logue--Community--Witness" says in this regard on p.
42, "Speaking of dialogue as a life-style, characterized by an open attitude to listen and learn from fel-
lowman [sic] of other religious traditions as well as
a readiness to witness to one's faith, we must affirm
that dialogue is a significant dimension in any Christian life and that it should be so also in the activities of the WCC as a whole."

[55]The group report on "Dialogue--Community--Wit-
ness" notes, therefore, (p. 42), ". . . references to
community when defining dialogue and mission and the
relationship between the two . . . . have significant
theological implications. In how far is God working in
the community which is the framework of dialogue? Is
there any salvific significance in the faiths and
truth-claims of the partner we meet in dialogue? If so,
how do these relate to the uniqueness of Christ? These
questions have to be further pursued."

[56]Ibid., p. 49. The text says, "There is no justification for Christian churches being closed communities seeking the security of the ghetto. Neither is
sufficient justification for a one-way mission. But
both one-way mission and closed ghettoes belong to the
reality of the empirical churches and this points to
errors in Christian self-understanding. A fresh theological framework where the imperative of love clearly demands a two-way open-ness on the part of Christians needs to be worked out. Dialogue needs no defence. Ghettoism and one-way mission have no defence."

[57]"Observations by Paul Verghese," Apendix IV,
"Seeking Community: The Common Search of People of Various Faiths, Cultures and Ideologies," in Minutes, New
Delhi, p. 58. See also the remarks of Carl Hallencreutz, pp. 51-52, and the summary of this discussion

on p. 15. The latter reads, "The 'provisional' approach
to world community explored by the Colombo dialogue
should be contributed to Section iii [the discussion on
seeking community in the Nairobi assembly], showing how
a 'kingdom of love' can grow from a universal theology of creation and a universal eschatology both of
which fully honour the uniqueness of Christ."

58"Muslims and Christians in Society: Towards
Goodwill, Consultation, and Working Together in South-
East Asia," the Hong Kong memorandum, Study Encounter
74/1 (1975): 6. The text reads, "Our purpose in Hong
Kong has been to face up to the fact that we come from
religiously pluralistic societies in South-East Asia,
wherein not only is conflict clearly disastrous but
even peaceful co-existence is an inadequate condition
for the urgent needs of our developing societies. Our
respective national societies, we feel, have a right to
expect from the faithful communities of Christians and
Muslims not conflict, not mere coexistence, but good-
will, a readiness to confer with each other and an
eagerness to cooperate in every possible way. Muslims
and Christians need each other's help to ease tension,
secure justice, relieve pain, and otherwise promote the
social, material and spiritual wellbeing of all people."

59Ibid., p. 7.

60Ibid.

61Ibid., p. 9.

62Jesus Christ Frees and Unites. Section III:
Seeking Community--The Search of People of Various
Faiths, Cultures and Ideologies. Preparatory dossier
for the 5th General Assembly of the WCC (Geneva: WCC,
1974), p. 15.

63Work Book for the Fifth Assembly of the World
Council of Churches, Nairobi, Kenya, 23 November-10 December 1975 (Geneva: WCC, 1975), pp. 37-38.

64"Appendix 3. The Report of the Moderator of the
Central Committee," in Breaking Barriers: Nairobi 1975.
The Official Report of the Fifth Assembly of the World
Council of Churches, Nairobi, 23 November--10 December
1975, ed. David M. Paton (London: SCM, 1976), p. 235.

65Ibid., pp. 235-236. See "The Lausanne Covenant,"
International Review of Mission 63 (1974): 570 which
reads, "We recognize that all men may have some knowledge of God through his general revelation in nature.
But we deny that this can save, for men suppress the
truth by their unrighteousness . . . . To proclaim Je-

sus as 'the Saviour of the world' is not to affirm that all men are either automatically or ultimately saved, still less to affirm that all religions offer salvation in Christ."

[66]"Report of the Moderator," p. 236.

[67]For an analysis of this debate over dialogue at the assembly, see Samuel Rayan, "'The Ultimate Blasphemy': On Putting God in a Box. Reflections on Section III: 'Seeking Community'," International Review of Mission 65 (1976): 129-133.

[68]See ibid., p. 133.

[69]Quoted from the report of the discussions, "Section III: Seeking Community: The Common Search of People of Various Faiths, Cultures, and Ideologies," in Breaking Barriers, p. 71.

[70]Ibid.

[71]Ibid., pp. 72-73.

[72]See Rayan's remarks in "Ultimate Blasphemy," p. 131. The official record of Chandran's remarks reads as follows: "We would like our brethren who are concerned about the commitment to the great commission of our Lord and the dangers of syncretism to be willing to listen to the testimony and insights of those who have more intimate knowledge of [other] faiths and are in no way less committed to Jesus Christ and his mission." Quoted from "Seeking Community," pp. 71-72.

[73]Thus Chandran remarked, p. 72, "We plead that they [namely European theologians] avoid the mistake of making judgments on the basis of traditional doctrines, without the knowledge of other peoples and their faiths, and thus failing to grow into the fullness of Christ."

[74]The official report of the proceedings states, in ibid., p. 70, "the majority of speakers were not happy with [the declaration] and believed it would be understood as spiritual compromise (Dr. Per Lonning, Church of Norway) or opposition to the mission of the Church (Bishop Michael, Russian Orthodox)."

[75]See "Seeking Community," no. 4.

[76]Ibid., no. 3. The text reads, "We are all agreed that the Great Commission of Jesus Christ which asks us to go out into all the world and make disciples of all nations, and to baptize them in the Triune Name, should not be abandoned or betrayed, disobeyed or compromised, neither should it be misused. Dialogue is both a mat-

ter of hearing and understanding the faith of others, and also of witnessing to the gospel of Jesus Christ."

[77]Ibid., no. 8. The text reads, "There is a great urgency for seeking community beyond our own. Whether we like it or not, we find ourselves thrown in with all of humanity in a common concern for peace and justice. We have been thrown together in an interdependent world, in which the urgency is that of survival or ex- tinction."

[78]Ibid., no. 9.

[79]Ibid., no. 10.

[80]Ibid., no. 16. The text reads, "But is there also a theological basis on which Christians should seek community with their neighbours of other faiths and convictions? Several answers were given to this question. Many stressed that all people have been created by God in his image and that God loves all hu- manity. Many believed that in a world broken by sin it is the incarnation of God in Jesus Christ which pro- vides the basis for the restoration of the creation to wholeness. Others would seek this basis for community in the trinitarian understanding of God. Still others would find theological meaning in the fact that history has removed and is removing geographical and cultural barriers which once kept us isolated and so is moving us towards one interdependent humanity. In all this discussion we encountered the question of a possible double basis for our search for community. Christians have a specifically theological basis for such a search. Is there also a common basis which should be mutually acceptable to people of differing faiths and ideologies?"

[81]Ibid., no. 20.

[82]Ibid., no. 29. The text reads, "Is there a spe- cific Christian culture? The question is pertinent, and loaded with the cultural imperialism associated with missionary history. Sharing our Christian commitment in different cultural contexts we realized joyfully that Jesus Christ both affirms and judges culture. As our Jewish guest affirmed, Jesus was an historical person, sharing a specific culture. At the same time Christian experience affirms that no culture is closer to Jesus Christ than any other culture. Jesus Christ restores what is truly human in any culture and frees us to be open to other cultures. Resources for world community are no Christian monopoly. We must be ready to acknowl- edge the presence of such resources wherever they are found. He offers us liberation from attitudes of cul-

tural superiority and from self-sufficience. He unites us in a community which transcends any particular culture."

83Ibid., no. 30.

84Ibid., no. 17.

NOTES TO CHAPTER SIX

1It was common practice after a general assembly for the Central Committee to replace the members serving on various Working Groups.

2The reports of these two meetings appear in a DFI pamphlet entitled Where Are We After Nairobi? Report of Core Group Meeting, Chambésy, Switzerland, May 17-20, 1976. Where Do We Go From Nairobi? Report of Core Group Meeting, Glion, Switzerland, January 24-28, 1977 (Geneva: WCC, 1976).

3Report of Core Group, Chambésy, p. 6.

4Ibid. The text reads, "It must be made clear again that this quest [for community] is to a large extent the necessity of human and humane neighbourly life in a world like ours that calls for that community which we call dialogue. We cannot treat our neighbours, our fellow human beings, as human beings without the openness of exchange at the deep level of encounter for which dialogue stands."

5Ibid., p. 9.

6Ibid.

7Ibid., pp. 4-5.

8Ibid., p. 5.

9Ibid., p. 15.

10Ibid., pp. 17-18.

11Ibid., pp. 19-20.

12Ibid., p. 11.

13Report of Core Group, Glion, p. 29.

14The aide-mémoire of this planning meeting appears in Christians Meeting Muslims. WCC Papers on Ten Years of Christian-Muslim Dialogue (Geneva: WCC, 1977), pp. 143-155.

[15]Report of Core Group, Glion, p. 28.

[16]Ibid.

[17]A collection of the papers presented, a list of participants, and the final statement issued appear in Stanley J. Samartha, ed., Faith in the Midst of Faiths: Reflections on Dialogue in Community (Geneva: WCC, 1977).

[18]Stanley J. Samartha, "A Pause for Reflection," in Faith in the Midst of Faiths, p. 11.

[19]The final statement of the consultation, entitled "Dialogue in Community," appears in Faith in the Midst of Faiths, pp. 134-169.

[20]See, for example, the remarks of Peter Beyerhaus in chapter 5 above.

[21]In an assessment of the Chiang Mai consultation, Dr. Samartha commented, ". . . people in the West, despite all evidence to the contrary, saw in the talk about 'world community' a creeping syncretism that might lead to one religion for the world--a soup in which all pieces of toast would eventually become soggy." Quoted from Stanley J. Samartha, "Dialogue in Community: A Step Forward. An Interpretation of the Chiang Mai Consultation," in Faith in the Midst of Faiths, p. 187.

[22]"Part I: On Community," no. 8, in "Dialogue in Community," p. 139.

[23]Ibid., no. 9, p. 140.

[24]Thus the statement says in "Part II: On Dialogue," no. 19, p. 143, "It [namely, dialogue] is our joyful affirmation of life against chaos, and our participation with all who are allies of life in seeking the provisional goals of a better human community. Thus we soundly reject any idea of 'dialogue in community' as a secret weapon of an aggressive Christian militancy. We adopt it rather as a means of living our faith in Christ in service of community with our neighbours."

[25]Ibid., no. 20, pp. 144-145.

[26]Ibid., no. 17, p. 143.

[27]"Part I: On Community," no. 1, p. 136.

[28]"Part II: On Dialogue," no. 19, p. 144.

[29]See "Introduction," to "Dialogue in Community," pp. 135-136. See also "Part II: On Dialogue," no. 21, p. 145.

[30]"Part II: On Dialogue," no. 21, p. 145.

[31]Ibid., no. 24, p. 147.

[32]Ibid., no. 27, p. 148.

[33]Ibid., no. 30, p. 149.

[34]The then Assistant Director of the DFI, John B. Taylor, was in fact given the special responsibility of directing the DFI's dialogue activity with Muslims when he joined the DFI staff in 1973.

[35]"Part III: Group Report A: Christian-Jewish-Muslim Relations," nos. 2(a) and 2(b), in "Dialogue in Community," pp. 152-153.

[36]Ibid., no. 2(c), p. 153.

[37]Ibid., no. 3(c), p. 154.

[38]Ibid., no. 3(d), pp. 154-155. The text reads, ". . . as Christians we are acutely aware of the missio Dei, and in addition acknowledge our inescapable responsibility in seeking deeper understanding of God's work in the world; we are convinced that not only is our inter-dependence crucial for the health and improvement of the communities we happen to share, but it is in the long term an essential part of our understanding of God's demands upon us."

[39]"Part III: Group Report B: Christian-Buddhist-Hindu Relations," nos. 4(a) and 4(b), in "Dialogue in Community," p. 159.

[40]Ibid., no. 4(f), p. 160.

[41]Note that the term "traditional" slips into usage here, despite what was said at the Ibadan consultation in 1973.

[42]"Part III: Group Report C: Christian Concern in Traditional Religions and Cultures," nos. 2(a) and 2(c), in "Dialogue in Community," p. 161. No. 2(c) reads, "In this report we wish to underline positive aspects of primal world-views because these can provide Christian communities with a basis for a dialogue which helps to build community. It may for example be possible to incorporate some aspects of such traditional cultures into services of worship, and to celebrate events in the 'rites of passage' in a particularly Christian way."

[43]Ibid., no. 3(c), p. 163.

[44]Ibid., no. 4(c), p. 165.

[45]Stanley J. Samartha, "Guidelines on Dialogue," Ecumenical Review 31 (1979):157.

[46]Ibid.

[47]Interview with Dr. Lonning, reprinted in Inside Out. A Style for Dialogue (Geneva: WCC, 1977), p. 43.

[48]Samartha, "Guidelines on Dialogue," pp. 157-158. In a report to the dialogue Working Group later in 1978, Dr. Samartha made the following comment about the Chiang Mai consultation: "The theological issues to which the attention of the churches is directed are the right ones. This is particularly because of the recognition that what is required is less a theology of religions than an ethics of community relationships." Quoted from "Responses to the Chiang Mai Statement: An Interim Report," in DFI, Minutes of the Third Meeting of the Working Group, Trinidad, May 1978 (Geneva: WCC, 1978), p. 98.

[49]The concluding memorandum, list of participants, and a summary account of the consultation appear in DFI, Minutes, Trinidad, pp. 72-83. The talks presented were: Wilfred C. Smith, "A Historian Looks at Faith, Science and Technology;" Dr. Naim Attiyah, "The Humanization of Technology;" S.L. Bonting, "Creation Viewed by Theology and Science: Attempt at a Synthesis;" G.M. Teutsch, "Man's Responsibility for the Created World, According to the Christian View." These are available upon request from the WCC headquarters at Geneva.

[50]"Memorandum," "Consultation of Christians and Muslims on Faith, Science and Technology and the Future of Humanity," in Minutes, Trinidad, p. 72.

[51]Ibid., p. 74. The text reads, "The role of suffering and of willingness to suffer, of potential defeat and ultimate victory for persons as they plunge into the present crises, received considerable attention. We addressed the specific question of the connotations of the Cross for not only person but city, for society and social justice. While Muslims spoke of the potential significance of the Christ figure for their community, Christians spoke of the Qur'an as reminder to their's of social covenant, of corporate justice and racial equality. Members of both communities were moved by the deep expressions of mutual involvement and genuine 'thank you's' to each other."

[52]The papers presented, the memorandum, and the list of participants appear in Stanley J. Samartha and Lynn de Silva, eds., Man in Nature: Guest or Engineer? A Preliminary Enquiry by Christians and Buddhists into

the Religious Dimensions in Humanity's Relation to Nature (Colombo: Ecumenical Institute for Study and Dialogue, 1979). The memorandum and list of participants
also appear in Minutes, Trinidad, pp. 84-95.

[53]See Samartha, "Man in Nature: Guest or Engineer?
Opening Address," in Samartha and Silva, Man in Nature,
p. 5.

[54]Ibid., p. 6.

[55]Thus the memorandum says, ibid., p. 104, "It was
affirmed that both Buddhism and Christianity have resources to enable man to overcome fragmentations and
brokenness such as we find in the world. How Buddhists
and Christians can help one another to achieve this in
facing the crises created by an unbalanced view of science and technology needs further thought."

[56]Ibid., p. 105.

[57]Stanley J. Samartha, "Director's Report: Priorities and Directions," in Minutes, Trinidad, p. 29.

[58]John B. Taylor, "Christian-Muslim Relations," in
Minutes, Trinidad, p. 43.

[59]"Director's Report," p. 29.

[60]"Group Report on Christian-Muslim Relations," in
Minutes, Trinidad, p. 17.

[61]"Director's Report," p. 30.

[62]"Group Report on Hindu/Buddhist Concerns," in
Minutes, Trinidad, p. 19.

[63]Ibid.

[64]Ibid., pp. 18-19.

[65]"Director's Report," p. 31.

[66]"Group Report on Cultures," in Minutes, Trinidad, pp. 22-23.

[67]For a brief summary of the discussions, the recommendations to the churches, and the list of participants, see Religious Experience in Humanity's Relation
with Nature: A Consultation, Yaoundé, Cameroon 1978
(Geneva: WCC, 1979).

[68]The following papers, available from the WCC,
were presented under this theme: N.K. Dzobo, "The Theory of Origin and Destiny of Man as Found Among the Ewe
of West Africa;" E. Tizal, "A Melanesian Cosmological
Process;" H.W. Turner, "Prolegomena to a Christian Examination of Primal Religions in Relation to the Natural Environment;" K.O. Opoku, "Time in the African Per-

spective;" J. Agossou, "Appropriation et maîtrise du temps par le négro-africain."

[69]The following papers, available from the WCC, were presented under this theme: E. Mveng, "Essai d'anthropologie négro-africaine: La personne humaine;" P. Abega, "La vision du monde du bati traditionnel;" C. Wright, "Causality and Liberation;" T. Ahrens, "Healing and Wholeness for the Human Person in a Melanesian Society;" M. Makang, "L'expérience religieuse dans la relation de l'homme avec la nature;" K. Appiah-Kubi, "Healing and Wholeness for the Human Person in an African Society--the Akan of Ghana;" A. Byaruhange-Akiiki, "Medicine and Wholeness Among the Bantu;" B. Kisembo, "Procreation and Responsible Parenthood;" D.N. Lartum, "Healing and Wholeness;" B. Senza-Masa, "Expériences religieuses dans la culture africaine;" H. Hebga, "Role de la sorcellerie."

[70]The following papers, available from the WCC, were presented under this theme: C. Wright, "Education Among People Within and Emerging From Primal World-Views;" J.N. Kudadjie, "Reflections on the Need to Harmonize the Healing Experience of Africa: A Pastoral Concern;" E. Rutiba, "Faith in Traditional Healing in Bufumbira, Uganda;" R. Rakotondraibe, "L'Eglise et la culture traditionnelle."

[71]"Recommendations," in Religious Experience in Humanity's Relation with Nature, p. 32.

[72]Ibid., p. 31.

[73]WCC, Guidelines on Dialogue With People of Living Faiths and Ideologies (Geneva: WCC, 1979), no. 1. Cf. "Dialogue in Community," no. 1.

[74]Guidelines on Dialogue, no. 7. Cf. "Dialogue in Community," no. 8.

[75]Guidelines on Dialogue, no. 8. Cf. "Dialogue in Community," no. 9: "The vision of a worldwide 'community of communities' commended itself to us as a means of seeking community in a pluralistic world. This vision is not one of homogeneous unity or totalitarian uniformity . . . ."

[76]Guidelines on Dialogue, no. 17. See also "Part III: Guidelines Recommended to the Churches for Study and Action," no. 6 of these guidelines. Cf. "Dialogue in Community," no. 18.

[77]Thus the guidelines (no. 18) say, "Dialogue, therefore, is a fundamental part of Christian service within community. In dialogue Christians actively re-

spond to the command to 'love God and your neighbour as yourself'. As an expression of love, engagement in dialogue testifies to the love experienced in Christ. It is a joyful affirmation of life against chaos, and a participation with all who are allies of life in seeking the provisional goals of a better human community." Cf. "Dialogue in Community," no. 19.

[78]"Introduction" in Guidelines on Dialogue. Cf. "Dialogue in Community," p. 136. See also Guidelines on Dialogue, no. 19: ". . . we do not see dialogue and the giving of witness as standing in any contradiction to one another. Indeed, as Christians enter dialogue with their commitment to Jesus Christ, time and again the relationship of dialogue gives opportunity for authentic witness. Thus, to the member churches of the WCC we feel able with integrity to commend the way of dialogue as one in which Jesus Christ can be confessed in the world today . . . ." Cf. "Dialogue in Community," no. 20.

[79]Guidelines on Dialogue, no. 23. Emphasis added. The Chiang Mai statement says simply (no. 24), "What is the relationship between God's universal action in creation and his redemptive action in Jesus Christ?"

[80]Guidelines on Dialogue, no. 23. The text says, "Are Christians to speak of God's work in the lives of all men and women only in tentative terms of hope that they may experience something of Him, or more positively in terms of God's self-disclosure to people of living faiths and ideologies and in the struggles of human life?"

[81]Ibid.

[82]Ibid., no. 28. The text says, "Despite the recognized dangers, Christians should welcome and gladly engage in the venture of exploratory faith. The particular risks of syncretism in the modern world should not lead Christians to refrain from dialogue, but are an additional reason for engaging in dialogue so that issues may be clarified."

NOTES TO CHAPTER SEVEN

[1]Rossano, "The Secretariat for Non-Christian Religions," p. 104.

[2]See again the remarks of bishop Per Lonning of Norway who represents the "evangelical" viewpoint in

chapter 6 above. This position fails to recognize suf-
ficiently, however, the profound human dimension to the
Christian message

[3]For an expression of this accusation, see the remarks of Wilfred Cantwell Smith in Towards a World Theology. Faith and the Comparative History of Religions
(Philadelphia: Fortress, 1981), pp. 132-134.

[4]The Secretariat's statements and the reflections
of its officials continue the schema enunciated by Paul
VI in his encyclical Ecclesiam suam, that is, the Catholic Church stands at the center of the world's religious history, all other churches and religions being
arranged in concentric circles around it. See the discussion of this encyclical in chapter 1.

[5]Rossano, "La Bible et les religions," pp. 24-25.

[6]Rahner, "Christianity and the Non-Christian Religions," p. 131.

[7]See the remarks of Hans Kung on this point in
Truthfulness: The Future of the Church (New York: Sheed
and Ward, 1968), pp. 141-154.

[8]See the remarks to this effect by Pope Paul VI in
his encyclical, Ecclesiam suam, chapter 1 above.

[9]John Hick, God and the Universe of Faiths. Essays
in the Philosophy of Religion (London: Macmillan,
1973), pp. 122-123.

[10]For a more detailed treatment of the universal
saving work of God in the biblical and later Christian
tradition, see Charles DeCelles, The Unbound Spirit:
God's Universal Sanctifying Works (New York: Alba
House, 1985).

[11]See Rom. 3:21-26: "But now, quite independently
of law, God's justice has been brought to light. The
Law and the prophets both bear witness to it: it is
God's way of righting wrong--all, without distinction.
For all alike have sinned, and are deprived of the divine splendour, and all are justified by God's free
gift alone, through his act of liberation in the person of Christ Jesus. For God designed him to be the
means of expiating sins by his sacrificial death, effective through faith. God meant by this to demonstrate
his justice, because in his forbearance he had over-
looked the sins of the past--to demonstrate his justice
in the present, showing that he himself is just and
also justifies any man who puts his faith in Jesus."

[12]See Acts 4:12: "For of all the names in the
world given to men, this is the only one by which we

can be saved." This is perhaps the key scriptural reference to the exclusive saving work of Christ

[13]See, for example, Sir. 1:8; 24:3-5; Wis. 7:12.

[14]See, for example, Sir. 24. For a study of the figure of Wisdom in the Jewish tradition, see Gerhard von Rad, Wisdom of Israel (New York: Abingdon, 1974).

[15]See, for example, Edward Schillebeeckx, Jesus: An Experiment in Christology, trans. Hubert Hoskins (New York: Seabury; Crossroad Books, 1979), pp. 429-432.

[16]See John 1:1-14.

[17]Justin the Martyr, First Apology, quoted in Vincent Zamoyta, ed., A Theology of Christ: Sources (Milwaukee: Bruce, 1967).

[18]See the discussion in Capéran, Le problème du salut, pp. 172-173 and 191-199. Thomas Aquinas uses this passage and explains implicit faith in his Summa Theologiae, 2a, 2ae, 1,7 as follows: ". . . on the basis of Hebrews, He that cometh to God must believe that he is and is a rewarder of them that seek him, all the articles of faith are implicit in certain primary ones, namely that God exists and that he has providence over man's salvation. For the truth that God is includes everything that we believe to exist eternally in God and that will comprise our beatitude. Faith in God's providence comprises all those things that God arranges in history for man's salvation and that make up our way towards beatitude." The quotation is from the Blackfriar's 1974 edition of the Summa.

[19]The letter of the Holy Office to Archbishop Cushing of Boston dated August 8, 1949 referred to in chapter one above illustrates this. For example, the letter says, "To gain salvation it is not always required that a person be incorporated in fact as a member of the Church, but it is required that he belong to it at least in desire and longing. It is not always necessary that this desire be explicit as it is with catechumens. When a man is invincibly ignorant, God also accepts an implicit desire, so called because it is contained in the good disposition of soul by which a man wants his will to be conformed to God's will." Quoted from the English translation of the letter in The Church Teaches, p. 120.

[20]I am borrowing the phrase "relatively adequate" from David Tracy, The Analogical Imagination. Christian Theology and the Culture of Pluralism (New York: Crossroad, 1981).

[21]"The Pastoral Constitution on the Church in the Modern World," no. 5, in Abbott, Documents of Vatican II, p. 203. Madathilparambil M. Thomas has identified this growing sense of the unity of humankind as one of the dominant characteristics of the contemporary era. See his views in M.M. Thomas, Man and the Universe of Faiths (Madras: Christian Literature Society, 1975), pp. 28-30.

[22]See John Macquarrie, Principles of Christian Theology, 2nd ed. (New York: Scribner's, 1977), p. 64.

[23]Thus Macquarrie remarks on pp. 97-98 of Principles of Christian Theology, using his "existential-ontological" language, "It is only through our total experience of being in the world that we reach any understanding of being; and for us, being in the world means existing, that kind of being which is open to itself and which already has some understanding of its being implicit in it. Being, then, gets disclosed in existing. But existing is not just beholding or contemplating or perceiving, for it is also concern and involvement and participation. Feeling is always a constituent factor in existing. At any given time, feeling, understanding, and willing--or, if one prefers a more latinized terminology, affection cognition, and willing--are all there together in existing. They are distinguishable aspects in the mental life of the existent, but they cannot be separated in the manner that was attempted in old-fashioned psychologies. We are, however, disclosed to ourselves, and being is disclosed, in affection and volition, as well as cognition, or, perhaps better expressed, all affective and conative experience has its own understanding. In particular, feeling and understanding cannot be sharply separated, and consequently one cannot sharply separate so-called 'emotive' and 'informative' language."

[24]In a way that I think overstates the point but which raises an important question in its recognition of this, John Hick writes, ". . . can we be so entirely confident that to have been born in our particular part of the world carries with it the privilege of knowing the full religious truth, whereas to be born elsewhere involves the liklihood of having only partial and inferior truth?" Quoted from Hick, God and the Universe of Faiths, p. 132.

[25]John Hick has indeed called upon Christians to recognize that Jesus is but one of many mediators of God, having the same importance as other great mediators such as Moses or Mohammed. This is the "Copernican revolution" he talks about. See his remarks in

ibid., pp. 120-132. See also the remarks in a summary of a Christology seminar held during the 1976 meeting the the Catholic Theological Society of America by Monika Hellwig: ". . . a non-exclusivist christology only becomes possible with a positive answer to the most radical question: can we change the 'story' substantially from what was handed down to us from the beginning? There is no doubt that the Christian 'story' makes claims of uniqueness, universal mediatorship, and unsurpassability for Jesus . . . . [O]ur 'story' as well as our 'doctrine' is constantly modified by theological discussion, but only to the extent that the community recognizes the new version as 'essentially unchanged', substantially continuous with previous versions. It seems, in this context, impossible to concede a non-exclusivist christology, although the meta-theological questions must be raised and the work of theology done with a critical awareness of these metaphysical questions." Quoted from "Seminar on Christology: Exclusive Claims and the Conflict of Faiths," <u>Catholic Theological Society of America: Proceedings</u> 31 (1976): 131-132. The term "non-exclusivist" is used here to mean a christology in which Christ is but one of many mediators of divine grace, definitive only for a particular cultural context, other cultures having their own mediators.

²⁶Paul Knitter, <u>No Other Name? A Critical Survey of Christian Attitudes Toward the World Religions</u> (American Society of Missiology Series, No. 7) (Maryknoll: Orbis, 1984), pp. 203-204.

²⁷See, for example, the recent works on Christology by following Catholic scholars: Walter Kasper, <u>Jesus the Christ</u>, trans. V. Green (New York: Paulist, 1977); Hans Kung, <u>On Being A Christian</u>, trans. Edward Quinn (Garden City, NY: Doubleday, 1976); James P. Mackey, <u>Jesus, the Man and the Myth: A Contemporary Christology</u> (Ramsey, NJ: Paulist, 1979); Gerald O'Collins, <u>Interpreting Jesus</u> (Ramsey, NJ: Paulist, 1983).

²⁸Macquarrie, <u>Principles of Christian Theology</u>, p. 302.

²⁹See ibid., p. 305.

³⁰John Macquarrie asks this question in ibid., p. 446.

³¹See ibid., pp. 170-173.

SELECTED BIBLIOGRAPHY

SELECTED BIBLIOGRAPHY

I. PRIMARY SOURCES

1. THE SECRETARIAT FOR NON-CHRISTIANS

(a) Publications of the Secretariat for Non-Christians (in chronological order)

Information for the Most Reverend Conciliar Fathers. Vatican City: Polyglot, 1964.

"A propos du salut des non-chrétiens." Summary of a 1965 Consultors' meeting, found in the archives of the Secretariat for Non-Christians.

Raccolta di testi di S.S. Paolo VI concernenti i rapporti con le religioni non cristiane. Vatican City: Polyglot, 1965.

The Hope Which Is In Us. A Brief Presentation of the Catholic Faith. 1st Supplement to the Bulletin. Vatican City: Polyglot, 1967.

Towards the Meeting of Religions. Suggestions for Dialogue: General Section. 3rd Supplement to the Bulletin. Vatican City: Polyglot, 1967.

Visions of Hope: Towards a Dialogue in Japan Thirty Years Ago. 4th Supplement to the Bulletin. Vatican City: Polyglot, 1967.

Rossano, Pietro. L'uomo e la religione. Rome: Esperienze, [1968].

Guidelines for a Dialogue Between Muslims and Christians. Rome: Ancora, 1969.

Meeting the African Religions. Rome: Ancora, 1969.

For a Dialogue With Hinduism. Rome: Ancora, [1969?].

Religions. Fundamental Themes for a Dialogistic Understanding. Rome: Ancora, 1970.

Religions in the World. Vatican City: Polyglot, [1970?].

Secunda raccolta di testi di S.S. Paolo VI concernenti i rapporti con le religioni non cristiane. Vatican City: Polyglot, [1970?].

Towards the Meeting with Buddhism. 2 vols. Rome: Ancora, 1970.

**(b) Articles, Addresses, and Letters of Key Secretari-
   at Personnel (in chronological order)**

(i) Fr. Pierre Humbertclaude

"Role spécifique du Secrétariat pour les non-chrétiennes et sa place dans l'Eglise." Bulletin 4
   (1967): 29-39.

"Clarification of the Nature and Role of the Secretariat for Non-Christians." Bulletin 11 (1969):
   77-96.

"Taking a Right View of the Founders of Religions."
   Bulletin 17 (1971): 99-102.

(ii) Cardinal Paolo Marella

"L'Eglise et les non-chrétiens. Dialogue et mission."
   Bulletin 10 (1969): 3-19.

(iii) Cardinal Sergio Pignedoli

"Letter From the New President." Bulletin 22 (1973):
   12-16.

"Perspectives of the Secretariat." Bulletin 23-24
   (1973): 84-86.

"Pentecostal Letter of the President of the Secretariat." Bulletin 26 (1974): 91-94.

"Come To Our House As Friends: An Account of the Work
   and Thinking of the Secretariat for Non-Christians." Worldmission 26 (1975): 4-16.

"A Japanese Encounter." Bulletin 28-29 (1975): 186-191.

"Relation de S.E. le cardinal Sergio Pignedoli." Bulletin 28-29 (1975): 12-15.

"Letter of Cardinal President of the Secretariat to the
   Bishops." Bulletin 36 (1977): 89-92.

"Message to the Muslim World at the End of Ramadan
   1977." Bulletin 39 (1978): 179-180.

"Introductory Address." Bulletin 41-42 (1979): 85-87.

(iv) Mgr. Jean Jadot

"The Growth in Roman Catholic Commitment to Interreli-
    gious Dialogue Since Vatican II." Journal of Ec-
    umenical Studies 20 (1983): 365-378.

(v) Fr. Pietro Rossano

"Il Segretariato per i non cristiani e la missione."
    Euntes Docete 19 (1966): 265-271.

"La Bible et les religions non-chrétiennes." Bulletin 4
    (1967): 18-28.

"Dialogue." Bulletin 7 (1968): 35-38.

"Is There Authentic Revelation Outside of the Judaeo-
    Christian Revelation?" Bulletin 8 (1968): 84-87.

"Christianity and the Religions." Bulletin 11 (1969):
    97-101.

"L'Eglise catholique et les religions non-chrétiennes."
    Address presented at a Joint Working Group meet-
    ing at Gwatt in 1969. Found in the archives of the
    Secretariat.

"Dialogue, Maieutic and Kerygma in St. Paul." Bulletin
    13 (1970): 46-51.

"God, Israel and the Peoples. Theological Meditation on
    JEPD." Bulletin 14 (1970): 93-101.

"Presentation of the Volume 'Religions' Published by
    the Secretariat." Bulletin 16 (1971): 36-40.

"Dialogue With Non-Christian Religions." Bulletin 17
    (1971): 103-108.

"Inter-Religious Dialogue." Talk given at Bombay, Jan-
    uary 21, 1973. Found in the archives of the Sec-
    retariat.

"The Spirit of Dialogue." Keynote address given at the
    Shantivanam Ashram during a Hindu-Christian "live-
    together," January 17, 1974. Found in the archives
    of the Secretariat.

"Clarifications." Bulletin 26 (1974): 137-139.

"Our Programme and Method." Bulletin 26 (1974):
    143-144.

"Contents of Dialogue With Non-Christians." Bulletin 26
    (1974): 143-144.

"The Theological Problem of the Religions." Bulletin 27
    (1974): 164-175.

"Dialogue avec les religions non-chrétiennes: contenu, finalité, conditions, limites." Talk given at the Abidjan colloquy, July 29, 1974. Bulletin 28-29 (1975): 26-28.

"Opening Address." Address given at the Kampala colloquy, August 5, 1974. Bulletin 28-29 (1975): 108-110.

"Introductory Address." Address given at the general meeting of Consultors at Grottaferrata (Rome), October 12, 1975. Bulletin 30 (1975): 211-213.

"Guiding Rule and Methodology of the Secretariat." Talk given during a meeting with WCC officials in Rome, May 28, 1976. Found in the archives of the Secretariat.

"Mgr. Rossano's Remarks at the Closing Session." Address given at the Chiang Mai consultation, April 27, 1977. Bulletin 36 (1977): 140-141.

"Interfaith, Its Importance and Implications." Bulletin 37 (1978): 29-39.

"Problème théologique du dialogue entre le christianisme et les religions non-chrétiennes." Talk given at Kinshasa, January 29, 1978. Bulletin 38 (1978): 87-93.

"Convergences spirituelles et humanistes entre l'Islam et le christianisme." Bulletin 40 (1979): 15-19.

"The Secretariat for Non-Christian Religions From the Beginnings to the Present Day: History, Ideas, Problems." Address given at the plenary meeting of Consultors at Rome, April 24, 1979. Bulletin 41-42 (1979): 88-109.

(iv) Other

Archives of the Secretariat for Non-Christians (consisting of file boxes arranged chronologically with the material inside likewise arranged chronologically).

Secretariatus pro Non Christianis, Bulletin (1964-1985) 1-59.

(c) Conciliar and Papal Sources

(i) Conciliar Documents (from Vatican Council II)

"Declaration on the Relationship of the Church to Non-Christian Religions." In Documents of Vatican II, pp. 660-668. Gen. ed. Walter M. Abbott. New York: America, 1966.

"Decree on the Missionary Activity of the Church." In Documents of Vatican II, pp. 584-630.

"Dogmatic Constitution on the Church." In Documents of Vatican II, pp. 14-101.

(ii) Papal Addresses, Letters, and Statements (in chronological order)

Paul VI. "Ad E.mum P.D. Eugenium S.R.E. Card. Tisserant, Episcopum Ostiensem, Portuensem et Sanctae Rufinae, Sacri Cardinalium Collegii Decanum et Collegio Praesidum Concilii Oecumenici Vaticani II antestantem." Acta Apostolicae Sedis 55 (1963): 740-744.

Paul VI. "The Encyclical Letter 'Ecclesiam Suam'." The Pope Speaks 10 (1964): 253-292.

Paul VI. "To the College of Cardinals." Catholic Mind 62 (1964): 54-60.

Paul VI. "Homilia habita in Basilica Vaticana, die Dominica Pentecostes, ad E.mos Patres Cardinales, Exc.mos Praesules, Clerum et Christifideles, praesertim sacrorum alumnos quamplurimos, inter Missarum sollemnia a Summo Pontifice ritu pontificali peracta." Acta Apostolicae Sedis 56 (1964): 428-433.

Paul VI. "Secretariatus de non Christianis erigitur, cuius Praeses E.mus P.D. Paulus S.R.E. Presbyter Cardinalis Marella renuntiatur." Acta Apostolicae Sedis 56 (1964): 560.

Paul VI. "Moderatoribus et Consultoribus e Secretariatu pro non Christianis, Romae Coetum habentibus." Acta Apostolicae Sedis 60 (1968): 568-569.

John Paul II. "The Attitude of the Church Towards the Followers of Other Religions: Reflections and Orientations on Dialogue and Mission." Bulletin 56 (1984): 126-141.

2. The World Council of Churches and the Sub-Unit for Dialogue With People of Living Faiths and Ideologies

(a) WCC and DFI Publications (in chronological order)

"Christians in Dialogue With Men of Other Faiths. Statement Drawn Up by the Protestant/Orthodox/ Catholic Consultation Convened by the WCC at Kandy, Ceylon, February 27-March 5, 1967." Study Encounter 3/2 (1967): 52-58.

New Delhi to Uppsala 1961-1968. Report of the Central Committee to the Fourth Assembly of the World Council of Churches. Geneva: WCC, 1968.

Goodall, Norman, ed. The Uppsala Report 1968. Official Report of the Fourth Assembly of the World Council of Churches, Uppsala, July 4-20, 1968. Geneva: WCC, 1968.

Hallencreutz, Carl F. New Approaches to Men of Other Faiths, 1938-1968: A Theological Discussion. Research pamphlet no. 18. Geneva: WCC, 1970.

Samartha, Stanley J., ed. Dialogue Between Men of Living Faiths. Papers Presented at a Consultation Held at Ajaltoun, Lebanon, March 1970. Geneva: WCC, 1971.

Samartha, Stanley J., ed. Living Faiths and the Ecumenical Movement. Geneva: WCC, 1972.

Samartha, Stanley J. and Taylor, John B., eds. Christian-Muslim Dialogue. Papers Presented at the Broumana Consultation, 12-18 July 1972. Geneva: WCC, 1973.

"The Wholeness of Human Life: Christian Involvement in Mankind's Inner Dialogue With Primal World-Views." Study Encounter 9/4 (1973): 1-20.

Samartha, Stanley J., ed. Living Faiths and Ultimate Goals. Geneva: WCC, 1974.

The Unity of God and the Community of Mankind: Co-Operation Between Muslims and African Christians in Work and Witness. Memorandum: Muslim-Christian Dialogue, University of Ghana, Legon, 17-21 July 1974. Muslims and Christians in Society: Towards Good-Will, Consultation and Working Together in Southeast Asia. Memorandum: Muslim-Christian Dialogue, Morrison House, Hongkong, 4-10 January 1975. Geneva: WCC, 1975.

Samartha, Stanley J., ed. Towards World Community: Resources and Responsibilities for Living Together. Geneva: WCC, 1975.

Work Book for the Fifth Assembly of the World Council of Churches, Nairobi, Kenya, 23 November-10 December 1975. Geneva: WCC, 1975.

Uppsala to Nairobi 1968-1975. Report of the Central Committee to the Fifth Assembly of the World Council of Churches. London: SPCK, 1975.

Paton, David M., ed. Breaking Barriers: Nairobi 1975. The Official Report of the Fifth Assembly of the World Council of Churches, Nairobi, 23 November-10 December, 1975. London: SPCK, 1976.

Taylor, John B., ed. Primal World Views. Christian Dialogue With Traditional Thought Forms. Ibadan Consultation 1973. Ibadan: Daystar, 1976.

Christians Meeting Muslims. WCC Papers on Ten Years of Christian-Muslim Dialogue. Geneva: WCC, 1977.

Hallencreutz, Carl F. Dialogue in Community: Ecumenical Issues in Inter-Religious Relationships. Uppsala: Swedish Institute of Missionary Research, 1977.

Taylor, John B. Dialogue, Community and Culture. Geneva: WCC, 1977.

Dialogue in Community. Statement and Reports of a Theological Consultation, Chiang Mai, Thailand, 18-27 April 1977. Geneva: WCC, 1977.

Samartha, Stanley J., ed. Faith in the Midst of Faiths. Reflections on Dialogue in Community. Geneva: WCC, 1977.

Religious Experience in Humanity's Relationship With Nature. A Consultation, Yaoundé, Cameroon 1978. Geneva: WCC, 1979.

Samartha, Stanley J. and de Silva, Lynn, eds. Man In Nature: Guest or Engineer? A Preliminary Enquiry By Christians and Buddhists Into the Religious Dimensions in Humanity's Relation to Nature. Colombo: Ecumenical Institute for Study and Dialogue, 1979.

Guidelines on Dialogue With People of Living Faiths and Ideologies. Geneva: WCC, 1979.

Samartha, Stanley J. Courage for Dialogue. Ecumenical Issues in Inter-Religious Relationships. Geneva: WCC, 1981.

(b) WCC and DFI Minutes and Reports (in chronological order)

Central Committee of the World Council of Churches. Minutes and Reports of the Twenty-Third Meeting. University of Kent at Canterbury, Canterbury, Great Britain, August 12-22, 1969. Geneva: WCC, 1969.

Central Committee of the World Council of Churches. Minutes and Reports of the Twenty-Fourth Meeting. Addis Ababa, Ethiopia, January 10th-21st, 1971. Geneva: WCC, 1971.

Bangkok Assembly 1973. Minutes and Reports of the Assembly of the Commission on World Mission and Evangelism of the World Council of Churches, December 31, 1972 and January 9-12, 1973. Geneva: WCC, 1973.

Sub-Unit on Dialogue With People of Living Faiths and Ideologies. Minutes of the Meeting of the Working Group, Pendeli Near Athens, March 1973. Geneva: WCC, 1973.

Sub-Unit on Dialogue With People of Living Faiths and Ideologies. Minutes of the Second Meeting of the Working Group, New Delhi, September 1974. Geneva: WCC, 1974.

Where Are We After Nairobi? Report of Core Group Meeting, Chambésy, Switzerland, May 17-20, 1976. Where Do We Go From Nairobi? Report of Core Group Meeting, Glion, Switzerland, January 24-28, 1977. Geneva: WCC, 1977.

Sub-Unit on Dialogue With People of Living Faiths and Ideologies. Minutes of the Third Meeting of the Working Group, Trinidad, May 1978. Geneva: WCC, 1978.

(c) Other

Archives of the Sub-Unit for Dialogue With People of Living Faiths and Ideologies (consisting of boxes containing various papers arranged in general chronological order).

II. SECONDARY LITERATURE

1. DIALOGUE

Aykara, Thomas A., ed. Meeting of Religions: New Orien-
      tations and Perspectives. Bangalore: Dharmaram
      Publications, 1978.

Barnes, Michael A. "In Dialogue With World Religions."
      The Month (1980): 158-162.

Bleeker, Claas J. Christ in Modern Athens. The Confron-
      tation of Christianity With Modern Culture and the
      Non-Christian Religions. Leiden: Brill, 1965.

Carman, John B. "Continuing Tasks in Inter-Religious
      Dialogue." The Ecumenical Review 22 (1970):
      199-209.

Christian, William A. Opposition of Religious Doc-
      trines: A Study in the Logic of Dialogue Among Re-
      ligions. New York: Herder and Herder, 1972.

"Consultors for Secretariat for Non-Christians." Tablet
      219, 18 September 1965, p. 1044.

Cragg, Kenneth. "Encounter With Non-Christian Faiths."
      Union Seminary Quarterly Review 19 (1964):
      249-309.

Culpepper, Hugo H. "The Incarnation in the Dialogue of
      the Religions." Review and Expositor 71 (1974):
      75-84.

Daniélou, Jean. "Les règles du dialogue." Axes 4,1
      (1971): 5-8.

Davies, Rupert E. "Multilateral and Bilateral Conversa-
      tions." One In Christ 15 (1979): 334-335.

Devanandan, Nalini and Thomas, Madathilparampil M.,
      eds. Preparation for Dialogue: A Collection of Es-
      says on Hinduism and Christianity in New India, by
      P.D. Devanandan. Bangalore: Christian Institute
      for the Study of Religion and Society, 1964.

Devanandan, Paul D. and Thomas, M. M., eds. Christian
      Participation in Nation-Building. Bangalore:
      Christian Institute for the Study of Religion and
      Society, 1960.

Dhavamony, Mariasusai. Evangelization, Dialogue and De-
      velopment. Documenta Missionalia 5. Rome: Univer-
      sita Gregoriana, 1972.

Divarkar, Parmananda. "Ecumenical Dialogue With Muslims." The Clergy Monthly Supplement 31 (1967): 177-181.

Dumoulin, Henri. "En dialogue avec le Bouddhisme Zen." Concilium 29 (1967): 115-147.

Duncan, Bruce. "Conversion or Dialogue." Lumen Vitae 28 (1973): 649-660.

Fitzgerald, Michael. "Muslim-Christian Dialogue in Libya." African Ecclesiastical Review 18 (1976): 186-193.

Girault, René. Croire en dialogue. Limoges: Droguet & Ardant, 1979.

Gregorios, Paulos Mar. "Dialogue With World Religions. Basic Approaches and Practical Experiences." Indian Journal of Theology 29 (1980): 1-11.

Griffiths, Bede. Christian Ashram. Essays Towards a Hindu-Christian Dialogue. London: Darton, Longman & Todd, 1966.

Hallencreutz, Carl F. "Dialogue and Community: Reflections From a European Periphery." Ecumenical Review 29 (1977): 12-17.

Hellwig, Monika K. "Bases and Boundaries for Interfaith Dialogue: A Christian Viewpoint." Journal of Ecumenical Studies 14 (1977): 419-431.

Hillman, Eugene. "Evangelization in a Wider Ecumenism: Theological Grounds for Dialogue With Other Religions." Journal of Ecumenical Studies 12 (1975): 1-12.

King, Ursula. "Religion and the Future: Teilhard de Chardin's Analysis of Religion as a Contribution to Inter-Religious Dialogue." Religious Studies 7 (1971): 307-323.

Klostermaier, Klaus K. "Hindu-Christian Dialogue." Journal of Ecumenical Studies 5 (1968): 21-44.

Idem. "A Hindu-Christian Dialogue on Truth." Journal of Ecumenical Studies 12 (1975): 157-171.

Idem. Hindu and Christian in Vrindaban. London: SCM, 1969.

Knitter, Paul F. "Horizons on Christianity's New Dialogue With Buddhism." Horizons 8 (1981): 40-61.

Masson, Jean. "Vers un rencontre du bouddhisme et du christianisme?" Gregorianum 45 (1964): 306-326.

Minz, Nirmal. "Theologies of Dialogue: A Critique." Religion and Society 14 (1967): 8-13.

Neill, Stephen. Christian Faith and Other Faiths. The Christian Dialogue With Other Religions. London: Oxford University Press, 1961.

"Non-Christian Observers and a Non-Christian Secretariat?" Tablet 217, 20 April 1963, pp. 439-440.

"Non-Christian Secretariat to Defend Religious Values." Catholic Messenger 82, 28 May 1964, p. 2.

"Non-Christians Unit Observes 10th Year." National Catholic Reporter 10, 8 March 1974, p. 5.

Rossano, Pietro. "Africa and Its Religions: A Note on Pope Paul's Journey." L'Osservatore Romano (Eng.), 11 September 1969, p. 5.

Idem. "The Gospel and African Culture: Report on Talks Promoted by the Secretariat for Non-Christians at Yaoundé, Cameroon." L'Osservatore Romano (Eng.), 5 August 1976, p. 4.

Idem. "Mission of the Secretariat for Non-Christians in Iran." L'Osservatore Romano (Eng.), 8 July 1976, p. 4.

Idem. "Missione e dialogo." Oikoumenikon 13 (1973): 229-239.

Idem. "Religions and Human Advancement." L'Osservatore Romano (Eng.), 25 November 1976, p. 8.

Samartha, Stanley J. "Christian-Muslim Dialogue in the Perspective of Recent History." Islam and the Modern Age 3 (1972): 43-48.

Idem. "Courage for Dialogue: An Interpretation of the Nairobi Debate." Religion and Society 23 (1976): 22-35.

Idem. "Dialogue as a Continuing Christian Concern." The Ecumenical Review 23 (1971): 129-142.

Idem. "Dialogue: Significant Issues in the Continuing Debate." The Ecumenical Review 24 (1972): 327-340.

Idem. "More Than An Encounter of Commitments. An Interpretation of the Ajaltoun Consultation on 'Dialogue Between Men of Living Faiths'." International Review of Mission 59 (1970): 393-403.

Idem. "The Progress and Promise of Inter-Religious Dialogue." Journal of Ecumenical Studies 9 (1972): 463-476.

Idem. "The Quest for Salvation and the Dialogue Between Religions." International Review of Missions 57 (1968): 424-432.

Idem. "Reflections on a Multilateral Dialogue." The Ecumenical Review 26 (1974): 637-646.

Idem. "The World Council of Churches and Men of Other Faiths and Ideologies." The Ecumenical Review 22 (1970): 190-198.

"The Secretariat for Non-Christian Religions." Tablet 218, 23 May 1964, p. 591.

"A Secretariat for Non-Christians." Christ to the World 9 (1964): 338-341.

"Secretariat for Non-Christians." Commonweal 80, 29 May, 1964, pp. 280-281.

Smart, Ninian. World Religions: A Dialogue. Baltimore: Penguin, 1966.

Smith, Wilfred Cantwell. "On Dialogue and 'Faith'; A Rejoinder." Religion 3 (1973): 106-114.

Spae, Joseph. Christian Corridors to Japan. Tokyo: Oriens Institute for Religious Research, 1965.

Idem. Christianity Encounters Japan. Tokyo: Oriens Institute for Religious Research, 1968.

Swidler, Leonard. "Ground Rules for Interreligious Dialogue." Journal of Ecumenical Studies 15 (1978): 413-414.

Taylor, John V. "The Theological Basis of Interfaith Dialogue." International Review of Mission 68 (1979): 373-384.

Weiser, Thomas. "Giving Account of the Hope: From Bangkok to Nairobi." International Review of Mission 67 (1978): 127-136.

Wickremesinghe, Lakshman. "Living Faiths in Dialogue." International Review of Mission 68 (1979): 385-393.

2. THEOLOGY OF RELIGIONS

Aagard, Johannes. "Revelation and Religion. The Influence of Dialectical Theology on the Understanding of the Relationship Between Christianity and Other Religions." Studia Theologica 14 (1960): 148-185.

Agus, Jacob B. "Revelation As Quest. A Contribution to
    Ecumenical Thought." Journal of Ecumenical Studies
    9 (1972): 521-543.

Aldwinckle, Russell. Jesus--A Saviour or the Saviour.
    Religious Pluralism in Christian Perspective. Ma-
    con, GA: Mercer, 1980.

Allen, Edgar Leonard. Christianity Among the Religions.
    London: Allen & Unwin, 1960.

Amirthan, Samuel. "The Challenge of New Religions to
    Christian Theological Thought." International Re-
    view of Mission 67 (1978): 399-406.

"Attitudes Towards Other Religions, a Corrective from
    the Secretariat for Non-Christians." Christ to the
    World 12 (1967): 355-356.

Augros, Louis. "Comportement de l'Eglise envers les re-
    ligions non chrétiennes. Réflexion critique sur le
    passé." Lumière et vie 80 (1966): 5-40.

Barth, Karl. "The Revelation of God as the Abolition of
    Religion." In Church Dogmatics, volume 1, part 2:
    The Doctrine of the Word of God, pp. 280-361.
    Translated by G.T. Thomson and Harold Knight.
    Edinburgh: T. & T. Clark, 1956.

Baum, Gregory. "Christianity and Other Religions. A
    Catholic Problem." Cross Currents 16 (1966):
    447-463.

Idem. "The Convictions of Others." The Ecumenist 10
    (1972): 49-52.

Idem. "The Jews, Faith and Ideology." The Ecumenist 11
    (1973): 71-76.

Beyerhaus, Peter. Bangkok '73. The Beginning or End of
    World Mission? Grand Rapids, Michigan: Zondervan,
    1974.

Blomjous, Joseph. "The Christian Significance of Reli-
    gious Pluralism and the Mission of the Church."
    Lumen Vitae 21 (1966): 543-551.

Brooke, Odo. "Natural Religion in the Supernatural
    Existential." The Downside Review 83 (1965):
    201-212.

Bruls, Jean. "Un nouveau regard de l'Eglise catholique:
    La déclaration conciliaire 'Nostra aetate'."
    Lumière et vie 80 (1966): 41-58.

Burkle, Howard. "Jesus Christ and Religious Pluralism."
    Journal of Ecumenical Studies 16 (1979): 457-471.

Capéran, Louis. Le problème du salut des infidèles. Essai historique. Toulouse: Grand Séminaire, 1934.

Cenkner, William. "The Convergence of Religions." Cross Currents 22 (1973): 429-437.

Cornélis, Etienne. Valeurs chrétiennes des religions non-chrétiennes. Histoire du salut et histoire des religions. Christianisme et bouddhisme. Paris: Editions du Cerf, 1965.

Cousins, Ewert. "Bonaventure and World Religions." The Cord 22 (1972): 55-63.

Idem. "The Trinity and World Religions." Journal of Ecumenical Studies 7 (1970): 476-498.

Cunningham, Adrian. "A Third Reformation?: R.C. Zaehner and Charles Davis on World Religions." New Blackfriars 53 (1972): 7-14.

Cuoq, Joseph. "Les croyants non chrétiens." Parole et mission 9 (1966): 279-290.

Cuttat, Jacques Albert. La rencontre des religions. Paris: Aubier, 1957.

Daniélou, Jean. The Advent of Salvation. A Comparative Study of Non-Christian Religions and Christianity. Translated by Rosemary Sheed. New York: Paulist, 1962.

Idem. "Christianisme et religions non chrétiennes." Etudes 321 (1964): 323-336.

Idem. "Christianity and the Non-Christian Religions." In Introduction to the Great Religions, pp. 7-28. Translated by Albert J. LaMothe. Notre Dame, Indiana: Fides, 1964.

Idem. Dieu et nous. Paris: Grasset, 1956.

Idem. "Is It the Purpose of the Mission to Bring Salvation? In Connection With the Theological Seminar in Bombay." Christ to the World 10 (1965): 221-231.

Idem. The Lord of History. Reflections on the Inner Meaning of History. Translated by Nigel Abercrombie. London: Longmans, 1958.

Idem. "Missionary Nature of the Church." Christ to the World 12 (1967): 336-345.

Idem. "Non-Christians and Christ." The Month 223 (1967): 137-144.

Idem. Les saints paiens de l'Ancien Testament. Paris: Le Seuil, 1956.

Davis, Charles. Christ and the World Religions. London: Hodder & Stoughton, 1970.

DeCelles, Charles. The Unbound Spirit: God's Universal Sanctifying Work. New York: Alba House, 1985.

Devanandan, Paul D. The Gospel and Renascent Hinduism. London: SCM, 1959.

Dhavamony, Mariasusai. "Self-Understanding of World Religions as Religion." Gregorianum 54 (1973): 91-130.

Erickson, Millard J. "Hope For Those Who Haven't Heard? Yes, But . . ." Evangelical Missions Quarterly (1975): 122-125.

Frick, Eugene G. "The World Religions: Four Dimensions of a Catholic Hermeneutic." Journal of Ecumenical Studies 11 (1974): 661-675.

Geernaert, Donna. "Christian Claim and Religious Pluralism in the Light of Teilhard de Chardin's Evolutionary Perspective." Ph.D. dissertation, University of St. Michael's College (Toronto), 1980.

Geffre, Claude and Jossua, Jean-Pierre, eds. True and False Universality of Christianity. Concilium 135. Edinburgh: Clark, 1980.

Gomez, Anastasio. "Theology of Non-Christian Religions." Euntes Docete 24 (1971): 372-391.

Greenwood, Robert P. "'Extra ecclesiam nulla salus'. Its Treatment in Recent Roman Catholic Theology." Theology 76 (1973): 416-425.

Gualtieri, Antonio. "Confessional Theology in the Context of the History of Religions." Sciences religieuses/Studies in Religion 1 (1971-71): 347-360.

Idem. "Descriptive and Evaluative Formulae for Comparative Religion." Theological Studies 29 (1968): 52-71.

Idem. "The Failure of Dialectic in Hendrik Kraemer's Evaluation of Non-Christian Faiths." Journal of Ecumenical Studies 15 (1978): 274-290.

Hacker, Paul. "The Christian Attitude Toward Non-Christian Religions." Zeitschrift fur Missionswissenschaft und Religionswissenschaft (Munster) 55 (1971): 81-97.

Idem. "The Religions of the Gentiles as Viewed by the Fathers of the Church." Zeitschrift fur Missionswissenschaft und Religionswissenschaft (Munster) 54 (1970): 253-278.

Idem. "The Religions of the Nations in the Light of
    Holy Scripture." Zeitschrift fur Missionswissen-
    schaft und Religionswissenschaft (Munster) 54
    (1970): 161-185.

Hebblethwaite, Peter. "On Non-Christian Religions." The
    Month 223 (1967): 144-152.

Hellwig, Monika. "Seminar on Christology: Exclusivist
    Claims and the Conflict of Faiths." Catholic Theo-
    logical Society of America: Proceedings 31 (1976):
    129-132.

Henry, Antonin Marcel, ed. Les relations de l'Eglise
    avec les religions non chréyennes: Declaration
    'Nostra aetate'. Unam Sanctam 61. Paris: Editions
    du Cerf, 1966.

Hick, John. God and the Universe of Faiths. Essays in
    the Philosophy of Religion. New York: St. Martin's
    Press, 1973.

Idem, ed. Truth and Dialogue: The Relationship Between
    World Religions. London: Sheldon Press, 1974.

Hick, John and Hebblethwaite, Brian, eds. Christianity
    and Other Religions: Selected Readings. London:
    Collins; Fount, 1980.

Hillmen, Eugene. "Anonymous Christianity and the Mis-
    sions." The Downside Review 84 (1966): 361-380.

Idem. The Wider Ecumenism. Anonymous Christianity and
    the Church. London: Burns & Oates, 1968.

Hinwood, Bonaventure. "Revelation in Non-Christian Re-
    ligions." Journal of Theology for Southern Africa
    11 (1975): 50-70.

Humbertclaude, Pierre. "Christianisme et religions."
    Seminarium 24 (1972): 374-392.

Khodr, Georges. "Christianity in a Pluralistic World--
    The Economy of the Holy Spirit." The Ecumenical
    Review 23 (1971): 118-128.

Kilian, Sabbas J. "The Catholic Theologian and Non-
    Christian Religions." Thought 49 (1974): 21-42.

Knitter, Paul. "Christomonism in Karl Barth's Evalua-
    tion of the Non-Christian Religions." Neue Zeit-
    schrift fur systematische Theologie und Religions-
    philosophie 13 (1971): 99-121.

Idem. "European Protestant and Catholic Approaches to
    the World Religions: Complements and Contrasts."
    Journal of Ecumenical Studies 12 (1975): 13-28.

Idem. No Other Name? A Critical Survey of Christian At-
    titudes Toward the World Religions. American Soci-
    ety of Missiology Series, No. 7. Maryknoll, NY:
    Orbis, 1984.

Idem. Towards a Protestant Theology of Religions. A
    Case Study of Paul Althaus and Contemporary Atti-
    tudes. Marburger theologische Studien 11. Marburg:
    N.G. Elwert, 1974.

Idem. "What Is German Protestant Theology Saying About
    the Non-Christian Religions?" Neue Zeitschrift fur
    systematische Theologie und Religionsphilosophie
    15 (1973): 38-64.

Idem. "World Religions and the Finality of Christ: A
    Critique of Hans Kung's On Being A Christian."
    Horizons 5 (1978): 151-164.

Koenig, Franz. "The Council and the Non-Christians."
    Christ to the World 9 (1964): 59-68.

Kraemer, Hendrik. The Christian Message in a Non-Chris-
    tian World. London: Edinburgh House Press, 1938;
    reprint ed., London: James Clark & Co., 1961.

Laurentin,René and Neuner, Joseph. The Declaration on
    the Relation of the Church to Non-Christian Reli-
    gions. New York: Paulist, 1966.

Leonard, Augustin. "Toutes les religions ont-elles la
    même valeur?" Nouvelle revue théologique 79
    (1957): 704-714.

"Letter of the Holy Office to Archbishop Cushing of
    Boston, 1949." In The Church Teaches. Documents of
    the Church in English Translation, pp. 118-121.
    Edited and translated by John F. Clarkson et al.
    Rockford, Ill.: Tan, 1973.

Marlé, René. La singularité chrétienne. Paris: Caster-
    man, 1970.

Masson, Jean. "La déclaration sur les religions non-
    chrétiennes." Nouvelle revue théologique 87
    (1965): 1066-1083.

Idem. "Face aux religions non-chrétiennes." Spiritus 25
    (1965): 416-425.

Maurier, Henri. Essai d'une théologie du paganisme.
    Paris: Editions de l'Orante, 1965.

Moeller, Charles. "The Conciliar Declaration on Non-
    Christian Religions and the Decree on Ecumenism."
    Lumen Vitae 21 (1966): 506-528.

Moffitt, John. "A Christian Approach to Hindu Beliefs."
    Theological Studies 27 (1966): 58-78.

Idem. "Christianity Confronts Hinduism." Theological
    Studies 30 (1969): 207-224.

Neill, Stephen. Salvation Tomorrow. The Originality of
    Jesus Christ and the World's Religions. Nashville:
    Abingdon, 1976.

Neuner, Joseph, ed. Christian Revelation and World Re-
    ligions. London: Burns & Oates; Compass, 1967.

Idem. "The Place of World Religions in Theology." The
    Clergy Monthly 32 (1968): 102-115.

Newbigin, James Edward Leslie. A Faith for This One
    World. London: SCM, 1961.

Newell, William Lloyd. "Zaehner vs. the Unity of Reli-
    gions." The Ecumenist 16 (1978): 41-45.

Nigosian, Sol A. "The Challenge of Religious Plural-
    ism." The Ecumenist 16 (1978)58-62.

Oesterreicher, John M. "Declaration on the Relationship
    of the Church to Non-Christian Religions. Intro-
    duction and Commentary." In Commentary on the Doc-
    uments of Vatican II, volume 3, pp. 1-154. Edited
    by Herbert Vorgrimler. Various translators. New
    York: Herder, 1969.

Panikkar, Raymond. "Christians and So-Called 'Non-
    Christians'." Cross Currents 22 (1972): 281-308.

Idem. "Faith--A Constitutive Dimension of Man." Journal
    of Ecumenical Studies 8 (1971): 223-254.

Idem. The Trinity and the Religious Experiences of Man.
    London: Darton, Longman & Todd, 1973.

Idem. The Unkown Christ of Hinduism. London: Darton,
    Longman & Todd, 1967.

Pannenberg, Wolfhart. "Toward a Theology of the History
    of Religions." In Basic Questions in Theology,
    volume 2, pp. 65-118. Translated by G.H. Kehm.
    London: SCM, 1971.

Papali, Cyril B. "The Place of Non-Christian Religions
    in the Economy of Salvation." Seminarium 18
    (1966): 991-1003.

Rahner, Karl. "Anonymous Christianity and the Mission-
    ary Task of the Church." In Theological Investi-
    gations, volume 12: Confrontations 2, pp. 161-180.
    Translated by David Bourke. London: Darton, Long-
    man & Todd, 1974.

Idem. "Anonymous Christians." In Theological Investigations, volume 6: Concerning Vatican Council II,
pp. 390-398. Translated by Karl-H. and Boniface
Kruger. London: Darton, Longman & Todd, 1969.

Idem. "Christianity and the Non-Christian Religions."
In Theological Investigations, volume 5: Later
Writings, pp. 115-124. Translated by Karl-H. Kru-
ger. London: Darton, Longman & Todd, 1966.

Idem. "History of the World and Salvation History." In
Theological Investigations, volume 5: Later Writ-
ings, pp. 97-114. Translated by Karl-H. Kruger.
London: Darton, Longman & Todd, 1966.

Idem. "Observations on the Problem of the 'Anonymous
Christian'." In Theological Investigations, volume
14: Ecclesiology, Questions in the Church, The
Church in the World, pp. 280-294. Translated by
David Bourke. New York: Seabury; Crossroad, 1976.

Idem. "The One Christ and the Universality of Salvation." In Theological Investigations, volume 16:
Experience of the Spirit: Source of Theology, pp.
199-225. Translated by David Morland. New York:
Seabury; Crossroad, 1979.

Rayan, Samuel. "'The Ultimate Blasphemy': On Putting
God in a Box. Reflections on Section III: 'Seeking Community'." International Review of Mission
65 (1976): 129-133.

Roper, Anita. The Anonymous Christian. Translated by
Joseph Donceel. New York: Sheed & Ward, 1966.

Rossano, Pietro. "Le religione non cristiane e la seco-
larizzazione." Humanitas 26 (1971): 63-76.

Idem. "La rivelazione come dialogo di Dio con l'uomo."
Humanitas 23 (1968): 194-208.

Idem. "What the II Vatican Council Has Taught Regarding Non-Christians." Christ to the World 12
(1967): 428-436.

Rousseau, Richard W., ed. Interreligious Dialogue: Facing the Next Frontier. Volume 1: Modern Theological Themes: Selections From the Literature. Mont-
rose, PA: Ridge Row Press, 1981.

Rupp, George. Christologies and Cultures: Towards A
Typology of Religious Worldviews. The Hague:
Mouton, 1974.

Idem. "Religious Pluralism in the Context of an Emerging World Culture." Harvard Theological Review 66
(1973): 207-218.

Samartha, Stanley J. The Hindu Response to the Unbound
    Christ. Inter-Religious Dialogue Series, No. 6.
    Madras: Christian Literature Society, 1974.

Idem. "Other People's Faiths." Frontier 17 (1974):
    105-107.

Schineller, J. Peter. "Christ and Church: A Spectrum of
    Views." Theological Studies 37 (1976): 545-566.

Schreiner, Peter. "Roman Catholic Theology and Non-
    Christian Religions." Journal of Ecumenical
    Studies 6 (1969): 376-399.

Seumois, André. "Appréciation théologique des systèmes
    religieux de la gentilité post-chrétienne." Neue
    Zeitschrift fur Missionswissenschaft 29 (1973):
    93-104, 210-217.

Idem. "Théologie des religions et révélation primi-
    tive." Euntes Docete 24 (1971): 329-348.

Sharpe, Eric J. Not To Destroy But To Fulfill. The Con-
    tribution of John Nicol Farquhar to Protestant
    Missionary Thought in India Before 1914. Studia
    Missionalia Uppsalensia 5. Lund: Gleerup, 1965.

Simon, Marcel. "Early Christianity and Pagan Thought:
    Confluences and Conflicts." Religious Studies 9
    (1973): 385-399.

Smith, Wilfred Cantwell. The Meaning and End of Reli-
    gion. A New Approach to the Religious Traditions
    of Mankind. New York: Macmillan, 1963.

Idem. Towards a World Theology. Faith and the Compar-
    ative History of Religion. Philadelphia: Westmin-
    ster, 1981.

Souillard, Paul-Marie. "Les infidèles, peuvent-ils être
    sauvés? Etapes historiques de la question."
    Lumière et vie 16-18 (1954): 779-800.

Stadler, Anton Paul. "Mission--Dialogue. A Digest and
    Evaluation of the Discussion in the Roman Catho-
    lic Church and Within the World Council of
    Churches." Ph.D. dissertation, Union Theological
    Seminary, New York, 1977.

Straelen, Henricus von. The Catholic Encounter With
    World Religions. London: Burns & Oates, 1966.

Idem. "Our Attitude Towards Other Religions." Worldmis-
    sion 16 (1965): 71-98.

Thils, Gustave. Propos et problèmes de la théologie des
    religions non-chrétiennes. Collection Eglise vi-
    vante. Paris: Casterman, 1966.

Thomas, Madathilparampil M. The Acknowledged Christ of the Indian Renaissance. London: SCM, 1969.

Idem. Man and the Universe of Faiths. Madras: Christian Literature Society, 1975.

Thompson, William M. "The Risen Christ, Transcultural Consciousness, and the Encounter of the World Religions." Theological Studies 37 (1976): 381-409.

Tillich, Paul. Christianity and the Encounter of the World Religions. New York: Columbia University Press, 1963.

Idem. "Natural and Revealed Religion." Christendom 1 (1935): 158-170.

Vallée, Gérard. Mouvement oecuménique et religions non chrétiennes. Le débat oecuménique sur la rencontre interreligieuse de Tambaram à Uppsala (1938-1968). Montreal: Bellarmin, 1975.

Idem. "Word of God and the Living Faiths of Men. Chronology of a Study Process." Study Encounter 6/4 (1970): 207-214.

Veitch, John A. "The Case for a Theology of Religions." Scottish Journal of Theology 24 (1971): 407-423.

Idem. "Revelation and Religion in the Theology of Karl Barth." Scottish Journal of Theology 24 (1971): 1-22.

Verastegui, Raphael Esteban. "Christianisme et religions non-chrétiennes: Analyse de la 'tendance Daniélou'." Euntes Docete 23 (1970): 227-279.

Idem. "Les religions non-chrétiennes dans l'histoire du salut." Euntes Docete 24 (1971): 417-427.

Idem. "Les religions non-chrétiennes n'ont-elles aucune valeur salvifique? Evaluation critique de la position du cardinal Daniélou concernant les religions non-chrétiennes." Euntes Docete 27 (1974): 25-64.

Visser't Hooft, Willem H. No Other Name: The Choice Between Syncretism and Christian Universalism. Philadelphia: Westminster, 1963.

Whitson, Robley E. The Coming Convergence of Religions. Toronto: Newman, 1971.

Young, Robert Doran. Encounter With World Religions. Philadelphia: Westminster, 1970.

Zaehner, Robert Charles. The Catholic Church and World Religions. London: Burns & Oates, 1964.

Idem. Concordant Discord: The Interdependence of
       Faiths. Oxford: Oxford University Press, 1970.

INDEX

TORONTO STUDIES IN THEOLOGY

DATE DUE

NOV 02 1994			
			Printed in USA